T0311834

Aviation and Climate Change

This book analyses the political, economic and managerial challenges for policy makers and the air transport industry as they face climate change.

Based on an overview of the scientific background and technological options for emissions reduction, *Aviation and Climate Change* provides an in-depth assessment of environmental regulation and management. It provides an up-to-the-minute analysis of the effects of aviation on climate change, and an economic analysis of policies to reduce or eliminate greenhouse gas emissions. The main emphasis of the book is on the economic mechanisms used to lessen emissions – carbon taxes, emissions trading schemes and offset schemes. It pays particular attention to the ways these policies work, and to the interaction between them – for instance, the interaction between taxes and emissions trading schemes. One feature of the book is that it analyses the Carbon Offsetting and Reduction Scheme for International Aviation (CORSIA) which has been developed by ICAO for international aviation, and which is due to commence operation shortly. The advantages and disadvantages of this controversial scheme are discussed.

This book will be of interest to researchers in diverse areas (economics, political science, engineering, natural sciences), to air transport policy makers, and to managers in the aviation industry.

Frank Fichert is Professor of Economics and Transport Economics at Worms University of Applied Sciences, Germany. He has published many papers on the transport sector. His research focuses on competition and regulation in the air transport industry and the environmental issues of aviation.

Peter Forsyth is Adjunct Professor at Monash and Southern Cross Universities. He has published extensively in the economics of aviation and tourism. His recent research has involved economic and policy approaches to addressing carbon emissions from aviation and tourism.

Hans-Martin Niemeier is Director of the Institute for Transport and Development at Bremen University of Applied Sciences. He is Chairman of the German Aviation Research Society (GARS) and of the Advisory Board of the European Aviation Conference. He led COST Action "Air Transport and Regional Development".

Aviation and Climate Change

Economic Perspectives on Greenhouse
Gas Reduction Policies

Edited by **Frank Fichert,**
Peter Forsyth and
Hans-Martin Niemeier

Routledge
Taylor & Francis Group

LONDON AND NEW YORK

First published 2020
by Routledge
2 Park Square, Milton Park, Abingdon, Oxon OX14 4RN

and by Routledge
605 Third Avenue, New York, NY 10017

First issued in paperback 2022

Routledge is an imprint of the Taylor & Francis Group, an informa business

© 2020 selection and editorial matter, Frank Fichert, Peter Forsyth and
Hans-Martin Niemeier; individual chapters, the contributors

The right of Frank Fichert, Peter Forsyth and Hans-Martin Niemeier to
be identified as the authors of the editorial material, and of the authors for
their individual chapters, has been asserted in accordance with sections 77
and 78 of the Copyright, Designs and Patents Act 1988.

All rights reserved. No part of this book may be reprinted or reproduced or utilised
in any form or by any electronic, mechanical, or other means, now known or
hereafter invented, including photocopying and recording, or in any information
storage or retrieval system, without permission in writing from the publishers.

Trademark notice: Product or corporate names may be trademarks or
registered trademarks, and are used only for identification and explanation
without intent to infringe.

Publisher's Note
The publisher has gone to great lengths to ensure the quality of this reprint but
points out that some imperfections in the original copies may be apparent.

British Library Cataloguing-in-Publication Data
A catalogue record for this book is available from the British Library

Library of Congress Cataloging-in-Publication Data
A catalog record for this book has been requested

ISBN 13: 978−0−367−50594−3 (pbk)
ISBN 13: 978−1−472−47917−4 (hbk)
ISBN 13: 978−1−315−57240−6 (ebk)

DOI: 10.4324/9781315572406

Typeset in Bembo
by Apex CoVantage, LLC

Contents

Figures

Tables

Acknowledgements

This book is a compilation of selected papers, some of them presented at workshops organized by the German Aviation Research Society. We would like to thank the Amsterdam University of Applied Sciences, Dresden University of Technology, German Aerospace Center (DLR) in Cologne, International University of Applied Sciences Bad Honnef, University of Applied Sciences Bremen and the University of Applied Sciences Worms for acting as hosts. We are also grateful to the Wolfgang-Ritter-Stiftung.

We would like to thank contributors to this edition for carefully reviewing other chapters and providing helpful comments and suggestions. We are especially indebted to Florian Allroggen, Margaret Arblaster, Achim Czerny, Ian Douglas, David Gillen, Wolfgang Grimme, Sven Maertens, Robert Malina, and David Warnock-Smith for their extensive review activity.

Guy Loft and Matthew Ranscombe of Routledge Publishers were encouraging with their active promotion of this volume.

Our thanks also go to Shravan Kumar for carefully revising the English style and for assistance in editing.

Editors and contributors

Carlos Calvo Ambel (Director, Trends and Analysis) joined T&E in January 2015 after working at the European Commission's climate directorate and the Permanent Representation of Spain to the EU. He was previously employed as a climate change consultant, advising clients on the clean development mechanism, the EU emissions trading system and other carbon reduction programmes. Currently he leads the trends and analysis team at T&E, where he both coordinates the organisation's analytical work and ensures its quantitative analysis is of the highest standard. He studied environmental sciences in Seville and completed a master's degree in public administration at Columbia University.

Laura Buffet (Director, Energy) joined T&E in April 2013 after two years working as a parliamentary assistant in the European Parliament. Laura directs the energy campaigns of T&E and focuses on making European fuels policy more sustainable, moving away from oil towards better advanced alternatives, especially renewable electricity, and phasing out the support to land-based biofuels. She has worked extensively on campaigns around the Renewable Energy Directive and the Fuel Quality Directive, as well as the EU delegated act that labelled palm oil diesel unsustainable. She studied public administration at the Institute of Political Studies in Strasbourg, followed by environmental law at the University of Strasbourg.

Katrin Dahlmann (Dr.) received her diploma in meteorology at Ludwig-Maximilians-Universität München in 2007. In 2012 she received her Dr. rer. nat. by the Ludwig-Maximilians-Universität München. Dr. Katrin Dahlmann has been responsible for several research projects, studies and academic papers at the DLR Institute of Atmospheric Physics. Her main research field is the climate impact of aviation and the assessment of mitigation strategies.

Thomas Earl (Manager, Modelling and Data Analysis) joined Transport & Environment in October 2016. After obtaining his PhD in engineering at the University of Sydney, he spent two and a half years as a postdoctoral research fellow in France. His research was in the domain of environmental engineering and fluid mechanics, where he honed his programming skills and analysis of big data. At T&E, he analyses transport and climate data, conducts research, and has helped develop their transport model.

Alexander Eisenkopf (Prof. Dr.) holds the ZEPPELIN Chair for Economic and Transport Policy at Zeppelin University Friedrichshafen. His research topics are transport policy, transport economics, and transport and environment. He published mainly on regulatory issues of transport and the conflicts between environment and transport.

Frank Fichert (Prof. Dr.) is Professor of Economics and Transport Economics at Worms University of Applied Sciences. His PhD thesis, which he finished in 1999 at Mainz University, analyses different policy instruments for reducing negative externalities from air transportation. He worked as Managing Director of the Research Institute for Economic Policy at Mainz (1999–2004) and as Professor for Economics and Air Transportation at Heilbronn University of Applied Sciences (2004–2009). He has published several papers on the transport sector and is co-author of the leading German textbook on air transport management. He is member of the Competence Centre Aviation Management at Worms University and program director of the bachelor's degree program "Aviation Management and Piloting". He has participated in several applied research projects, including the H2020 project COCTA, the German Aviation Benchmarking study, and the report on the market power of Amsterdam Airport, as well as projects commissioned by federal and state ministries in Germany. His research focuses on competition and regulation in the air transport industry and the environmental issues of aviation.

Peter Forsyth has been at Monash University since 1997, originally as Professor of Economics and since 2014 as Adjunct Professor. He is also Adjunct Professor at Southern Cross University. Much of his research has been on transport economics, especially on the economics of aviation, and on the economics of tourism. In 2005 he delivered the Martin Kunz lecture at the Hamburg Aviation Conference. He has published widely in both tourism and aviation, including the book *Liberalization in Aviation* (2013, Ashgate). He has taught on cost benefit analysis, competition policy, the economics of regulation and public economics for many years. In recent years he has done considerable research on economic policies to reduce greenhouse gas emissions of aviation and tourism. He has also done extensive work using Computable General Equilibrium models to analyse tourism policy issues. In 2015 he was made a Fellow of the Air Transport Research Society.

Lucy Gilliam (Aviation and Shipping Campaigner) joined T&E in September 2017 after several years consulting on environmental campaigns and having previously working as a science adviser in the UK civil service. She also spent five months as a trainee at the European Commission's research and innovation directorate, working on SME policy. She holds a BSc in biological science and a PhD in molecular microbiology as well as a diploma in commercial coastal sailing vessels from Enkhuizen Nautical College.

Volker Grewe (Prof. Dr.) studied mathematics at the University Augsburg, Germany and meteorology at the Ludwig-Maximilians-University in Munich (Germany). He has been working as a scientist in the field of climate-chemistry interactions with focus on traffic and air traffic effects upon the atmosphere since 1993 at DLR-Oberpfaffenhofen. He also worked at NASA-GISS in New York, 1999–2000, and visited NCAR (Boulder, CO) NASA-Ames, NASA-GISS and CICERO (Oslo, Norway) during sabbaticals as a guest scientist. He is Topical Editor of the journal *Geoscientific Model Development*, was granted the "Aviation Award" in 2014, was Vice-Chair of the international association ECATS from 2015 to 2018 and became Full Professor for "Climate Impacts of Aviation" at the faculty of Aerospace Engineering at TU-Delft in 2016.

Wolfgang Grimme is a business economist at the DLR Institute of Air Transport and Airport Economics. He graduated in 2004 from the University of Giessen with a master's degree in business administration focusing on transport management and international management. He joined DLR in 2005 and has since then focused in his work on regulatory policy issues in air transport, impact analysis of political measures on the air transport system, environmental economics and intra- and intermodal competition.

Karlheinz Haag (Dr. Ing.) studied aerospace engineering at the Technical University Aachen (RWTH Aachen) from 1975 to 1981. From 1981 until 1988 he worked as a junior scientist at the Institute for Mechanics at the Technical University Aachen, where he completed his doctoral degree. Between 1988 and 2002 he held several management functions at German Aerospace Centre (DLR e.V.). As Program-Director Aeronautics he was responsible for the management of DLR's aeronautics research programs between 1998 and 2002. From April 2002 until June 2018 he was Vice President of the Department "Environmental Issues" at the Lufthansa Group. The portfolio of the position covered research-oriented activities, technical and operational aspects in combination with lobby activities. Since June 2018 he is retired.

Bill Hemmings (Advisor, Aviation and Shipping) was previously T&E's director of these campaigns from 2008 to 2019. He is Australian/Austrian and took science and arts degrees at the University of Tasmania before mastering in international relations at the University of Oxford. He brings business, political and negotiating experience to international aviation and shipping work acquired living and working on five continents first with the Australian and Canadian (on exchange) Foreign Services, then with Hong Kong's airline Cathay Pacific and in Europe with Rosenbluth International, later American Express Advisory Services.

Martin Jung is a research associate at the Institute of Air Transport and Airport Research of the German Aerospace Center. He holds a master's degree in computer science. His research interests include hybrid simulation, agent simulation, analysis and visualization of big data, complex and inhomogeneous architectures and aviation.

Hermann Keimel graduated at the University of Regensburg in April 1977. He holds a degree in economics with special focus on macroeconomics, economic and financial policy, statistics and econometrics. He joined the Air Transport and Airport Research Department of the German Aerospace Centre (DLR) in November 1977. First, he worked on scenarios for the development of economic systems of the EU. From 2001 to 2004, Hermann managed the subproject "Mobility and Transport" of the project "Sustainable Development – Perspectives for Germany" on behalf of the German Helmholtz Association. From 2006 to 2009, he was in charge of the subproject "Evaluation of Findings on Sustainable Strategies" of the project "Demography and Infrastructure – National and Regional Aspects of Demographic Change" on behalf of the German Helmholtz Association. Since 2010, Hermann has been focusing on economic impacts of the transport system in general and the air transport system in particular. He retired in 2017.

Andreas Knorr (Prof. Dr.) is Full Professor of Economics: Economic and Transport Policy at the German University of Administrative Sciences Speyer. He has published numerous articles in the field of transport economics with an emphasis on aviation- and railroad-related topics as well as on European economic integration and antitrust economics.

Sven Maertens (Dr.) holds a master's degree (2002) in business administration with special focus on transportation and spatial economics, marketing and controlling. He has been responsible for several research projects, studies and academic papers at the Institute of Air Transport and Airport Research at the German Aerospace Center (DLR). His main research fields are airline business models and environmental and economic impact assessments of the air transport sector.

Peter Morrell graduated in economics from Cambridge University and subsequently gained a master's in air transportation from the Massachusetts Institute of Technology, where he worked on NASA-sponsored research into airline forecasting and profitability. He has a doctorate in airline capital productivity from Cranfield University. He initially worked with merchant bank Lazard Brothers, in the City, before joining the Association of European Airlines in Brussels as an economist in 1971. He worked as an air transport consultant from 1978 to 1991, when he joined Cranfield's Department of Air Transport, retiring in 2011. He is a former Head of the Department of Air Transport at Cranfield University, where he had a chair in air transport economics and finance. He is now an independent aviation advisor and a visiting professor at Cranfield University, and on the editorial boards of the *Journal of Air Transport Management* and *Tourism Economics*. He is the author of the textbook *Airline Finance* (the fourth edition of which was published in 2013, and a Chinese edition in 2007), *Moving Boxes by Air: the Economics* *of International Air Cargo*, second edition, with Thomas Klein (2018) and has written many papers for both academic and industry journals.

Andrew Murphy (Manager, Aviation) joined T&E in June 2014 having previously worked for the Green European Foundation and interning at the European Commission's transport directorate. Andrew is Irish, with a bachelor of arts degree in political science and law and a bachelor of law from the National University of Ireland, Galway. Andrew manages T&E's work on sustainable aviation, including state aid and VAT taxation.

Hans-Martin Niemeier (Prof. Dr.) is a Director of the Institute for Transport and Development at Bremen University of Applied Sciences. He is Chairman of the German Aviation Research Society (GARS), Managing Member of the Advisory Board of the European Aviation Conference and Chair of the COST Action "Air Transport and Regional Development" (ATARD). He led the research projects "German Airport Performance" and "German Aviation Benchmarking" and conducted the studies "Airport Benchmarking by Economic Regulators", "Market Power of Amsterdam Airport" for the Netherlands Competition Authority and "Comparative Study (Benchmarking) of the Efficiency of Avinor's Airport Operations" for the Norwegian Ministry of Transport and Communication. From 2014 to May 2019 he was a member of the Performance Review Body of the Single European Sky. He has published on privatisation, regulation and competition of airports, the reform of slot allocation and on airline and airport alliances.

Hendrik Nieße completed his studies at the Osnabrueck University in 2008 with a degree in Systems Sciences, with focus on computer modelling and theoretical computer sciences. He worked within the project "New Approaches to Adaptive Water Management under Uncertainty", carried out a Social-Network Analysis project in Bolivia and developed special software for the assessment of pollutants inputs into watercourses. Hendrik joined the DLR Institute of Air Transport and Airport Research in 2011. His research focused on the quantification and analyses of the accessibility provided by air traffic, for which he has developed special software and indicators. These findings were also used in the study "Emirates Airlines and Germany". Hendrik's other activities are: modelling of the influence of climate policies on the global aviation emissions, information technology implementation and integration of different air traffic models. He left DLR in 2015.

Arne Roth (Dr.) joined Bauhaus Luftfahrt in 2010 where he leads the research focus area "Alternative Fuels". Important specific topics are fuel chemistry, the assessment of biomass potentials and the holistic evaluation and prioritization of renewable jet fuel alternatives produced from biomass and other regenerative feedstock and energy sources. He serves as active member and focal point for topics related to alternative fuels in the Working Group "Environment & Energy" of the "Advisory Council for Aviation Research and Innovation in Europe (ACARE)", and in other national and international expert committees. Before turning towards alternative fuels, he was concerned with chemical hydrogen storage in solid state materials. He studied chemistry at the Bielefeld University and holds a doctoral degree in bioinorganic chemistry from the Friedrich-Schiller-University Jena. Very recently (after having written the chapter for this volume) he has taken up a leading position at Fraunhofer Institute for Interfacial Engineering and Biotechnology in Straubing, Germany.

Werner Rothengatter (Prof. Dr.) served as Professor of Economics at Karlsruhe Institute of Technology (KIT) until his retirement in 2010. He was Dean of the Faculty of Technology 2003–2004. Earlier he served as Professor for Economic Theory and Policy at the Universities of Kiel and Ulm (1979–1986) and as Head of the Transport Division at the German Institute for Economic Research, Berlin (1986–1989). Dr. Rothengatter has published widely on transport-related issues, having published six books and more than a hundred articles in the field of transport economics and management, covering air, rail and road transport. His past projects have focused on issues of transport pricing and management, spatial development, the cost evaluation of public transportation schemes and trans-European networks. He served as President of the World Conference on Transport Research Society from 2001 to 2007 and was a member of the editorial board of several major transport journals. He is a co-editor of the Springer Series on Transportation Research, Economics and Policy. He has continued to provide consultancy services for various transport-related projects. He was a member of the Standing Advisory Committees of the German Ministry of Transport and of Deutsche Bahn AG and of the Reform Commission for the Construction of Large Projects of the German Ministry of Transport.

Robert Sausen (Prof. Dr.) received his diploma in physics at Eidgenössische Technische Hochschule (ETH) Zürich, Switzerland, in 1979. In 1983 he received his Dr. rer. nat. by the Technische Hochschule Darmstadt, Germany. He worked as a postdoc at the Max-Planck-Institut für Meteorologie, Hamburg. In 1986 he became a Hochschulassistent (assistant professor) at the Meteorologisches Institut of Universität Hamburg. In both positions he worked on coupling of atmosphere and ocean models, climate simulations, and atmospheric diagnostic. In 1991, he got his habilitation and venia legendi for meteorology at Universität Hamburg. In the same year he became head of the department Atmospheric Dynamics (now Earth System Modelling) of the DLR Institute of Atmospheric Physics at Oberpfaffenhofen, Germany. Since 1992 he is a member of the Fakultät für Physik of the Ludwig-Maximilians-Universität München, where he teaches meteorology, since 2000 as a professor. At DLR, the work of Prof. Sausen is dedicated to the impact of transport, in particular aviation, on the chemical composition of the atmosphere and on climate. He was Coordinating Lead Author of the IPCC Special Report "Aviation and the Global Atmosphere". In 2000 he was awarded the Otto-Lilienthal-Price. Prof. Sausen is author of more than 100 peer-reviewed papers.

Martin Schaefer (Dr.) graduated from Technische Universität Berlin in 2006 as an aeronautical engineer. In 2012 he obtained a doctoral degree in engineering from Ruhr-Universität Bochum. From 2006 to 2013 he worked as a research associate at the DLR Institute of Propulsion Technology with a focus on aircraft engine emissions and aviation scenarios. Between 2013 and 2018 he continued his career as a Technical Advisor at the German Federal Ministry of Transport and Digital Infrastructure (BMVI). He has joined the European Union Aviation Safety Agency (EASA) in 2018 as an environmental expert.

Janina Scheelhaase (Dr.) is an environmental economist at the DLR Institute of Air Transport and Airport Economics. She graduated in 1989 from the University of Wuppertal, Germany, with a master's degree in business administration. In 1994, she graduated with a PhD in environmental economics from the University of Aachen. She joined DLR in 2004. She is heading the Air Transport Economist research group since 2009 and has been responsible for a great number of research projects, studies and academic papers at the DLR Institute of Air Transport and Airport Research.

Jori Sihvonen (Clean Energy Officer) joined T&E in 2016. Jori is a master of forestry sciences and economics and has been working on sustainability issues since his graduation. At T&E Jori worked on the sustainability of biofuels, and other energy carriers. Jori followed aviation biofuel development at both EU and ICAO levels.

Florian Wolters (Dipl.-Ing.) received his degree in aerospace engineering from Stuttgart University in 2009. Since then he is a research associate at the Institute of Propulsion Technology at the German Aerospace Center (DLR). His research topics are in the fields of gas turbine performance simulation, future engine concepts and alternative fuels.

1 Introduction and overview

*Frank Fichert, Peter Forsyth
and Hans-Martin Niemeier*

Climate change is one of the crucial global problems of the 21st century. Nations have responded to this challenge by unilateral measures as well as international agreements on reducing greenhouse gas emissions. Important milestones have been the United Nations Framework Convention on Climate Change (UNF-CCC) of 1992, followed by the Kyoto Protocol in 1997. More recently, in the Paris 2016 agreement, the aim of keeping the global temperature rise well below 2 degrees Celsius above pre-industrial levels was formulated, with an additional ambition to limit the temperature increase even further to 1.5 degrees Celsius. Many jurisdictions have defined pathways for reducing CO_2 emissions, often aiming at a "decarbonisation" of the economy.

The economic aspects of climate change have been addressed in many publications. William Nordhaus analysed climate change already in the 1970s and received the Nobel Prize in Economic Sciences in 2018. The Stern report, published in 2007, had a major influence on the public debate on climate change policies. Nowadays, the economics of climate change are a common element in every textbook on environmental economics.

The aviation industries' contribution to climate change became a major topic by the 1990s. In 1999 the Intergovernmental Panel on Climate Change (IPCC) issued a special report on "Aviation and the Global Atmosphere". For several years, the International Civil Aviation Organization (ICAO) has discussed different ways to reduce international aviation's contribution to global warming. Technical options for more fuel-efficient aircraft and the potentials of renewable fuels have been analysed thoroughly throughout the world. Many initiatives have been formed to foster research and development; for example, the European research program "Clean Sky", which also looks into other environmental issues like noise reduction. Large airlines publish sustainability reports, explaining their initiatives to limit CO_2 and other emissions. The problem is made more complex because of the fact that it is not only carbon emissions which lead to global warming – other gases, such as nitrous oxides, also contribute to the problem. Carbon emissions may be responsible for only about a third of the overall problem.

Policy makers, as well as economists in particular, have been discussing the pros and cons of different policy instruments in the air transport market. From the 1990s, non-governmental organizations (NGOs) and also some political parties have been arguing in favour of higher taxes on aviation in order to limit air transport's growth and emissions. However, the international nature of aviation requires international cooperation in order to implement measures which are effective as well as efficient. For example, the European Union's initial approach to include not only intra-European flights but also flights from Europe to non-EU member states in its Emissions Trading Scheme (ETS) caused conflicts with countries affected by this measure. Finally, in 2016 ICAO initiated a global market-based scheme, CORSIA (Carbon Offsetting and Reduction Scheme for International Aviation), to achieve carbon-neutral growth of international air transport, which will be implemented stepwise beginning in 2021.

Given the intense debate and the many policy initiatives sketched here, it is not surprising that there are already some books on aviation and climate change; for example, Gössling and Upham (2009). Moreover, a large number of papers have been published in journals focusing on air transport and sustainability, respectively.

The focus of this volume is narrower than that of other more general books on climate change and air transport. The focus here is on policies, and on the economic analysis of those policies which are being used, or are suggested, to lessen or eliminate the greenhouse gas emissions of air transport. There have been a range of policies which rely on economic instruments and which have been used, or are being suggested, as ways of reducing emissions. These include taxation policies such as ticket taxes and fuel taxes, quantitative instruments such as Emissions Trading Schemes, voluntary schemes and new initiatives such as CORSIA. The objective of the volume is to explain what they involve and how they work, what problems they encounter, how effective they might be, and what alternatives there are to the use of air transport, such as the greater use of rail.

Several aspects of aviation and climate change are not considered, or are considered only in passing – these include the more technological aspects of policies, the geographical aspects and the political economy aspects of developing support for policies. These are important issues which are for others to explore. Most of the policies considered here are capable of being implemented in the short term, though they will not be, of their own, sufficient to address the emissions problem. The technological solutions, including engine and airframe developments and lower or zero emission fuels, will take time to develop, and they will become increasingly important over the longer run.

As a starting point, Grewe provides an up-to-date overview on the contribution of aviation to climate change. The potentials of renewable fuels are analysed by Roth. The majority of the papers deal with different instruments for environmental protection, combining theoretical models, empirical analysis, and policy aspects. Fichert, Forsyth and Niemeier set the scene by providing an overview of the different instruments which have been used or suggested, and they discuss interdependencies between the instruments. Knorr and Eisenkopf also compare several instruments, with a special focus on voluntary carbon offsets offered by airlines. Morrell focusses on Emissions Trading Schemes, concentrating on the EU scheme. An important development has been the development of CORSIA. Haag provides an insight into the role of ICAO in the decision-making process leading to the development of this, and Maertens, Grimme and Scheelhaase analyse how CORSIA will work.

The chapter by Scheelhaase et al. contains a model-based comparison of different market-based measures which covers not only carbon emissions, but also other climate relevant emissions of aviation like NO_x and contrails. The analysis favours an Emissions Trading Scheme on a global level compared to a climate tax and a NO_x emission charge combined with an open CO_2 trading scheme and operational measures. Hemmings et al. of Transport and Environment describe the view of a NGO on aviation and climate change. They address a key policy question of the European Union, namely a potential pathway for the European Union to support decarbonisation of the aviation sector to meet the goals of the Paris Agreement. The roadmap to decarbonising European aviation combines measures such as a carbon pricing of €150 per tonne to reduce fuel demand from aviation either by improving efficiency or reducing demand, and then proposes how the remaining fuel demand can be decarbonised by alternative biofuels and electrofuels.

Rothengatter discusses the intermodal issue, in particular with respect to high-speed rail, which is a substitute for air travel. He argues that under economic and environmental criteria, high-speed rail is advantageous over air travel for distances between 300 and 800 km in densely populated corridors. He is sceptical about a high-density, high-speed rail network.

In political and even in academic discussions, the special treatment of aviation (and also shipping) has been taken as given. Murphy questions the political decision of the current policy which goes back to the Kyoto Protocol. He shows a simple way to include aviation and shipping emissions in the Nationally Determined Contributions (NDC) of the Paris Agreement. Finally, Forsyth summarises the discussion on aviation and climate change and provides directions for future research.

The editors hope that this volume will not only provide new insights for academics as well as practitioners interested into aviation and climate change, but also encourage future research on the issue.

References

Gössling, S. and Upham, P., eds. (2009). *Climate change and aviation: Issues, challenges and solutions*. London: Earthscan.

IPCC – Intergovernmental Panel on Climate Change. (1999). *Aviation and the global atmosphere*. Cambridge: Cambridge University Press.

Stern, N. (2007). *The economics of climate change: The Stern Review*. Cambridge: Cambridge University Press.

2 Aviation emissions and climate impacts

Volker Grewe

1. Introduction

Air traffic emissions contribute to climate warming in a very complex way. The emitted species alter the atmospheric composition and cloudiness, lead to changes in Earth's radiation budget and finally contribute to human-made climate change. This chain of physical processes depends on a variety of meteorological parameters and includes a wide range of time-scales. For example, the climate impact of a today's carbon dioxide emission prevails for centuries, while contrails may exist for hours only. Here, a short overview is given, showing how emitted carbon dioxide affects the atmosphere, what kind of other, non-CO_2 effects are caused by aviation, and how these impacts can be assessed by using so-called climate metrics. Finally, examples are given to show how a reduction of air traffic's climate impacts might be achieved.

2. Aviation CO_2: from the emission to global warming

The most prominent anthropogenic greenhouse gas is carbon dioxide. It originates from kerosene, i.e. fossil fuel, combustion. Air traffic CO_2 emissions contribute to the total anthropogenic CO_2 emissions by about 2.5% (Figure 2.1). Aviation emissions have grown since the middle of the last century, when civil aviation became more important. Major international crises have reduced the growth in emissions. However, air traffic and its emissions have grown overproportionally after these crises (Figure 2.1).

The carbon dioxide emissions lead to an increase in the atmospheric CO_2 concentration. This CO_2 enhancement remains in the atmosphere and decays only slowly. The decay is controlled by several physical processes, such as the oceanic CO_2 uptake, and hence can only be insufficiently described by a single lifetime; although, for illustration purposes, a lifetime for this perturbation of 80 to 100 years provides a reasonable illustration of the long-term effect of CO_2 emissions on the CO_2 concentration.

The relation between an emission of CO_2 and the corresponding impact on the near surface temperature originates from a sequence of effects which is illustrated exemplarily in Figure 2.2. It shows, in a thought experiment, the effect of an imagined new fleet, which would go into service in 2015. The fleet

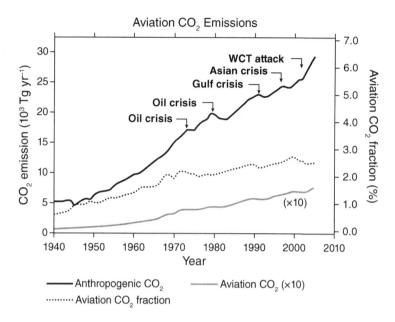

Figure 2.1 Growth in CO₂ emissions in Tg CO₂ yr-1 (left-hand axis) for all anthropogenic activities (top solid line) and from aviation fuel burn (lower solid line), and the fraction of aviation CO₂ emissions (%, right hand axis). Note that the aviation CO₂ emissions are depicted ten-fold.

Source: Figure adapted from Lee et al. (2009).

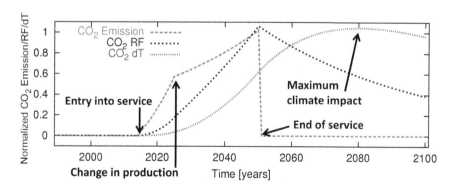

Figure 2.2 CO₂ emissions and global warming (thought experiment). Thought experiment showing the relation between CO₂ emissions and resulting global warming. Non-dimensional temporal development of an imagined fleet scenario to illustrate the principle relation between CO₂ emissions (long dashed), CO₂ concentration change and radiative forcing (short dashed) and induced temperature change (dotted). Entry into service is 2015, a lower production rate from 2025 to 2050 and a full stop of service in 2050. For all data, the maximum value is normalised to 1.

Source: Figure adapted from Grewe and Stenke (2008).

size is pictured to increase until 2050 with a change in the amount of produced aircraft in 2025. In 2050 the service of all aircraft of this type is shut down. This leads to emissions from the fleet, which follow the fleet size, peaking in 2050 and being zero afterwards. The CO_2 concentration change, and equally the impact on radiation, induced by these emissions, also peak in 2050, but the curve is much smoother and concentration changes prevail long after the emissions have stopped. The change in radiation (RF) affects the atmosphere-ocean system and leads to an increase in atmospheric temperatures, which, due to the considerable inertia of the system, peaks around 2080 – long after the emissions have stopped. An impact on climate still exists decades after the last emission happened.

3. Non-CO_2 effects from aviation

Besides carbon dioxide, there are other air traffic impacts on climate, which are equally important. These non-CO_2 air traffic impacts (Figure 2.3; see also IPCC, 1999; Wuebbles, Gupta and Ko, 2007, for more detailed sketches) can either directly affect climate, since their emission alters greenhouse gas concentrations, or they affect climate agents chemically or micro-physically, such as ozone, methane and contrails. In the following, the chemical and (micro-) physical processes, which are presented briefly in Figure 2.3, are described in more detail. The importance of the individual processes is assessed in Figure 2.4

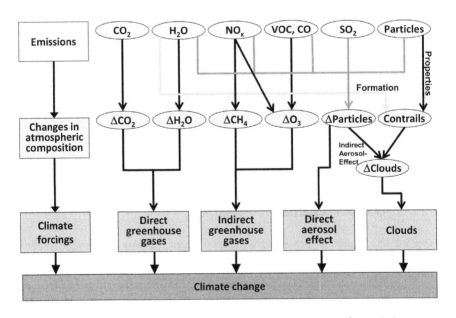

Figure 2.3 Schematic view on the processes leading to climate impacts from aviation.

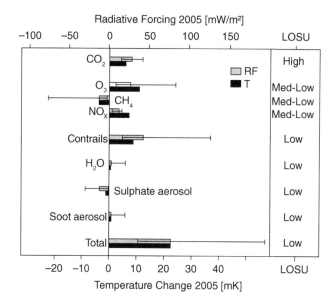

Figure 2.4: Radiative forcing and temperature change from global aviation. Radiative forcing (grey bars) from global aviation (mW/m²) and the respective temperature change (black bars) considering all emissions from 1940 to 2005 and evaluating the radiation changes and temperature changes in 2005. Error bars represent the 90% likelihood range for each RF estimate.

Source: Data are taken from Lee et al. (2009) for all climate agents except for contrail-cirrus, which are based on more recent studies summarized in IPCC (2013). Level of scientific understanding (LOSU; a subjective assessment, including both, a combination of the understanding of underlying physical processes and the range of RF quantifications) is shown on the right.

in terms of units of radiative forcing caused by aviation and in terms of the associated estimated temperature change. Note that all emissions from aviation since 1940 are considered and the RF is evaluated for the concentration changes in 2005.

The non-CO_2 climate agents have a much shorter lifetime, which implies that the location (longitude, latitude, and altitude) and time, and also the meteorology at the time of emission, determine the lifetime of the perturbation. Water vapour (Figure 2.3) is the most important natural greenhouse gas, but its lifetime in the troposphere is small, and water vapour emitted by aircraft rains out within days to weeks. It has a considerable climate impact only when it is emitted well above the tropopause. That region, the stratosphere, is strongly stratified, implying a low vertical exchange, and hence leads to an accumulation of water vapour (Grewe and Stenke, 2008). Nitrogen oxide emissions, although emitted only in a very low concentration, are controlling the ozone production, since one NO_x molecule emitted by air traffic produces around 50 to 60 ozone molecules (Dahlmann et al., 2011). The most important ozone production reaction is

$$NO + HO_2 \rightarrow OH + NO_2, \qquad\qquad (R1)$$

where the NO_2 molecule photolyses and recombines with molecular oxygen (air) to form ozone. This reaction also includes an enhancement of OH and a reduction in HO_2 (hydroperoxyl radical). The OH radical easily reacts with methane and hence reduces the concentration of this greenhouse gas. In addition, the formed ozone also leads to an OH increase (Grewe, Tsati, et al., 2017).

Volatile organic compounds (RO_2, where R stands for a carbon chain) resulting from unburned hydrocarbons are precursors for ozone similar to reaction (R1), where HO_2 and OH are replaced by RO_2 and RO. However, they are emitted only in a very low quantity by air traffic during cruise, and this air traffic emission does not significantly affect air chemistry during cruise. The impact of air traffic emissions on radiation via changes in the chemical composition are in a similar order of magnitude as those from CO_2. The warming effect from ozone production clearly dominates over the cooling from methane (Figure 2.4).

Particles in the atmosphere are both reflecting sunlight (cooling effect) and absorbing terrestrial radiation (warming effect). Their physical characteristics determine which of the processes dominates. A number of emissions are precursors for particles (Figure 2.3), such as sulphur and nitrogen oxides. Most important are soot and sulphate particle emissions, the latter depending on the sulphur content of the fuel. These emissions lead directly to changes in particle concentrations and radiative transfer. This effect is called direct aerosol effect (Figure 2.3), and it is regarded to be small compare to other effects (Figure 2.4). On the other hand, when these particles act as cloud nuclei, they change cloud cover, albedo and the absorption of terrestrial radiation and hence have an indirect effect. The relevant physical and micro-physical processes for most of these effects are, theoretically, reasonably well understood. However, it is unclear how important individual processes are and which of them occur how frequently (Righi, Hendricks and Sausen, 2016; Penner et al., 2018).

One of the most prominent climate impacts from aviation are contrails and the transition into cirrus (contrail-cirrus), which here are referred to as "contrails". They form when the hot and humid exhaust becomes saturated with respect to water during the mixing of the exhaust with surrounding air. Droplets form, which freeze when the air is cold enough. They can persist when the air is supersaturated with respect to ice and take up water from the environment; otherwise, the contrail dissolves after seconds. In the case of persistence, water vapour from the environment deposits on the ice particles. Water vapour from the exhaust has only a minor contribution to the total water vapour content of the contrail. Since the jet vortices, which capture the exhaust, subside significantly due to their dynamics, the contrail has a significant vertical extension. Vertical wind shear spreads the contrails significantly. Contrails can survive in the order of hours to around a day. Studies showed that this impact is as important for radiation changes as the CO_2 impact (Burkhardt and Kärcher, 2011; Bock and Burkhardt, 2016; references in Grewe, Dahlmann, et al., 2017; Figure 2.4).

This description of the chemical and (micro-) physical processes from air traffic (Figure 2.3) and the assessment of their importance for radiative forcing (Figure 2.4) clearly shows that some climate impacts, such as CO_2, NO_x (= NO + NO_2) and contrails are more important than others. In this regard, two major issues have to be kept in mind. First, this assessment is valid only for the air traffic system as it has been evolved; any other technology and any specific aircraft or routing will have a different climate impact, especially relation between the individual climate agents. And second, the so-called "Level Of Scientific Understanding" (LOSU), which is a combination of the understanding of physical processes and the spread in available estimates for RF, is very different for different processes, with the lowest rating for the indirect aerosol effect.

The impact of aviation on climate was illustrated in Figure 2.2, describing also the relation between RF and near surface temperature change. This relation, the so-called climate sensitivity parameter, is not equal for all climate forcings but depends on the location of the radiation change. Studies suggest that this parameter might be significantly larger for ozone and methane compared to contrails. Within the uncertainties in the quantification, the impact from CO_2 emissions, NO_x emissions, and contrails have to be seen as basically equally important (Figure 2.4). The contribution of air traffic since its beginning to current climate change is around 5%. Depending on the assumption for future scenarios, the contribution might stay at this 5% level (Skeie et al., 2009).

A range of measures to reduce the climate impact from aviation has been discussed, which includes new technologies, alternative fuels, alternative routing and economic incentives. To guide decision processes, it is indispensable to actually assess their potential to reduce the impact on climate. The process chain is laid out in Figure 2.5. Any measure will have an impact on the emissions, which in turn change the concentration of atmospheric constituents, such as greenhouse gases, contrails and clouds, which then alter the radiation and impact climate (here the near surface temperature changes are taken as a well-accepted climate change indicator). Climate change affects agriculture, forestry and energy production, to name some, and hence impacts society. Finally, damages and costs emerge. Both the political relevance and the scientific uncertainty in quantifying these effects are increasing along this process chain. Detailed calculations of this chain require an immense amount of computing and turnaround time, largely limiting the feasibility of performing routinely climate impact assessments. Hence tools or methods are required, which deliver a "shortcut"; an easy to handle and easy to understand climate metric. They have a number of requirements, e.g. they should be based on all individual

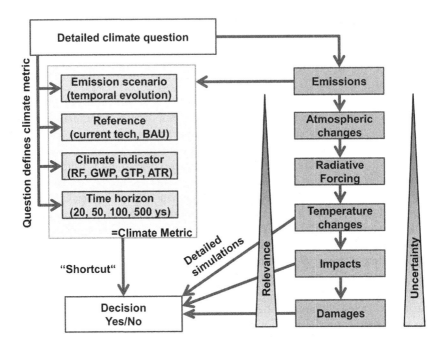

Figure 2.5 Schematic view on the process chain from emissions to damages and the role of climate metrics. RF = Radiative Forcing, GWP = Global Warming Potential, GTP = Global Temperature Potential, ATR = Average Temperature Response, BAU = Business as usual. See text for further explanations.

Source: Adapted from Fuglestvedt et al. (2003); Grewe and Dahlmann (2015).

emissions, such as CO_2, NO_x, etc., rather than on CO_2 emissions only (Forster, Shine and Stuber, 2006).

Any assessment requires a careful consideration of the respective addressed question (Grewe and Dahlmann, 2015). For example, "Does a given new aircraft concept has the potential to significantly reduce the long term climate impact, when introduced into the world's aircraft fleet?" From this question, a number of specifications can be deduced immediately (see also Figure 2.5). First, an emission scenario can be identified with an entry into service, number of aircraft produced, and lifetime of the aircraft. Second, the reference is implicitly addressed in the question, current comparable technology, where some foreseen or suggested improvements might be included. Third and fourth, the climate change indicator and time horizon can adequately be chosen. Since the mean long-term climate impact is addressed in the question, the ATR with 100 years' time span/horizon is suitable (see also the Info Box for a variety of climate indicators).

Info Box: Climate Indicators

Radiative Forcing (RF): RF is defined as the change in net irradiance at the boundary between troposphere and stratosphere (i.e. tropopause) caused by a concentration change and relative to pre-industrial times.[*]
   Absolute Global Warming Potential (AGWP): AGWP is defined as temporal integral over RF from time of emission until a given time horizon.
   Absolute Global Temperature Potential (AGTP): AGTP is equal to the near surface temperature change at a given time horizon.
   Average Temperature Response (ATR): Mean temperature change over a certain time span/horizon.
   GWP, GTP, ATR-P: The Global Warming Potential, Global Temperature Potential and the Average Temperature Response-Potential are the respective absolute climate indicators of a regarded species (AGWP, AGTP, ATR) in relation to the absolute climate indicator of a reference species (mostly CO_2) with the same mass.

[*] See IPCC (2013) for various other definitions of RF.

Generally, any approach should suit the purpose. In this context, this means that the assessment of future technologies or measures has to include a forward-looking climate indicator. Hence the radiative forcing is problematic, since it includes impacts of the past emissions. A frequently used climate change indicator is the so-called radiative forcing index (RFI), which is the ratio of the RF of all effects relative to that of CO_2. However, the RFI brings about a couple of well-known and severe disadvantages. Firstly, it is solely based on CO_2 emissions and hence not applicable in any assessment, which addresses non-CO_2 impacts. Hence, it is not emission-based (Forster, Shine and Stuber, 2006). Secondly, RF (and therefore also RFI) is an indicator for the future equilibrium temperature change, only for constant future concentrations. But constant concentrations imply a severe inconsistency between the future CO_2 and non-CO_2 emissions, because of the different lifetimes of CO_2 and non-CO_2 constituents.

4. Example for mitigation options: alternative routing

Currently a number of options to mitigate the climate impact of air traffic are discussed. They include technical changes, such as the open rotor concept, alternative fuels such as biofuels and liquid hydrogen, more efficient air traffic management and climate friendly routing. Most options are associated with increased fuel efficiency. An exemption is climate optimised routing, where a trade-off between CO_2 and non-CO_2 impacts is regarded. A strong decrease in non-CO$_2$ impacts is achieved at a relatively low expense of CO$_2$ emissions and hence decreases in fuel efficiency. The implementation of those options requires supporting economic measures.

Koch (2013), Dahlmann (2012) and Dahlmann et al. (2016) presented a study, which combines aircraft design, engine performance, trajectory calculation, cash operating costs and climate impact calculations. They focused on the roughly 1200 international routes, flown with the Airbus 330–200 in 2006. A variation of both speed (faster and slower) and initial cruise altitude (higher, when possible and lower) shows that there is a potential to reduce the climate impact (here: ATR over 100 years applying emissions over the aircraft's whole life span) by flying generally lower (Figure 2.6, dashed curve). In Figure 2.6 the current relation between the fleet's costs (fuel and crew) and the climate impact is normalised by 1 each. It shows that a 30% climate impact reduction can be achieved by flying lower at an increase of costs of around 5%. A higher climate impact reduction is feasible, though at much higher costs. The aircraft, however, was not initially optimized for that cruise altitude and speed. Hence, when redesigning the aircraft (Figure 2.6, left), it becomes much more efficient at this lower flight altitude, and a reduction of the climate impact of 30% without any increase in costs is feasible (Figure 2.6, solid line).

This approach takes into account not a rerouting for specific weather situations, but a general change in the aircraft trajectory which is applied to all

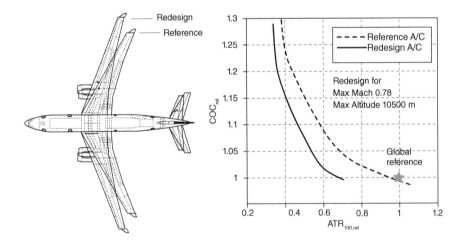

Figure 2.6 Example of aircraft design and fleet composition. Left: Design of an Airbus 330–200 and redesign for lower flight altitude and speed. Right: Optimal cost-benefit relation for two fleets of aircraft: the original aircraft (dashed) and redesigned aircraft (solid). Costs are given as relative changes of the cash operating costs (fuel and crew) and benefits are given in relative changes of the average temperature response over 100 years for cruise emission during the lifespan of the aircraft. Values are relative to the aircraft's reference trajectories.

Source: Figures are taken from Dahlmann et al. (2016).

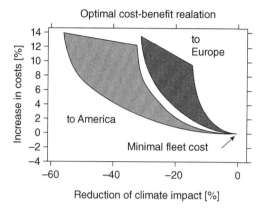

Figure 2.7 Relation of economic cost changes and climate impact changes for trans-Atlantic air traffic of one specific winter day. Relations for westbound and eastbound flights are in light and dark grey, respectively. Several climate metrics are used to indicate ranges (shaded area).

Source: Figure based on results from Grewe et al. (2014).

weather situations. However, since the non-CO_2 effects are often very regional, especially the formation of persistent contrails, it is worth considering changes in the aircraft trajectory, which take into account the specific weather situation and the variations in the climate impact from aircraft emissions depending on the location and time of these emissions. Grewe et al. (2014) analysed for one day the trans-Atlantic air traffic, i.e. roughly 400 flights in either direction. They changed the vertical and lateral routing to obtain a smaller impact on climate and found large reductions in the climate impact of about 25% with an increase in costs (mainly fuel) of 0.5% for westbound flights (Figure 2.7). The jet stream for that day was very west-east oriented. This implies that eastward flights largely profit from the jet stream's tail winds and that leaving the jet stream area includes large penalties for fuel consumption, emissions and climate impact. On the other side, westbound flights, which avoid the jet stream, have more routing options and hence a much larger climate reduction potential. However, taking all occurring weather situations into account, this difference of climate impact depending on the flight direction is becoming significantly smaller (Grewe, Matthes, et al., 2017).

5. Summary

Emissions from air traffic contribute to climate change via a number of atmospheric processes which alter the abundances of so-called climate agents. Besides CO_2, there are impacts from contrail-cirrus, NO_x emissions which lead to ozone formation and methane depletion, water vapour and particles. The atmospheric processes are complex, and although for many processes there is a good understanding and a good observational basis, the quantification is associated with large uncertainties. One reason is the large variability of the atmosphere. A detailed description of the air traffic related atmospheric changes can be found in Lee et al. (2010) and Grewe, Dahlmann, et al. (2017).

A number of options to mitigate the air traffic's climate impact are currently discussed. Most mitigation options are concentrating on the reduction of the CO_2 emissions, e.g. by introducing more efficient technologies or alternative fuels such as biofuels. A mitigation option, which appears more intriguing, is making use of the high variability in space and time of non-CO_2 climate impacts, simply by avoiding regions which are very climate sensitive, i.e. re-routing.

References

Bock, L. and Burkhardt, U. (2016). Reassessing properties and radiative forcing of contrail cirrus using a climate model. *Journal of Geophysical Research Atmospheres*, p. 121. doi:10.1002/2016JD025112.

Burkhardt, U. and Kärcher, B. (2011). Global radiative forcing from contrail cirrus. *Nature Climate Change*, 1, pp. 54–58. doi:10.1038/nclimate1068.

Dahlmann, K. (2012). *Eine Methode zur effizienten Bewertung von Maßnahmen zur Klimaoptimierung des Luftverkehrs*. Dissertation, LMU München, Fakultät für Physik, also available as DLR-Forschungsbericht, DLR-FB-2012-05.

Dahlmann, K., Grewe, V., Ponater, M. and Matthes, S. (2011). Quantifying the contributions of individual NO_x sources to the trend in ozone radiative forcing. *Atmospheric Environment*, 45(17), pp. 2860–2868. doi:10.1016/j.atmosenv.2011.02.071.

Dahlmann, K., Koch, A., Linke, F., Lührs, B., Grewe, V., Otten, T., Seider, D., Gollnick, V. and Schumann, U. (2016). Climate-compatible air transport system – climate impact mitigation potential for actual and future aircraft. *Aerospace*, 3(38). doi:10.3390/aerospace3040038.

Forster, P.M.d.F., Shine, K.P. and Stuber, N. (2006). It is premature to include non-CO_2 effects of aviation in emission trading schemes. *Atmospheric Environment*, 40, pp. 1117–1121.

Fuglestvedt, J.S., Berntsen, T.K., Godal, O., Sausen, R., Shine, K.P. and Skodvin, T. (2003). Metrics of climate change: Assessing radiative forcing and emission indices. *Climatic Change*, 58, pp. 267–331.

Grewe, V., Champougny, T., Matthes, S., Frömming, C., Brinkop, S., Søvde, A.O., Irvine, E.A. and Halscheidt, L. (2014). Reduction of the air traffic's contribution to climate change: A REACT4C case study. *Atmospheric Environment*, 94, pp. 616–625. doi:10.1016/j.atmosenv.2014.05.059.

Grewe, V. and Dahlmann, K. (2015). How ambiguous are climate metrics? And are we prepared to assess and compare the climate impact of new air traffic technologies? *Atmospheric Environment*, 106, pp. 373–374. doi:10.1016/j.atmosenv.2015.02.039.

Grewe, V., Dahlmann, K., Flink, J., Frömming, C., Ghosh, R., Gierens, K., Heller, R., Hendricks, J., Jöckel, P., Kaufmann, S., Kölker, K., Linke, F., Luchkova, T., Lührs, B., van Manen, J., Matthes, S., Minikin, A., Niklaß, M., Plohr, M., Righi, M., Rosanka, S., Schmitt, A., Schumann, U., Terekhov, I., Unterstrasser, S., Vázquez-Navarro, M., Voigt, C., Wicke, K., Yamashita, H., Zahn, A. and Ziereis, H. (2017). Mitigating the climate impact from aviation: Achievements and results of the DLR WeCare project. *Aerospace*, 4(3), pp. 1–50. doi:10.3390/aerospace4030034.

Grewe, V., Matthes, S., Frömming, C., Brinkop, S., Jöckel, P., Gierens, K., Champougny, T., Fuglestvedt, J., Haslerud, A., Irvine, E. and Shine, K. (2017). Feasibility of climate-optimized air traffic routing for trans-Atlantic flights. *Environmental Research Letters*, 12(3), p. 034003. doi:10.1088/1748-9326/aa5ba0.

Grewe, V. and Stenke, A. (2008). AirClim: An efficient climate impact assessment tool. *Atmospheric Chemistry and Physics*, 8, pp. 4621–4639.

Grewe, V., Tsati, E., Mertens, M., Frömming, C. and Jöckel, P. (2017). Contribution of emissions to concentrations: The TAGGING 1.0 submodel based on the Modular Earth Submodel System (MESSy 2.52). *Geoscientific Model Development*, 10, pp. 2615–2633. doi:10.5194/gmd-2016-298.

IPCC. (1999). *Aviation and the global atmosphere: A special report of IPCC working groups I and III.* Cambridge: Cambridge University Press.

IPCC. (2013). *Climate change 2013 – the physical science basis, intergovernmental panel on climate change, working group I contribution to the fifth assessment report*, T.F. Stocker, D. Qin, G-K. Plattner, M.M.B. Tignor, S.K. Allen, J. Boschung, A. Nauels, Y. Xia, V. Bex and P.M. Midgley, eds. Cambridge: Cambridge University Press.

Koch, A. (2013). *Climate impact mitigation potential given by flight profile and aircraft optimization*. Dissertation, also DLR-Forschungsbericht, FB-2013-37.

Lee, D.S., Fahey, D.W., Forster, P.M., Newton, P.J., Wit, R.C.N., Lim, L.L., Owen, B. and Sausen, R. (2009). Aviation and global climate change in the 21st century. *Atmospheric Environment*, 43(22–23), pp. 3520–3537. doi:10.1016/j.atmosenv.2009.04.024.

Lee, D.S., Pitari, G., Grewe, V., Gierens, K., Penner, J.E., Petzold, A., Prather, M.J., Schumann, U., Bais, A., Berntsen, T., Iachetti, D., Lim, L.L. and Sausen, R. (2010). Transport impacts on atmosphere and climate: Aviation. *Atmospheric Environment*, 44, pp. 4678–4734.

Penner, J.E., Zhou, C., Garnier, A. and Mitchell, D.L. (2018). Anthropogenic aerosol indirect effects in cirrus clouds. *Journal of Geophysical Research: Atmospheres*, 123(11), pp. 652–677. doi:10.1029/2018JD029204.

Righi, M., Hendricks, J. and Sausen, R. (2016). The global impact of the transport sectors on atmospheric aerosol in 2030 – part 2: Aviation. *Atmospheric Chemistry and Physics*, 16, pp. 4481–4495. doi:10.5194/acp-16-4481-2016.

Skeie, R.B., et al. (2009). Global temperature change from the transport sectors: Historical development and future scenarios. *Atmospheric Environment*, pp. 6260–6270. doi:10.1016/j.atmosenv.2009.05.025.

Wuebbles, D., Gupta, M. and Ko, M. (2007). Evaluating the impacts of aviation on climate change. *Eos Transactions American Geophysical Union*, 88, pp. 157–160. doi:10.1029/2007EO 140001.

3 Renewable fuels for aviation

Arne Roth

1. Introduction

Renewable and drop-in capable jet fuels are needed to meet the industry's self-imposed targets for greenhouse gas (GHG) emission reductions. This contribution addresses the potentials of renewable jet fuels as an important pillar of a future sustainable aviation sector. First, aviation-specific targets in the context of internationally agreed goals to limit global warming are described. Then, the issue of drop-in capability and technical approval of synthetic jet fuel is addressed, and a brief overview of selected production pathways and the current use of renewable jet fuel is presented. Several production pathways, based on biomass feedstock as well as non-biogenic options, are under development but have not yet been industrially demonstrated. The specific GHG balance of renewable jet fuels and the scalability of production are discussed as key factors determining the potential of renewable jet fuel alternatives to facilitate the energy transition in the aviation sector. Many pathways show very favourable GHG performances and production potentials that are in principle sufficient to supply the worldwide fleet with renewable fuel. Finally, the economic competitiveness of renewable jet fuel is discussed as a key challenge for large-scale market uptake, and a concluding outlook on further developments is presented.

2. The need for renewable jet fuel

The world's economy has to be "decarbonized" in the long term. While this expression in its literal sense is misleading, as carbonaceous materials will always be eaten, burnt, consumed and used in many ways, it transports a serious and urgent meaning: The carbon loop of our economy and our daily life has to be closed, thus stopping the accumulation of carbon in Earth's atmosphere, biosphere and the oceans through combusting fossil fuels.

At the 2015 United Nations Climate Change Conference (COP 21) held in Paris, the parties agreed on the long-term target of "holding the increase in the global average temperature to well below 2 °C above pre-industrial levels and to pursue efforts to limit the temperature increase to 1.5 °C above pre-industrial levels" (UN, 2015). In order to achieve this target, enormous efforts are required worldwide and by all sectors. It should nevertheless be noted that international aviation is not *explicitly* included in the Paris Agreement – the mandate for emissions abatement from international aviation has been assigned to ICAO as responsible UN body. ICAO has defined a "basket of measures to reduce aviation CO_2 emissions" (described in ICAO, 2016a: Chapter 4), and, as part of that, decided in 2016 "to implement a GMBM[1] scheme in the form of the Carbon Offsetting and Reduction Scheme for International Aviation (CORSIA) to address any annual increase in total CO_2 emissions from international civil aviation" (ICAO, 2016b). However, the Paris Agreement of course *implicitly* includes the entire (national and international) aviation sector through the specification of the overarching goal of limiting global warming to 2 °C or even 1.5 °C.

The fifth assessment report (AR5) of the Intergovernmental Panel on Climate Change (IPCC) assesses various mitigation scenarios and their compatibility with targets to limit global warming. According to AR5, the 2 °C target is met with a probability of greater than 66%, if the CO_2 concentration in the atmosphere does not exceed the range of 430 to 480 ppm at the end of this century (IPCC, 2014: Chapter 6). This compares to a global average level of already 410 ppm today (NOAA, 2018a) and an annual increase of well above 2 ppm in the past five years (NOAA, 2018b). In terms of emission trajectories, this means that by 2050 the global annual GHG emissions have to be reduced by 41% to 72% relative to 2010 and even by 78 to 118% by the end of this century (IPCC, 2014). To meet the 1.5 °C goal, the reductions have to be substantially more severe, with annual emissions peaking already in 2020, reaching values below today's level by 2030 and even more strongly declining beyond 2030 (Millar et al., 2017).

The IPCC emission trajectories are global and include emissions from all sectors. However, it is obvious that any sector or any nation failing to meet the required average emission reduction would translate into even higher reductions required in the other sectors or nations. While there are currently no binding emission reduction targets in place for commercial aviation, the aviation industry itself, recognizing its responsibility to contribute to the global efforts to limit global warming, has announced a set of ambitious, albeit non-binding targets to reduce its carbon footprint (illustrated in Figure 3.1, top). Specifically, the aviation industry committed to increase the fleet's fuel efficiency by 1.5% per year until 2020, to reach carbon-neutral growth[2] from 2020 onwards and to halve the net CO_2 emissions of the aviation sector by 2050 relative to the level of 2005 (ATAG, 2012). This target for 2050 lies well within the required emission reduction corridor associated with a greater than 66% probability of keeping global warming below 2 °C, according to the IPCC (2014) assessment. Please note that the reference year for quoted IPCC scenarios is 2010, while the aviation industry's reduction targets are defined relative to 2005; as emissions in 2005 were lower than in 2010, this means that a reduction of 50% relative to 2005, as targeted by the aviation industry, would correspond to an even higher reduction relative to 2010. However, it must also be emphasized that

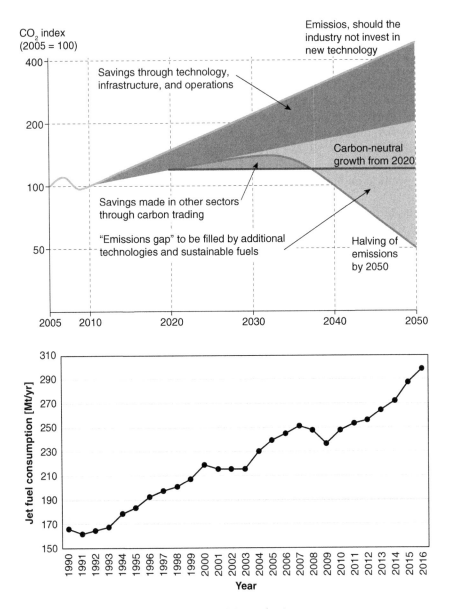

Figure 3.1 Jet fuel consumption and CO_2 emission reduction targets.

Top: Schematic illustration of the CO_2 emission reduction targets of the aviation industry. Bottom: Historic global jet fuel consumption.

Sources: Top: Adapted from ATAG (2012). Carbon-neutral growth from 2020 and halving of fleet-wide emissions relative to 2005 levels by 2050; emission reductions envisioned through improvements in technology and operations as well as through market-based measures (carbon trading or offsetting); an "emissions gap" remains to be filled through use of sustainable fuels and "additional technologies". Bottom: EIA (2018). The 2005 level of consumption is indicated as reference for the ATAG target of halving emissions relative to 2005 level by 2050.

according to the IPCC assessment, even higher reductions are required for the second half of the century, essentially resulting in a complete decarbonization of all sectors by 2100. In this sense, the goal of halving emissions by 2050 can be only an intermediate step on the pathway of the aviation sector towards the 2 °C target (or even the 1.5 °C target).

To understand the challenges associated with the aviation industry's emissions reduction goals, it is useful to look at the recent development of the sector's fuel consumption (Figure 3.1, bottom). From the plotted data it is apparent that fuel consumption of global aviation is rapidly increasing, albeit with temporary declines following the Gulf War in 1991, the September 11 attacks in New York in 2001 and the global economic crisis in 2008. But apart from these temporary declines, global jet fuel consumption has grown annually by 1% to 8% since 1992. As the jet fuel consumed today is essentially 100% conventional (i.e., fossil), this means that CO_2 emissions of aviation have increased approximately with the same rate.

The extent of the problem associated with the future development of the aviation sector's emissions vs. the targeted emission reductions becomes clearly visible when studying the market development forecasts of the industry. For example, aircraft manufacturers Boeing (2017) and Airbus (2017) forecast a global annual air traffic growth (in revenue kilometres) of 4.7% and 4.4%, respectively, for the next 20 years (2017–2036). Such growth rates would substantially surpass the sector's ambitious targets in terms of increased fuel efficiency, for example 1.5% annual efficiency gains until 2020, as expressed by the global aviation industry (ATAG, 2012), or even 2% annual gains until 2050, as set forth by ICAO (2011).

Such a development would, if it becomes reality, result in a future situation where the growth in air traffic continues to outpace gains in efficiency, translating into a net growth in fuel consumption and, consequently, in rising GHG emissions, if the consumed jet fuel remains largely conventional. For international aviation, ICAO (2016a) projects a more than fourfold increase in CO_2 emissions from fuel combustion by 2050 when compared to 2005 levels, even under optimistic assumptions with respect to development and implementation of fuel-efficient technologies. It can therefore be concluded that an energy transition is needed in the aviation sector, in the course of which essentially the entire volume of currently fossil kerosene is replaced in the long-term future by renewable energy carriers with very low specific GHG emissions. In this context, however, aviation's contribution to global warming cannot be measured only by the emitted quantities of CO_2 and other GHGs; another relevant contribution comes from the fact that aircraft cause emissions of soot, water, nitrogen oxides, sulphur oxides and other species in high altitudes, thereby affecting atmospheric physico-chemical processes and impacting the global radiation budget (Lee et al., 2010; IPCC, 2013: Chapter 7; Grewe in this volume).

Several technology options enabling an energy transition in aviation are currently discussed and researched, such as electric propulsion using batteries and/or hydrogen fuel cells, hybrid electric solutions and liquefied gaseous or synthetic liquid fuels. However, given the long development and product cycles of aircraft, the high cost associated with the implementation of disruptive technologies and the to-date limited performance of required key technologies, e.g. batteries with sufficient storage capacities, it is generally acknowledged that the only feasible renewable energy option for aviation in the near- to medium-term future are synthetic liquid fuels. Such fuels should be designed in a way that allows direct use without requiring any changes of aircraft and fuel systems and are therefore commonly referred to as *drop-in* fuels.

3. Drop-in capability

For safety reasons, aviation is a sector with rigid national and international standards and specifications. A specific standard specification (ASTM D7566) for "aviation turbine fuel containing synthesized hydrocarbons" has been developed (ASTM International, 2019). This specification lists approved types of synthetic fuel components and specific production technologies and specifies all technical requirements for the synthetic components as well as for the final jet fuel blend. Meanwhile, several types of synthetic fuels have been approved according to ASTM D7566; for example, Fischer-Tropsch Hydroprocessed Synthesized Paraffinic Kerosene (FT-SPK), approved in 2009, and Hydroprocessed Esters and Fatty Acids (HEFA), approved in 2011. More recently, other fuel pathways have been technically approved, such as Alcohol-to-Jet (AtJ), based on alcohols as intermediate products, and synthetic isoparaffinic (SIP) jet fuel produced via the so-called Direct-Sugar-to-Hydrocarbon (DSHC) pathway. A brief description of these (and selected other) production pathways is presented in Section 4.

Once approved according to ASTM D7566, alternative jet fuels can be used in civil aviation, albeit to date only in blends with conventional jet fuel. The reason for this limitation is that the alternative jet fuels that have been technically approved so far differ in their chemical composition from conventional jet fuel. Even though the chemical compounds found in alternative jet fuels are also found in conventional kerosene, the chemical composition of conventional jet fuel is broader and more complex, generally representing mixtures of linear, branched and cyclic alkanes, aromatic species and traces of other compounds. Overall, it is estimated that conventional jet fuel consists of about 1000 or even more chemical compounds (Hemighaus et al., 2006). This complexity of conventional jet fuel is a consequence of the diverse composition of crude oil, from which it is produced. Alternative production pathways, in contrast, often rely on specific synthetic procedures that yield a specific class of products, sometimes even specific product compounds. The narrower distribution of chemical constituents affects the macroscopic properties (physico-chemical properties and properties related to storage and handling) of a fuel. The relation between jet fuel composition and macroscopic properties was recently described in a comprehensive report (Zschocke, Scheuermann and Ortner, 2017).

In this context, it is important to understand that fuel systems and engines used today in aviation have been developed and optimized for the use of conventional jet fuel. In the absence of detailed knowledge about the relation between chemical and macroscopic properties and in order to ensure flawless operation of engine and fuel systems, usage of jet fuels produced from sources other than crude oil is limited to blends with conventional jet fuel. However, this limitation can be revised depending on future developments, e.g., in production pathways or engine technologies. In principle, also approval of 100% alternative jet fuel (i.e. fully drop-in capable alternative jet fuel) is conceivable.

4. Renewable aviation fuels: technology options and current use

As argued previously, the aviation sector is in great need of tremendous quantities of renewable drop-in fuels to achieve its self-imposed GHG emission reduction targets and to comply with the internationally adopted COP 21 climate protection targets. However, while renewable fuels for road transport in the form of, e.g., ethanol and biodiesel produced from biogenic feedstock represent long-established renewable energy options, the increasing interest in alternative jet fuel is a comparably new phenomenon. Motivated by this growing interest, a diverse landscape of production technologies is currently under development, with maturity levels ranging from research at laboratory scale to already successful industrial implementation. A detailed review of viable production pathways can be found in the relevant literature, e.g., in Kaltschmitt and Neuling (2018) and Mawhood et al. (2016). In Section 4 a high-level description of the most prominent technical approaches to produce renewable jet fuel is given. This description is in part based on a technology review conducted in the EU-funded coordination and support action CORE-JetFuel (Coordinating research and innovation of jet and other sustainable aviation fuel–Grant Agreement No. 605716). Text passages of the CORE-JetFuel report "Report on compilation, mapping and evaluation of R&D activities in the field of conversion technologies of biogenic feedstock and biomass-independent pathways" (Roth, Sizmann and Jeßberger, 2016), exclusively written by the author of this chapter, have been used for this purpose and were adapted, updated and shortened where necessary.

4.1 Hydroprocessed Esters and Fatty Acids (HEFA)

The production of Hydroprocessed Esters and Fatty Acids (HEFA) fuels is based on hydroprocessing of fats and oils (triacylglycerols; also named triglycerides) of biogenic origin, i.e. from plants or animals. The HEFA conversion process is schematically illustrated in Figure 3.2. In this context, hydroprocessing (a process well established in classical petrochemical industry) is generally understood to include a family of thermochemical processes under hydrogen atmosphere, namely hydrogenation, hydrocracking and hydroisomerization. These processes

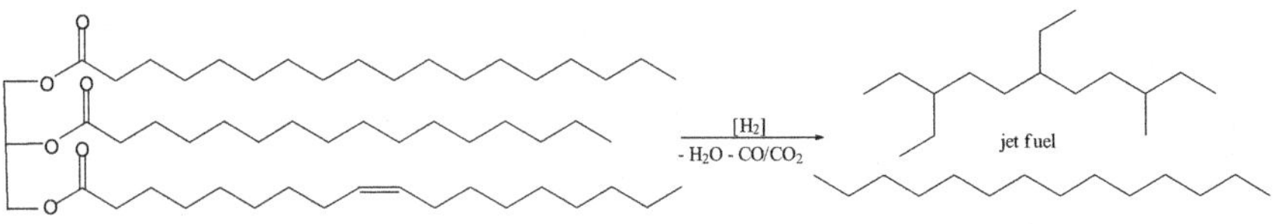

Figure 3.2 Schematic illustration of HEFA jet fuel production from oils and fats (triacylglycerols) via hydroprocessing.

Note: Displayed compounds are shown as exemplary representatives of triacylglycerols (educts) as well as branched (iso) and linear (*n*) alkanes as products in the jet fuel range. In reality, the educts and produced fuels contain a large number of different compounds; in addition to middle distillate fuels (jet fuel, diesel), lighter naphtha fractions and propane are generated.

can occur in parallel, i.e., in a single reactor at the same time. Please note that readily usable jet fuel (conventional or containing synthetic blending components) is far more complex than shown here and contains a wide variety of linear, branched and cyclic hydrocarbons.

As exclusively unbranched alkanes (*n*-alkanes) are unsuitable for jet fuel (or diesel) applications mainly due to disadvantageous cold flow properties, the yielded *n*-alkanes have to undergo hydrocracking (leading to a reduction of molecular weight through shortening of the average chain length) and hydroisomerization (conversion of linear into branched compounds) in order to meet specifications (ASTM International, 2019).

HEFA was approved for use in commercial aviation in blends of up to 50% with conventional jet fuel in 2011 and is currently the only production process of renewable jet fuel that has been industrially implemented at substantial scale. Consequently, HEFA is the only renewable jet fuel commercially available in relevant quantities at the moment. A limited number of HEFA refineries are operational worldwide with production capacities of up to 800,000 t of middle distillate fuels per year. The most important producers are Neste Oil, with plants in Finland, Singapore and the Netherlands, and AltAir Fuels, with a plant in Paramount, California, that was recently acquired by World Energy. It is important to note that the targeted product in the mentioned production facilities is mainly diesel, while jet fuel is usually produced only on demand and in limited quantities. An exception is the AltAir Fuels plant in Paramount that has an integrated jet fuel production capability (see also Section 4.5).

4.2 Thermochemical pathways

In contrast to the HEFA pathway that depends on fats and oils as single energy-dense type of feedstock, thermochemical technologies are capable of converting a broad range of heterogeneous biomass materials, importantly including lignocellulosic materials that are ubiquitous and highly abundant in the biosphere. Two examples of such thermochemical technologies are introduced here, namely the gasification of biomass followed by Fischer-Tropsch synthesis and hydrothermal liquefaction (HTL). It must be emphasized, however, that there are far more technologies at various stages of development, for example technologies based on pyrolysis. Comprehensive reviews of thermochemical conversion pathways can be found in the pertinent literature (Kaltschmitt and Neuling, 2018; Zhang, Xu and Champagne, 2010).

4.2.1 Gasification and Fischer-Tropsch synthesis

The process of gasification of biomass and subsequent Fischer-Tropsch (FT) synthesis, often referred to as Biomass-to-Liquid (BtL), is closely related to the conventional Coal-to-Liquid (CtL) technology that has been long established at industrial scale, e.g., by SASOL in South Africa. In a sense, BtL represents a renewable variation of the conventional CtL process. However, utilization of biomass as feedstock poses specific challenges, particularly related to the heterogeneity of the starting material, its content of heteroelements (sulphur, nitrogen, phosphorous and metals) as well as its varying water content and mechanical properties.

The BtL technology is based on the generation of syngas (synthesis gas, a mixture of hydrogen and carbon monoxide) via gasification of biogenic carbonaceous feedstock and subsequent FT synthesis, as schematically depicted in Figure 3.3. The raw FT product, often termed FT crude, is hydroprocessed to saturate all C-C bonds, to maximize yields of the desired product fractions and to adjust the ratio of branched and linear alkanes. For more detailed information on Fischer-Tropsch technologies, refer to the existing rich literature, e.g., Steynberg and Dry (2004) or de Klerk (2011).

To date, no commercial BtL production facility has become operational. Several industrial projects have recently been announced, e.g., by Red Rock Biofuels (Liedtke, 2018) and Fulcrum (GreenAir, 2018b), but none of them has entered the operational phase yet.

Jet fuel produced via gasification and FT synthesis, so-called FT-SPK (Fischer-Tropsch Hydroprocessed Synthesized Paraffinic Kerosene), was the first synthetic fuel approved according to ASTM D7566 for use in commercial aviation

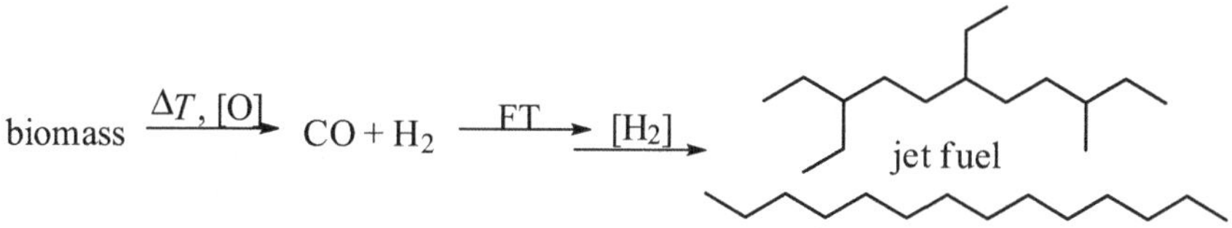

Figure 3.3 Schematic illustration of the BtL process via gasification at high temperatures and in the presence of an oxidizing agent (oxygen and/or steam), Fischer-Tropsch (FT) synthesis and hydroprocessing.

Note: Displayed product compounds are shown as exemplary representatives of branched (iso) and linear (n) paraffins in the jet fuel range. In reality, the produced fuels contain a large number of different compounds.

(see also Section 3). It can be used in blends with conventional jet fuel containing up to 50% of the synthetic component.

4.2.2 Hydrothermal liquefaction (HTL)

Hydrothermal liquefaction (HTL) of biogenic feedstock represents a special case of hydrothermal processing where biomass is treated in an aqueous medium at high temperatures and pressures, usually in the sub or near-critical regime, i.e., below 374°C and 220 bar (Biller and Roth, 2018; Elliott et al., 2014). Virtually all types of carbonaceous biogenic feedstock can be processed via HTL, rendering this technology highly flexible. As a particular advantage, no energy-intensive drying of the feedstock is required, as HTL is conducted in aqueous phase with water as reacting agent and solvent. Feedstock is applied as slurry, usually containing 10%–30% solid material. This means that very wet feedstock with about 80% water content can be readily used. Microalgae, for example, represent a suitable feedstock that is otherwise challenging to convert. But also other types of feedstock with high moisture and ash content can be applied in HTL, including waste streams, such as residues of anaerobic digestion (AD), manures, sewage sludge, dried distiller grains with solubles (DDGS), food wastes and municipal wastes. However, also "classical" types of biomass, including dedicated energy crops such as energy grasses or woody biomass from short-rotation coppice, can be used.

The targeted raw product of HTL is a black and viscous oil phase usually referred to as biocrude (see Figure 3.4). In addition, an aqueous phase, a gas phase (mainly CO and CO_2) and a solid fraction are formed in the process. To produce transportation-grade fuels, biocrude requires upgrading, e.g., through hydrotreatment to remove heteroelements, similar to the upgrading of fossil crude oil in conventional refineries (Ramirez, Brown and Rainey, 2015).

The chemistry behind the HTL process is complex and the composition and product distribution of the formed phases are highly dependent on the applied feedstock and the specific reaction conditions. These dependencies are not yet fully understood and subject of ongoing research efforts.

The product distribution is largely affected by the biochemical composition of the feedstock. Lipids, for example, are almost entirely fractionated to the biocrude in the form of fatty acids and alkanes as reaction products. Carbohydrates, on the other hand, tend to form undesired char. This can be avoided by keeping the pH value of the reaction mixture in the alkaline regime to increase biocrude yields. Addition of alkaline catalysts is particularly important when processing lignocellulosic feedstock to achieve satisfactory conversion of carbohydrates to biocrude and to avoid excessive char formation. The yielded biocrude can be upgraded via hydroprocessing to fuel products in the gasoline, kerosene and diesel range.

Several companies are currently striving to bring HTL technology to industrial maturity. Examples are Licella, located in Australia, and Steeper Energy, located in Denmark and Canada. Licella operates a pilot facility where it has

Figure 3.4 Biocrude produced via continuous HTL in a pilot-scale research reactor.
Source: Picture courtesy of P. Biller, Aarhus University, Denmark.

developed and demonstrated its Cat-HTR™ technology, while Steeper Energy recently announced a partnership with Silva Green Fuel, a Norwegian–Swedish joint venture, to construct an industrial-scale demonstration plant with an investment of EUR 50.6 million at a former pulp mill located in Tofte, Norway (Steeper Energy, 2017). The planned facility has a targeted production capacity of 4000 litres of biocrude per day and will use forestry residues as feedstock (Lane, 2018). However, despite the promising commercialization projects, no industrial-scale facility applying HTL processes has yet become operational.

Moreover, all commercial projects are focusing exclusively on HTL as a primary conversion step, while none includes the subsequently required upgrading and refining steps in order to yield transport-grade fuel products.

As no industrial projects are dedicated to upgrading and refining of biocrude, little is known about the properties and potential suitability of fuel products refined from biocrude. However, scientific studies show that aliphatic as well as aromatic compounds potentially suitable as jet fuel components are present in the upgraded products in substantial quantities. Therefore, it is likely that HTL-derived fuels prove suitable for application as renewable jet fuel.

4.3 Pathways involving fermentation

4.3.1 Alcohol-to-Jet (AtJ)

The pathway Alcohol-to-Jet (AtJ) essentially consists of two independent processes, namely the production of alcohols, typically via microbial fermentation of carbohydrates from biomass, and the subsequent chemical conversion of alcohols (the actual AtJ process) into hydrocarbons, such as diesel and jet fuel. Here, the description is limited to the AtJ step, as the fermentative production of alcohol (at least of ethanol) from various biomass feedstock can be considered industrially mature.

For the conversion of alcohols into liquid hydrocarbon fuels, alcohols are typically first dehydrated, yielding the corresponding alkanes, which are subsequently oligomerized to the desired chain length. Final hydrogenation yields saturated hydrocarbons (alkanes) that could serve, e.g., as blendstock in jet fuel production, if process conditions are chosen accordingly. A simplified AtJ reaction scheme for the alcohols ethanol and isobutanol is presented in Figure 3.5.

In this process, the molecular structure of the products are specific for the alcoholic educt and the chosen process pathway. This means that an AtJ process starting from ethanol yields products that differ from AtJ conversion starting from isobutanol. In case of both alcohols, product molecules show even carbon

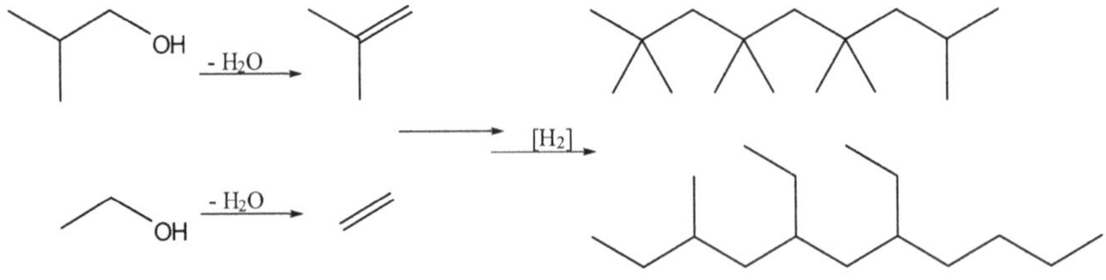

Figure 3.5 Schematic illustration of the AtJ conversion of isobutanol (top) and ethanol (bottom) into hydrocarbon compounds in the jet fuel range.

Note: Displayed product compounds are shown as exemplary representatives of alkanes typically generated in the respective process. However, in reality, conversion efficiency and selectivity are not 100%, i.e. other products than the depicted ones are formed as well.

numbers (multiples of C_2 for ethanol and of C_4 for isobutanol). Formation of the branched AtJ product based on ethanol as feedstock, as shown in Figure 3.5 (bottom), assumes dimerization of ethylene to 1-butene and 2-butene which are then oligomerized and hydrogenated, yielding C_8, C_{12} and C_{16} (as in Figure 3.5) *iso*-alkanes in the jet fuel range. Alternatively, ethylene can be oligomerized directly, resulting in linear alkanes from C_8 to C_{16} in the jet fuel range. In contrast, in case of isobutanol as feedstock, oligomerization and hydrogenation also yields C_8, C_{12} and C_{16} *iso*-alkanes, but with a higher degree of branching (Figure 3.5, top).

Several companies are pursuing commercialization of AtJ production, e.g. Gevo, LanzaTech and Swedish Biofuels, even though industrial-scale production has not yet been realized. Nevertheless, substantial progress has been achieved in the past years with the technical approval of AtJ-derived jet fuel in commercial aviation (ASTM D7566, Annex 5). Being originally limited to a maximum blending ratio of 30% and isobutanol as feedstock, approval was recently extended to 50% maximum blending ratio and now also includes ethanol as starting material (Green Car Congress, 2018).

4.3.2 Direct microbial conversion to hydrocarbons

The approach of using microorganisms to directly convert carbohydrates into pure hydrocarbons (not alcohols) is pursued by several companies, most prominently by Amyris (in collaboration with Total) and by Global Bioenergies. As the Amyris pathway is the most developed one, it is briefly described in the following.

In the conversion route developed by Amyris, sugar (mainly glucose or sucrose) is converted by genetically engineered microorganisms into the C_{15}-alkene farnesene. In a second step, farnesene is saturated *via* hydrogenation, yielding the final fuel product farnesane. The overall process is also termed Direct-Sugar-to-Hydrocarbon (DSHC) and is schematically depicted in Figure 3.6.

A unique feature of this synthetic jet fuel is the fact that it represents only a single compound (farnesane). This compares to a highly diverse composition of conventional jet fuel that is likely to contain more than 1000 different chemical compounds (Hemighaus et al., 2006). In 2014, farnesane produced via the Amyris process[3] was approved according to ASTM D7566 for use in civil aviation at a maximum blending ratio of 10%. This comparably low blending limit

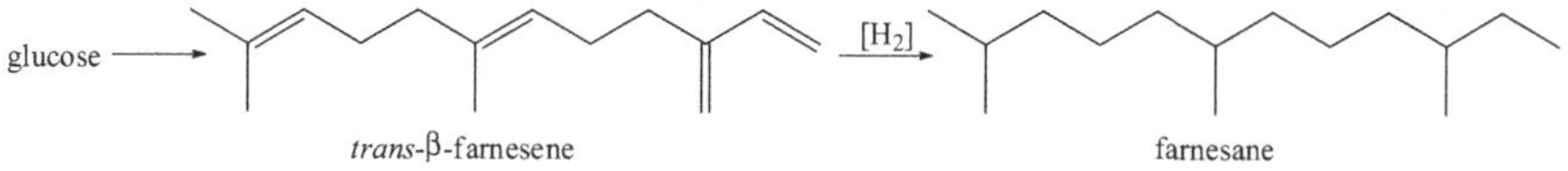

glucose ⟶ *trans*-β-farnesene [H₂] ⟶ farnesane

Figure 3.6 Schematic representation of the DSHC conversion route developed by Amyris.

Note: Sugar (here: glucose) is converted into farnesene (an unsaturated C_{15} compound) and subsequently hydrogenated to yield the saturated hydrocarbon (a branched iso-alkane) farnesane ($C_{15}H_{32}$).

results from the described unique composition of the fuel (100% farnesane). Amyris' jet fuel production technology has been demonstrated in Brazil based on sugar from sugarcane, but it has not yet been commercialized.

4.4 Renewable non-biogenic processes

Most of the production technologies that are currently researched and developed (and all of the pathways described earlier in this chapter) depend on biogenic feedstock, i.e. biomass. In this context, biomass represents an intermediate storage system for solar energy, which is chemically stored via photosynthesis in plants in the form of biomass. However, the concept of relying on natural photosynthesis as an energy harvesting system suffers from the inherent low energy efficiency of photosynthesis. While the theoretical limit of the photosynthetic efficiency ranges from 4.6% for so-called C_3 plants to 6% for C_4 plants (Zhu, Long and Ort, 2008), actual efficiencies of only about 1% or lower are achieved under natural growth conditions. This low efficiency translates into low area-specific yields (corresponding to an inefficient use of land) and other critical issues, such as high water consumption for biomass production. In the light of increasing concerns related to environmental and social sustainability, it is therefore of great interest to develop production technologies that do not depend on the use of biomass feedstock and, thus, to diversify the renewable fuel technology portfolio (Stechel and Miller, 2013). Two examples of such non-biogenic pathways, namely Power-to-Liquids (PtL) and solar-thermochemical fuel production, are introduced in the following.

4.4.1 Power-to-Liquids (PtL)

Power-to-Liquids (PtL) is a production pathway for liquid hydrocarbons based on electric energy, water and carbon dioxide (CO_2) as main resources. A schematic illustration of the PtL process is presented in Figure 3.7. If the electric energy and CO_2 are generated from renewable sources, PtL represents a renewable, but biomass-independent (non-biogenic) pathway to produce liquid fuels. Detailed descriptions of technical aspects, techno-economic and environmental potentials, in particular with respect to jet fuel production, can be found in the relevant literature (Schmidt et al., 2016, 2018; Terwel and Kerkhoven, 2018; Malins, 2017).

The basic principle of PtL is to re-energize the combustion products carbon dioxide and water by electric energy in a synthetic process, finally yielding fuel products. The PtL process comprises three main steps:

1   Hydrogen production from renewable electricity using the electrolysis of water.
2   Provision and conversion of renewable CO_2.
3   Synthesis of liquid hydrocarbons, e.g. via Fischer-Tropsch synthesis, with subsequent upgrading/conversion to fuels.

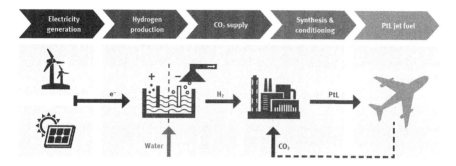

Figure 3.7 Schematic illustration of the Power-to-Liquids (PtL) production pathway.

Renewable electric energy is used to generate hydrogen via electrolysis of water; hydrogen is then reacted with CO_2 to produce hydrocarbon fuels. The liquefaction process ("synthesis & conditioning") includes several reaction and refining steps, e.g. Fischer-Tropsch synthesis.

Source: Schmidt et al. (2016); reproduced with permission of Ludwig-Bölkow-Systemtechnik GmbH and Umweltbundesamt.

Electrolysis of water results in the electrochemical splitting of water into hydrogen and oxygen, here shown for the case of alkaline electrolysis:

$$4H_2O + 4e^- \rightarrow 2H_2 + 4OH^-$$
$$4OH^- \rightarrow O_2 + 2H_2O + 4e^-$$

The net reaction of these two half-cell reactions is the generation of hydrogen and oxygen according to:

$$2 H_2O \rightarrow 2H_2 + O_2$$

Electrolysis of water represents the key process step in the PtL pathway, where electric energy is chemically stored in the form of the gaseous fuel hydrogen. In the following process step, carbon dioxide (CO_2) is supplied from a renewable point source, such as biogas power plants or bioethanol production plants, or from direct air capture (DAC). CO_2 is then reduced by some of the generated hydrogen in a reverse water gas shift (RWGS) reaction, yielding the more reactive carbon monoxide (CO):

$$CO_2 + H_2 \rightleftharpoons CO + H_2O$$

A mixture of CO and the remaining H_2 (synthesis gas) is then liquefied, e.g., through Fischer-Tropsch (FT) synthesis (as in case of biomass gasification/FT synthesis; see Section 4.2.1) and refined into liquid fuel products. Even though FT synthesis is generally discussed as most straightforward liquefaction technology for PtL, if targeting long-chain hydrocarbon products, other pathways are conceivable. For example, syngas can also be liquefied through methanol synthesis, with the methanol being further converted into hydrocarbons (Schmidt et al., 2018).

Substantial R&D efforts are currently dedicated to PtL technologies worldwide. However, production of liquid hydrocarbon fuels via PtL has not yet been demonstrated at an industrially relevant scale. A small demonstration unit has been constructed and successfully operated by Sunfire in Dresden, and the construction of an industrial-scale demonstration facility by Nordic Blue Crude is planned in Norway, scheduled to start operation in 2020 with an initial production capacity of 8000 t/yr (Sorge, 2017).

If Fischer-Tropsch synthesis is applied as liquefaction process, the yielded jet fuel fractions are already approved for use in commercial aviation, according to the ASTM D7566 standard specification. This is an important advantage for the endeavour of bringing PtL-based jet fuel production to commercial application.

4.4.2 Solar-thermochemical fuels

In the solar-thermochemical fuel production pathway, solar heat is used to drive the splitting of the low-energy compounds water (H_2O) and carbon dioxide (CO_2):

$$H_2O \xrightarrow{\Delta T} H_2 + 1/2O_2$$
$$CO_2 \xrightarrow{\Delta T} CO + 1/2O_2$$

The heat is supplied through solar tower or dish concentrating systems, enhancing solar irradiation by 1500 times or more. A schematic illustration of the process of solar-thermochemical fuel production is presented in Figure 3.8. Detailed descriptions on solar-thermochemical production systems can be found in the relevant literature (Chueh et al., 2010; Romero and Steinfeld, 2012; Batteiger et al., 2015).

In a nutshell, the high-energy compounds hydrogen (H_2) and carbon monoxide (CO) generated in the splitting reaction are separated as synthesis gas from the by-product oxygen (O_2) and further processed in a liquefaction unit, e.g. via Fischer-Tropsch synthesis, just as in the case of PtL (Section 4.4.1) and that of gasification of biomass (Section 4.2.1). While in principle the splitting of water could be conducted thermolytically, i.e. through thermally induced breakage of C-O and O-H bonds, this would require unfavourably high temperatures. Therefore, the splitting is mediated by metal oxides, without altering the net reactions (the splitting of H_2O and CO_2 into H_2, CO and O_2) but with decreasing the reaction temperatures to manageable regimes. For example, utilization of cerium dioxide (CeO_2, often referred to as ceria) enables operation of the splitting process at temperatures of 1100 to 1800 K (Furler, Scheffe and Steinfeld, 2012).

The concept of this process chain was proven in the EU-funded collaborative project SOLAR-JET (n.d.), where the first-ever sample of hydrocarbons in the jet fuel range was produced through solar-thermochemical splitting of

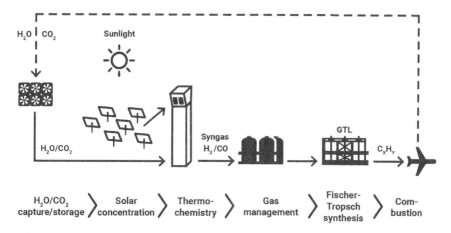

Figure 3.8 Schematic illustration of solar-thermochemical fuel production. Solar heat, generated in a solar tower concentrating system, is used to drive the generation of synthesis gas (syngas, a mixture of H_2 and CO) from water and CO_2. Syngas is liquefied, e.g., through Fischer-Tropsch synthesis and refined into hydrocarbon fuels, such as jet fuel.

Source: Reproduced with permission of Arttic/SUN-to-LIQUID: Integrated solar-thermochemical synthesis of liquid hydrocarbon fuels. Grant agreement no. 654408. http://www.sun-to-liquid.eu.

water and CO_2 in laboratory-scale experiments and by using an artificial sun (Marxer et al., 2015). The field validation of the process under relevant operational conditions represents the central objective of the succeeding EU-funded project SUN-to-LIQUID: A dedicated solar tower concentration facility has been constructed at IMDEA Energy Institute in Mostoles (Spain), as shown in Figure 3.9. The facility is now operational and has been presented to the public in June 2019. In both projects, the thermochemical reactors (developed at ETH Zurich) were based on CeO_2 as reaction mediator.

Solar-thermochemical fuel production represents a technology that is still far from industrial maturity. However, it shows promising techno-economic and environmental performance potentials (Falter, Batteiger and Sizmann, 2016; Falter and Pitz-Paal, 2017) and should be further researched as a technology option that offers both sustainability and scalability. As in the case of biomass gasification (Section 4.2.1) and PtL (Section 4.4.1), the yielded jet fuel fraction is already approved for use in commercial aviation, if Fischer-Tropsch synthesis is used as liquefaction technology.

4.5 Current commercial use of renewable jet fuel

In the past near ten years, as several production pathways were approved and added to the standard specification ASTM D7566 (see Section 3), there has been a considerable number of projects and initiatives by numerous airlines to

Figure 3.9 Solar tower concentration facility for field validation of the solar-thermochemical fuel production process as part of the EU-funded collaborative project SUN-to-LIQUID. The facility is located at IMDEA Energy Institute, Mostoles, Spain.

Source: Picture courtesy of E. Koepf/© ETH Zürich 2017.

use renewable jet fuels in commercial flights. A pioneering example was the project burnFAIR in Germany, where Lufthansa operated 1188 regular commercial flights between Hamburg and Frankfurt over a period of six months in 2011. In that project, one engine of a single Airbus A321 was fuelled with a 50% blend of HEFA-SPK (Zschocke, 2014). This was the first time that an airline used renewable jet fuel in a series of scheduled commercial flights. Many projects by other airlines followed. Information about current activities and flights powered by renewable jet fuel is provided by the ICAO Global Framework for Aviation Alternative Fuels (GFAAF) (ICAO, 2018).

In all of the early demonstration projects, the used renewable fuel was supplied from dedicated storage systems to the aircraft; it was not delivered through the common fuel hydrant systems at airports. Thereby it was ensured that the renewable jet fuel could be supplied to the specific aircraft (or even specific engine) of the airline that had purchased the renewable fuel batch. However, such a procedure is impracticable for day-to-day business, considering a future large-scale deployment of renewable jet fuel. Consequently, recent developments have been focused on introducing renewable jet fuel into the common fuel hydrant systems of selected airports.

Oslo Airport was the first example, where kerosene produced from biomass was distributed through the hydrant system, thereby supplying all aircraft departing from Oslo with small quantities of renewable jet fuel (Larsen, 2017; McKenna, 2017). Other airports followed, such as Los Angeles and Toronto (GreenAir, 2018a), or announced to do so (Port of Seattle, 2018; SkyNRG, 2018).

Nevertheless, despite these encouraging developments, the current share of renewable jet fuel in the total volume of jet fuel consumed worldwide (about 270 Mt per year (IATA, 2017)) is negligibly small. This is mainly a consequence of unfavourably high cost of production of renewable jet fuel, as will be discussed in more detail in the next section.

It is also interesting to note that in almost all demonstration projects, HEFA fuel (see Section 4.1) was used. Only in a very few cases were other fuel options applied, e.g. synthetic isoparaffinic (SIP) jet fuel produced by Amyris on a few national Air France flights in France in 2014 (GreenAir, 2014a) and AtJ fuel produced by Gevo on singular flights by several airlines in 2017 (GreenAir, 2017). This reflects the fact that today HEFA is the only industrially mature production technology, while other pathways have been realized only at demonstration scale (SIP and AtJ) or are not ready for production at all. The portfolio of fully developed production technologies that can contribute to short-term deployment of renewable jet fuel is very limited, and more development efforts are required to enlarge this portfolio and, thus, enable the future ramp-up of production through sustainable and scalable technologies.

5. The potential of renewable jet fuel

The foremost objective of using renewable jet fuel is to reduce the carbon footprint of the aviation sector, as laid out in Section 2. In the previous sections it was discussed that there are several promising pathways to produce renewable jet fuels under development. A crucial question now concerns to what extent the various pathways can contribute towards achieving the objective of reducing aviation's carbon footprint.

The following three criteria are key to evaluate a specific pathway's potential:

1   **Specific greenhouse gas (GHG) emissions,** i.e., the GHG emissions released per unit of fuel over its entire life cycle from production (also of the feedstock) to combustion. Specific GHG emissions can also be expressed as specific GHG emission reduction potential, i.e., in relation to specific GHG emissions of conventional jet fuel.
2   **Production potential,** i.e., the volumes that can be produced based on the potential availability of all required resources (including energy). The production potential describes the scalability of fuel production pathways.
3   **Economic competitiveness.**

While economic issues are addressed separately in Section 6, the specific GHG emissions of renewable jet fuels and their production potential are briefly discussed in the following.

5.1 Specific greenhouse gas emissions

The specific greenhouse gas (GHG) emissions of renewable jet fuels strongly depend on the feedstock used and the conversion technology applied. Moreover, the results of life-cycle assessments can vary substantially, depending on the underlying assumptions, methods and boundary conditions. Nevertheless, specific GHG emissions (absolute values and in comparison to emissions of conventional jet fuel) for the production pathways described in Section 4 have been extracted from selected published sources and listed in Table 3.1. Please note that this is an exemplary compilation and not at all an exhaustive review of available data that can often span a broad range, even for a single production pathway.

An important aspect apparent from the listed data is the fact that utilization of renewable feedstock, particularly biomass, does not necessarily result in a favourable GHG balance. The values in Table 3.1 range from GHG reduction of over 90% (compared to conventional jet fuel) for gasification/FT of forestry residues to zero for HTL of microalgae. Considering the tremendous

Table 3.1 Specific greenhouse gas (GHG) emissions of selected production pathways for renewable jet fuel

Production pathway	Feedstock	Specific GHG emissions $[gCO_{2,eq} MJ_{fuel}^{-1}]$		Reference
HEFA	Jatropha	55–60	(31–37%)	a, b
	Used cooking oil	27	(69%)	b
Gasification/FT	Forestry residues	6	(93%)	b
	Corn stover	13	(85%)	b
HTL	Forestry residues	18–20	(77–79%)	b
	Microalgae	87	(0%)	c
AtJ	Corn stover	35	(60%)	b
	Sugar cane	26	(70%)	b
DSHC (SIP)	Sugar cane	44	(50%)	b
Power-to-Liquids (PtL)	Electric energy, CO_2, water	11–28	(68–87%)	d
Solar-thermochemical	Solar heat, CO_2, water	15	(83%)	e

References for Table 3.1:
a: Zschocke (2014); b: de Jong et al. (2017); c: Fortier et al. (2014); d: Schmidt et al. (2018); e: Falter, Batteiger and Sizmann (2016)

Note: Specific reductions of GHG emissions relative to conventional jet fuel (specific GHG emissions; Stratton, Wong and Hileman, 2010): 87.5 $gCO_{2,eq} MJ_{fuel}^{-1}$) are given in parentheses as percent values. Electricity input for Power-to-Liquids (PtL) production assumed to be completely renewable (PV/wind in Germany). Emissions from land use change are not included.

challenges associated with reducing the climate impact of aviation to the targeted levels (Section 2), renewable fuel pathways promising less than a 60% GHG reduction compared to conventional jet fuel do not seem to be expedient options. Accordingly, pathways based on lignocellulosic feedstock, such as forestry residues (but also many other materials not listed here) and renewable non-biogenic pathways (PtL and solar-thermochemical production) are highly promising options. It must be emphasized, however, that the GHG balance of non-biogenic options strongly depends on the source of the utilized energy and CO_2: only if input energy and CO_2 from *renewable* sources are used is a favourable GHG balance achieved. Low specific GHG emissions, as listed in Table 3.1 for PtL fuels, require electricity input from completely renewable sources. It should also be noted that fuel production from biogenic sources, particularly from energy crops, can induce substantial GHG emissions from land use change (LUC) (Qin, Mishra and Hastings, 2017). LUC-induced GHG emissions are not included in values listed in Table 3.1.

5.2 Production potential

The scalability of production pathways of renewable fuels is ultimately limited by the sustainable availability of feedstock. This is particularly important for fuel options depending on biomass, where increasing demand for energy crops can result in, e.g., land-use change issues with environmental and social implications.

Many studies have been conducted on the assessment of the potential availability of different types of biomass feedstock, such as land-based energy crops, algae, wastes and residues. A comprehensive review of the rich pertinent literature has been published recently (Roth, Riegel and Batteiger, 2018). Therefore, the discussion of production potentials is restricted to a few key issues here.

First, it must be clearly stated that production of food and feed to secure the sufficient nutrition of the population generally represents the purpose of use with the highest priority; only resources not required to meet this demand can be considered potentially available for energy purposes.

Furthermore, the potential availability of biomass for energy purposes is limited by sustainability issues. This includes environmental as well as socio-economic sustainability. Concerns are raised in particular for agricultural and silvicultural production of dedicated energy crops, for example, in terms of negative impacts on biodiversity, use of pesticides and fertilizers, water consumption, conversion of formerly natural habitats and other issues. But the use of wastes and residues is also limited for sustainability reasons (Searle and Malins, 2016). For example, a certain share of residues from agriculture and forestry need to be left unused to maintain the quality of the soils and protect biodiversity. Furthermore, competing uses of such residues, e.g. as fuel wood or animal feed, have to be considered.

Depending on assumptions with regard to sustainability-related land-use restrictions, a broad span of biomass potentials has been reported. The more conservative estimations resulted in global future biomass potentials from the cultivation of land-based energy crops of about 30–125 EJ[4] per year (Roth, Riegel and Batteiger, 2018), from which roughly 100–425 Mt of jet fuel could be produced.

The potential of wastes and residues for energy purposes has recently been assessed for the European Union, with overall 157 Mt (dry mass) sustainably available per year (Searle and Malins, 2016; Malins et al., 2014). This roughly corresponds to an annual production potential of jet fuel of about 10 Mt. About 50% of this potential comes from agricultural residues.

As an additional class of biomass feedstock, microalgae have attracted substantial attention in recent years. Microalgae can be cultivated in various types of photobioreactors (Apel and Weuster-Botz, 2015), but a techno-economically viable and environmentally advantageous pathway of cultivation and conversion has not yet been established. In principle, microalgae do not require fertile land for cultivation, and consequently, the potential of microalgae can be considered complementary to the potential of land-based energy crops. However, the viability of fuel production from microalgae is uncertain.

Overall, there is a considerable potential for the production of jet fuel from biomass feedstock (energy crops, wastes and residues), if compared to the current global jet fuel consumption of about 270 Mt per year (IATA, 2017) (see Figure 3.1). However, it is uncertain whether this potential can be fully leveraged in a sustainable way. Even though conservative studies take certain sustainability principles into account, sustainability of biomass cultivation depends on many specific local conditions and has environmental, economic and social dimensions. Strict and coherent sustainability standards have to be implemented to ensure that the use of biomass for energy purposes does not compromise its intentional purpose, i.e. to establish a sustainable energy basis for aviation and other sectors. Extensive deployment of biogenic jet fuel would also require political prioritization of jet fuel production over other uses of biomass feedstock (Staples et al., 2018).

Moving to renewable pathways that do not depend on biomass feedstock, such as PtL (Section 4.4.1) and solar-thermochemical fuels (Section 4.4.2), production potentials are essentially unlimited with respect to the required input streams water, CO_2 and renewable energy. Water and CO_2 can be sustainably sourced in the required quantities, e.g. from desalination of sea water (Falter and Pitz-Paal, 2017) and direct capture from air (Sanz-Pérez et al., 2016), respectively. And the potential of renewable energy is surpassing the energy demand of aviation by orders of magnitude. For example, a geo-scientific assessment of concentrated solar power (CSP) generation on suitable land areas with high local solar irradiation showed a technical potential of 3,000,000 TWh$_{el}$ per year (Trieb et al., 2009). For comparison, the global annual electricity consumption in 2014 amounted to about 23,000 TWh$_{el}$ (IEA, 2014), while about 6,600 TWh$_{el}$ per year would be required to meet the entire global annual jet fuel demand of 270 Mt through PtL production (assuming a conversion efficiency of 50%). Importantly, the potential of renewable (non-biogenic) energy is widely complementary to biomass and bioenergy potentials, as no fertile land is needed for its harvesting. For example, the land areas most suitable for solar electricity generation are located in arid regions with low humidity and high solar irradiation, i.e., regions unsuitable for efficient agriculture.

It can be concluded from this brief discussion of the scalability of production pathways that the theoretical potential of renewable jet fuel is sufficient to sustainably supply the entire global fleet and to meet the aviation sector's emission reduction targets. However, it must also be emphasized that such an energy transition in aviation is associated with substantial investments in the construction of required fuel production capacities (Staples et al., 2018).

6. Economic aspects

The costs for airlines associated with the procurement of jet fuel are substantial. According to IATA, the annual expenses of global commercial airlines for fuel in the time between 2006 and 2016 ranged from 127 billion to 230 billion USD (IATA, 2017), representing a major share of the airlines' operating costs. The major obstacle for large-scale use of renewable jet fuel lies in the fact that it is substantially more costly to produce than conventional jet fuel. The exact difference in cost of production depends on many factors, such as the price of crude oil vs. local cost of feedstock, labour and energy, and varies strongly for different production pathways. Nevertheless, and in spite of the broad range of cost estimations reported throughout the scientific literature, published studies are quite coherent in the general finding that renewable jet fuel is more expensive than the conventional one.

An overview of the minimum fuel selling price (MFSP) of renewable jet fuel produced via various pathways (conversion technologies and feedstock), according to a few selected recent studies, is shown in Table 3.2. Interestingly, the lowest MFSP (of the pathways assessed in the cited studies) was found for jet fuel produced via HTL from forestry residues (921 EUR t^{-1}; see Table 3.2). However, at the same time, jet fuel production from woody biomass via HTL (the same conversion technology) was reported in another study to result in a substantially higher MFSP of 3,023 EUR t^{-1}, which is also the consequence of very high investment cost assumed in that specific study (Bann et al., 2017) for the construction of the HTL production facility.

Without going further into detail on the assumptions and specific accounting methodologies in the cited publications (and acknowledging that this is by far not an exhaustive list of relevant studies in this field), it is interesting to note that the MFSPs (mean values) of renewable jet fuels listed in Table 3.2 range from about 900 EUR t^{-1} to more than 6,000 EUR t^{-1}. This compares to today's average market prices (IATA, 2018) of conventional jet fuel of about 540 EUR t^{-1}, confirming the previously stated problem of an unfavourable "cost premium" of renewable vs. conventional jet fuel.

As mentioned in the beginning of this section, this unfavourable cost performance of renewable jet fuel poses a severe challenge for large-scale deployment.

Table 3.2 Minimum fuel selling price (MFSP) for various renewable jet fuels

Production pathway	Feedstock	MFSP (EUR t⁻¹)	Ref.
HEFA	Soybean oil	1,395 (1,013–1,868)	a
	Used cooking oil	1,272 (938–1,795)[a]	b
Gasification/FT	Municipal solid waste	1,342 (1,105–1,618)	a
	Forestry residues	1,666 (816–3,754)[a]	b
	Wheat straw	2,412 (1,346–4,978)[a]	b
HTL	Woody biomass	3,224 (2,421–4,145)	a
	Forestry residues	921 (734–2,407)[a]	b
	Wheat straw	1,272 (979–3,346)[a]	b
AtJ	Forestry residues	2,280 (1,265–3,550)[a]	b
	Wheat straw	3,420 (1,877–5,263)[a]	b
DSHC (SIP)	Forestry residues	4,560 (2,530–7,018)[a]	b
	Wheat straw	6,140 (3,305–9,746)[a]	b
Power-to-Liquids (PtL)	Electric energy, CO_2, water	1,841 (1,086–1,926)[b]	c
		1,348–4,165[c]	d
Solar-thermochemical	Solar heat, CO_2, water	2,513–2,934[d]	e

a min and max values estimated from sensitivity analysis; b based on 2050 technologies; c based on 2030 technologies; d low value: CO_2 from point source; high value: CO_2 from direct air capture.

References Table 3.2:
a: Bann et al. (2017); b: de Jong et al. (2015); c: Schmidt et al. (2018); d: Brynolf et al. (2018); e: Falter, Batteiger and Sizmann (2016)

Note: Values were extracted from selected published studies (cited in the table) and converted into EUR t⁻¹, where necessary; wherever available, mean values are given, with min and max values in parentheses.

On the demand side, most (if not all) airlines will not be willing to purchase renewable fuel at substantially higher prices than for conventional jet fuel, at least not in large quantities and on a regular basis, unless they gain a compensating monetary benefit from doing so or are forced by regulative measures. Monetary benefits could come from, e.g., emission trading or carbon offsetting schemes. On the supply side, companies are reluctant to risk the large investments required to build up industrial production facilities, unless sufficient demand for their fuel products can be expected at prices that ensure the return of investments and to achieve a reasonable profit. However, without the build-up of industrial production facilities, cost reduction through learning effects cannot be achieved. This situation is commonly referred to as the "hen-and-egg problem", and it is argued that public support through funding, price guaranties or other measures would be required to break this circle and enable ramp-up of industrial production. But even though there is no doubt that cost reduction through learning effects would occur, it is not clear when (if at all) production of renewable jet fuel at competitive cost (compared to conventional jet fuel) will be possible. Firstly, it is uncertain to what extent production cost of renewable jet fuel can be reduced through process optimization, even for an *n*th plant production case. And secondly, cost competitiveness of renewable fuels strongly depends on the market price of crude oil as the main cost driver for the conventional reference, which is notoriously difficult to predict.

Looking at the development of the conventional jet fuel price over the past 30 years (illustrated in Figure 3.10 for the U.S. market) shows that large alterations can occur within a few years, with prices above 800 EUR t^{-1} in 2008 and in 2011–2013. Even though today's jet fuel price lies far below these levels (at about 540 EUR t^{-1}, according to IATA, 2018), it is conceivable, based on the historic data, that prices around 900 EUR t^{-1} could again become reality within a few years from now. Such prices would not be too far away from (even if still below) the MFSP of several renewable fuels, as listed in Table 3.2.

In any case, it is very likely that in the short- and medium-term future, it will remain more expensive to produce renewable than conventional jet fuel. In order to facilitate the deployment of renewable jet fuel in spite of this disadvantage, external adjustment of the market conditions will be required. Various options for such an adjustment are frequently and controversially discussed in the aviation community, e.g., mandatory quota for renewable jet fuel or even a ban on conventional kerosene, subsidies for producers or consumers, introduction of carbon or fuel taxes, market-based measures (such as the Emissions Trading Scheme – ETS – in the EU) or carbon offsetting schemes (such as ICAO's CORSIA); see also the respective chapters in this volume. The fact that aviation is a highly international sector with a global network renders any implementation of regulative measures very complicated and challenging. International actions require international agreements, while national measures are easier to implement, but generally pose risks of market distortion, as is often argued.

Apart from regulative measures, offtake agreements between producers and consumers appear to be effective instruments to de-risk investments in production facilities and to help bridging the so-called valley of death between the stage of R&D and industrial implementation. For example, the airline Cathay Pacific and fuel supplier BP agreed to buy 1.14 Mt and 1.52 Mt, respectively,

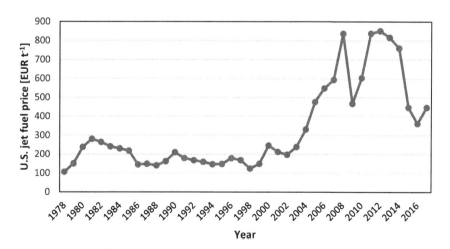

Figure 3.10 Historic jet fuel prices in the U.S.

Data Source: EIA (2018).

over 10 years from Fulcrum (GreenAir, 2014b, 2016). Fulcrum plans to construct a first industrial facility to produce liquid fuels via gasification of municipal solid waste and FT synthesis (Section 4.2.1). Similarly, Red Rock Biofuels (producing fuels from forestry residues; see Section 4.2.1) has offtake agreements in place with FedEx and Southwest Airlines over eight years (Biofuels Digest, 2018). Particularly for capital-intensive renewable non-biogenic production pathways, such as PtL (Section 4.4.1), offtake contracts could help to de-risk investments. Nordic Blue Crude reports to have multiple offtake agreements in place (Holen, 2019).

However, it has to be noted that none of the three mentioned examples has started construction of the production facilities at the time of this writing. Therefore, it remains to be seen, if those projects will be successful and actually produce and supply the promised fuel volumes.

7. Outlook

Renewable and drop-in capable jet fuels will have to play a central role in the endeavour of aviation to substantially reduce its climate footprint. Considering the projected growth of air traffic, a near-complete substitution of conventional by renewable jet fuel will be required in the long term to enable aviation to meet the industry's self-imposed GHG emission reduction targets and to develop in a way that is consistent with the internationally agreed target of limiting global warming to well below 2 °C (or even below 1.5 °C).

Various promising technologies for the production of renewable jet fuel are currently under development. Many of these technologies are based on the use of biomass feedstock, while others facilitate renewable production without using biogenic feedstock, such as Power-Liquids (PtL) and solar-thermochemical fuels. It is encouraging that many production pathways show very low specific GHG emissions, when compared to conventional jet fuel. Equally important, the potential availability of feedstock and renewable energy is, in principle, sufficient to facilitate a sustainable energy transition of the aviation sector.

However, no production pathway offering both, highly favourable GHG balance (sustainability) and large production potentials (scalability), have reached industrial maturity to date. Substantial R&D efforts are therefore required to explore the potentials of new and novel technologies and, at the same time, to demonstrate more established options under industrially relevant operational conditions.

Unfortunately, production of renewable and truly sustainable jet fuel will likely remain substantially more expensive than conventional jet fuel. The lack of economic competitiveness under the current market conditions represents the main obstacle on the way towards large-scale deployment. External economic or regulative measures will be required to facilitate significant market uptake. Examples of such measures reach from mandatory quota, subsidies and carbon taxes to emissions trading and carbon offsetting schemes. Currently the subject of controversial discussions is which measures are most suitable in terms of effectiveness and cost efficiency. Nevertheless, some measures will be needed, as it is unlikely that economic competitiveness can be achieved alone through technical developments and lessons learnt from industrial demonstration projects.

In summary, renewable jet fuels have the potential to facilitate the transition of the aviation sector from a conventional to a renewable energy basis. Promising technologies, depending on biomass as well as renewable non-biogenic options, are currently under development but have not yet reached industrial maturity. The main obstacle for the large-scale deployment of renewable jet fuels is the lack of economic competitiveness, as renewable jet fuels are more costly to produce than conventional kerosene. Substantial efforts to further develop promising production technologies and the installation of regulative and policy measures are required to enable the economically competitive large-scale production of renewable jet fuels.

The author gratefully acknowledges funding from the European Union's Seventh Programme for Research Technological Development and Demonstration under Grant Agreement No 605716 (Project CORE-JetFuel). He would also like to thank Dr. V. Batteiger, Dr. C. Falter and Dr. A. Sizmann from Bauhaus Luftfahrt e. V. for critically reviewing the manuscript.

Notes

1 Global Market-Based Measures
2 Carbon-neutral growth means that aviation's CO_2 emissions shall be capped, not exceeding the level of 2020, despite the expected growth of transport capacity. However, it is envisioned that this target will not be met through emission reductions within the aviation sector alone, but also through market-based measures, such as emissions trading or offsetting, i.e. through additional reductions in other sectors.
3 Now named SIP (synthetic isoparaffinic) jet fuel.
4 1 EJ (exajoule) corresponds to 10^{18} J.

References

Airbus. (2017). *Global market forecast – growing horizons 2017 / 2036.* Blagnac Cedex.
Apel, A.C. and Weuster-Botz, D. (2015). Engineering solutions for open microalgae mass cultivation and realistic indoor simulation of outdoor environments. *Bioprocess and Biosystems Engineering*, 38(6), pp. 995–1008.
ASTM International. (2019). *ASTM D7566-19b, Standard Specification for Aviation Turbine Fuel Containing Synthesized Hydrocarbons.* West Conshohocken, PA: ASTM International.
ATAG – Air Transport Action Group. (2012). *A sustainable flightpath towards reducing emissions.*
Bann, S.J., Malina, R., Staples, M.D., Suresh, P., Pearlson, M., Tyner, W.E., Hileman, J.I. and Barrett, S. (2017). The costs of production of alternative jet fuel: A harmonized stochastic assessment. *Bioresource Technology*, 227, pp. 179–187.
Batteiger, V., Bauldreay, J., Falter, C., Furler, P., Geerlings, H., Le Clercq, P., Marxer, D., Pandi, P., Reinalda, D., Scheffe, J., Sizmann, A. and Steinfeld, A. (2015). Progress and perspectives of

solar fuels. In: *Aviation in Europe innovating for growth: Proceedings of the 7th European Aeronautics Days 20–23 October, London.* pp. 167–173.

Biller, P. and Roth, A. (2018). Hydrothermal liquefaction: A promising pathway towards renewable jet fuel. In: M. Kaltschmitt and U. Neuling, eds., *Biokerosene – status and prospects.* Berlin, Heidelberg: Springer, pp. 607–635.

Biofuels Digest. (2018). *The story of Red Rock Biofuels and the bond market breakthroughs.* [Online] Available at: http://www.biofuelsdigest.com/bdigest/2018/01/11/it-takes-a-village-to-raise-a-biorefinery-the-story-of-red-rock-biofuels-and-all-those-others-shifting-to-bond-market-financing/ [Accessed 25 May 2018].

Boeing. (2017). *Current market outlook 2017–2036.* Seattle.

Brynolf, S., Taljegard, M., Grahn, M. and Hansson, J. (2018). Electrofuels for the transport sector: A review of production costs. *Renewable & Sustainable Energy Review*, 81, pp. 1887–1905.

Chueh, W.C., Falter, C., Abbott, M., Scipio, D., Furler, P., Haile, S.M. and Steinfeld, A. (2010). High-flux solar-driven thermochemical dissociation of CO_2 and H_2O using nonstoichiometric ceria. *Science*, 330(6012), pp. 1797–1801.

de Jong, S., Antonissen, K., Hoefnagels, R., Lonza, L., Wang, M., Faaij, A. and Junginger, M. (2017). Life-cycle analysis of greenhouse gas emissions from renewable jet fuel production. *Biotechnology for Biofuels*, 10, p. 64.

de Jong, S., Hoefnagels, R., Faaij, A., Slade, R., Mawhood, R. and Junginger, M. (2015). The feasibility of short-term production strategies for renewable jet fuels – a comprehensive techno-economic comparison. *Biofuels, Bioproducts and Biorefining*, 9(6), pp. 778–800.

de Klerk, A. (2011). Fischer – Tropsch fuels refinery design. *Energy and Environmental Science*, 4(4), pp. 1177–1205.

EIA – U.S. Energy Information Administration. (2018). *International energy statistics.* [Online] Available at: https://www.eia.gov [Accessed 14 May 2018].

Elliott, D.C., Biller, P., Ross, A.B., Schmidt, A.J. and Jones, S.B. (2014). Hydrothermal liquefaction of biomass: Developments from batch to continuous process. *Bioresource Technology*, 178, pp. 147–156.

Falter, C., Batteiger, V. and Sizmann, A. (2016). Climate impact and economic feasibility of solar thermochemical jet fuel production. *Environmental Science & Technology*, 50(1), pp. 470–477.

Falter, C. and Pitz-Paal, R. (2017). Water footprint and land requirement of solar thermochemical jet-fuel production. *Environmental Science & Technology*, 51(21), pp. 12938–12947.

Fortier, M-O.P., Roberts, G.W., Stagg-Williams, S.M. and Sturm, B.S.M. (2014). Life cycle assessment of bio-jet fuel from hydrothermal liquefaction of microalgae. *Applied Energy*, 122, pp. 73–82.

Furler, P., Scheffe, J.R. and Steinfeld, A. (2012). Syngas production by simultaneous splitting of H_2O and CO_2 via ceria redox reactions in a high-temperature solar reactor. *Energy & Environmental Science*, 5(3), pp. 6098–6103.

GreenAir. (2014a). *Air France launches one-year sustainable development showcase project involving weekly biofuel flight.* [Online] Available at: http://www.greenaironline.com/news.php?viewStory=1998 [Accessed 17 May 2018].

GreenAir. (2014b). *Cathay Pacific enters equity deal and 10-year offtake agreement with MSW-to-biojet developer Fulcrum.* [Online] Available at: http://www.greenaironline.com/news.php?viewStory=1963 [Accessed 25 May 2018].

GreenAir. (2016). *Oil giant BP makes significant entry into sustainable aviation fuel production with investment in Fulcrum.* [Online] Available at: http://www.greenaironline.com/news.php?viewStory=2303 [Accessed 25 May 2018].

GreenAir. (2017). *Eight airlines join 'Fly Green Day' to use Gevo's alcohol- to-jet fuel on flights out of Chicago.* [Online] Available at: http://www.greenaironline.com/news.php?viewStory= 2426 [Accessed 16 Nov. 2017].

GreenAir. (2018a). *Air Canada, Red Rock and SkyNRG move forward on biofuel initiatives while Air New Zealand takes longer view.* [Online] Available at: http://www.greenaironline.com/ news.php?viewStory=2473 [Accessed 2 May 2018].

GreenAir. (2018b). *Fulcrum BioEnergy breaks ground on 10.5 million gallon waste to jet fuel Sierra plant.* [Online] Available at: http://www.greenaironline.com/news.php?viewStory=2486 [Accessed 22 May 2018].

Green Car Congress. (2018). *ASTM greenlights ethanol as feedstock for alcohol-to-jet synthetic fuel; blend level up to 50%.* [Online] Available at: http://www.greencarcongress.com/2018/ 04/20180416-atj.html [Accessed 23 May 2018].

Hemighaus, G., Boval, T., Bacha, J., Barnes, F., Franklin, M., Gibbs, L., Hogue, N., Jones, J., Lesnini, D., Lind, J. and Morris, J. (2006). *Aviation fuels technical review (FTR-3).* Chevron Corporation.

Holen, G. (2019). Producing Fischer-Tropsch-based Kerosene and Naphtha on Commercial Scale. *Mitigating the Impact on Climate Change in Air Transport.* 10th International Conference on Sustainable Aviation and the Future of Air Transport, 19 November, Bonn, Germany.

IATA – International Air Transport Association. (2017). *Fact sheet industry statistics.*

IATA – International Air Transport Association. (2018). *Jet fuel price monitor.* [Online] Available at: http://www.iata.org/publications/economics/fuel-monitor/Pages/index.aspx [Accessed 8 May 2018].

ICAO – International Civil Aviation Organization. (2011). *Resolution A37–19: Consolidated statement of continuing ICAO policies and practices related to environmental protection – climate change.* Montreal.

ICAO – International Civil Aviation Organization. (2016a). *On board a sustainable future – ICAO environmental report 2016.* Montreal.

ICAO – International Civil Aviation Organization. (2016b). *Resolution A39–3: Consolidated statement of continuing ICAO policies and practices related to environmental protection – global market-based measure (MBM) scheme.* Montreal.

ICAO – International Civil Aviation Organization. (2018). *ICAO global framework for aviation alternative fuels.* [Online] Available at: https://www.icao.int/environmental-protection/ GFAAF/Pages/default.aspx [Accessed 17 May 2018].

IEA – International Energy Agency. (2014). *Key world energy statistics 2014.*

IPCC – Intergovernmental Panel on Climate Change. (2013). Clouds and aerosols. (Boucher, O., Randall, D., Artaxo, P., Bretherton, C., Feingold, G., Forster, P., Kerminen, V-M., Kondo, Y., Liao, H., Lohmann, U., Rasch, P., Satheesh, S.K., Sherwood, S., Stevens, B. and Zhang, X.Y.) In: T.F. Stocker, D. Qin, G-K. Plattner, M. Tignor, S.K. Allen, J. Boschung, A. Nauels, Y. Xia, V. Bex and P.M. Midgley, eds., *Climate change 2013: The physical science basis. Contribution of working group I to the fifth assessment report of the intergovernmental panel on climate change.* Cambridge, UK and New York: Cambridge University Press.

IPCC – Intergovernmental Panel on Climate Change. (2014). Assessing transformation pathways. (L. Clarke, K. Jiang, K. Akimoto, M. Babiker, G. Blanford, K. Fisher-Vanden, J-C. Hourcade, V. Krey, E. Kriegler, A. Löschel, D. McCollum, S. Paltsev, S. Rose, P.R. Shukla, M. Tavoni, B.C.C. van der Zwaan and D.P. van Vuure). In: O. Edenhofer, R. Pichs-Madruga, Y. Sokona, E. Farahani, S. Kadner, K. Seyboth, A. Adler, I. Baum, S. Brunner, P. Eickemeier, B. Kriemann, J. Savolainen, S. Schlömer, C. von Stechow, T. Zwickel and J.C. Minx, eds., *Climate change 2014: Mitigation of climate change. contribution of working group III to the fifth assessment report of the intergovernmental panel on climate change.* Cambridge, UK and New York: Cambridge University Press.

Kaltschmitt, M. and Neuling, U., eds. (2018). *Biokerosene – status and prospects.* Berlin, Heidelberg: Springer.

Lane, J. (2018). The silver in silva: The Story of steeper energy and SGF's's $59M advanced biofuels project in Norway. *Biofuels Digest.* [Online] Available at: http://www.biofuelsdigest.com/bdigest/2018/01/16/the-silver-in-silva-the-story-of-steeper-energys-59m-advanced-biofuels-project-in-norway/ [Accessed 3 May 2018].

Larsen, O.M. (2017). Aviation biofuels at Oslo Airport. In: *ICAO Seminar on Alternative Fuels.* International Civil Aviation Organization (ICAO), 8-9 February, Montreal, Canada.

Lee, D.S., Pitari, G., Grewe, V., Gierens, K., Penner, J.E., Petzold, A., Prather, M.J., Schumann, U., Bais, A., Berntsen, T., Iachetti, D., Lim, L.L. and Sausen, R. (2010). Transport impacts on atmosphere and climate: Aviation. *Atmospheric Environment,* 44, pp. 4678–4734.

Liedtke, K. (2018). Red rock gets go-ahead for lakeview. *Herald and News.* [Online] Available at: https://www.heraldandnews.com/news/local_news/red-rock-gets-go-ahead-for-lakeview/article_253409ba-63aa-5c42-becd-ea9ac2711805.html [Accessed 24 May 2018].

Malins, C. (2017). *What role is there for electrofuel technologies in European transport's low carbon future?* Cerulogy.

Malins, C., Searle, S., Baral, A., Turley, D. and Hopwood, L. (2014). *Wasted – Europe's untapped resource.* International Council on Clean Transportation (ICCT) and NNFCC.

Marxer, D., Furler, P., Scheffe, J., Geerlings, H., Falter, C., Batteiger, V., Sizmann, A. and Steinfeld, A. (2015). Demonstration of the entire production chain to renewable kerosene via solar thermochemical splitting of H_2O and CO_2. *Energy & Fuels,* 29(5), pp. 3241–3250.

Mawhood, R., Gazis, E., de Jong, S., Hoefnagels, R. and Slade, R. (2016). Production pathways for renewable jet fuel: A review of commercialization status and future prospects. *Biofuels, Bioproducts and Biorefining,* 10(4), pp. 462–484.

McKenna, J. (2017). *Norway's airports refuel aircraft with biofuels.* World Economic Forum. [Online] Available at: https://www.weforum.org/agenda/2017/11/norway-airports-biofuels-avinor/ [Accessed 17 May 2018].

Millar, R.J., Fuglestvedt, J.S., Friedlingstein, P., Rogelj, J., Grubb, M.J., Matthews, H.D., Skeie, R.B., Forster, P.M., Frame, D.J. and Allen, M.R. (2017). Emission budgets and pathways consistent with limiting warming to 1.5 °C. *Nature Geoscience,* 10, pp. 741–747.

NOAA – National Oceanic and Atmospheric Administration. (2018a). *Recent global CO_2 trend.* Global Monitoring Division of the National Oceanic and Atmospheric Administration. [Online] Available at: https://www.esrl.noaa.gov/gmd/ccgg/trends/gl_trend.html [Accessed 13 June 2018].

NOAA – National Oceanic and Atmospheric Administration. (2018b). *Annual mean global carbon dioxide growth rates.* Global Monitoring Division of the National Oceanic and Atmospheric Administration. [Online] Available at: https://www.esrl.noaa.gov/gmd/ccgg/trends/gl_gr.html [Accessed 20 June 2018].

Port of Seattle. (2018). *Port of Seattle announces partnership for sustainable aviation fuels at Sea-Tac airport.* [Online] Available at: https://www.portseattle.org/news/port-seattle-announces-partnership-sustainable-aviation-fuels-sea-tac-airport [Accessed 17 May 2018].

Qin, Z., Mishra, U. and Hastings, A., eds. (2017). *Bioenergy and land use change.* Hoboken, NJ: John Wiley & Sons.

Ramirez, J., Brown, R. and Rainey, T. (2015). A review of hydrothermal liquefaction bio-crude properties and prospects for upgrading to transportation fuels. *Energies,* 8(7), pp. 6765–6794.

Romero, M. and Steinfeld, A. (2012). Concentrating solar thermal power and thermochemical fuels. *Energy & Environmental Science,* 5(11), pp. 9234–9245.

Roth, A., Riegel, F. and Batteiger, V. (2018). Potentials of biomass and renewable energy: The question of sustainable availability. In: M. Kaltschmitt and U. Neuling, eds., *Biokerosene – status and prospects*. Berlin, Heidelberg: Springer, pp. 95–122.

Roth, A., Sizmann, A. and Jeßberger, C. (2016). *Report on compilation, mapping and evaluation of R&D activities in the field of conversion technologies of biogenic feedstock and biomass-independent pathways (Final report)*. EU-FP7 project CORE-JetFuel.

Sanz-Pérez, E.S., Murdock, C.R., Didas, S.A. and Jones, C.W. (2016). Direct capture of CO_2 from ambient air. *Chemical Reviews*, 116(19), pp. 11840–11876.

Schmidt, P., Batteiger, V., Roth, A., Weindorf, W. and Raksha, T. (2018). Power-to-liquids as renewable fuel option for aviation: A review. *Chemie Ingenieur Technik*, 90(1–2), pp. 127–140.

Schmidt, P., Weindorf, W., Roth, A., Batteiger, V. and Riegel, F. (2016). *Power-to-liquids: Potentials and perspectives for the future supply of renewable – aviation fuel*. Dessau: German Environment Agency.

Searle, S.Y. and Malins, C.J. (2016). Waste and residue availability for advanced biofuel production in EU member states. *Biomass and Bioenergy*, 89, pp. 2–10.

SkyNRG. (2018). *KLM, Växjö Småland Airport, Södra, SkyNRG and partners sign LOI to investigate the feasibility of producing sustainable aviation fuels in the Växjö region*. Press Release. [Online] Available at: http://skynrg.com/wp-content/uploads/2018/05/20180514_Press-Release-KLM-Växjö-Småland-Airport-Södra-SkyNRG-and-partners-sign-LOI-to-investigate-the-feasibility-of-producing-sustainable-aviation-fuels-in-the-Växjö-region-FINAL.pdf. [Accessed 17 May 2018].

SOLAR-JET. (2015). *SOLAR-JET: Solar chemical reactor demonstration and optimization for long-term availability of renewable jet fuel*. Grant agreement no. 285098. [Online] Availabe at: https://cordis.europa.eu/project/rcn/99761_en.html. [Accessed 19 March 2020].

Sorge, N-V. (2017). Norweger bauen gigantische Fabrik für Wunder-Diesel. *Manager Magazin*. [Online] Available at: http://www.manager-magazin.de/unternehmen/autoindustrie/norwegen-investoren-bauen-fabrik-fuer-wunder-diesel-a-1156215.html [Accessed 14 July 2017].

Staples, M.D., Malina, R., Suresh, P., Hileman, J.I. and Barrett, S.R.H. (2018). Aviation CO_2 emissions reductions from the use of alternative jet fuels. *Energy Policy*, 114(Nov.), pp. 342–354.

Stechel, E.B. and Miller, J.E. (2013). Re-energizing CO_2 to fuels with the sun: Issues of efficiency, scale, and economics. *Journal of CO_2 Utilization*, 1, pp. 28–36.

Steeper Energy. (2017). *Steeper energy announces EUR 50.6 M (DKK 377 M) advanced biofuel project with Norwegian-Swedish joint venture silva green fuel in licensing deal*. [Online] Available at: http://steeperenergy.com/2017/12/15/steeper-energy-announces-eur-50-6-m-dkk-377-m-advanced-biofuel-project-with-norwegian-swedish-joint-venture-silva-green-fuel-in-licensing-deal/. [Accessed 3 May 2018].

Steynberg, A.P. and Dry, M.E., eds. (2004). *Fischer-Tropsch technology*. Amsterdam: Elsevier.

Stratton, R.W., Wong, H.M. and Hileman, J.I. (2010). *Life cycle greenhouse gas emissions from alternative jet fuels*. Partnership for AiR Transportation Noise and Emissions Reduction (PARTNER).

Terwel, R. and Kerkhoven, J. (2018). *Carbon neutral aviation with current engine technology: The take-off of synthetic kerosene production in the Netherlands*. Quintel Intelligence B.V. (Amsterdam, Netherlands) and Kalavasta B.V. (Lochem and Rotterdam, Netherlands).

Trieb, F., Schillings, C., Sullivan, M.O., Pregger, T. and Hoyer-Klick, C. (2009). Global potential of concentrating solar power. In: *15th SolarPaces Conference, 15–18 September, Berlin, Germany*.

UN – United Nations. (2015). *Framework convention on climate change (FCCC)*. In *Conference of the Parties*. Paris: Adoption of the Paris Agreement.

Zhang, L., Xu, C. and Champagne, P. (2010). Overview of recent advances in thermochemical conversion of biomass. *Energy Conversion and Management*, 51(5), pp. 969–982.

Zhu, X-G., Long, S.P. and Ort, D.R. (2008). What is the maximum efficiency with which photosynthesis can convert solar energy into biomass? *Current Opinion in Biotechnology*, 19(2), pp. 153–159.

Zschocke, A. (2014). *Abschlussbericht BurnFAIR*. Deutsche Lufthansa.

Zschocke, A., Scheuermann, S. and Ortner, J. (2017). *High biofuel blends in aviation (HBBA) – final report*. Deutsche Lufthansa AG and Wehrwissenschaftliches Institut für Werk- und Betriebsstoffe.

4 Air transport and the challenge of climate change – how aviation climate change policies work

Frank Fichert, Peter Forsyth and Hans-Martin Niemeier

1. Introduction

While nearly all countries seem to agree that climate change should be managed, there are considerable disagreements over how the emissions of greenhouse gases (GHGs) should be limited, and by which instruments. This chapter discusses the instruments of relevance from an economic perspective and pays particular attention to mechanisms which are used, or are proposed, for air transport. In Section 2 we provide a framework for economic efficiency and climate change mitigation policy, focusing on the static efficiency of measures to control GHGs by prices (like taxes) or quantities (like cap and trade). While both instruments have their pros and cons in terms of efficiency, this is typically not the case with command and control measures. These mandatory restrictions are analysed in Section 3, namely emission standards for aircraft.[1] International transport is generally less taxed than most other sectors, which has negative effects in terms of GHG emissions as well as economic welfare. Ideally, there should be a similar tax rate on all goods and services on government revenue grounds (though see Chapter 13, Section 3.4), and the same tax on externalities, such as greenhouse gas emissions. These problems as well as the disadvantages of unilateral measures in an international industry are discussed in Section 4, focusing on fuel taxes and air passenger taxes (e.g. the UK air passenger duty (APD)).

The workings of an emission trading scheme (ETS) as applied to air transport are analysed in Section 5. In Section 6, the workings of the CORSIA scheme, which has been proposed for international air transport, are examined. Due to be commenced in 2021, it is a hybrid scheme which combines elements of limits to emissions like an ETS, an "implicit" price on emissions, and an offset scheme. The ways the different policies interact is analysed in Section 7, and specific issues are discussed in Section 8. In Section 9, the different policy options which have been suggested are compared and contrasted.

2. Economic efficiency and climate change mitigation policies

Environmental policy seeks to correct market failure due to externalities. It deals with emissions because they are causing damage – and it is usually assumed that the marginal damage of emissions (MD) is increasing with an increasing amount of total emissions (see Figure 4.1). Emissions are always a by-product of a production and/or consumption activity. Firms and households do not have an incentive to emit more than necessary, but since avoiding emissions is costly, there is also no incentive to reduce emissions, unless there is a specific framework set by the government, or clear property rights have been defined so that polluters can negotiate with those impacted by the pollution to reduce emissions. In general, the amount of emissions (assuming a hypothetical situation without any environmental policy) is determined by the equilibrium of the respective markets for goods and services. In Figure 4.1, the marginal abatement cost curve (MAC) has to be read from right to left, with q_0 indicating the amount of emissions without an environmental policy constraint, and increasing marginal costs of emissions reductions. From an overall perspective, environmental policy should reduce emissions up to point q_{opt}, at which the marginal benefits of reducing emissions (= avoiding damage) equals the marginal abatement costs.

Due to the derived nature of emissions, a change in the level of economic activity, e.g. due to economic growth or a recession, leads to a shift of the MAC curve, changing also the overall optimum. Moreover, changes in the costs of emissions reductions, which might be a by-product of technological progress, also shift the MAC curve and therefore also move the intersection of the two curves.

Environmental measures are usually classified into two broad categories – command and control policies on the one hand, and economic instruments, including taxes and emission trading schemes, on the other. The instruments are often assessed in terms of environmental effectiveness and static as well as dynamic efficiency (Requate, 2005), complemented by distributional aspects and political feasibility. Very often the instruments are assessed in a textbook style, assuming that the costs and benefits of emissions reductions are known or can be estimated with sufficient accuracy.

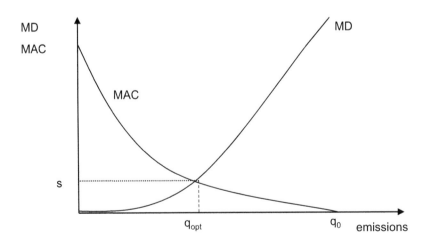

Figure 4.1 Marginal abatement costs and marginal damage.

In Figure 4.1, the optimum can be reached either by a cap and trade system, limiting the amount of greenhouse gases to q_{opt}, or by a tax with a price of s per unit of greenhouse gas. Both instruments are equally effective as well as efficient, or as Helm (2005) summarises: "The choice between price and quantity is not determined, because information is perfect" (p. 211). Textbooks (see, for example, Fritsch, 2018) then look at other criteria, like practicability to favour one instrument over the other.

However, "[u]ncertainty is central to environmental policy" (Pindyck, 2007, p. 62), and we lack knowledge about the ecological and economic processes of climate change. Moreover, the costs of emissions as well as of emissions reductions are typically nonlinear and (especially with respect to damage) often irreversible.

Uncertainty has important implications for the design of an optimum oriented mitigation policy, because the equivalence between emission trading and taxes does not hold any more. If the marginal damage and the marginal abatement costs are not known, the target as well as the tax rate can be set at a wrong level. While uncertainty related to the marginal benefits of emission reductions leads to the same welfare loss irrespective of the choice of instrument (Adar and Griffin, 1976), uncertainty of the marginal cost of emission reduction leads to different welfare losses for each instrument (Weitzman, 1974; Stavins, 1996; Hepburn, 2006; Sturm and Vogt, 2018), depending on the slope of the MAC and the MD curve.

Assume that an error of the same relative magnitude has occurred in setting the tax rate and the target. The tax rate was set 20 per cent below the optimal level at t_1. In the case of Figure 4.2, "tax better than target", the excessively low tax rate leads to higher than optimal emissions of q_1. Hence it results in a

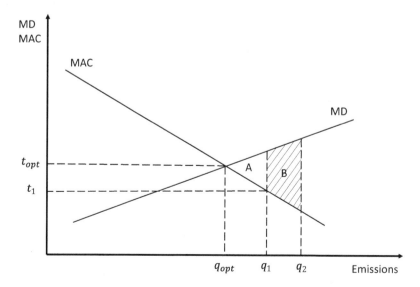

Figure 4.2 Efficiency comparison – tax better than target.

welfare loss of the area A. This needs to be compared with the welfare loss of a 20 per cent error in setting the target. If the target was set 20 per cent above the optimal level at q_2, then a welfare loss of A plus B occurs. Hence the tax is better than a target.

The results are reversed in the case of Figure 4.3, "target better than tax". Here the 20 per cent error in setting the target leads to the emissions of q_2 and to a welfare loss of C. The same error in setting the tax rate leads to emissions of q_1 which are larger than q_2 and which leads to a welfare loss of C plus D.

The different results can be easily explained by comparing the relative steepness of the marginal abatement costs and the marginal damage costs of emissions in the two figures. In the case "tax better than target", the marginal abatement cost is much steeper than the marginal damage cost while in the case of "target better than tax", this is reversed. As long as the absolute change in the marginal abatement costs is greater than the absolute change in the marginal damage cost, an error of the same relative size leads to lower welfare loss if a tax is used (Weitzman, 1974).

Weitzman's analysis of price versus quantity influenced the debate on taxes versus cap and trade substantially. It showed that under uncertainty, the choice between the two market-based instruments (tax and "cap and trade") might lead to substantial differences in terms of welfare. Among others, Nordhaus (2008, 2017), Pizer (2002), Goulder and Pizer (2008) and Helm (2008) have argued in favour of a carbon tax. Pizer has modelled the marginal cost curves of emission reduction and the marginal benefits of emission reductions (i.e. marginal damage curves). As the latter are relatively flat, he estimates that taxes are five times more efficient. The logic behind this is that if an error in an additional amount

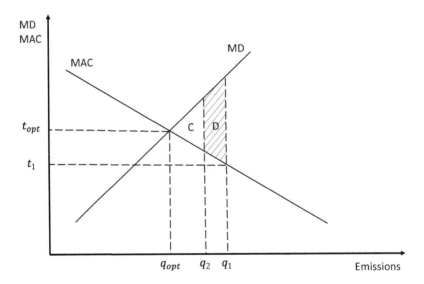

Figure 4.3 Efficiency comparison – target better than tax.

of emissions is less costly than an error in the costs of reducing emissions, a tax is the better choice. If severe or even catastrophic damages occur due to rising temperatures, i.e. a rather steep marginal damage curve, emission trading would be better than a tax, but so far all calculations of the cost and benefits of climate change have shown that this is not (yet) the case (Nordhaus, 2017).

While from a purely economic viewpoint – and given the assumptions mentioned here – a price instrument such as a carbon tax is superior to a quantity measure such as a cap and trade, the political success of the latter has lead economists to discuss ways how to improve the quantity measure with price elements. Pizer (2002) is one author who argues in favour of combining emission trading with other price instruments. One option is to combine emission trading with setting a price ceiling and a price floor. Under uncertainty, such hybrid instruments perform substantially better in terms of economic welfare than a pure systems of emission trading. An interesting proposal is also to set the price floor by a carbon tax, as allowance prices in the EU ETS have been variable and at times so low that they discouraged long-term investment in carbon-reducing energy and infrastructure (Helm, 2009). These hybrid instruments are to be distinguished from additional instruments such as bans on airport expansion or reform of ATC, which, under an emission trading system, are redundant to manage carbon emissions, unless the "waterbed" effect is specifically addressed (see Section 7).

The previous discussion on economic efficiency was based on the assumption that the optimum level of emissions could be reached either by a tax or by a cap-and-trade scheme. With respect to climate change, many states – based on multilateral agreements or national decisions – have set specific reduction targets for CO_2 emissions. One might question whether these objectives have been set in an efficient way. However, if those objectives shall be reached, Baumol and Oates have pointed out that a cap and trade scheme is effective in reaching a defined emissions target, whereas a tax will always be a "trial and error" process, since governments are not informed about the marginal abatement cost curve. However, for practical policy making also other aspects might matter. One might discuss, for example, which instrument might be more vulnerable for lobbying activities from different stakeholder groups, or whether tax revenues (or revenues from auctioning allowances) will be spent by the government in an efficient way.

3. Command and control policy

Command and control measures are widely used instruments in environmental policy. GHGs could be limited by setting a technology standard for aircraft in terms of emissions. The IPCC report in 1999 discusses "engine emission stringency" as one of the measures, since ICAO has set such standards for pollutants since 1981 (exclusively focussing on the emissions affecting local air quality during the landing–take-off-cycle). These standards should reflect the "best achievable technology by all manufacturers" (IPCC, 1999, p. 343). The ICAO

Council adopts recommendations of ICAO's Committee on Aviation Environmental Protection (CAEP). These standards[2] define the emissions maxima for new aircraft in Annex 16, Vol. II (Environmental Protection) to the Convention on International Civil Aviation. In 1981 the first ICAO standard was defined for engines produced after 1985. These standards have been strengthened stepwise (Ahmad, 2016).

Annex 16 Vol. III introduced standards for CO_2 emissions for the first time. These rules were adopted on 6 March 2017 (ICAO, 2017) and apply to new aircraft designs from 2020 and to aircraft type designs already in production as of 2023. After 2028, engines which do not comply with the standard must not be produced anymore. Since fuel consumption is strongly influenced by the weight of an aircraft, the standards are complex and differ between different phases of the flight (begin, middle, and end of the cruise phase). Moreover, they are also based on the payload, the available floor space, and the range of an aircraft.

Command and control measures are typically seen as cost inefficient (see, for example, the textbook by Field and Field, 2002). However, inefficiency occurs only if the same standard is set for firms with different abatement costs, e.g., if all polluters are required to reduce emissions by the same percentage. With respect to subsonic jet aircraft and their engines, it can be assumed that technology is rather similar, and therefore the efficiency argument is not very strong. However, the effectiveness of such standards is lacking, as they only limit the emissions per flight (CO_2 standards) or per kg of fuel burnt (standards for pollutants). In other words, in spite of these standards, an overall growth of the market might lead to increasing total emissions. Moreover, unlike in the case of noise emissions and pollutants, airlines have an economic incentive to reduce fuel consumption and therefore CO_2 emissions. Consequently, the new CO_2-standard has an effect only if it goes beyond the optimum fuel efficiency from an airline's perspective, i.e., if the additional costs of the new engines are above the savings which can be achieved by operating them.

To the best of our knowledge, the effects of the CAEP/ICAO standards have not been analysed rigorously by any academic study.[3] The IPCC is very careful and "suggests that ICAO stringency requirements have 'pushed' engine emissions reduction technology or, at a minimum, have ensured its incorporation into new and derivative engine designs" (p. 344). The IPCC report also reflects on a parallel debate on so-called "technology forcing versus technology following standards", which started by a World Bank report on automobile standards in 1996 (Faiz, Weaver, and Walsh, 1996; Gerard and Lave, 2005; Hascic, de Vries, Johnstone, and Medhi, 2009). Given the fact that ICAO can set only recommendations which reflect compromises among the various stakeholders, with engine manufacturers and aircraft producers amongst them, it is very doubtful that the standards force new technology. This is also reflected in the IPCC report:

> the best technology concept has a specific meaning for aviation. The airworthiness concern is that setting standards based on unproved, anticipated,

or non-existent technology might result in untenable solutions, as might requirements that all engines meet a single, extremely low emissions threshold.

(p. 344)[4]

Another option for command and control policies are operational regulations on routes and trajectories. Since the effects of some emissions depend on the actual location of the emissions (e.g., with respect to the global warming effect of NO_x emissions, and the formation of contrails), areas where emissions lead to a strong impact on the environment might have to be avoided. However, this type of operational regulation has to be based on a profound understanding of the interactions between environmental conditions and the climate effect of aircraft emissions, as well as on a reliable forecast of the relevant environmental conditions. Moreover, there is a general trade-off between the reduction of the greenhouse effects of non-CO_2 emissions and fuel consumption, since these operational regulations lead to a deviation from the flight path that minimizes fuel consumption. Currently, there is some research on flightpaths which might minimize the climate effects of aviation (DLR, 2016; Rosenow et al., 2018), but there are no governmental initiatives to introduce such a scheme into practical air traffic management.

4. Taxes

There is a long and ongoing debate on the taxation of the air transport industry. First, a distinction has to be made between taxes on the air transport service itself (including Value Added Taxes as well as specific "ticket taxes"), taxes on fuel, and taxes on emissions. Due to the proportional relation between fuel burn and CO_2 emissions, a fuel tax is basically the same as a tax on carbon emissions (only with a different tax rate). Other emissions, like NO_x and noise, are not directly linked to fuel burn.

Taxes on air transport services (as distinct from fuel or emissions) primarily have an effect on overall demand, and the effect on fuel consumption and emissions is due only to a smaller number of movements. From an environmental perspective, these instruments are not very specific. Furthermore, empirical estimations of demand elasticities show that overall demand can be inelastic and only some market segments of leisure traffic are elastic (InterVISTAS, 2007). In the case of non-congested airports, a tax will lead to a reduction in demand (either due to a modal shift, especially on short-haul markets, or a smaller number of journeys). For airports facing excess demand and subject to slot allocation, imposing a tax will not increase the price to the passenger (unless the tax is so high that it eliminates the slot rent). Airline costs will rise with the tax, but not airfares, and the airlines' slot rents are transformed into tax revenue, with no immediate demand effect at all. This issue is quite relevant for taxes imposed in a number of countries with airports subject to excess demand, in Europe and elsewhere (e.g. Japan).

Within the European Union, there is hardly any common approach to the taxation of air transport services. No European state levies a Value Added Tax (VAT) on international flights (this includes intra-EU-flights), though in some states domestic flights are subject to VAT, either applying the regular rate (e.g. Germany), or the reduced rate (e.g. Austria). Moreover, some countries have introduced a specific tax on air transport services, which might be seen as an (imperfect) substitute for the VAT.[5] Examples include the UK Air Passenger Duty (APD), the (abandoned) Dutch "ticket tax" of 2008–09, and the German "Air Transport Tax". Irrespective of their different names, all these taxes are quantity taxes, levied on departing passengers (with the general exemption of transfer passengers originating from foreign airports). Design options include a uniform tax for all passengers, a differentiation based on the length (or final destination)[6] of the journey (usually with different "distance bands") and/or the class of travel. In some cases, there is even a double taxation of domestic flights, e.g. in Germany which levies the VAT as well as the Air Transport Tax on domestic flights. Different market segments (short/long haul, economy/business class), as well as airlines following different business models (low-cost carrier vs. network carrier), are affected in a different way. Furthermore, almost all European taxes cover only passengers: except for the French civil aviation tax, there is no tax on air cargo in Europe. In addition, other countries and regions, such as Australia and Hong Kong, impose taxes on international air transport, though in several cases the taxes imposed are mainly to recover airport related costs (European Commission, 2019). Table 4.1 provides an overview of different designs and gives examples for the respective options.

Table 4.1 Options for design of air transport taxes and examples

Only international flights (uniform rate)	Domestic and international flights			
	Uniform rate	Differentiation based on distance/destination		
		Uniform rate per destination/distance class		Additional differentiation based on class of travel
		Two distance classes/ destination types	More than two distance classes	
Australia (AUD 60)	Norway (NOK 82)	France–Civil aviation tax (EUR 4.48 for EEA, EUR 8.06 all other)	Germany (EUR 7.47 short haul, EUR 23.32 medium haul, EUR 41.99 long haul)	France–Solidarity tax (EUR 1.13 EEA economy class, EUR 4.51 all other economy class, EUR 11.27 EEA business class, EUR 45.07 all other business class)

Own table. Data source: European Commission, 2019. Tax rates for 2018.

There are several studies which analyse the effects of introducing or abolishing a passenger tax. Apart from the underlying price elasticity of demand and the market structure on the relevant air transport segments, other assumptions also matter. For example, Mayor and Tol (2008) assume that domestic holidays and holidays abroad are not substitutes. In this case, increasing the UK APD would even lead to higher CO_2 emissions. The rationale is as follows: a quantity tax like the APD favours flights to destinations farther abroad since it reduces the relative price difference, and the respective demand model assumes that tourism demand is influenced by relative rather than absolute price differences between different destinations.

In border regions, some passengers might switch to foreign airports in order to avoid a tax. In the Netherlands, a ticket tax was introduced in July 2008 (coincidentally in a period where the economic crisis already hit the air transport markets) and abolished one year later. There were two tax rates: EUR 11.25 for flights within the European Economic Area (EEA) and EUR 45 for all other flights. Gordijn and Kolkman (2011) provide some "rough estimates" that the tax led to a decrease in the number of passengers at Amsterdam Schiphol Airport of about two million, with half of them switching to airports in Belgium and Germany. Based on Schiphol's passenger number of around 47.4 million in 2008, the tax led to a demand reduction of approximately 4 per cent.

Several studies have been conducted of the German air transport tax, which was introduced on 1 January 2011. These usually compare actual traffic numbers in 2011 with a forecast of a hypothetical situation without the tax (taking into account other determinants such as GDP growth, fuel price development, and specific effects like the closing of parts of the European airspace on same days in 2010 caused by the Icelandic volcano eruption). Fichert, Forsyth and Niemeier (2014) provide an overview of other studies and estimate that the tax led to a reduction in demand between 1.2 and 2.8 per cent in the origin-destination market, depending on the assumed income elasticity of demand. They argue that at hub airports, origin and destination passengers were to some degree replaced by international transfer passengers, which provided a higher net revenue for the hub carrier.

A recent CE Delft study (European Commission, 2019) analyses the potential effects of the introduction/abolition of a ticket tax, as well as the introduction of a VAT on all international flights. Based on this model, abolishing the German ticket tax would increase passenger numbers by 4 per cent. Levying VAT on all international flights (standard rate 19 per cent) would reduce demand in Germany by 16 percent according to this study. For the UK, the CE Delft study assumes that abolishing the APD would increase passenger numbers by 9 per cent.

Most studies, including the CE Delft study, assume that taxes (ticket taxes as well as fuel taxes which are discussed next) are fully passed on to the passenger. Given capacity restrictions at many large airports, as well as monopolistic market structures (where the pass-through rate is typically below 100 per cent), the average pass through rate is below 100 per cent. Consequently, many studies tend to overestimate the effects of the introduction or abolishment of taxes (see Section 8).

An alternative tax is a fuel tax. Due to the linear relation between fuel consumption and CO_2 emissions, an aviation fuel tax would be almost exactly the same as a carbon tax for aviation. The EU directive on energy taxation (2003/96/EC) gives EU member states the right to introduce an aviation fuel tax on domestic flights as well as on a bilateral basis, if two states agree on it. However, with the exception of the Dutch tax on fuel used on domestic flights (which is a very small market), there is no example of fuel taxation in the EU (and the Dutch tax, which was introduced in 2005, was abolished in 2011; Rijksoverheid, 2012). With respect to other emissions, pollutants like NO_x[7] are rarely taxed, and a tax based on the climate effect of these pollutants would be very complex, since this effect depends on flight altitudes and latitudes as well as on weather conditions.

In Europe, with its relatively small countries and open borders, each unilateral approach to taxation has to take competitive developments (or "distortions") into account. In particular, ticket taxes have had an above average effect in border regions, leading to "carbon leakages" rather than to carbon reductions. If a larger country (e.g., France, Germany, Italy, or Spain) introduces a fuel (or carbon) tax on domestic flights, the respective carriers would be put at a disadvantage with respect to their competitors abroad, since passengers from secondary airports might transfer abroad instead of using the domestic airports. For a bilateral fuel tax (which might be levied e.g. between Germany and Greece), the same argument applies (Greek passengers headed for North America might fly via Amsterdam, Paris, or London instead of transferring at Frankfurt or Munich). Moreover, German tourists might replace Greece with other holiday destinations such as Spain or Portugal. Against this background, the reluctance of European countries to introduce taxes on the air transport industry unilaterally is not surprising, and only a European-wide implementation might be effective as well as efficient.[8]

If a tax on aviation fuel were introduced at the European level, the effects on demand would be very similar to an overall increase in the fuel price. In the short term, fares would increase, demand would drop, and airlines would have a stronger incentive to save fuel by operational measures. In the longer term, airlines would have an incentive to invest in more fuel-efficient aircraft. As tax rates are usually relatively stable, at least compared to fluctuating permit/allowance prices, airlines would face less uncertainty and could invest in such long-term projects.

With respect to extra-EU flights, most bilateral Air Service Agreements prohibit the taxation of fuel which is purchased by foreign airlines. As long as these clauses remain, the introduction of a fuel tax for intra-European flights might have the somehow strange effect that the fares on long-haul flights would not change, whereas intra-EU flights would be more expensive.

Given that aviation (and also maritime) has been exempted from Value Added Tax (VAT) and emission taxes for many decades, this creates distortion, as other activities are more heavily taxed. This provides a rationale for taxing aviation. Welfare losses have been quantified in two studies (Keen and Strand, 2007; Keen, Parry and Strand, 2013). They modelled the welfare effects from a worldwide tax of 25 US dollars per tonne of CO_2. The results show an increase in economic welfare consisting of two distinct effects, namely higher fuel prices reducing the externality of aviation emissions and the welfare gain from correcting the price distortion from the VAT exemption through a reduction in air services due to higher air fares. Keen, Parry and Strand (2013) highlight that "the tax-subsidy distortion is much larger (about 3.5 times as large) than the environmental distortion" (p. 18) so that taxing aviation "would be warranted even in the absence of climate concerns, as an imperfect correction for failure to levy VAT or other sales tax on international leisure travel" (p. 37).

5. Emissions trading schemes (ETSs)

One of the most discussed and controversial policies being currently implemented around the world is the ETS, particularly the European ETS. In terms of geographical coverage and ambition, this is the largest actual policy instrument currently being applied to aviation. However, other countries, such as New Zealand are implementing or planning ETSs (see Morrell in this volume).

5.1 The workings of an ETS

An ETS of the "cap and trade" form involves setting a target (in reality, an allowable maximum) on greenhouse gas emissions for a specific period (say 2019) and issuing permits to emit up to this level. Firms which generate emissions would need a permit to do so, or else risk a potentially prohibitive fine. Permits could be issued free to firms, sold at a set price, or auctioned to the highest bidders. In principle, permits could be issued to firms on the basis of their past emissions ("grandfathering"), or on quite different criteria, such as their output, value added, or employment. Permits could even be issued to consumers. Most likely, they would be issued either to emissions-producing firms or to upstream suppliers of energy.

A critical aspect is that permits should be tradable amongst firms to minimize the cost of reducing emissions. Ideally (in terms of promotion of efficiency), they would have to be issued on a non-industry-specific basis, and a firm in one industry would be able to sell unused permits to a firm in another industry – thus an airline could buy permits from a power station (and vice versa, if permitted by the regulation). There might be different classes of permits, e.g. for carbon and NO_x emissions. Granted that permits are limited, they would be in demand, and they would sell for a price, and a market for them would develop (just as a market for water rights has developed in several countries). With a well-functioning market, the firms which can reduce emissions for a lower cost than the permit price will do so, while other firms, which find emission reduction costly, will buy permits and not reduce their emissions as much. This would result in achieving a target at minimum cost to the economy.

If a target is set at a level below the amount of emissions which would result under normal circumstances, i.e. with no constraint, permits will be valuable. If a firm wishes to produce products in a way which causes emissions, it will need permits to do so. It may have to purchase them in the market, or it may be able to use permits which have been allocated to it free of charge. If it uses free permits, it will suffer a cost in that it passes up the opportunity to sell them at a profit. Thus, a cost is imposed on a firm whenever it generates emissions, and it will seek to pass these costs onto its customers. Subject to the extent of pass through, an ETS will have a similar effect on prices to a carbon tax. The difference is that an ETS is like a tax which can be returned all or in part to the firm, and the rate of tax varies according to the demand for permits.

An ETS is shown in Figure 4.4. There is an initial demand for the ability to generate emissions as shown by D. For simplicity, we assume that airline output and emissions vary together, and they are shown on the x axis. If an ETS is imposed on the industry, airlines will not be able to generate their preferred level of emissions; rather, they will be constrained to a level of K permits to generate emissions. Suppose that the costs (long-run average costs) of the airlines are shown by LAC, and these are equal to long run marginal costs, LMC. In this case, the scarce permits will be valued at P_1. Assume that there is full pass through of costs – the case of less than full pass through is considered in Section 8. If these permits are auctioned, airlines will cover just the costs of production and permits. However, if airlines are given the permits free of charge,

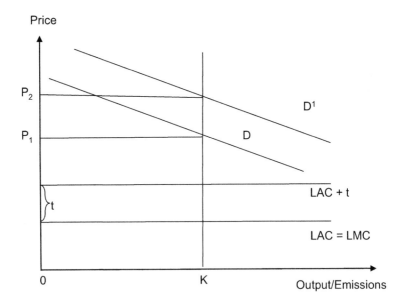

Figure 4.4 Emissions Trading Scheme.

they will enjoy a profit equal to P_1-LAC per permit. If, over time, demand for permits increases to D^1, and if the number of permits is unchanged, the value of the permits will increase, and either the government, as issuer of the permits, or the airlines will gain. If the government were to impose a tax of t on emissions (or passengers), the value of the permits would fall, but the emissions will stay unaltered. This is an example of where additional policies are redundant – see Section 7.

Several countries are implementing ETSs for aviation. The first country to do so was New Zealand, which included domestic aviation in an economy-wide scheme in 2010. The EU has had an ETS which applied to a range of industries, such as energy, since 2005. In 2012 it was extended to aviation. Domestic and intra-European aviation are included, though flights to and from Europe have not been included – something which has been controversial, since the EU originally proposed to include all flights landing or departing at an EU airport with the entire emissions of each flight, no matter whether CO_2 was emitted in EU airspace or not, being subject to the scheme.

A major problem of an ETS is setting the right level of permits initially and over time to reduce emissions on levels to stabilize climate change. Emission reduction requires long-term investment and research in low carbon technologies over a long time. These investments have to be efficiently timed, which can happen only if the prices correctly reflect the incremental abatement costs over time. Investments must be guided by credible initial and future caps, and price stability should be established, to avoid uncertainty. The European ETS has so far more or less failed in this respect (for a comprehensive assessment, see Hepburn and Teytelboym, 2017). In the first phase of the EU ETS (covering industries other than aviation), from 2005 to 2007 emission allowances were over-allocated. For the third phase from 2013 to 2020 (when aviation was covered), the cap was reduced by 1.74 per cent annually, and other measures such as a market stability reserve (MSR) were implemented. In spite of this, carbon prices were still regarded as too low and too unstable, so that Hepburn and Teytelboym (2017) recommend price floors and ceilings. Since then, the prices of allowances have risen significantly, to be around 25 Euro per tonne of CO_2 in late 2019.

One of the issues to be settled when an ETS is established is whether it will be an aviation-specific scheme, or whether aviation is to be part of a more general scheme. The ETSs in place so far have handled aviation as part of a more general ETS. Other things being equal, this is the more efficient approach – efficiency is increased when airlines can buy or sell permits to non-airline businesses, thus lowering the cost of achieving a given reduction in CO_2 (however, the EU ETS has limitations on trading between aviation and non-aviation industries).[9] Overall an ETS is regarded as a very efficient way of reducing emissions. However, setting up the institutions which enable trade in permits may be costly, at least in the short run.

Trading between industries is shown in Figure 4.5. Suppose that initially no trade is permitted, and that the demand for permits by the air transport industry is

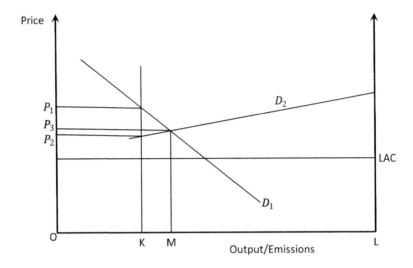

Figure 4.5 Emissions Trading Scheme with trade between two industries.

shown by D_1. If the industry is allocated K permits, there will be excess demand, and permits will be valuable – the price will be P_1. Suppose that another industry is generating emissions. The demand for permits by this industry can be shown as D_2, with the x axis being from right to left. Suppose that the amount of emissions permitted from this industry is shown by the distance KL. The price for permits in this industry will be P_2, which is clearly less than P_1. In this case, the two industries will trade if they are permitted to do so. They will arrive at an equilibrium at P_3, air transport will be a buyer of KM permits, and the other industry will be a seller of KM permits. Since the airline industry is a willing buyer of permits up to the point where it reaches M, and the other industry is a willing seller, both industries gain, even though no more emissions are generated.

Thus, as a general rule, trade in permits benefits both industries, and their consumers – trade promotes efficiency. This result would be similar to that where a uniform carbon tax is applying in both industries. This has strong implications for the discussion of climate control measures generally. It is very likely that aviation will be the net buyer of permits from other industries. If the goal is to achieve climate objectives at minimum cost, trading should be permitted, and some industries will be buyers, and others sellers, of permits.

5.2 Free permits or not?

One important aspect of the design of an ETS concerns whether permits should be free or not.

In the EU scheme, most of the permits were given away free to airlines, at least in the early years of the scheme. Thus, the airlines had a chance to adjust to potentially large changes in their costs and ways they face in doing business. At the time of the extension to aviation, the market price of permits was low, and thus the cost of gaining permits was only a small proportion of the overall cost of operating. The presence of free permits poses a number of questions related to the design of the scheme and how it will work, however.

One of these, which was important in the years prior to the introduction of the extension, was that of who would gain the free allowances. Different rules of allocation will create winners and losers. The EU developed a set of rules for allocation, based on previous outputs of the airlines, with an attempt to ensure that there were some incentives for airlines to reduce their pre-scheme CO_2 emissions. Not all the free allowances were allocated to existing airlines – there has been some provision for new entrant airlines. Different business models of airlines were treated differently, and the worst off were regional airlines with short flights. As with all systems of allocation of valuable resources, there have been disputes about the allocations, though these have been moderate (see the chapter by Morrell in this volume).

The other important question concerns how the airlines will behave when granted free, but quite valuable permits – will they pass on opportunity costs to their passengers and profit from the free permits, or will they base their fares on actual payments only?

Take the case of non-free permits first. How would an airline offering a fare on 100 Euro respond to a 5 Euro tax or permit price? In a competitive market, it may not pass on the whole 5 Euro in the short run, though it is likely to pass on the whole amount soon. If the airline market is monopolist or oligopolistic, it may not pass on the whole 5 Euro (see Section 8). Full pass through need not occur when the airline market is constrained by airport slots or regulatory limits on capacity.

It is far from clear how airlines will behave if they are given free permits. Suppose that, on this flight, the airline requires five permits (valued at 5 Euro) but receives four of them free. How will it respond? If it sets its price according to its costs, it will raise the fare by 1 Euro – even though it requires five permits, it will pass on the benefits of the free permits to its passengers.

Alternatively, it may behave in a profit-maximising manner. The opportunity cost of the permits is 5 Euro, even though it gains four of them free. The average cost of the flight is 101 Euro, but the marginal cost is 105 Euro. Under competition, the profit-maximising fare for the flight will be 105 Euro. If all airlines behave as profit maximisers, fares for this route will rise to 105 Euro, and airlines will gain profits to the value of the free permits they receive. However, demand will drop due to the increased fare, which will probably lead to further changes in the markets.

Most of the discussions of airline behaviour in the context of the EU ETS assume that airlines will behave as average cost fare setters (e.g., see Scheelhaase and Grimme, 2007). In this case, fares will rise only to the extent that airlines need to pay for the permits they use. Indeed, the airlines themselves are saying that they will raise their fares only as needed to buy permits. In a competitive market, it is difficult for one firm to raise fares if all around, its competitors are keeping fares low. However, one should not necessarily assume that this is the whole story.

Suppose that airline products are not perfect substitutes, and airlines have some discretion over the fares they charge. An airline will be aware of the marginal cost of its services. It will have an incentive to reduce services and sell off the permits if the fare it is receiving is less than the marginal cost of the flight. The airline's behaviour under the ETS under (partly) free permits will be an interesting test case of the profit-maximising assumption. At least for the next few years, there will be a big difference between profit maximising prices and prices set at cost (especially in the EU case if allowance prices remain at around 25 Euro per tonne). Cost-based pricing will cost the airlines a lot – especially in that airlines are not a very profitable industry. Will airlines be able to convert free permits into profits, or will they be too competitive to do so? If they do, there may be a problem of rent seeking developing over time (see Flues and van Dender, 2017).

An ETS has an effect on emissions from both the direct and supply side. There is a constraint on emissions which, regardless of the elasticity of demand, has an effect of reducing emissions. An ETS also gives the airlines an incentive to reduce emissions through the supply side. Creating emissions is costly for airlines, and they gain by developing ways, such as through improved engines, to lower emissions.

A further aspect of the airlines' behaviour (whether airlines set their price at average cost or opportunity/marginal cost) needs to be recognized. Some commentators have expressed concern that free permits or subsidised permits sold at lower than the market price lead airlines to respond too little to the ETS, and that if the airlines were required to pay the full price for their permits, they would reduce emissions more (see Hemmings et al. in this volume).

However, an ETS works by setting a fixed limit on emissions – this will stay the same no matter how the industries and airlines act. Different airlines may respond differently to the imposition of the limit, but overall, airlines will generate the same total of emissions. If trading of permits is not permitted, each industry will be required to keep to the emissions cap, including air transport. When trading is permitted, whether firms set prices at average cost or opportunity/marginal cost will be irrelevant for the total emissions generated of CO_2. The firms' behaviour can make a difference as to the allocation of emissions and a difference to the amounts of permits traded, and possibly the direction of the trade, but not the total amount of emissions of CO_2. If airlines behave as profit maximisers, the price of air travel will be higher, and the emissions from air transport will be lower, than if the airlines only cover cost, and emissions from air transport will be higher (and emissions from other industries correspondingly lower). Total emissions of CO_2 will be the same, though total emissions of non-CO_2 gases are likely to be higher if air transport emits more of these than other industries.

6. The CORSIA scheme

The Kyoto Protocol included only domestic aviation emissions into climate change policy and did not systematically treat aviation. The task to control greenhouse gases (GHGs) from international air transport was delegated to the International Civil Organization (ICAO), which in turn asked the International Panel for Climate Change (IPCC) to assess the impact of aviation on climate change (see Haag in this volume). The IPCC report "Aviation and the Global Atmosphere" (1999) also discussed various measures to reduce GHGs. However, it took almost two decades for member states to agree on measures to mitigate greenhouse gases of aviation, namely, to adopt a Carbon Offsetting and Reduction Scheme for International Aviation (CORSIA) in October 2016, and new CO_2 emissions standards for aircraft in March 2017. In 2011 and 2016 the IMF (2011, 2016) favoured a tax on air transport – an alternative market-based measure to emission trading that has been disregarded by most ICAO member states and has been heavily criticised by the industry (ICAO). The CORSIA scheme is a hybrid scheme, which combines aspects of a quantitative limit, an implicit tax, and an offset scheme. It is a mechanism to ensure carbon-neutral growth of aviation.

CORSIA might be described as a mandatory marginal offset scheme (see also Maertens et al. in this volume). It will start with participating countries volunteering to offset emissions once they have exceeded 2020 levels. Later on, the scheme will require mandatory offsets for those countries in the scheme. Initially not all countries will be part of CORSIA; the intention is that more and more countries will sign up for it. Also, initially, the scheme will work at a country level, but the intention is that it will later work at an individual airline level. The base period for the scheme is the average emissions of 2019 and 2020. A country and its airlines will be permitted CO_2 emissions up to the emissions of the 2019–2020 average. As emissions grow, it will need to purchase offsets for the excess emissions above the 2019–2020 average level. In this way, taking into account the offsets, carbon-neutral growth will be achieved.

The CORSIA scheme is a hybrid, in as much as there are several elements to it. There is a limit to the emissions which may be produced without further action or charge. If a country's airlines are able to keep their emissions below the limit, perhaps by using alternatives such as biofuels (in ICAO's terminology, "eligible fuels"), there will be no further costs. If a country's airlines exceed the limit, they will be required to purchase offsets. This is rather like a marginal tax – the more the airlines emit, the more they will have to pay through purchasing offsets. Over time, as the airlines grow, they will be required to purchase more and more offsets. The "tax" will be used to purchase offsets, not government revenue, and taking into account the additional carbon emissions from the additional aviation output, will result in no net change in global carbon emissions.

The workings of a CORSIA system are shown in Figure 4.6. Costs, price, and emissions per unit are shown on the y axis, and output and emissions on the x axis. At the beginning, airlines are free to create emissions until they reach an output of X_1 (for example, in 2019–2020). This corresponds to a demand of D_1. As demand grows, say to D_2, airlines will be required to purchase offsets for the additional emissions. These cost P_2 minus P_1 (= LAC). The marginal cost of air travel is equal to this amount. If airlines are profit maximisers, the price

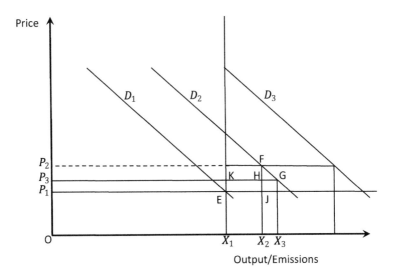

Figure 4.6 Working of CORSIA scheme.

of air travel will rise to P_2, and the equilibrium will move from E to F. In this situation the airlines will gain a rent or profit, equal to $P_1 P_2 KE$. This is because they have a right to create emissions free of charge – they only have to pay KEJF by way of offsets.

It is also possible that the airlines will set their prices at average cost, not marginal cost (as with an ETS). In this case, the airlines do not gain any rents as a result of being able to create emissions up to x_3. In this situation, the airlines will price at p_3, which will be sufficient to cover the cost of the offsets which they need to buy, but no more. In this case, the airlines will need to buy more offsets because their demand will be greater. Actual emissions from airlines will be higher, though this will be exactly matched by the greater use of offsets.

Over time, demand for air travel will increase to D_3. If the price for offsets stays the same, the marginal cost of travel will be unaltered, and the airlines will charge the same price, p_2 if they are profit maximisers. They will gain the same profit or rent, but they will need to buy more offsets. In this case, the cost of offsets will form a higher proportion of the price to travellers, p_2. If the airlines set prices at average cost, including the cost of offsets, the price to travellers will rise, because the cost of offsets will become a higher proportion of the overall price. The price will rise from p_3. As demand and output increase over time, the costs of the offsets will rise. This will have no impact on price if the airlines are profit maximisers, but it will mean that the price of air travel will rise if the airlines set prices at average cost.

The CORSIA system will be effective in reducing (offsetted) emissions on both the demand and supply side. On the demand side, the higher cost of travel will reduce demand – as shown in Figure 4.6. Airlines as a group until end

2029, and then individually from 2030, will also have an incentive to create fewer emissions by lessening the emissions intensiveness of their operations, such as by using more biofuels or using more fuel-efficient aircraft and engines, since they will lessen the amount of the offsets which they will need to buy. However, the effect which is likely to prove strongest quantitatively will be the direct effect, forcing airlines to reduce their emissions by purchasing offsets. Aviation will be still a major source of emissions, but an increasing proportion of those emissions will be offset.

As noted before, the CORSIA system will be effective regardless of whether airlines behave as profit maximisers and gain rents from the introduction of the system, or whether they price at average cost. In the early days, all the airlines will be operating on more or less equal terms. In this situation, competition may force them to keep prices low by setting the prices at average cost. In the longer run, there will be entry and exit of airlines. New airlines will need to use offsets for all of their operations since they were not around when the system came into being, and airlines were grandfathered the rights to create emissions without having to pay for offsets for all of them. The newer airlines will be at a disadvantage vis-à-vis the older airlines, especially if offsets become costly over time. While the marginal cost will be the same for all airlines, if existing airlines price at average cost, CORSIA might be seen as an entry barrier which impedes competition.

In principle, the CORSIA approach is a promising approach to limiting the emissions from air transport while enabling aircraft to fly. It allows for a gradual adjustment to higher costs of air travel if airlines price at average cost (and a quicker adjustment if airlines are profit maximisers). But it relies very heavily on the offset system. If offsets are unreliable and questionable, it will not achieve the promised constraints to global emissions – thus offsets will have to be carefully monitored. Some (e.g., Warnecke et al., 2019) have argued that there is an abundance of "junk" offsets, and that the requirements for CORSIA can be filled at very low cost – perhaps 1 Euro per tonne. This suggests that CORSIA seems to be too good to be true. It is not surprising that the EU is reluctant to replace the ETS by CORSIA for intra-Europe flights. Several questions need to be answered concerning the reliability and cost of offsets before there is a rigorous evaluation of CORSIA.

There are other limitations. For example, why emissions in the year 2020? The 2020 starting date might create a problem of gaming – it may be in the interest of airlines to increase emissions up till 2020, to increase the base and maximise the level of emissions for which they do not need to purchase offsets. It shares several of the features of the ETS system. As with the ETS approach, there are important qualifications on how it will work which need to be recognised. These are discussed in the next section.

7. Interactions between policies – the waterbed effect

Price methods such as taxes, and quantity methods such as ETSs and CORSIA, differ in several ways, but one important way is how they interact with other policies. This has sometimes been called the "waterbed" effect. If a tax is imposed, this does not have any implications for the effectiveness of other policies – for example, voluntary actions to curb emissions will also work, adding to the effect of the tax (though quantity constraints, such as airport slots, can change this). By contrast, a comprehensive ETS and CORSIA will work differently. The ETS puts a maximum on the emissions that can be emitted. Other measures can be implemented, such as a passenger tax, but they will have no impact on emissions, since the ETS sets the allowable emissions, and the actual emissions will equal the allowable emissions (unless the limit is slack) (Forsyth, Dwyer and Spurr, 2007; Fankhauser, Hepburn and Park, 2011). Additional policies will have some effects, such as reducing the price in the market for permits. However, they will not have any effect in reducing carbon emissions, unless the waterbed effect is specifically addressed.

This means that, in the presence of an ETS, additional policy measures are redundant. This has strong implications for climate change policies. Often a mixture of policies is advocated, in the belief that a broad menu of policy measures will help reducing emissions. In fact, it will not, since the ETS limits are binding. Thus, for example:

- Passenger taxes will cease to have any effect in terms of reducing emissions while an ETS is in operation.
- Bans on airport expansion, such as those demanded by some pressure groups, will not have any effect on emissions if an ETS is working. They will have a cost to the home economy, however.

Complementary measures do sound appealing – they *appear* to reduce emissions. There may be reasons why specific measures could be desirable, though reasons other than their effect on emissions. Thus, for example, a government may choose to subsidise biofuels as a fuel for aviation – perhaps because it believes that there are production externalities in the development of new techniques. Governments may believe that there are R&D spillovers in engine research (for a critical discussion of market failure in the R&D market for clean technologies, see Dechezlepretre and Popp, 2017). For some countries, there may be distributional aspects to aviation measures. If this is the case, then these complementary measures need to be assessed in terms of these other objectives, such as raising government revenues, not the impact on emissions, which remain at nil.

This is shown in Figure 4.4. The effective rationing mechanism once an ETS is in operation is to put a limit on permits available – in this case, it is K. If the government imposes a tax, be it a passenger tax or a fuel tax, such as t, there will be no effect on emissions. The value of permits will fall, but not their quantity.

It is worth noting that only a comprehensive ETS (and CORSIA) create this property of redundancy of other policies. Other policies, such as a carbon tax, or specific measures, such as voluntary offsets or improvements to ATM, do not have this property. An ETS achieves a specific level of emissions and no more, no matter what other policies are implemented. By contrast, if a carbon tax is imposed, additional measures such as voluntary offsets and improvements to ATM have an additional effect on emissions, in addition to the effect of a carbon tax. For some, this property of the ETS would be regarded as a drawback of the ETS. However, this should be seen in context; all polices have particular properties, and the objective should be on choosing the best policy in the circumstances. For example, an ETS has the property that it sets the actual emissions to a set target, which can be a desirable property – other options such as a carbon tax do not guarantee that emissions will be at the target level – they could be way below or way above.

The waterbed effect of an ETS does mean that policy makers should be aware of the effectiveness of complementary measures once an ETS is in operation. Many countries in the EU had policies which had, at least in part, the rationale of reducing emissions. Once the EU ETS came into being and before recent reforms, this rationale was no longer viable. These options, which seem reasonable, created real costs for no benefit in terms of emissions reduction. Most likely, the persistently low prices of allowances in the EU system have been partly due to countries adopting emissions reduction policies – evidence that the waterbed effect is present. In addition, a variant of the waterbed effect also occurs with the CORSIA type of system.

As with the ETS, the CORSIA system involves a fixed limit. In this case, the airlines can create emissions, but they are required to essentially cancel them out by buying offsets. This can be shown by considering an aviation tax in addition to a CORSIA mechanism. This tax raises the price which travellers must pay (adding to the cost of the service and the cost of the offsets). With the higher price, emissions from the airlines will fall, and it may appear that the tax is working to lessen emissions. However, the tax also reduces the airlines' need for offsets. This will exactly cancel out the effect of the tax on emissions. As long as the offsets are working as they should, there will be zero net global emission reduction. It is not possible.

The waterbed effect has been recognised in recent changes to the EU ETS. In particular, a market stability reserve (MSR) has been established and set in operation from 2019, and this will affect the operation of the waterbed effect (see Hepburn et al., 2016). The MSR is a mechanism to reduce price volatility in the market for allowances/permits. However, it also works to reduce the number of allowances in the market when there are too many allowances, given specific criteria. Thus, if an aviation tax lessens the demand for allowances, a number of allowances may be withdrawn. This will have the effect of reducing or eliminating the waterbed effect. The criteria for withdrawal of allowances have been arbitrarily set, and thus there is no guarantee that a tax which results in a reduction of x tonnes of emissions will result in x tonnes of allowances being withdrawn.

The precise quantitative effects on the number of allowances of the MSR have yet to be analysed, and observers disagree as to what extent they will eliminate the waterbed effect. Nevertheless, there will be a change in the right direction which will lessen the waterbed effect. The issue of the interplay between the EU ETS and aviation taxation will need to be resolved if countries and the EU choose to impose both the ETS and aviation taxes.

8. Specific issues

8.1 Aviation and intermodal competition

Aviation climate change policies will affect intermodal competition, and this will have a range of effects (see Rothengatter in this volume). Ideally, all modes should be treated in the same way – for example, if there is a carbon tax which applies to one mode, such as aviation, then it should apply to all modes. In this way, climate change objectives can be met at minimum cost. Some countries are seeking to impose a fairly general climate change policy. Thus, for example, the New Zealand ETS applies to all (domestic) modes, and the short-lived Australian carbon tax applied to several modes.

Some aviation climate change policies will apply only to aviation – the most prominent of these is the EU ETS, which will apply to aviation on its own, though it is linked to the EU ETS which covers energy (this affects the cost of running electric trains) though not road transport (see De Borger and Proost, 2017). Given that, for the most part, aviation is a substitute for other modes, and also given that aviation is the most carbon intensive of transport modes, applying a policy which applies to aviation but not other modes will reduce carbon emissions overall. With both an ETS and a carbon tax, increasing the price of aviation will increase the demand for other modes, and increase their emissions. The net effect on emissions from implementing the policy will be negative, however. The net effect will be smallest for modes which are relatively high emitters of CO_2, such as high-speed trains (which rely on electricity, which may be generated by using fossil fuels or renewable sources).

Some policies may, in fact, add to emissions. An example might be air passenger taxes which are imposed by some countries such as Germany. Passengers who are close to the border may choose to drive to another airport which is outside the country imposing the tax – they will still fly and generate emissions, but they will also create emissions when accessing the airport. This was a consideration when the Netherlands removed its air passenger tax.

The handling of motor fuel is a tricky one. Most countries already impose high taxes on fuel, primarily for revenue raising reasons. The taxes reduce emissions – should an additional tax be levied on fuel? This is an issue which needs to be addressed when determining the overall best policy for transport, not just aviation, though what is done will affect aviation's output and emissions.

8.2 Indirect emissions

Aviation produces emissions directly but also indirectly, through its use of other goods and services such as electricity. In spite of the enormous interest in and concern for aviation's direct emissions, there has been very little interest in its *indirect* emissions. Indeed, very little is available on how large these are. One measure, done in the context of a measure of the carbon footprint in tourism in Australia, suggests that the indirect emissions from aviation could be as high as a quarter of its direct emissions (Dwyer, Forsyth and Spurr, 2010). Furthermore, the Australian case may be an outlier, given that flights to Australia are long and direct fuel use per kilometre is relatively low – this means that the indirect emissions will be high relatively to the direct. The indirect emissions from air transport are unlikely to be insignificant in most cases.

Most aviation climate change policies target only direct emissions and ignore indirect emissions. The situation is not quite as challenging as it seems, because aviation is partly captured in the EU ETS for energy. Already, aviation is affected by its use of electricity – thus British Airways is paying, indirectly, for its use of energy. If a country has a comprehensive ETS, as does New Zealand, aviation (in this case domestic but not international) pays for both its direct and indirect emissions. In measuring the impact on travel demand and a country's competitiveness of a policy, it is important to factor in not just the direct effect but also the indirect effect.

8.3 Pass through

The pass-through issue is an important one for climate change policies since the extent to which costs are passed through determines how effectively the policy works. Pass through is about the extent that a cost increase imposed by a policy is passed through by the airline to the passenger. In many cases, we cannot assume that a cost which is initially imposed on the airline gets fully passed through to the passenger. Competitive conditions can mean that only some of the cost is passed through – the airline may need to absorb some of the cost itself. Pass through is likely to be greater in the long run than in the short run, as airlines adjust their capacity on offer if it is not profitable. Some examples of incomplete pass through are as follows:

- In oligopoly or monopoly, a tax will not be passed on to passengers in full in the short run, or possibly in the long run.
- Where airports are subject to excess demand, and slots are used, an air passenger tax, such as those of the UK (Heathrow Airport), the Netherlands (Schiphol), and Germany (Düsseldorf Airport), will not be passed on – airlines will bear the full burden of the tax and there will be no impact of the tax on output or emissions.
- When airlines are subject to an ETS for which some permits are allocated free of charge, they have the choice between setting fares at profit-maximising levels, or lower fares based on average costs. If the latter is the case, there is incomplete pass through.

The first case, that of monopoly or oligopoly, is considered when airlines are subject to an ETS. In Figure 4.7, the profit maximum is characterized by

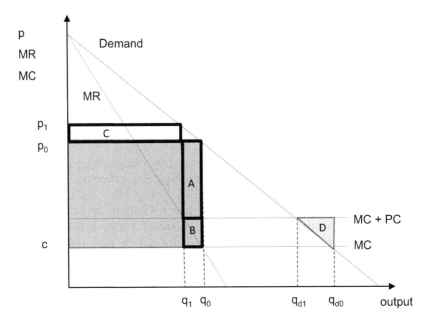

Figure 4.7 Cost pass through of opportunity costs of free allowances – monopoly case.

p_0 and q_0. With a linear relation between output and emissions, the introduction of an ETS leads to a parallel shift of the MC function, with p_1 and q_1 as the new profit-maximising situation. The profit contribution on the market for air transport services is reduced by (A+B−C). On the other hand, B is the additional revenue from selling q_0−q_1 permits to other firms. Consequently, if C is larger than A, passing through opportunity costs of free permits is a profit-maximising strategy. On the other hand, if A is larger than C, the airline would be better off not to pass through these opportunity costs. Many possibilities exist to change the assumptions of the model to make it more realistic. First, price differentiation is common in the air transport industry. If the airline would apply perfect price differentiation, every customer with a willingness to pay above "c" would pay a fare equal to his maximum willingness to pay. If free permits are introduced, total output would be reduced from q_{d0} to q_{d1}. For all remaining passengers, the price would remain the same; the airline's profits would increase by D. Second, CO_2 emissions (and therefore the demand for CO_2 permits) are not proportional to output. Therefore, they might be considered to be fixed costs (per flight) rather than variable costs per passenger.

The second case is where airlines are operating out of slot constrained airports, such as London Heathrow, Dusseldorf, and Amsterdam Schiphol. There is excess demand and airlines gain a slot rent from the constrained capacity, manifest in airfares being above costs (the slot rent). If the airline faces an increase in costs, be it due to an aviation tax or the workings of an ETS, it will face the whole of the cost increase itself – its slot rents will be reduced. In this case, there will be no reduction in the airline's output, and no reduction in emissions. Passengers will be unaffected, and there will be zero pass through.

A third case of partial pass through is that with free permits in an ETS. When aviation is included in an ETS, which has a proportion of free permits, will airlines raise prices by the amount that they need to pay for the non-free permits, or base prices on cost and recover only the value of all the permits which they need in order to make a flight, including free and non-free permits? At the margin, airlines can trade permits at their full value. A profit-maximising airline will factor its permits at their full value. Permits will be rather like airport slots – and airlines do not give their slots away just because they did not pay anything for them.

In spite of this, many discussions assume that the airlines will simply charge the passengers the amount they have to pay for the non-free permits and effectively give the free permits to the passengers. In short, they will set prices at below the profit-maximising level – they will behave as size maximisers. It is an empirical question as to how they will behave. This assumption lies behind the opposition of the non-European airlines to their inclusion in the EU ETS. Airlines from several countries, particularly the US and China, were very vocal about this, and instituting legal action and threating retaliation. In spite of this, the airlines might have profited substantially from their inclusion, especially if airlines act as profit maximisers.

The pass-through issue raises the issue of whether a policy actually works effectively to reduce emissions. Sometimes it will not. In order to have the full impact on demand and emissions, it is necessary that the passenger faces the cost of the impost. If pass through is incomplete or zero, the effect of the policy on emissions will be incomplete or in some cases zero. There is, however, an important difference between ticket taxes and an ETS. If a tax is imposed, the cost to the airline will rise, and all or some of this cost will be passed on to the passenger. If aviation is part of a multi-industry ETS, the introduction of the aviation ETS raises the allowable emissions from an amount X to X + Y, the emissions will rise from X to X + Y. The amount of emissions reduction from aviation may be smaller than Y – aviation will simply purchase permits from other industries. Thus, the European aviation ETS will have the effect of reducing emissions by the targeted amount, though much of the reductions in emissions may come from other industries. This has implications for the effect on *non-carbon* emissions, which will not be reduced by as much because of this effect (see Chapter 13, Section 3.3).

9. Assessing policies

In this discussion, we have set out a range of aspects of the various policies which have been adopted or suggested for aviation. In this section we attempt to draw together the different strands of the discussion and provide an overall assessment. We try to highlight the positive and negative aspects of the main policies and, in doing so, make it possible for a reader to assess how well they will work. Several aspects are important.

The first of these is efficiency – it is desirable that the policy works efficiently. In the context of climate change policies, this means that the policy achieves a reduction of CO_2 or other greenhouse gas emissions at minimum cost. For present purposes, we are not particularly concerned about who bears this cost – distributional aspects of policies could be important, especially since they might affect the impact on emissions (see later in this section). In this assessment we take the view that efficient climate change mitigation policies are applied to substitute modes and other activities – clearly this may not be the case (e.g. surface modes may not be subjected to efficient policies), and this will affect the desirability of the policies.

A second aspect is that of transaction costs. A policy may be efficient in principle, but there may be large costs in setting it up. If so, then these transaction costs should be factored into the overall assessment. Thus, an ETS may be efficient, but it may be expensive to set up.

Effectiveness is another basic, but important aspect. Some command and control instruments, such as bans on airport expansion, could be very effective, but they reach the target at higher costs than efficient ones. On the other hand, there are policies that have a clear impact, though others do not. There might be uncertainty as to how the policy works, and how large the impact is. There might also be policies which have no or only a negligible impact and are purely symbolic (Böhringer and Vogt, 2004).

Governments will be interested in the revenue aspects of policies they are implementing. Some policies yield revenues for the government – an obvious case is a carbon tax. Other policies such as R&D subsidies cost the government revenue.

In Table 4.2 we assess the different policies in terms of these various aspects. We also give actual examples where available.

We discuss these options briefly in turn. The assessment of the strength of the effects on objectives is subjective and indicative.

ETS with Paid Permits. This is one of the most efficient options. An ETS with Paid Permits tackles the problem of emissions directly, and it is effective in limiting the emissions. The ETS may be costly to set up and run. It is more efficient and effective if the scheme is a general multi-industry scheme rather than an aviation-specific scheme. The government gains considerable revenue.

ETS with Free/Subsidised Permits. This option may be less efficient than the paid permit option in that it may have a smaller-than-expected impact on aviation emissions, meaning that a larger burden will fall on other industries. It is not clear how airlines will react and what the level of pass through will be. The transaction costs of allocating free permits could be significant. There would be some government revenue, though it would not be as large as with the paid permits. It is more efficient and effective if it is a multi-industry rather than an aviation-specific scheme. Free permits increase stakeholder acceptance.

Table 4.2 Assessment of policy options

Policy	Efficiency	Transaction Cost	Effectiveness	Impact on Government Revenue	Examples
ETS – Paid Permits Part of Multi-Industry Scheme	Very high, but sensitive to errors	High	Very high	Positive	New Zealand
Part of Aviation-Specific Scheme	High		High		
ETS– Free or Subsidised Permits Part of Multi-Industry Scheme	High but sensitive to errors	Very high	High	Small	EU
Part of Aviation-Specific Scheme	Moderately high		Low		
CORSIA	High though subject to errors	High	High if most countries join the scheme and offsets are genuine	Small	Planned but yet to be implemented by ICAO
Carbon Tax	Very high except when airport slots are limited	Low	High	Positive	Australia, 2012–2014
Passenger Taxes	Moderate except when airport slots are limited	Low	Low	Positive	UK, Germany
Limits to Airport Expansion	Very Low	Low	Low if other policies are in place	None	Suggested for London Airports: considered for Vienna airport
Reducing Airport Congestion	Moderate	Low	Moderate	None	US airports a possible application
Reforming ATC	Moderate	High	Unknown	None	Possible reform of European ATC
Requirements on New Engines	Low	Low	Low to moderate	None	CAEP/ICAO stringency requirements
Subsidies for Biofuels	Low	Moderate	Moderate	High	Voluntary trials
Voluntary Actions by Airlines, Airports and Passengers	Moderate	Low to moderate	Low to moderate	None	Many examples of airline offset schemes

Carbon Taxes (e.g., fuel taxes). Under uncertainty this instrument is superior to ETS in some cases though not all. Carbon taxes are an efficient option, and the transaction costs should not be large. As with all carbon taxes, the impact on emissions is uncertain – the tax might be an ineffective means of reducing emissions. Government revenues will be large. These taxes will have little or no effect when airports are slot constrained (Forsyth, 2008).

Passenger Taxes. A passenger tax affects emissions only though affecting demand and if there are low elasticities the impacts on emissions are much more uncertain than carbon taxes – most likely, the impact on emissions will be small. They are relatively easy to set up, and they produce revenues for the government (their main rationale). These taxes will have little or no effect if airports are slot constrained (Forsyth, 2008).

Limits to Airport Expansion. This is suggested by some (e.g. Committee on Climate Change (UK), 2009) but it is a very oblique way of lessening emissions – it is not clear whether it will actually reduce emissions by much, especially if an ETS or a CORSIA scheme is in place. It is easy to implement but there may be large efficiency costs of distorting passengers' travel patterns.

Reducing Airport Congestion. This is only an option where there is inefficient operation of airports – which is often the case in the US but not in Europe or other areas, where slots ration airports. Introduction of slots or pricing will lessen fuel use and reduce emissions. In spite of this, policy makers have been reluctant to do this.

Reforming ATM. Reforming ATM is likely to be an efficient policy (if not combined with an ETS). In Europe, for example, reform might lead to a 10%–12% reduction in fuel use and CO_2 emissions. It has often been advocated, but it has been difficult to achieve, since individual countries control their airspace, and coordination is required. In practical terms, it is not clear how big a reduction in CO_2 can be expected.

Requirements on New Engines. New engines will lead to reductions in CO_2. Requirements that airlines use aircraft which are more advanced than they would otherwise use will further reduce emissions, but at a cost. Given these costs and the need to establish international rules, transaction costs are high.

Subsidies for Low Carbon Fuels. This option is quite similar to the engine option in that it might be moderately effective in reducing emissions, but it is high cost in terms of efficiency – there are more cost-effective ways of achieving the same reductions. However, it would be more costly than regulations on equipment in terms of government budgets.

Voluntary Actions. Passengers, airlines, and airports have been willing to reduce their emissions. This, of course, will be at some cost to them. Such actions will solve only a small proportion of the problem. They are low cost and valuable for this reason.

A comprehensive and well-designed ETS system emissions caps emissions efficiently. There may be reasons for having additional instruments (e.g. to generate revenues) or for combining instruments (e.g. cap and trade with price floors) – however, as argued in Section 7, combinations of policies need to be carefully designed so that they actually work together to reduce emissions. These considerations lead to important political economy questions which have been less well studied than the pure economic question of optimal instruments.

10. Choosing amongst policies: the political economy dimension

Mankiw has criticised US policies for favouring emission trading over a tax. "Convincing China of the virtues of a carbon tax, however, may prove to be the easy part. The first and more difficult step is to convince American voters, and therefore political consultants, that 'tax' is not a four-letter word" (Mankiw, 2007). No doubt ideology plays an important role in the choice of instruments, but more important is rent seeking (Helm, 2015). According to Helm (2005, 2009) the choice by the EU in favour of the instrument of an ETS was based almost entirely on political grounds, because policy does not value so much the efficiency effects, but the income effects of taxes and ETS. He argues that well-designed carbon taxes and permits will lead to substitution and income effects. Economists may look only at the efficiency effects, but business will focus on the latter effect and try to develop strategies to improve their competitive position by raising rivals' costs. He argues that business will try to minimize the substitution effects and will lobby to receive the income generated from environmental instruments. "Under taxes, it goes to the governments; under permits, if they are grandfathered, the companies keep it". It is hardly surprising that for as long as the polluters expected grandfathering, they lobbied hard for this approach (2009, p. 230). Furthermore, permits can be designed to erect barriers to entry and raise rival costs.

Rent seeking also explains many of the shortcomings of the European Emissions Trading system – for example, the lack of a credible long-term reduction target, grandfathering of initial permits with relative high administrative costs, a volatile carbon price with an over-allocation of emissions permits, which resulted in a emissions price of almost zero and a lack of covering all sectors of the economy (see, for example, Helm, 2009, 2010; Kemfert and Schneider, 2009). While the hope is that these problems can be resolved in time, the question of how well this can be achieved in a political process of rent seeking remains to be seen.

Notes

1 We do not discuss voluntary targets, which do not rely on command, as they play a rather minor role in aviation. See Knorr and Eisenkopf in this volume.
2 It is important to note that ICAO standards are not mandatory, but recommendations.
3 ICCT (2016) shows that all aircraft remaining in production in 2023 match the CO_2 standard. Hence, it is a good example that ICAO regulated something that the industry can easily achieve.
4 The reluctance to force technology has been criticized by organisations like Transport & Environment (2010, p. 7): "Accelerate work on a meaningful CO_2 standard for all new aircraft, not by type, that goes significantly beyond business as usual."

5 Tax deductibility is another difference between a VAT and a ticket tax. Whereas most business travellers can deduct VAT, this is not possible with a ticket tax.
6 For originating passengers, the tax rate is based on the final destination as stated on the ticket. Consequently, passengers cannot reduce the tax burden by choosing transfer flights via hubs in countries without a ticket tax instead of direct flights. The only option to avoid the tax would be self-connecting, which brings other disadvantages, especially the risk of missed connections.
7 In Germany, some airports have introduced surcharges on the emissions of NO_x and other pollutants during the LTO cycle. However, like the German surcharges on noise emissions, the entire scheme is revenue neutral; i.e., when the surcharges on emissions were introduced, other (movement-based) charges were reduced.
8 Another unwanted side effect of a fuel tax might be an incentive for fuel tankering (Eurocontrol, 2019). In order to avoid this effect, the tax would have to be based on the fuel consumed on a flight between A and B, and not on the quantity of fuel purchased at A.
9 Airlines can purchase allowances from other industries, but they may not sell their permits to other industries. Since the air transport industry is expected to grow and options for reducing CO_2 emissions are rather limited, airlines will have to purchase allowances anyway, so in practice the limitation of the EU ETS does not have an effect on efficiency.

References

Adar, Z. and Griffin, J.M. (1976). Uncertainty and the choice of pollution control instruments. *Journal of Environmental Economics and Management*, 3, pp. 178–188.

Ahmad, M.T. (2016). *Global Civil aviation emissions standards – from noise to greener fuels*. Occasional Paper Series: Sustainable International Civil Aviation, Institute of Air and Space Law (IASL) at McGill University.

Böhringer, C. and Vogt, C. (2004). The dismantling of a breakthrough – the Kyoto Protocol as symbolic policy. *European Journal of Political Economy*, 20(3), pp. 597–617.

Committee on Climate Change (UK). (2009). *Meeting the UK aviation target – options for reducing emissions to 2050*. Committee on Climate Change.

De Borger, B. and Proost, S. (2017). Tax and regulatory policies for European transport: Getting there, but in slow lane. In: I. Parry, K. Pittel and H. Vollebergh, eds., *Energy tax and regulatory policy in Europe: Reform priorities*. London: MIT Press, pp. 259–296.

Dechezlepretre, A. and Popp, D. (2017). Fiscal and regulatory instruments for clean technology development. In: I. Parry, K. Pittel and H. Vollebergh, eds., *Energy tax and regulatory policy in Europe: Reform priorities*. London: MIT Press, pp. 167–214.

DLR German Aerospace Center. (2016). *CATS – climate compatible air transport system*. [Online] Available at: https://www.dlr.de/lk/en/desktopdefault.aspx/tabid-8596/14795_read-37386/ [Accessed 24 Nov. 2019].

Dwyer, L., Forsyth, P. and Spurr, R. (2010). Estimating the carbon footprint of Australian tourism. *Journal of Sustainable Tourism*, 8(3), pp. 355–376.

Eurocontrol. (2019). *Fuel tankering: Economic benefits and environmental impact*. Aviation Intelligence Unit – Think Paper, Brussels.

European Commission. (2019). *Taxes in the field of aviation and their impact*. Final Report, Brussels, June.

Faiz, A., Weaver, C.S. and Walsh, M.P. (1996). *Air pollution from motor vehicles: Standards and technologies for controlling emissions*. Washington, DC: World Bank.

Fankhauser, S., Hepburn, C. and Park, J. (2011). *Combining multiple climate policy instruments: How not to do it*. Centre for Climate Change Economics and Policy, Working Paper No 48 and Grantham Research Institute on Climate Change and the Environment Working Paper No 38.

Fichert, F., Forsyth, P. and Niemeier, H-M. (2014). Auswirkungen der deutschen Luft-verkehrsteuer auf das Passagieraufkommen – Eine Zwischenbilanz. *Zeitschrift für Verkehrswissenschaft*, 85(3), pp. 167–193.

Field, B.C. and Field, M.K. (2002). *Environmental economics*. 3rd ed. Boston: McGraw-Hill.

Flues, F. and van Dender, K. (2017). *Permit allocation rules and investment incentives in emissions trading systems*. OECD Taxation Working Papers No 33. Paris: OECD.

Forsyth, P. (2008). Airport slots: Perspectives and policies. In: P. Forsyth, D. Gillen and H-M. Niemeier, eds., *Airport slots: International experiences and options for reform*. Aldershot: Ashgate, pp. 379–405.

Forsyth, P., Dwyer, L. and Spurr, R. (2007). *Climate change policies and Australian tourism scoping study of the economic aspects*. Sustainable Tourism Cooperative Research Centre.

Fritsch, M. (2018). *Marktversagen und Wirtschaftspolitik*. 10th ed. München: Vahlen.

Gerard, D. and Lave, L.B. (2005). Implementing technology-forcing Policies: The 1970 clean air act amendments and the introduction of advanced automotive emissions controls in the United States. *Technological Forecasting and Social Change*, 72, pp. 761–778.

Gordijn, H. and Kolkman, J. (2011). *Effects of the air passenger tax*. KiM Netherlands Institute for Transport Policy Analysis, Den Haag.

Goulder, L.H. and Pizer, W.A. (2008). Climate change, economics of. In: Palgrave Macmil-lan, ed., *The new Palgrave dictionary of economics*. doi:10.1057/978-1-349-95121-5_2595-1.

Hascic, I., de Vries, F., Johnstone, N. and Medhi, N. (2009). Effects of environmental policy the type of innovation: The case of automotive emission-control technologies. *OECD Journal: Economic Studies*, 1, pp. 49–66.

Helm, D. (2005). Economic instruments and environmental policy. *Economic and Social Review*, 36, pp. 205–228.

Helm, D. (2008). Climate-change policy: Why has so little been achieved? *Oxford Review of Economic Policy*, 24, pp. 211–238.

Helm, D. (2009). EU climate – change policy – a critique. In: D. Helm and C. Hepburn, eds., *The economics and politics of climate change*. Oxford: Oxford University Press, pp. 222–244.

Helm, D. (2010). Government failure rent-seeking, and capture: The design of climate change policy. *Oxford Review of Economic Policy*, 26, pp. 182–196.

Helm, D. (2015). *The carbon crunch, revised and updated edition*. New Haven: Yale University Press.

Hepburn, C. (2006). Regulation by prices, quantities, or both: A review of instrument choice. *Oxford Review of Economic Policy*, 22, pp. 226–247.

Hepburn, C., Neuhoff, K., Acworth, W., Burtraw, D. and Jotzo, F. (2016). Introduction – the economics of the EU market stability reserve. *The Journal of Environmental Economics and Management*, 80, pp. 1–5.

Hepburn, C. and Teytelboym, A. (2017). Reforming the EU ETS – where are we now? In: I. Parry, K. Pittel and H. Vollebergh, eds., *Energy tax and regulatory policy in Europe: Reform priorities*. London: MIT Press, pp. 1–28.

ICAO – International Civil Aviation Organization. (2017). *Council adopts new CO_2 emissions standard for aircraft*. Montreal: Press Release, 6 Mar.

ICCT – International Council on Clean Transportation. (2016). *International civil aviation organization's CO_2 standard for new aircraft*. [Online] Available at: https://theicct.org/pub lications/international-civil-aviation-organization-co2-standard-new-aircraft [Accessed 24 Nov. 2019].

IMF – International Monetary Fund. (2011). Promising domestic fiscal instruments for cli-mate finance. Background Paper for the Report to the G20 on – mobilizing sources of climate finance, prepared by staff of the International Monetary Fund. [Online] Available at: https://www.imf.org/external/np/g20/pdf/110411b.pdf. [Accessed 24 Nov. 2019].

IMF – International Monetary Fund. (2016). *After Paris: Fiscal, macroeconomic, and financial implications of climate change*. IMF Staff Discussion Note. [Online] Available at: https:// www.imf.org/external/pubs/ft/sdn/2016/sdn1601.pdf. [Accessed 24 Nov. 2019].

InterVISTAS. (2007). *Estimating air travel demand elasticities*. [Online] Available at: https:// www.iata.org/en/iata-repository/publications/economic-reports/estimating-air-travel-demand-elasticities---by-intervistas/ [Accessed 11 Mar. 2020].

IPCC – Intergovernmental Panel on Climate Change. (1999). *Aviation and the global atmosphere*. Cambridge: Cambridge University Press.

Keen, M., Parry, I. and Strand, J. (2013). *Planes, ships, and taxes: Charging for international aviation and maritime emissions*. Economic Policy, 57th Panel Meeting, Trinity College Dublin, Apr.

Keen, M. and Strand, J. (2007). Indirect taxes on international aviation. *Fiscal Studies*, 28, pp. 1–41.

Kemfert, C. and Schneider, F. (2009). Der Emissionshandel in Deutschland und Österreich – ein wirksames Instrument des Klimaschutzes? *Perspektiven der Wirtschaftspolitik*, 10(1), pp. 92–122.

Mankiw, G. (2007). Economic view: One answer to global warming: A new tax. *New York Times*, 16 Sept.

Mayor, K. and Tol, R.S.J. (2008). The impact of the EU-US Open Skies agreement on international travel and carbon dioxide emissions. *Journal of Air Transport Management*, 14(1), pp. 1–7.

Nordhaus, W.D. (2008). *A question of balance: Weighing the options on global warming policies*. New Haven: Yale University Press.

Nordhaus, W.D. (2017). Revisiting the social cost of carbon. *Proceedings of the National Academy of Sciences*, 114, pp. 1518–1523.

Pindyck, R. (2007). Irreversibility, uncertainty, and investment. *Journal of Economic Literature*, 29, pp. 1110–1148.

Pizer, W.A. (2002). Combining price and quantity controls to mitigate global climate change. *Journal of Public Economics*, 85, pp. 409–434.

Requate, T. (2005). Dynamic incentives by environmental policy instruments – a survey. *Ecological Economics*, 54, pp. 175–193.

Rijksoverheid. (2012). *Overige fiscale maatregelen 2012*. [Online] Available at: http://www. rijksbegroting.nl/2012/voorbereiding/begroting,kst160738.html [Accessed 24 Nov. 2019].

Rosenow, J., Fricke, H., Luchkova, T. and Schulz, M. (2018). Minimizing contrail formation by rerouting around dynamic ice-supersaturated regions. *Aeronautics and Aerospace Open Access Journal*, 2(3), pp. 105–111.

Scheelhaase, J. and Grimme, W. (2007). Emissions trading for international aviation – an estimation of the economic impact on selected European airlines. *Journal of Air Transport Management*, 13(5), pp. 253–263.

Stavins, R.N. (1996). Correlated uncertainty and policy instrument choice. *Journal of Environmental Economics and Management*, 30, pp. 218–232.

Sturm, B. and Vogt, C. (2018). *Umweltökonomik*. 2nd ed. Heidelberg: Springer Gabler.

Transport & Environment. (2010). *Grounded: How ICAO failed to tackle aviation and climate change and what should happen now*. Published to coincide with the ICAO Triennial Assembly, Montreal, European Federation for Transport and Environment AISBL. Brussels.

Warnecke, C., Schneider, L., Day, T., Theuer, S. and Fearnehough, H. (2019). Robust eligibility criteria essential for new global scheme to offset aviation emissions. *Nature Climate Change*, 9, pp. 218–221.

Weitzman, M. (1974). Prices vs quantities. *Review of Economic Studies*, 41, pp. 477–491.

5 ETSs and aviation

Implementation of schemes in the EU and other countries

Peter Morrell

1. Introduction

This chapter describes the application of an emissions trading scheme (ETS) to aviation, principally looking at the case of the (original) EU scheme. This is a scheme that covers aviation, has been implemented and has by far the largest international coverage. However, aviation schemes in other countries are discussed at the end of the chapter. Fierce opposition to the full EU ETS from countries such as the USA, India and China forced the EU to scale down its coverage pending a satisfactory global solution being found through the International Civil Aviation Organisation (ICAO). The preliminary results from the scaled-down version are also described here. Although the original concept of the EU ETS has never been applied, it will be discussed in depth. This is because the original design raised a lot of competitive concerns, an important issue when analysing ETSs.

ICAO finally reached an agreement at its General Assembly in October 2016 after three years of negotiations on a global market-based measure (MBM) to reduce international aviation emissions: emissions exceeding 2019–20 levels will have to be offset by investment in green projects and programmes; a pilot and voluntary phase of the scheme will start in 2021, becoming compulsory from 2027. This scheme is known as the CORSIA scheme (see Maertens et al. in this volume). The EU ETS is in operation, but it is not clear how it will be changed when CORSIA becomes operational.

The overall objective of an ETS is to use the price mechanism to reduce greenhouse gas emissions, in the light of Kyoto and subsequent targets. Such market-based measures should be much more effective than voluntary measures. For example, voluntary carbon offsetting is widely available on airline booking websites, but few take up this option. An ETS provides incentives to reduce emissions at the *lowest cost*. However, care needs to be taken to avoid schemes that merely transfer wealth between taxpayers and emitters, or between emitters in some parts of the world and those in other regions. The latter danger applies particularly to aviation and is relevant to the present EU reduced scale scheme that will be described later in this chapter.

2. The rationale of an aviation ETS

The need for a global aviation mechanism to reduce emissions was recognised in the Kyoto Protocol but excluded from its targets. Instead ICAO was tasked with devising such a scheme, recognising the fact that aviation emitters were largely not ground-based in a specific country and must be dealt with internationally. Kyoto came into force in February 2005, while the ICAO scheme was only agreed towards the end of 2016, coming into force on a voluntary basis from 2021 and obligatory from 2027. Emissions data started to be collected from January 2019, and the baseline emissions will be an average of calendar years 2019 and 2020. Offsetting will be required for each year's emissions that are above the baseline. Growth factors will be calculated for each year compared to the baseline initially on all industry operations and later based on each airline's own emissions growth. Unlike the EU ETS described in this chapter, there will be no cap, but they will need to offset any additional emissions (versus the baseline) by purchasing emissions reductions from projects or buying them on the EUA exchange (see later in this chapter). The difficulty here is the possibility that emissions reductions actually take place and would not have done so without such a purchase.

Following the Kyoto direction, ICAO's Committee for Aviation Environmental Protection (CAEP) considered and evaluated measures to reduce aviation emissions, including the possible introduction of an ETS. It concluded that fuel taxes were impossible to introduce and encouraged regional emissions trading initiatives (subject to third country agreement). Thus nothing was likely to be introduced on a global scale at least for some time. In the meantime, the EU moved ahead with the incorporation of aviation into their existing ETS.

The most common form of emissions trading is the "cap and trade" model. A cap is placed on emissions within the scheme by requiring all emissions to be reported and matched by a tradable permit, allowance or emission unit, whose supply is limited. International agreements or national governments determine how many emission units are provided to emitters, and these can be given to participants without charge or charged for, usually through an auction. If their emissions overshoot their allocation of allowances, they must purchase additional units from other participants either at periodic auctions or on a trading exchange. If they have spare units because they reduce their emissions below their allocation, they can sell those to other participants or hold them and use them in future years. This trading ensures that emissions are reduced at the lowest possible cost.

Participants to the scheme are those that emit greenhouse gases or those that supply products that create emissions when used by operators or consumers. In the aviation context, participants could be:

- Final consumers (passengers, cargo shippers or consolidators)
- Operators (airlines)
- Aviation fuel suppliers

Targeting passengers is too complex to administer, but the two other types of participant could be considered. The New Zealand scheme that includes domestic aviation includes fuel suppliers, while the EU and Chinese schemes target operators. The latter provides the best incentive direct to the entity that is responsible for aircraft selection and thus emissions. Airlines can invest in new, low emission aircraft, thus reducing their need for expensive allowances, or use cheaper older, inefficient aircraft and pay for others to reduce emissions.

The EU added aviation to its existing ETS (started in 2005) which covered 45% of total EU ground-based CO_2 emissions and applied to more than 11,000 heavy energy-using installations in power generation and manufacturing industry.

The EU issued general allowances, to installation operators under the original scheme, and aviation allowances, to aviation operators. Installation operators must surrender general allowances to cover their verified emissions. But they are not allowed to hold or surrender aviation allowances. Aviation operators can hold and surrender both aviation allowances and general allowances.

3. How ETSs are applied to aviation

This section will examine how an ETS has been applied to aviation, with particular reference to the (original) EU scheme. This is because the EU scheme was one of the first to target aviation on a large scale and also shows how a scheme can work across borders. Individual country schemes can realistically apply only to domestic aviation, which (apart from the USA) do not account for a huge share of greenhouse gases emitted (for a fuller discussion, see Kopsch, 2012).

3.1 Which greenhouse gases?

The cap and trade model outlined earlier can be applied to any of the greenhouse gases, the most important being CO_2 and NO_x. So far only CO_2 has been included, although aviation NO_x emissions have for some years been addressed through ICAO on a global scale through gradually improved and tighter aero-engine emission standards. In aviation, CO_2 is emitted when fuel is burnt in aero-engines, and the generally agreed conversion factor is 3.15 kg of CO_2 produced from every kilogram of jet kerosene burnt (IPCC, 1999).

3.2 The inclusion of aviation in the EU ETS

The EU Directive for aviation was introduced in January 2009, and its provisions were expected to be incorporated into the legislation of each member country by the end of the year (European Parliament and Council, 2009). This took somewhat longer, with, for example, the UK regulations coming into force at the end of August 2011 (UK, 2010). The main parameters agreed for the EU ETS were:

- To include aviation in the existing scheme for greenhouse gas (only CO_2) emission allowance trading

- First year 2012
- All flights to/from European Union airports
- Various exemptions including smaller aircraft (emitting less than 10,000 tonnes CO_2 per year or operating less than 243 flights per three-month period), military, training and rescue flights
- Cap based on actual emissions averaged across calendar years 2004, 2005 and 2006
- Cap set at 97% of baseline in 2012, and 95% for 2013 to 2020
- Emissions allocation based on a benchmark
- Initially 15% of allowance to be auctioned
- Provisions for free allowance (3% of the total) to be given to start-up airlines (with no operations in 2010) and those whose Revenue Tonne-kilometres (RTKs) are growing by more than 18% pa

Some details were still to be finalised, such as the method of auctioning and the percentage of auctioning in subsequent years. These activities and the implementation of the scheme were to be undertaken by the relevant agencies in each member state. The baseline 2004–06 cap was expected to be published later in 2009, and the actual amounts allocated to airlines would have to await the 2010 shares of RTKs.

The decision on the cap was in fact finally published by the European Commission in March 2011, the 2005–06 average annual emissions estimated at 219,476,343 tonnes of CO_2 (European Commission, 2011). This was calculated using Eurocontrol data for flights and actual fuel consumption from operators. Based on this figure for average annual aviation emissions in 2004–06, the number of aviation allowances to be created in 2012 amounted to 212,892,052 tonnes of CO_2 (97% of the base) and the number of aviation allowances to be created each year from 2013 onwards 208,502,525 tonnes of CO_2 (95% of the base).

From the time of publication of the European Commission's first proposal (2006) and the emergence of the Directive, there was considerable industry lobbying and studies, and the stronger role of the European Parliament is also reflected in the outcome. The latter proposed that the Commission's original proposal of a 100% cap was reduced to 90%, with all flights included from 2011 (not just the intra-EU flights in the original).[1] The European Parliament Green Party was advocating 100% auctioning, with the Parliament settling on 25%. This crucial variable was initially set at 15% for 2012 but left open for 2013 to 2020, presumably dependent on how other industries in the scheme are treated, but it was later fixed at 15% until 2020.

Table 5.1 shows estimates of the likely expected shortfall in allocated aviation allowances (based on the originally intended overall coverage), after those allocated free of charge and available to buy at auction. The shortfall would have to be purchased in the market from aviation or other industry participants who had a surplus. This could be, for example, a power generator that had switched fuel from "dirty" coal to cleaner gas.

Table 5.1 Expected aviation sector allowance (EUAA) shortfall, 2012 to 2020 (million tonnes CO_2) based on the originally intended overall coverage

	2012	2013	2014	2015	2016	2017	2018	2019	2020
Annual allowances allocated free of charge – > A(Free)	182.56	172.49	172.49	172.49	172.49	172.49	172.49	172.49	172.49
Special Reserve – > A(Res)	None	6.31	6.31	6.31	6.31	6.31	6.31	6.31	6.31
Auctioned Allowances – > A(Auc)	32.22	31.55	31.55	31.55	31.55	31.55	31.55	31.55	31.55
Total amount of allowances to be distributed annually	214.78	210.35	210.35	210.35	210.35	210.35	210.35	210.35	210.35
Forecast Annual Aviation[a] Emissions	264.7	270.8	278.1	285.6	294.2	33.0	312.1	321.4	331.1
Expected Shortage	**49.92**	**60.45**	**67.75**	**72.25**	**83.85**	**92.65**	**101.75**	**111.05**	**120.75**

Source: Point Carbon and UniCredit internal research

a Starting from 2016, assumed aviation emissions assumed to grow by 3% annually in line with IATA traffic forecasts).

3.2.1 Benchmarking

There are two different approaches to the allocation of the free allowances: grandfathering and benchmarking. The former gives airlines allowances in proportion to their emissions in the base year or years, while the latter seeks to reward those airlines that have already taken steps to reduce their emissions through investment or improved operations. Benchmarking penalises those airlines that are less efficient than the "average" and rewards those that do better. The "average" can be formulated in different ways.

Benchmarking using a traffic rather than capacity metric has the advantage of rewarding airlines that have already introduced efficient aircraft and those that achieve higher efficiency than their competitors. It is thus favoured by airlines that have high passenger load factors, e.g. low-cost carriers (Frontier Economics, 2006).

Benchmarking involves the determination of a baseline efficiency measure, say RTKs per tonne CO_2, fixing an overall CO_2 cap and allocating CO_2 allowances depending on an airline's share of RTKs. This was the EU aviation ETS approach:

$$RTK_{total} = \sum_{i=1}^{n} RTK_i \tag{1}$$

$$E_{total} = \sum_{i=1}^{n} E_i \tag{2}$$

$$A_i = \frac{(E_{total})}{RTK_{total}} * RTK_i \tag{3}$$

n = Number of airlines taking part
RTK_{total} = Total RTKs in the reference year (calendar 2010) for those taking part
RTK_i = Total RTKs performed by the airline i in 2010
E_{total} = Emissions assigned to all airlines in the base period 2004–06 (average)
E_i = Emissions assigned to airline i in the base period times 97% (less amounts reserved for new entrants and fast growers) in the first year and 95% subsequently
A_i = Emission allowances (certificates) assigned to each airline for each of the years 2012 to 2020

The benchmark was published by the European Commission once it had totalled the RTKs for all those taking part in the reference year (RTK_{total}). This was divided into the total free allowance to give a ratio that could be applied to individual operator RTKs (RTK_i) to give its free allowance. The total of free allowance to be allocated in 2012 was the cap of 219.5 million tonnes multiplied by 97% to give the total allowance available multiplied by 82% to arrive at the amount to be allocated free of charge, i.e. 181.0 million tonnes.

- In 2012 (trading period from 1 January to 31 December 2012) an airline would have received 0.6797 allowances per 1,000 tonne-kilometres (original scheme)
- In 2013 to 2020 (trading period 1 January 2013 to 31 December 2020) an airline would have received 0.6422 allowances per 1,000 tonne-kilometres (original scheme)

Reporting of RTK data is crucial for the scheme to work, and a system has been established of verification by registered specialists. The administering member state ensures that each aircraft operator submits to the competent authority in that member state a monitoring plan setting out measures to monitor and report emissions and tonne kilometre data for the purpose of an application under Article 3e and that such plans are approved by the competent authority in accordance with the guidelines adopted pursuant to Article 14 (2008/101/EC and European Commission, 2010).

As a cap and trade system, the EU ETS sets an emissions cap or limit on the total emissions allowed by all EU ETS operators, but within that limit the carbon market allows participants in the system to buy and sell allowances as they require.

The carbon price signifies the amount participants in the EU ETS are willing to pay per EU allowance (1 allowance (EUA) equals 1 tonne of CO_2 or its equivalent) given demand and supply. In addition, EU Aviation allowances (EUAAs) have been created to be used for compliance by airline operators. Operators also have the option to use certain Kyoto Units generated from emissions reducing projects: Emission Reduction Units (ERUs) and Certified Emission Reductions (CERs) to offset their EU ETS requirements, subject to a limit of 15% in any year.

In addition to the auctioning of units, an EU ETS operator can access the secondary carbon market to buy allowances or Kyoto Units through multiple routes:

- Trading directly with other companies covered by the system
- Buying or selling from intermediaries, e.g. banks and specialist traders
- Using the services of a broker
- Joining one of the several exchanges that list carbon allowance products

The European Union Registry is an online database hosted and managed by the European Commission by which EUAs, EUAAs and Kyoto Units are held, traded and surrendered for compliance purposes.

3.2.2 Auctioning

Auctioning was selected as the best option for allocation of the majority of allowances (EUAAs), although, as for the ground-based emissions scheme, the share of total allowance to be auctioned was very low. This was because it was the most efficient method, it treated new entrants and incumbents equally, it provided credit to airlines taking early action and it involved the issuing authority with lower data requirements. On the other hand, it imposes a greater financial burden on the industry, hence the phased introduction. Their second-best option was benchmarking, and the least attractive was grandfathering, although either of these could be combined with the other method.

The European Commission's Auctioning Regulation governs the auctioning of Phase III (2013–16) EUAs and EUAAs. It provided for the establishment of a common EU auction platform and granted member states the right to opt out and set up national platforms – the UK, Germany and Poland exercised this right. The UK was the first EU member state to hold an auction in Phase II (2008 to 2012) and auctioned 10% of allowances compared to the EU average of 3% (includes not just aviation but all the other industries covered). Over the course of Phase III, 50% of allowances will be auctioned. ICE Futures Europe is conducting auctions of EU ETS Phase III EUAs and EUAAs on behalf of the UK's Department of Energy and Climate Change (DECC). The percentage of aviation allowances auctioned will remain at 15%.

According to Article 7 of Commission Regulation (EU) No. 1031/2010 of 12 November 2010, the volumes bid shall be added up, starting with the highest bid price. The price of the bid at which the sum of the volumes bid matches or exceeds the volume of allowances auctioned shall be the auction clearing price. All bids making up the sum of the volumes bid determined pursuant to paragraph 2 shall be allocated at the auction clearing price.

3.2.3 The special reserve

Operators eligible to receive free allocation from the special reserve are those which started air services after 2010 (new entrants), or whose RTK data increased by an average of more than 18% annually between 2010 and 2014. These RTKs must not be a continuation of air services performed by another aircraft.

New entrants might be deterred in a limited way by this free allocation. However, a fund will be established both for new entrants and those airlines growing by more than 18% a year. The Directive states that 3% of the total allocation of allowances shall be reserved for such applications, with a maximum of 1 million allowances per airline. Since there are unlikely to be any fast-growing airlines, all or most of this should be available to start-ups, with the upper limit allowing the new entrant up to between 2 million and 5 million passengers a year, depending on business model and length of haul.

3.2.4 Penalties

The submission by operators of the data needed by authorities has to be verified by one of the registered specialist firms. Operators that do not comply with the terms of the scheme face penalties, starting with a fine of €100 per tonne CO_2 if sufficient allowance is not surrendered by the cut-off date. Accounts could also be frozen, and ultimately the operator could be banned from EU airspace.

3.3 Implementation: reduced geographical scope

Opposition to the EU ETS increased over 2011 and 2012 as implementation approached and even once the scheme had officially started:

- The US Congress considered a law that would it make illegal for US carriers to comply with EU ETS; Russia was considering taking similar steps
- Representatives from 32 countries, such as the United States, China and India, convened in Moscow in February 2012 and expressed their opposition to the EU ETS
- Seven leading European air carriers wrote to the continent's political leaders asking for a balanced solution to avoid a major trade conflict
- LH Cargo maintained that Russian refusal to issue sufficient rights to overfly is related to EU ETS conflict

A new Regulation 421/2014 was adopted on 16 April 2014 reflecting the opposition to the ETS that had been introduced and the progress on agreement of global measures in ICAO.[2] The major change was the reduction in its scope from "all flights *to/from* EU airports" to "all flights *between* EU airports". It inserted the following in Article 28a of the original Directive 2003/87/EC:

1 By way of derogation from Articles 12(2a), 14(3) and Article 16, Member States shall consider the requirements set out in those provisions to be satisfied and shall take no action against aircraft operators in respect of:

a all emissions from flights to and from aerodromes located in countries outside the European Economic Area (EEA) in each calendar year from 1 January 2013 to 31 December 2016;

b all emissions from flights between an aerodrome located in an outermost region within the meaning of Article 349 of the Treaty on the Functioning of the European Union (TFEU) and an aerodrome located in another region of the EEA in each calendar year from 1 January 2013 to 31 December 2016;

c the surrender of allowances, corresponding to verified 2013 emissions from flights between aerodromes located in States in the EEA, taking place by 30 April 2015 instead of 30 April 2014, and verified 2013 emissions for those flights being reported by 31 March 2015 instead of 31 March 2014.

The Regulation also exempted non-commercial aircraft operators emitting less than 1,000 tonnes CO_2 per annum until 31 December 2020. Aircraft operators are required to report 2013 and 2014 aviation emissions, based on the reduced scope of the EU ETS, by 31 March 2015 and to surrender a corresponding amount of allowances by 30 April 2015. The reporting and surrendering dead-lines for aviation emissions in respect of the calendar years 2013 and 2014 therefore were the same dates in 2015 (but separate reports).

After the 2016 ICAO Assembly, the European Commission was required under Regulation 421/2014 to report to the European Parliament and to the Council. The report considered all the options for reducing emissions from aviation and presumably the extent that these can be addressed by the long expected ICAO way forward, once the details have been agreed.

3.3.1 Benchmarks

Free aviation allowances are allocated to more than 900 aircraft operators who applied for free allocation by reporting their verified tonne-km data for 2010. The free allocation is calculated on the basis of benchmark values established in European Commission and EEA Joint Committee decisions taken in 2011. In Phase III, an airline receives 0.6422 allowances per 1,000 tonne-kilometres flown (original scheme).

The benchmark was calculated by dividing the total annual amount of free allowances available by the sum of tonne-kilometre data included in applica-tions by aircraft operators submitted to the Commission. The submissions by aircraft operators were based on independently verified tonne-kilometre activ-ity data recorded throughout the 2010 calendar year.

The allocation of free allowances to each aircraft operator is carried out by member states. They calculate the allocation by multiplying the benchmark by the verified 2010 tonne-kilometre data of each eligible aircraft operator who applied.

It has to be noted, however, that between 2013 and 2016, according to Article 28a of Directive 2003/87/EC, as amended by Regulation (EU) No 421/2014, aircraft operators shall be issued a number of free allowances reduced in propor-tion to the reduction of surrender obligation provided for in the same article.

3.3.2 Auctioning

The percentage of aviation allowances to be auctioned remained at 15% as laid down in the original directive. The new Regulation 421/2014 stipulated that member states will auction allowances that are reduced in proportion to the reduction in the total number of aviation allowances to be issued (resulting from the reduced geographical coverage).

3.3.3 The special reserve

The number of allowances allocated through the special reserve mechanism was reduced in proportion to the reduced scope of the scheme. Applications had to be submitted before 30 June 2015. The share of free allowances handed out was initially set at 85% with the remaining 15% auctioned off.

When the original scheme was suspended in the face of opposition and the potential for developments in ICAO, a legal challenge to the European Court of Justice was mounted by the low-cost airline association (ELFAA). Now that an amended regulation has been passed based on the reduced scope of the scheme, the challenge was resumed but ultimately was unsuccessful. The case is based on a number of arguments, perhaps the most important being the fact that the revised scheme discriminates between intra- and extra-EU flights.

3.4 Progress of intra-EU scheme

The scaled-down version of the original Aviation ETS is clearly far from ideal. Much is expected of an ICAO agreement to set up global market-based measures, or find a way to integrate the EU scheme into an acceptable global scheme. The interim solution introduces more distortions and also requires compliance by the airlines that are included. Quite a few non-EU carriers are still required to report and submit allowances under the reduced scheme, since they operate intra-EU flights. One such example, Saudi Arabian Airlines, has been fined €1.4 million (US$1.6 million) for breaching EU carbon emissions rules, making it the first big non-EU carrier to be fined for breaking EU regulations. The airline comes under the Belgian government for administrative purposes, and it is obliged to apply fines of €100 for each tonne of carbon dioxide equivalent that it emitted for which it has not surrendered allowances.

At least in the beginning of the scheme, the European authorities have been very relaxed about breaches in reporting. The German Emissions Trading Authority (DEHSt) published a list of 44 non-compliant operators it fined for not surrendering carbon allowances in 2012, which included Air Berlin.

3.5 Impact on airline costs

Most of the studies and estimates of the impact of ETS on airline costs applied to the broader-scope scheme that was suspended. However, Table 5.2 shows some that looked at more limited coverage. At the time, the final cost of acquiring the necessary allowances for the first year of the scheme was not known, and the initial free allowance was announced for the restricted scope for the Phase 3 period only in 2014. For most of the airlines that will have a shortfall, the cost of auction or market purchases of allowance will not be published. A key consideration is how far the value of free allowances is recovered from higher fares.

Table 5.2 shows the range of possible impacts of ETS allowance costs on air fares and profits. The earlier studies assumed that only departing flights from EU airports would be included. Even if 100% of the cost of allowances is passed on, the impact on an intra-EU flight is unlikely to exceed €5 per passenger at what are historically relatively high market prices of CO_2. Long-haul passengers could pay up to €40 on these assumptions, but this attributes none of the costs to the cargo shippers (see later in this section).

Table 5.2 Summary of previous EU aviation ETS impact studies (assuming all allowances paid for)

	Short-haul	Medium-haul	Long-haul
European Commission (2006)[1]			
€ per return ticket impact:			
Allowance price: €6 per tonne	0.90	1.80	7.90
Allowance price: €30 per tonne	4.60	9.00	39.60
CE Delft (2005)[1]			
€ per return ticket impact:[2]			
Allowance price: €10 per tonne	0.20	0.40	1.00
Allowance price: €30 per tonne	0.70	1.30	2.90
Ernst & Young–York Aviation (2007)			
€ per return ticket impact:	*Low-cost*		
Allowance price: €30 per tonne	0.81		
Average one-way fare €	47.44		
Percent increase in fare	1.7%		
Change in demand (elasticity −1.5)	−2.6%		
UK Defra (2008)			
Impact on airline profits			
Price elasticity 1.1–1.3	8–18%		9–20%
Price elasticity: 0.6–0.7			15–20%
Frontier Economics for ELFAA (2006)			
€ per return ticket impact:	*Low-cost*	*Full service*	
Allowance price: €27 per tonne	2.72	5% of av. fare	
Allowance price: €40 per tonne	4.00	8% of av. fare	
Change in demand (elasticity −1.5)			
Allowance price: €27 per tonne	−7.5%	−2.0%	
Allowance price: €40 per tonne	−12.0%	−3.0%	
Merrill Lynch (2008)			
€ per return ticket impact:	*Low-cost*	*Full service*	
Allowance price: €30 per tonne	1.54	3.52	

1 ETS scope restricted to only departing flights from EU airports
2 Assuming that the 100% free allowance is not valued and passed on in higher fares.

The European Commission (2006) commented that at an allowance price of €30, "these ticket price increases are modest. Their modesty is also demonstrated by the very limited impact they have on reducing forecasted demand".

The allowance prices assumed are generally based on past market prices. However, studies have suggested that air transport is likely to be a purchaser of allowances given its growth rate and its marginal cost of abatement. This and a tighter scheme for ground-based emitters could have pushed up the market price of CO_2 to well above the €30–40 assumed earlier. Consultants Green Aviation (2009) forecasted prices in the range of €30–50 in the 2012–13 timeframe. Airlines can purchase CO_2 emissions derivatives well in advance of the first year in which allowance for their own emissions needs to be found. There will therefore be winners and losers in such trading activity, in the same way as fuel hedging. Auction prices for European Aviation Allowances (EUAAs) are unlikely to go above the market or futures prices for European Allowances (EUAs) at the time, since the former can be used only by other airlines.

As Figure 5.1 shows, there is quite a strong correlation between oil and carbon prices. Electricity generators have a large influence on the carbon market price, and when the price of oil is high they switch to "dirtier" coal, which needs to be covered by a greater number of allowances which are likely to have to be purchased in the market. This means that airlines could be faced by increased volatility of combined fuel and fuel emissions costs, some of which will be smoothed out by hedging. It should be noted that the CO_2 prices quoted here are for EUAs. The price is thus heavily dependent on the free allocation to other industries in the scheme. Higher recent prices (e.g. 24 euros in January 2019) will thus reflect the reduction in free allocation and the overall tightening of the ETS scheme. EUAs are used by ground-based emitters in the scheme but can be purchased in the market and submitted by airlines. Airlines are allocated EUAAs which can be submitted only by airlines and not by the other emitters.

The aforementioned studies generally concluded that the impact on LCCs would be lower per passenger, but higher in terms of percentage reduction in traffic. This conclusion is arrived at using similar elasticities and the higher share of ETS surcharge in relation to their average fare, which could be as low as €40–50.

None of the studies passed on the allowance cost for each flight to the cargo shippers, even though they account for a sizeable part of the payload on long-haul flights. The European Commission's analysis (based on CE Delft, 2005) took a B777–300 for their long-haul assessment and passed on the estimated

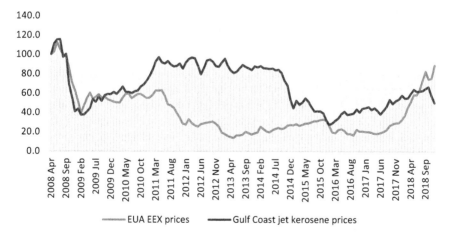

Figure 5.1 Jet kerosene (US Gulf) spot and carbon futures (EUA) market price (€/tonne CO_2, and US$ per gallon).

Source: Indexed: 100 = April 2008; data sources: US EIA and EEX exchange (own figure).

long-haul allocation of €9,422 per flight to the 238 passengers carried (340 seats at a passenger load factor of 70%), giving €39.60 per passenger at a CO_2 price of €30 (see Table 5.2). These should be doubled to allow for the fact that the scheme covered both arrivals and departures at EU airports (which would affect only flights between EU and non-EU airports). However, the long-range B777–300 can carry up to just over 25 tonnes of cargo in the lower deck compartment (depending on cargo density), or around 40% of total payload. If only 60% of ETS costs are allocated to passengers rather than the full 100%, the impact on the long-haul ticket price would be €47 rather than just under €79. This should be viewed against airline fuel surcharges which in June 2008 reached a peak of £218 (€275) per long-haul flights of more than nine hours on British Airways (2008b).

The Ernst & Young and York Aviation study (2007) was commissioned by airline trade associations covering all business models. It concluded that a large part of the ETS costs would have to be absorbed in reduced profits, with network airline operating margins reduced from 4% to 2.4% (for a CO_2 price of €30 per tonne), passing on around 35% of ETS costs to passengers. Low-cost carriers would face margins reduced from 15% to 11.1%, passing on 30% of costs.

3.6 Distortions and effects

First, this method puts a smaller burden on those airlines operating with high load factors and over longer sectors. Second, those airlines flying shorter sectors would tend to be penalised, although Sentance and Pulles (2005) argue that this would encourage passengers to take less polluting forms of transport such as rail. The latter effects could be addressed in alternative benchmark approaches, but with increased complexity (Morrell, 2007). Other distortions are addressed in Faber, Vreede and Lee (2007).

Figure 5.2 shows a hypothetical example of the difference in allocation using the EU ETS proposed method of benchmarking. The average fuel efficiency used in the allocation (assuming the base and reference year emissions are the same) is likely to reflect a relatively long sector length, given the inclusion of routes to/from non-EU countries. Taking 1,000 nm or 1,852 km as the average, operators of identical aircraft types could get 1.4 tonnes of free CO_2 allowance more than it actually emitted over its longer-than-average sector length or 2.6 tonnes less than it emitted. A similar relationship would apply to the latest technology aircraft of this size (B737 MAX) and equivalent Airbus types (e.g. the A320 neo family). It should be added that for routes of this traffic density a more fuel-efficient aircraft would not be currently available. If these allowance shortfalls are monetised using a CO_2 price of €40 per tonne, the extra costs incurred by the 230 km operator would be €103 per flight, or less than one euro per passenger.

The use of RTKs rather than ATKs might be considered to favour low-cost carriers (LCCs) at the expense of network carriers. LCCs would favour the RTK metric which would inflate their share of the reference RTK total used

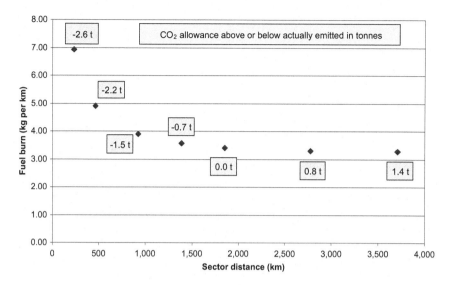

Figure 5.2 Impact of benchmarking on B737–400 flight with hypothetical average at 1,850 km sector length.

Source: Own exhibit.

for allocation relative to the network, lower load factor airline. However, the cost of additional allowance required by the LCC would be a higher share of its average ticket price. Furthermore, the network airline would have fewer passengers to pass on the cost to, but more passengers that were less price-sensitive and the cost would be a lower percentage of the average ticket price. The network carrier is making a choice to offer fewer seats and operate at a lower load factor to encourage higher-yielding (less price-sensitive) passengers.

There were a number of complications, particularly emanating from the problem of ensuring a level playing field between EU and non-EU carriers, which have been avoided by the decision to implement only an EU-wide scheme, which does not involve flights to and from the EU – the "stop the clock" decision. Air travel markets are often served on a multiple sector basis, especially longer-haul ones. Such markets cannot always be operated non-stop, but a one-stop service can be attractive in terms of price, timing, earning frequent flyer awards, etc. An example given by EU carrier Finnair (Ihamäki, 2009) is the New York/Delhi market:

- New York–Helsinki–Delhi (11,821 km) served by Finnair
- New York–Dubai–Delhi (13,229 km) served by Emirates Airlines

There is no non-stop flight serving this market. The two sectors operated by Finnair would emit an estimated 294 tonnes of CO_2, while the Emirates flights would emit 326 tonnes. Finnair would have to submit an equivalent amount of allowances under the original EU ETS, while both Emirates sectors would be outside the ETS scope. Taking €40 per tonne CO_2 would result in Finnair paying €11,740 or €43 per passenger.

It should be added that the Finnair is serving the New York/Delhi market using more fuel-efficient sector lengths. Fuel burn per kilometre flown generally declines up to around 4,000 km to 6,000 km in length and then starts to increase due to the additional fuel required to carry the larger fuel load (Peeters, Middel and Hoolhorst, 2005; Egelhofer, 2008, on more technical aspects related to aircraft design). This is more pronounced and at the lower end of this range for flights with very high load factors, as is often the case today. One estimate suggests that serving the market with one long non-stop flight might add 4% to total fuel burn, allowing for the landing and taking off at the intermediate stop (Green, 2002).[3] Thus in the earlier example an additional 13 t of CO_2 is emitted due to this effect (+4%), the remainder due to the longer overall distance flown (+1,408 km).

On the other hand, Emirates would burn an extra 32.2 t of jet kerosene, or 3,292 US gallons from its indirect routing. At the peak mid-2008 price of US$4 per US gallon, this would mean extra costs of $13,168, or $48 (€34) per passenger. Thus Finnair's ETS cost disadvantage is offset to some extent by the extra fuel cost incurred by Emirates, assuming the high fuel prices experienced in 2008. Other flight time-related costs such as aircraft and engine maintenance would also be higher for Emirates. It should also be noted that other costs should also be taken into account, notably landing and handling fees at the intermediate point and any passenger time costs.

An alternative and probably more common pattern would be to locate the sixth freedom traffic hub to the East of the EU rather than within it (as per the last example). These are hubs such as Dubai, Mumbai, Singapore, and Bangkok, that can attract traffic between Australia, the Far East and to a lesser extent Africa and the EU. An example that does not require much extra flying is London/Singapore:

- London–Singapore (10,851 km) served by British Airways non-stop
- London–Dubai–Singapore (11,304 km) served by Emirates Airlines via its hub

The two sectors operated by Emirates would emit an estimated 519 tonnes of CO_2 using an A380 aircraft while the non-stop British Airways Airbus 380 would emit 484 t. Emirates would have to submit allowances only for its first sector under the (original) EU ETS, or 250 tonnes. British Airways' entire flight would be within the (original) ETS scope, with allowances required for 484 t of CO_2. Taking €40 per tonne CO_2 would result in an Emirates London/Singapore passenger paying an ETS charge of €25 and a British Airways passenger €48.[4] In this example, Emirates would consume an additional 11 tonnes of fuel, which would approximately cancel the difference at fuel prices of US$4 per US gallon of jet fuel. In this case the one-stop route provides the most fuel-efficient mode of operation. Longer routes such as between the EU and Sydney might confer an even larger advantage on sixth freedom carriers located outside Europe along this "Kangaroo" route (assuming the original EU scheme).

The question arises as to whether EU carriers could have overcome this disadvantage by making use of their own or their partners' non-EU hubs. Setting up their own hubs outside the EU is at present severely restricted by their lack of traffic rights under third country Air Services Agreements. Most major network airlines are members of strategic alliances and could make use of such hubs through code sharing or joint ventures.

An example of this is the Hamburg/Los Angeles market, which Lufthansa currently serves via its Frankfurt hub. This involves a two-sector operation, but with the economies of scope that are available from combining other markets through the hub (e.g. Berlin/Los Angeles, Bremen/Los Angeles, etc). A non-stop Hamburg/Los Angeles flight has very limited feed at both ends of the market and is unlikely to be economic. The relative viability of the non-stop flight would only be marginally improved from the saving of ETS allowance costs as a result of more direct flying without the extra take-off and landing.

Lufthansa's major US alliance partner is United Airlines, and it could operate a joint service, say, Hamburg–Washington, DC–Los Angeles, with the first sector operated by Lufthansa (and subject to ETS in the original proposal) and the second sector by United (not subject to ETS) with its own code. The Washington–Hamburg flight might be operated by a reasonably fuel-efficient aircraft since it would benefit from feed traffic from the Americas to/from Hamburg, but this is already available to United without ETS or Lufthansa involvement. Lufthansa would have limited feed to provide from the Hamburg end, and thus United would gain little from such co-operation with the EU carrier.

Overall, EU carriers' increased use of non-EU hubs operated by alliance partners would not have been much of a solution for them, given that the net cost incentive would have been small. It would weaken their own strategic position and probably reduce the number of viable long-haul flights that they could operate, with limited alliance benefits. Any attempt by the EU to try to levy a charge on the non-EU sectors connecting to flights to/from EU airports would achieve little environmental gain in return for a serious diplomatic backlash.

Finally, since rail is not included in the ETS, there is the potential for some change in the distortion between the two modes, especially high-speed rail (apart from that stemming from other taxes or subsidies). Little research has been done on any likely impact, but a recent study of the effect of the Dutch government tax on air tickets of €11.25 per departing European passenger estimated only a "slight shift to car and train" (Jorritsma, 2009). The tax was subsequently withdrawn.

3.7 The impact on airline pricing

The costs incurred by airlines as a result of the EU ETS can either be absorbed in reduced profits, passed on to the consumer in higher fares and rates or a combination of the two. Profits could also be enhanced by passing on the value of free allowance received (opportunity costs), or passing on over 100% of the costs incurred. Previous studies do not always make it clear whether they also include these opportunity costs, and it is assumed they do not where they are not specifically identified.

One consideration is the possible marketing advantages of including the ETS charge as a separate add-on to the fare. This might be attractive to some passengers in confirming that the polluter is paying (and to the airline in withdrawing its voluntary offset mechanism). In this case, and assuming the original EU ETS, the non-EU airline gets a clearer signal from its competitor and can include a similar charge but reduce the underlying fare accordingly.[5]

The European Commission's impact assessment assumed that airlines would be able to pass on all of the allowance costs incurred. This was based on CE Delft (2005) assumptions:

- All of the extra costs of ETS allowance would be passed on in markets subject to the ETS
- Cross-subsidisation between services subject to ETS and those outside it would not occur because this would imply raising fares in non-ETS markets to offset fare reductions in ETS markets; if this increased profits, it should be done regardless of the EU ETS
- There is no empirical evidence either way on the pass through of the opportunity costs, so their evaluation included both approaches

IATA (2007) assumed that 75% of the ETS allowance cost would be passed through to higher fares or a CO_2 surcharge. Merrill Lynch expected that operators would try to pass on "as much as possible of the cost of emissions allowances to customers". UK Defra (2007) concluded that "the rate of cost pass through is likely to be around 100%, for aviation as a whole, with variations by sub-market". The variations ranged "from 90% to 120% for most aviation services". This was based on a largely theoretical analysis by a consultancy, Vivid Economics, depending on the nature of demand, competition and whether firms seek to maximise profits, market share or sales.

Some studies differentiated between flights to/from congested airports, where none of the additional costs would be passed on, and uncongested airports, where all of the costs would be added to fares (Oxera, 2003). Frontier Economics (2006) calculated a differential impact on low-cost and network carriers, suggesting that not all of any increase in costs due to ETS would be passed on in higher prices by the LCC: "the impact of ETS on aviation prices in general and in any particular market would in practice depend on the elasticity of demand (and supply) in the relevant market". This study assumed a price elasticity of demand of −0.8 for the network carrier's short/medium haul network, and −1.5 for the LCC. This gave a 2–3% reduction in demand for the network carrier as a result of passing through all of the €4 per passenger ETS cost, but a 7.5%–12% drop for the LCC. The network carrier could pass on all of the €4 per passenger increase with no fall in revenues, but the LCC would suffer a revenue decline of 2.5%–4% if it did so. This analysis ignores the fact that the more price elastic passengers carried by airlines such as British Airways (a large part of its non-premium leisure passengers which accounted for 58% of total traffic in 2007; British Airways, 2008a), and the less price sensitive traffic on LCCs (e.g. foreign property owners).

Other studies took the more realistic line that ETS costs might be passed on to certain markets or market segments. This is cross-subsidisation which occurs where an airline uses profits it makes in one market or market segment where it has market power to support low prices in other markets or segments which are subject to greater competition. Markets are usually defined on a city or airport pair basis. But they could also be the various market segments travelling on the same city-pair, often simplified to premium and economy passengers. Cargo is another segment carried on the same flight but often disregarded.

Premium passengers are generally thought to be price inelastic and economy price elastic, although there are sub-groups within each category that behave differently. Increasing premium prices and reducing economy fares would thus be expected to increase revenues, other things being equal. Some commentators think that this has been exploited to the full and that premium or business passengers are becoming more price elastic. Airlines are also keen to increase their share of premium passengers on competitive routes because they are generally more profitable (apart from those travelling first class). In Europe, this is likely to take the form of discounting premium transfer passengers (those connecting at their hubs) but not non-stop markets to/from their hubs.

In the context of the original EU ETS, the routes in question will involve all airlines (EU and non-EU) incurring additional costs from the need to purchase emissions permits. These costs would lead initially to lower profits. All carriers could pass on the additional costs to the passengers in higher fares in the same way as fuel surcharges, but in highly competitive markets they may prefer to absorb the costs in lower profits or take steps to reduce other costs (such as labour) further to compensate. In this respect, airlines appeared much more successful in reducing non-fuel costs during periods of very high fuel prices. Reduced profits would also lead to a higher cost of borrowing, less ability to invest in more fuel-efficient aircraft and more competitive products. This would reduce their ability to compete with non-EU carriers in the future. Non-EU carriers could take a hit on profitability much more easily, since the markets in question will probably account for a small part of their total revenues. They could also much more easily absorb the costs across the rest of their network.

Some of the previous studies have discussed "profit maximisation" and an "equilibrium situation", but this is likely to be an oversimplification, and in reality airlines are responding to many changes in both demand and supply as the date of departure of the flight approaches. In the short term, airlines tend to try to maximise revenues, with costs relatively fixed. This amounts to profit maximisation but on a dynamic and network basis. Each market's revenues are spread over a number of sectors such that profit maximisation can be viewed only on a network basis; this offers considerable scope for cross-subsidisation that has nothing to do with ETS (e.g. short-haul feeder routes from profits from long-hauls).

The market segment that this is likely to focus on is the premium traffic, since the marginal revenue gained from attracting these passengers far exceeds marginal costs. However, price is only one of a number of important factors governing premium traffic purchase decisions, the ticket for which is usually purchased by the company rather than the individual (Brons et al., 2002). Others include:

- Frequent flyer programmes
- Corporate agent and travel manager incentives
- Product features (flight timings, service levels, frequency, etc.)

The last is difficult to adjust on a shorter-term basis, and one carrier may have a marked advantage that is already reflected in market share and yield. The first two factors are also very important and give the home carrier a built-in advantage that small price changes would not easily shift (e.g. British Airways in the markets with UK origin or destination). This applies to home market sales and explains why premium sales in adjacent markets (British Airways' sales in, for example, Germany connecting with their long-haul flights to/from London) are much less dependent on the first two bullet points and easier to attract. Thus cross price elasticity in the non-stop home markets is relatively low and in the multi-stop (hub-feed) markets much higher.

This example needs to be expanded to include non-EU carriers, assuming the original EU ETS. They will be competing in the non-stop flights to/from EU carrier hubs, but efforts to attract home market sales will be limited for the aforementioned reasons. The home carrier might also defend its premium point-to-point passengers by allocating more of the flight's ETS costs to other segments. On the other hand, the non-EU carrier will be able to cross-subsidise in all multi-stop markets travelling on the flight between its hub and the EU carrier hub, and also the non-stop market sold in its home country, although this may be quite small (e.g. Dubai and Singapore).

From time to time, the EU ETS is revised to improve its working. In recent years, several problems have emerged. One problem has been that allowance prices have been volatile at times, and another problem has been that allowance prices have tended to have been unexpectedly low. The response has been that a "market stability reserve" (MSR) was introduced in 2019. The MSR is a reserve price scheme, which withdraws allowances and puts them into a reserve when they are considered excessive, and thus pushes the price up. When the amount of allowances is regarded as being insufficient, allowances can be released from the reserve, pushing prices down. In certain circumstances, if the amount of allowances is regarded as excessive, allowances can be permanently removed from the scheme, having the effect of pushing prices up in the long run (see Hepburn et al., 2016).

These reforms have particular relevance for air transport. If there is an ETS in place, and governments impose additional policies, such as aviation taxes, this will have no effect on net carbon emissions, since the reduction in air transport emissions will be matched by an increase in emissions from other industries – this is sometimes called the "waterbed" effect (see Fichert, Forsyth and Niemeier in this volume). If the additional policies are to have the desired effect of lowering emissions, allowances need to be taken out of the scheme. To an extent, the MSR does this, though the extent to which it does so is subject to debate. This is important given that many countries which are covered by the EU ETS are introducing or planning to introduce specific policies to lower air transport emissions.

3.8 Price elasticities of demand

Previous studies have tried to estimate the impact of price increases or ETS surcharges on demand. Some have gone a step further in attempting to gauge the supply response and resultant changes in profitability. Price elasticities have been determined in past studies using econometric techniques over given historical periods of time. These have encompassed periods of economic growth and downturns. The estimates are shown separately for business travel and leisure travel, since these would be expected to show different reactions to price increases or reductions. They are often based on business and economy class or cabin passengers, and this is used as a proxy for purpose of trip data that is not reported on any regular basis.

UK Defra (2007) highlighted the range of elasticities determined in previous studies, while Brons et al. (2002) distilled some key findings from a survey of 37 studies and examined the impact on the estimates of such variables as class of travel, distance and level of income. Omitting income from the estimation resulted in an overestimation of price sensitivity. This seems to be supported by a more rigorous pass through of fuel surcharges by airlines during periods of strong economic growth.

Long-haul markets might be expected to show less price sensitivity since there are fewer substitutes, and this was apparent from the Brons et al. data. On the other hand, Defra (2007) concluded that there is "no evidence that long and short haul flights have different price elasticities".

Some feel that LCC passengers should be treated differently from leisure traffic in general; this was the view of the Defra study, but Frontier Economics (2006) disagreed. Some LCCs carry up to 20% of passengers on business trips in contrast to European charter flights which have almost none. LCCs differ from network carrier short-haul flights that also carry a mix of business and leisure passengers in having only one fare available at any point in time. This means that they cannot take advantage of price differentiation based on the difference in price elasticities confirmed by previous studies.

The impact on demand resulting from ETS induced price increased will vary depending on the elasticity used. Most previous estimates of the impact on demand are small and insufficient to prevent aviation emissions from continuing to rise in the future. For this reason, an open trading scheme is crucial in allowing aviation to pay for emissions reductions in more polluting industries or to encourage alternative technology energy. Anger et al. (2008) concluded that 100% pass through of aviation allowances would result in its emissions being 7.5% lower in 2020 than without the ETS.

4. Other aviation ETS schemes

4.1 New Zealand

The emissions trading scheme (ETS) was introduced in 2008 and from 2010 applied to liquid fossil fuels as far up the supply chain as possible, in other words, when refined oil products leave the refinery or are imported. This means that fuel suppliers who take fuel from the refinery or who import it are required to participate in the scheme by surrendering New Zealand Units (NZUs) to cover the emissions that result from the fuel they buy. Aviation fuel was included but only that which was used for domestic aviation since international fuel is exempt due to the country's treaty obligations. Four airlines registered as voluntary opt-in consumers of jet aviation fuel, but reporting only their domestic operations.

Liquid fossil fuel participants are only required to surrender one NZU for every two tonnes of emissions, and they can buy NZUs from the government to meet their obligations at a fixed price of NZ$25 per NZU if they wish, although they could acquire them from the forestry sector or ERU/CERs in the market for prices well below NZ$5 (IBRD/World Bank, 2014). This differs from the EU scheme which limits the use of offsets.

4.2 China (Shanghai)

The national Chinese emissions trading scheme (ETS) was expected to start in the second half of 2017, but was postponed until 2020. It will cover eight industries including aviation. No details have been published, and it may be adapted to the approaches taken by the EU and/or ICAO, at least for aviation. In the meantime the Shanghai ETS was designated as one of the seven Chinese ETS pilot programmes, starting from 2013, but as with the others it seems to have stalled. The other ETS pilots were Shenzhen, Guangdong, Hubei, Beijing, Chongqing and Tianjin, but none of these directly involve aviation.

The Shanghai ETS includes industrial sectors, but also covers non-industrial sectors such as aviation, ports, airports, railways and commercial buildings that emitted more than 10,000 tCO_2/year in 2010–2011. The objective of the Shanghai ETS was to cut carbon intensity by 19% below the 2010 level by 2015. The domestic flights of six airlines were included in the Shanghai ETS: China Eastern, Shanghai Airlines, China Cargo Airlines, Juneyao Airlines, Spring Airlines and Yangtze River Express. Apart from a growing cap, the Shanghai scheme was designed to work in a very similar way to the EU ETS, with grand-fathering, benchmarking and auctioning of allowances.

5. Summary and conclusions

The failure to get agreement for a global Emissions Trading Scheme for air transport through ICAO led the EU to finalise its own scheme. An emissions or fuel tax was ruled out given the hundreds of international aviation agreements that would have to be re-negotiated. The first international aviation ETS was due to be implemented in 2012 and be applied to all flights arriving in and departing from EU airports. Opposition from non-EU countries and renewed efforts through ICAO led to a scaled-down, intra-EU scheme.

Most studies of the impact of the EU ETS on airlines show a modest increase in cost per passenger even assuming all their allowance value is passed on in full. This cost is well below past fuel cost surcharges and may have a limited impact on air traffic growth. The degree to which these costs are passed on and which market segment takes the brunt of this will depend on the position in the economic cycle and the pricing strategies of the airlines involved. Given that many airlines take a network-wide approach to pricing it will also depend on the size of the costs in relation to their system-wide revenues. Almost none of the previous studies assumed any pass through of ETS costs to cargo shippers, even though cargo can account for almost 40% of payload on long-haul passenger flights.

The assumption on the cost of acquiring additional EUAAs or EUAs though auctioning or in the market has tended to be based on past market trends determined by the existing ground-based emitters. These may increase significantly as a result of a tighter scheme for ground-based emitters.

The approach to passing on ETS costs may be similar to fuel surcharges, which network airlines showed as a separate add-on (although some LCCs absorbed them in the underlying fares offered). This might be attractive to some passengers in confirming that the polluter is paying (and to the airline in withdrawing its voluntary offset mechanism). Previous studies also looked at the likely impact on demand of possible price increases. As expected there was a large range of elasticities used, and differing views on the differential impact on leisure versus business, long-haul versus short-haul and LCC versus other types of airline. None of them considered the economic context in which the airlines find themselves, or ETS cost increases acting as a driver to reduce other non-fuel costs.

Any scheme that uses benchmarking for allocation of free allowance will produce some distortions, and the EU approach tends to favour longer-haul carriers and LCCs. The regional coverage of the original EU scheme penalises EU hub carriers and favours those with hubs outside the EU, but this impact is not large. The extra fuel needed to carry passengers on indirect routings via non-EU hubs may more than outweigh any ETS costs avoided, and the EU carrier could market its competing service as the more environmentally friendly.

The revised, reduced scope, interim scheme introduces far more significant distortions. This is because only intra-EU flights are targeted, thus disadvantaging EU-based network carriers with a sizeable proportion of connecting traffic at their EU hubs.

Notes

1 Ironically, strong opposition from non-EU countries led to its reduction in scope to the original proposal, at least for the first years.
2 The regulation entered into force on 30 April 2014 and was immediately and simultaneously enforceable as law in all member states. A directive would have needed the slow process of being incorporated in each member country's national law.
3 The gain would be far higher if the long-haul aircraft were designed for a maximum range of, say, 7,500km, since weight would be saved from lighter structures.
4 Both are based on a passenger load of 400 in identical A380 aircraft.
5 As was the case with fuel surcharges.

References

Anger, A., Allen, P., Rubin, J. and Köhler, J. (2008). *Air transport in the European Union emissions trading scheme*. Study for the Omega Project.

British Airways. (2008a). *Investor day 2008*. [Online] Available at: http://media.corporate-ir.net/media_files/irol/24/240949/BAPres/Investor_Day_6March08_Pres.pdf [Accessed 26 Nov. 2019].

British Airways. (2008b). *Press release*. 29 May.

Brons, M., Pels, E., Nijkamp, P. and Rietveld, P. (2002). Price elasticities of demand for passenger air travel: A meta-analysis. *Journal of Air Transport Management*, 8(3), pp. 165–175.

CE Delft. (2005). *Giving wings to emission trading*. A study for the European Commission. DGTREN.

Egelhofer, R., Marizy, C. and Bickerstaff, C. (2008). On how to consider climate change in aircraft design. *Meteorologische Zeitschrift*, 17(2), pp. 173–179.

Ernst & Young–York Aviation. (2007). *Analysis of the EC proposal to include aviation activities in the emissions trading scheme*. 1 June.

European Commission. (2006). *Working document SEC(2006) 1684*. 20 Dec.

European Commission. (2010). *Regulation No. 1031/2010 on the timing, administration and other aspects of auctioning of greenhouse gas emission allowances pursuant to directive 2003/87/EC of the European Parliament and of the council establishing a scheme for greenhouse gas emission allowances trading within the community*.

European Commission. (2011). *Inclusion of aviation in the EU ETS: Commission publishes historical emissions data on which allocations will be based*. Press release, IP/11/259.

European Parliament and Council. (2009). *Directive 2008/101/EC amending Directive 2003/87/EC so as to include aviation activities in the scheme for greenhouse gas emission allowance trading within the Community*. 19 Nov.

European Parliament and Council. (2014). *Regulation No. 421/2014 amending directive 2003/87/EC establishing a scheme for greenhouse gas emission allowance trading within the community, in view of the implementation by 2020 of an international agreement applying a single global market-based measure to international aviation emissions*.

Faber, J., Vreede, G. and Lee, D. (2007). *The impacts of the use of different benchmarking methodologies on the initial allocation of Emissions Trading Scheme permits to airlines*. Final Report to DfT and the Environment Agency, UK.

Frontier Economics. (2006). *Economic consideration of extending the EU ETS to include aviation.* Report for ELFAA.

Green, J.E. (2002). Greener by design – the technology challenge. *The Aeronautical Journal,* 106(1056), pp. 57–113.

Green Aviation. (2009). [Online] Available at: www.greenaviation.com [Accessed 26 Nov. 2019].

Hepburn, C., Neuhoff, K., Acworth, W., Burtraw, D. and Jotzo, F. (2016). Introduction: The economics of the EU market stability reserve. *The Journal of Environmental Economics and Management,* 80, pp. 1–5.

IATA – International Air Transport Association. (2007). *Financial impact of extending the EU ETS to airlines.* 9 Jan.

IBRD/World Bank. (2014). *State and trends of carbon pricing.* Washington, DC.

Ihamäki, K. (2009). *EU ETS: How ready are the airlines?* Presentation to Green Aviation Airline ETS Masterclass, London, 1 June.

IPCC – Intergovernmental Panel on Climate Change. (1999). *Aviation and the global atmosphere: Summary for policymakers: A special report of IPCC working groups I and III.*

Jorritsma, P. (2009). Substitution opportunities of high speed train for air transport. *Aerlines.* [Online] Available at: https://aerlinesmagazine.wordpress.com/2009/05/01/substitution-opportunities-of-high-speed-train-for-air-transport/ [Accessed 26 Nov. 2019].

Kopsch, F. (2012). Aviation and the EU emissions trading scheme: Lessons learned from previous emissions trading schemes. *Energy Policy,* 49, pp. 770–773.

Merrill Lynch. (2008). *Aviation in EU ETS; an incentive for efficiency.* 8 Sept.

Morrell, P. (2007). An evaluation of possible EU air transport emissions trading scheme allocation methods. *Energy Policy,* 35, pp. 5562–5570.

Oxera. (2003). *Assessment of the financial impact on airlines of integration into the EU greenhouse gas emissions trading scheme.*

Peeters, P.M., Middel, J. and Hoolhorst, A. (2005). *Fuel efficiency of commercial aircraft: An overview of historical and future trends.* NLR-CR-2005-669, National Aerospace Research Laboratory NLR, Nov.

Sentance, A. and Pulles, H. (2005). *The initial allocation of permits at the beginning of each year (benchmarked allocation).* Discussion Paper for Working Group 5 of the Committee on Aviation Environmental Protection (CAEP), ICAO CAEP 5 –WG5 WP5-5/3.

UK. (2010). *Climate change. The aviation greenhouse gas emissions trading scheme regulations 2010 No. 1996.*

UK Defra. (2007). *A study to estimate ticket price changes for aviation in the EU ETS.* A report for the UK Department for Environment, Food and Rural Affairs Defra and the Department for Transport, London, Nov.

UK Defra. (2008). *A study to estimate the impacts of emissions trading on profits in aviation.* A report for the UK Department for Environment, Food and Rural Affairs Defra and the Department for Transport, London, Jan.

6 International action and the role of ICAO

Karlheinz Haag

1. The Kyoto process

The first international activities addressing climate change might be dated back to 1972 to the UN Conference on Human Environment in Stockholm. Twenty years later, in 1992 the UN Conference on Environment and Development took place in Rio de Janeiro and decided to address climate change and environmental issues by adopting the Rio Convention and the action plan named Agenda 21. This conference can be seen as a milestone to address climate change on a global level. The United Nations Framework Convention on Climate Change (UNFCCC), which is an international environmental treaty, was negotiated in Rio de Janeiro and entered into force on 21 March 1994. The UNFCCC objective is to "stabilize greenhouse gas concentrations in the atmosphere at a level that would prevent dangerous anthropogenic interference with the climate system". Since 1992, 195 countries have joined the UNFCCC and worked together in the process of developing an international agreement which led to the Kyoto Protocol (UN, 1998).

Art 2.3 of the Protocol commits the signatory states to reduce greenhouse gas emissions and their concentration in the atmosphere "to minimize adverse effects, including the adverse effects of climate change". The Kyoto Protocol was adopted in Kyoto, Japan, on 11 December 1997 and entered into force on 16 February 2005 after several years of discussion and negotiation.

The countries which have joined the UNFCCC hold regular annual meetings, the Conference of the Parties (COP), to improve the implementation of measures and design a frame for a Kyoto follow-on period; from the author's point of view not all time successful, if we take the Copenhagen Conference in 2009 and its output – the Copenhagen Accord – as an indicator.

The Protocol's first commitment period started in 2008 and ended in 2012. A second commitment period, after difficult negotiations, was agreed on in 2012, and known as the Doha Amendment to the Protocol.

One key principle of the Kyoto Protocol is the principle of "Common but Differentiated Responsibilities" (CBDR), which puts the obligation to reduce emissions based on defined reduction target only on developed countries (as defined in Annex 1 of the Protocol). The reduction obligations can vary significantly from country to country.

To support the achievement of the emissions reduction goals, the Kyoto Protocol defines three flexibility mechanisms that can be used. These mechanisms are Emissions Trading, the Clean Development Mechanism (CDM), and Joint Implementation (JI). An emission trading system allows Annex I Parties to "trade" the so-called "Assigned Amount Units" (AAUs) or "allowances" which represent "unused emissions reductions" with partners in the system. The CDM and JI are called "project-based mechanisms". They generate emission reductions from projects. The CDM is designed for emission reductions in non-Annex I Parties, while JI focuses on Annex I Parties.

The production of emission reductions generated by the CDM and JI can be used by Annex I Parties in meeting their emission limitation commitments. They can also be linked to an emission trading system and help that system to compensate or overcome shortfalls in availability of allowances. All three instruments had been and are in use. One example also for linking various elements is the emission trading system in Europe, but also several other countries have implemented or are considering implementing an ETS and/or carbon pricing (World Bank, 2018).

The negotiations addressing an international climate regulation framework beyond 2020 continued in the annual UNFCCC Conferences of the Parties (COP). After many years of complex and difficult negotiations, the 21st Conference of the Parties (COP 21) in Paris in 2015 finally delivered and agreed in the adoption of the Paris Agreement, a new global agreement on the reduction of climate change. The Paris Agreement is seen as milestone agreement. It includes many new elements for a future-oriented climate policy but also addresses continuity concerning the existing instruments and mechanisms to control climate change. Last but not least, it will be binding for the signatory states.

Interestingly, in contrast to earlier COP conferences, the international aviation and maritime sectors are not mentioned in the Paris Agreement. This fact has created different reactions in the outside world. There was some criticism especially from non-governmental organizations (NGOs) in certain regions of the world. Whether that criticism has its rationale or not can be decided by the reader. The essential aspect which should not be forgotten in this debate is that there was and still is a clear obligation and task for aviation to act on the basis of the Kyoto Protocol. Action was taken by the International Civil Aviation Organization (ICAO). ICAO delivered and approved the implementation of a carbon-neutral growth strategy, pushing for improvement in all technical, operational and legal aspects of aviation. The important new element in this strategy is the implementation of a mandatory "CARBON Offsetting and Reduction Scheme–CORSIA" at the general assembly in 2016. CORSIA supports the climate goal of ICAO to freeze the carbon dioxide emissions from international aviation on the level of the year 2020.

2. Kyoto process and aviation

The treatment of international aviation and maritime emissions was a real issue in the Kyoto process as these two industry sectors do not fit in the design scope of the Protocol, which allocates the responsibility for emissions or emissions reduction to single states. One of the key issues is that emissions from international aviation cannot be easily allocated to a single state.

Article 2.2 of the Kyoto Protocol addresses this issue and is clear and precise in describing the way forward. "The Parties . . . shall pursue limitation or reduction of emissions of greenhouse gases . . . from aviation and marine bunker fuels, working through the International Civil Aviation Organization and the International Maritime Organization, respectively."

In contrast to domestic aviation, greenhouse gas emissions from the international aviation and maritime sectors are excluded from the scope of the Kyoto Protocol. Governments agreed to work through the ICAO to find a solution to the allocation problem of emissions from international aviation.

The exclusion of international aviation was strongly criticized especially because of the assumed significant contribution of aviation to climate change; headlines like "climate killer No. 1" were created. This "hype" could probably be seen as irrational and unrealistic, but this would not be correct or fair. First of all, concerns that were formulated have only partly materialized, that the impact of aviation on the atmosphere is more than only CO_2 and that the growth of emissions would be out of control due to a lack of regulatory influence.

The aviation sector at that time was reacting more defensively, saying that the contribution was comparatively small. This indeed was and still is the case, but concerns were and still are about the quite strong annual growth rates over a long period. It is indeed both a general issue and an aviation issue that we still see growth in overall anthropogenic emissions as well as in the aviation sector. Interestingly, the proportion of aviation to the total CO_2 emissions from fuel combustion was slightly decreasing over the last ten years (from 2.92% in 2000 to 2.69% in 2015). Since the share of CO_2 emissions from international aviation has increased during that period (from 1.53% to 1.65%), this decreasing share is due to the smaller growth rate of emissions on domestic flights (data source: IEA). It must be mentioned that these numbers are looking backwards and are not appropriate for any forecasting.

3. Climate research

The interest in the anthropogenic influence on the atmosphere and its scientific analysis "sky-rocketed" with the observation of the depleting ozone layer. Aviation is known as an industry sector which not only produces emissions but produces them in regions where the atmosphere is potentially most sensitive to changes. In 1999 the Intergovernmental Panel on Climate Change (IPCC) published the "famous" special report on "Aviation and the Global Atmosphere". The report was prepared at the request of the ICAO. It synthesised the scientific knowledge, the level of understanding, quantified the major effects including the level of uncertainties and gave an outlook. In the coming years this basis was developed further, enriched and improved. The key messages of that report, from the author's point of view was: the climate impact of carbon dioxide is only one effect; there is the additional impact of NO_x, water vapour and especially contrails and cirrus clouds, which increase the overall climate impact of aviation. In comparing the various effects, and the quality of data describing the specific effects, there was a significant difference in quality, which also stimulated research in the following years.

The methodology that best describes a climate impact is not a simple story. A very interesting discussion on that issue is still ongoing within the scientific community. In particular, the metric used in the report was criticized for having deficiencies when used as a forecasting methodology. This is linked to the impact time of various species, which can be significantly different. As a consequence, the results can change depending on the time window under observation.

The longest lasting gas with impact on climate is carbon dioxide. Once emitted, on average, it remains for roughly 100 years in the atmosphere, while contrails, e.g., are effects measured in hours, days or weeks. Overall, the analysis concluded that the emissions of carbon dioxide by aircraft were 0.14 Gt C/year in 1992, which was about 2% of total anthropogenic carbon dioxide emissions in 1992, growing up to 3% in 2050. The range of increase in carbon dioxide emissions to 2050 in different scenarios was between 1.6 and 10 times the values in 1992. A rough estimate of the additional non-carbon impact could be derived. The total impact was roughly estimated as twice as high as carbon dioxide alone (see also Grewe in this volume). It is interesting to note that this special report on aviation is still the only sectoral analysis of an industry sector produced by the IPCC.

It might be of value to consider some comments and aspects from an airline operator's point of view. First of all, the impact of non-carbon emissions is seen as a given, but the magnitude is still under discussion, and the priority question of where to start arises too. The sector is currently concentrating on CO_2 emissions for several reasons. The most important is the fact of the lifetime of CO_2 in the atmosphere. The second one is the fact that the impact is well known and, because of its lifetime, equally spread all over the world – a real global issue. The third aspect is that the non-carbon effects under discussion have an operational, a regional, a seasonal and a time-of-day component, which makes treatment difficult but could potentially allow the development of avoidance or reduction strategies by taking the different influence factors into account. The last aspect might be more political – without having an agreement on the reduction of carbon emissions, it could be seen as premature to start discussions about additional measures.

4. ICAO

4.1 Overview

The International Civil Aviation Organization is an agency of the United Nations specializing in international aviation, with its headquarters located in Montreal, Canada. The legal basis of ICAO is the Convention on International

Civil Aviation (signed in 1944), also known as the Chicago Convention. ICAO develops Standards and Recommended Practices (SARPs) and policies for international civil aviation together with the Convention's 191 member states and industry groups to reach consensus on a safe, efficient, secure, economically sustainable and environmentally responsible civil aviation sector (ICAO, 2018a).

The ICAO organization consists of an Assembly, a Council of limited membership with various subordinate bodies and a Secretariat. The chief officers are the President of the Council and the Secretary General. *The Assembly* is the sovereign body of ICAO with representatives from all Contracting States, meeting every three years. *The Council* is the governing body, composed of 36 states and elected by the Assembly for a three-year period. The Council work is supported and assisted by various committees.

4.2 ICAO and environment

Environmental issues are addressed through the Committee on Aviation Environmental Protection (CAEP). This is a technical committee of the Council established in 1983. CAEP is composed of 23 members from all regions of the world and 16 observers. Additionally, more than 400 internationally renowned experts are involved in CAEP activities and in special working groups.

Environmental aspects of aviation are a challenge which ICAO takes very seriously. ICAO continuously develops and improves a range of standards, policies and guidance material to address aircraft noise and engine emissions, embracing technological improvements, operating procedures, proper organization of air traffic, appropriate airport and land-use planning, and the use of market-based options. For more than 40 years, ICAO has addressed environmental issues by developing new standards, guidance and policies (for an overview, see ICAO, 2016).

Traditionally, the environment-oriented activities of ICAO were based on technical analysis and then developed to standards, guidance and policies. With the Kyoto Protocol, ICAO had to fulfil a new role and new obligations concerning global climate change and emissions mitigation, a task which was and still is of high political sensitivity. For instance, the level of acceptance and acknowledgement of climate mitigation measures was not uniform around the world. Principles and criteria (like CBDR) probably appropriate for discussions on the UNFCCC level were not uniformly accepted and agreed for aviation. Last but not least, there might have been the perception that once a decision was taken for the special case of aviation at the ICAO level, it might then have influence on the complete UNFCCC process and the negotiations for a post-Kyoto agreement.

4.3 ICAO and climate change activities

In this complex and difficult political environment, ICAO started to examine various potential measures and developed guidance material around 2001, quite early after the Kyoto Protocol.

The 35th ICAO Assembly in 2004 addressed the highly political issue of environmental charges and taxes and urged "Contracting States to refrain from unilateral implementation of greenhouse gas emissions charges prior to the next regular session of the Assembly in 2007, where this matter will be considered and discussed again". The Assembly was effectively ruling out the use of this policy instrument because of its lack of environmental integrity and effect. The technical and analytical work underlying those decisions was prepared by CAEP. From 2007 on, ICAO published studies and guidance material on emissions trading.

In principle ICAO was using the well-established processes and procedures as developed in the past and applied it to this new field of action. ICAO in its technical work was always keen and usually successful in assessing various parameters and their potential interaction, and clearly worked along the message as formulated by Mr. Roberto Kobeh González (President of the Council) in the 2007 first environmental report of ICAO:

> As important as accurate and authoritative information is, cooperation among all stakeholders and parties concerned. Moving forward, we must ensure that whatever action is taken is done so in a harmonized manner, taking into account diverging views on addressing environmental matters. Our common focus must remain an appropriate balance between aviation and the environment.

This clearly says that ICAO is not operating on an issue in isolation; it is addressing the potential impact on other aspects of importance for the sector by trying to find a system optimization instead of a component optimization. Some examples to mention might be: fuel-saving procedures during approach (like continuous descent approach) and their link to safety aspects, fuel-saving procedures and noise, fuel-saving procedures and airport capacity, noise- or fuel-saving procedures and costs. Based on the mandate and preparatory technical expertise, ICAO was moving and developing its policy step by step as expressed in the Assembly resolutions from 2010 and 2013.

The work managed and monitored by the ICAO Council was supported by two types of working groups or committees. The Council has established policy-oriented working groups (with different names). In parallel, linked to and supervised by the policy work, the technical and/or scientific part and the supporting analysis were provided by the existing committees (mainly CAEP).

In the 37th Assembly resolution from 2010, action on climate mitigation played an important role. The following list of selected statements and positions from the resolution describes the scope of work.

- An aspirational goal was defined: "global annual average fuel efficiency improvement of 2 per cent until 2020 and an aspirational global fuel efficiency improvement rate of 2 per cent per annum from 2021 to 2050".

- An additional long-term perspective from 2020 and the option of carbon-neutral growth was addressed:

  Without any attribution of specific obligations to individual States, ICAO and its member States with relevant organizations will work together to strive to achieve a collective medium-term global aspirational goal of keeping the global net carbon emissions from international aviation from 2020 at the same level.

- A monitoring step was defined: "Encouraging States to submit their action plans outlining their respective policies and actions, and annual reporting on international aviation CO_2 emissions to ICAO".
- A global market-based measures system was addressed: "with the support of member States and international organizations, to continue to explore the feasibility of a global MBM scheme".
- The development of a global CO_2 standard for aircraft aiming for 2013 was announced.

The outcome was criticized by NGOs (some heavily), saying that ICAO had failed, that it had discussed for more than a decade without delivering. From the author's point of view, this criticism does not reflect some key aspects, and has some gaps in terms of a reality check.

- ICAO is an organization, which represents its member states. They define the scope of activities and the speed of implementation. These states had been (and still are) the same states that had signed the Kyoto Protocol (or not), the same states that negotiated for decades (without success) in the UNFCCC about the Kyoto Protocol and its prolongation.
- Methods and instruments as discussed and agreed in ICAO – like efficiency goals or market-based mechanisms – are accepted tools in the Kyoto process and the Paris Agreement. There is no logic in criticizing their application for aviation.

ICAO proceeded in the well-established and proven way with its analysis and action. ICAO has developed a framework for states to describe their climate mitigation action – the state action plans. In checking the output of the COP 21 in Paris, one might see some parallels. ICAO is also very active in its role of providing support to enable or educate countries to act. The area of sustainable alternative fuel is well addressed by ICAO not only in providing a platform of knowledge exchange but also in contributing to the development of sustainability criteria for the use of alternative fuels.

One could probably see two key elements in the carbon regime in which ICAO plays an even more active role. The first one is the development of a carbon standard for aircraft, in an analogy to the noise standards of ICAO. The second one was to continue the analysis on regulatory or market-based measures. One key lesson learned from earlier studies is of special importance: The recognition that levies (taxes and charges) are not an appropriate instrument to reduce the climate impact of aviation. The discussion consequently then focused on various market-based systems, mainly emissions trading or offsetting.

4.4 ICAO and a market-based measures system

An emission trading system (cap and trade system) places a cap on all emissions. The cap in this case is normally measured in tonnes of CO_2. Allowances are created and distributed to emitters by states' organizations. They define the frame in which a single emitter is allowed to produce emissions. A flexibility mechanism to adapt to changes is included through the option of trading allowances with other emitters. An ETS system could cover different industry sectors. The ETS process in Europe is also described in Morrell (in this volume).

An offsetting system has a lot of elements in common with an ETS system, especially the definition of emissions (units), the monitoring, reporting and verification procedures. The major difference is the way allowances are produced, or more precisely, the fact that allowances can be produced. An ETS defines a certain amount of allowances (i.e. by the government), while an offsetting system creates allowances through project-type activities, which basically means investment in other sectors or areas to create an emissions reduction that can be compared to the current status. This approach has a larger amount of flexibility and capability to adopt according to market developments. It is prerequisite that all the emissions reduction created by project-based mechanisms must be verified and certified. The Kyoto Protocol already has defined two types of project-based (flexible) mechanisms: a Clean Development Mechanism (CDM) and a Joint Implementation (JI), which are already in use and are also linked to ETS systems. This is attractive for aviation, in the sense that the sector can develop a system to treat emissions reduction via compensation based on existing methods, instruments and experience from the UNFCCC world.

The 38th ICAO Assembly in 2013 was again heavily involved in the climate change debate, not only by giving policy and technical guidance, but also agreeing on a landmark decision for aviation to tackle climate change. After having reaffirmed the goals and the activities as decided in 2010, the major decision was to agree on the development of a (mandatory) global market-based system from aviation to be ready for application from 2020 on. Based on past experience, a two-branch work program was started: one branch treating the political elements of the global market-based system; and the second branch working on the technical elements of that system.

5. IATA position and engagement

The International Air Transport Association (IATA) was formed in 1945 in Cuba. IATA is a trade association which can be seen as the voice of the international airlines business. The organization represents around 250 airlines operating about 84% of the air transport capacity available in the world.

IATA has been active from the very beginning in supporting ICAO in its environment-related activities. IATA has also closely followed the scientific analysis addressing climate change and the influence of aviation on climate. The Association was able to develop a response by developing a strategy to counteract the negative impact of aviation on the climate. Maintaining the socio-economic benefits of the aviation sector, the strategy is supported by the overwhelming majority of member airlines.

It is worthwhile to note that IATA was able to develop a concept which finds support from nearly all airlines, despite competition, despite different economic, social and political situations in different regions of the world and despite the variety of business models.

IATA focused on two areas:

•   Increase and improve the dialogue with stakeholders and create a better understanding of the sector and the boundary conditions under which the sector operates.
•   Develop a concept to counteract and reduce the impact of aviation on climate change, and to demonstrate responsibility and preserve the business. In other words, IATA's focus is to buy the license to survive and to grow.

The conclusions of the internal process in IATA can be described with three key elements.

•   Global Sectoral Approach.
•   Carbon Neutral Growth 2020.
•   Four Pillar Strategy.

The Global Sectoral Approach describes the preferred scope of application of a climate mitigation measure. Carbon Neutral Growth 2020 defines the targets, while the Four Pillar Strategy represents the toolbox to be used to achieve the goals.

The *Global Sectoral Approach* covers and addresses three key elements. It reflects the difficulty that arises attempting to attribute emissions of international aviation to states as discussed during the Kyoto process. It takes into account the competitive and distortive impact which isolated single state measures might have, as the impact on operators can vary significantly and might lead to carbon leakage. (This is the case, for example, in the current design of the European Emissions Trading System.) It strives to find a system that is both as administratively simple as possible and as credible as possible. The best-case solution to address these aspects is to design a harmonized global system for the sector.

It should be noted that all concepts developed are focused on international aviation and ICAO. But airlines have an interest in designing the system in a way that covers domestic aviation too. Should states decide to implement a system that controls domestic aviation emissions, the use of an existing and accepted methodology might be an approach to avoid or reduce the complexity and the administrative burden for operators.

The *Carbon Neutral Growth Concept 2020* (CNG 2020) is the condensation of various impact factors and the compromise goal which is overwhelmingly accepted by the industry. It is a three-step approach with different ambitious levels in the goals defined over time.

- An average improvement in fuel efficiency of 1.5% per year from 2009 to 2020.
- A cap on net aviation CO_2 emissions from 2020 (carbon-neutral growth).
- A reduction in net aviation CO_2 emissions of 50% by 2050, relative to 2005 levels.

The CNG concept is sometimes criticized as not being challenging enough. The counter-argument from the author's point of view is that this is a compromise which tries to best manage a large variety of positions held by airlines from different regions. It also tries to accommodate what could be seen as a technically feasible or realistic position in terms of application and implementation. Last but not least, it has been the accepted way forward by the overwhelming majority of airlines in IATA and has found its way into the ICAO processes (ATAG, 2015).

The first step prior to 2020 is an efficiency commitment that reflects the fact that airlines need time to adjust their strategy and their operations to a new boundary condition. The first step also reflects the situation that systems and the methods for CNG need to be developed and implemented, and it reflects the significant changes in the airline market, especially in developing regions. The second key step is to implement an upper limit based initially on the 2020 emissions and then for the long run on the 2050 perspective, to find a way to reduce emissions.

The third element is the *Four Pillar Strategy*, which is nothing but the toolbox of instruments and measures necessary to achieve carbon-neutral growth from 2020. The four pillars are:

- Improved technology, including the deployment of sustainable low-carbon fuels.
- More efficient aircraft operations.
- Infrastructure improvements, including modernized air traffic management systems.
- A single global market-based measure, to fill the remaining emissions gap.

The first of these four Pillars offers large potential and is critical in terms of achieving the desired objectives in emission reduction (see IATA, 2013, p. 34). Achievement depends heavily on the development and implementation of new technologies by manufacturers. These technologies (through better fuel efficiency and thus lower carbon emissions) will mostly become effective through airline fleet modernization and, to a minor degree, through retrofits to in-service aircraft. The CO_2 standard developed by ICAO is one instrument to stimulate new technologies.

The second Pillar covers elements like flexible routing, flying the shortest wind-adjusted routes, the use of most modern air traffic management technology to reduce separation and increase capacity, the use of collaborative decision-making, streamlining daily operations, "light-weighting" cabin equipment, maximizing load factors, utilising new landing and take-off procedures, and fitting fuel efficiency devices.

The third Pillar represents measures like investments in new air traffic management technology and airport capacity, as well as a better and more flexible use of airspace which will result in fewer delays and more direct and efficient routes. With the necessary financial and political commitments from governments, these efforts will also bring significant emissions reductions.

The fourth Pillar is an element which creates emissions reduction outside the aviation industry and therefore is of different quality in comparison to Pillars 1–3. The sector is committed to a global market-based measure, to be developed through ICAO and to be operational from 2020 onwards. In the industry's view, a single global carbon offsetting scheme offers the swiftest and most effective approach.

The reason for adding this fourth element to the strategy is mainly to avoid running into a type of dead-end situation in case the sectoral internal measures do not deliver enough reduction to reach a given goal. If there is no alternative, the blunt potential consequence could be operational restrictions, which is in nobody's interest because this would restrict business. The key approach is to decouple the growth of transport from the growth of emissions. A second aspect which might create interest in the global market is the fact that operators can potentially have a certain flexibility to balance between an engagement in Pillars 1–3 or alternatively/additionally in Pillar 4, depending on a cost analysis. In other words, the operator has a choice to select the most cost-efficient approach from his point of view. A comprehensive overview over the CNG 2020 concept including the elements of the Four Pillars Strategy can be found in IATA (2013, p. 8).

These concepts were agreed upon at the 65th IATA Annual General Meeting in 2009 in Kuala Lumpur, at which IATA announced that the airline industry is committed to achieving carbon-neutral growth by 2020. These concepts were and are the basis for the industry's participation and engagement and found their way into ICAO negotiations (IATA, 2019). The industry has demonstrated the capability to act and to compromise. This does not mean that everything is on track, that there is no discussion. There is still a long way to go, and a lot of issues remain to be solved before a system to control international aviation emissions is agreed and active and in force.

6. Current status and the way forward

While the work in Pillars 1–3, in which past experience is available, is quite well established and shows progress, the new area of market-based measures needed special attention. Based on the resolution of the 38th Assembly, the

ICAO Council has organized ICAO's work and had to focus intensively on developing a global market-based measures system.

The Council established the Environment Advisory Group (EAG), composed of 17 Council members plus an industry (IATA) and NGO representative. The major role of EAG was, to give political guidance and to oversee the technical work, provided by the Global Market Based Measures Task Force (GMTF) of CAEP.

The result of this process was the development Standards and Recommended Practices (SARPs) for CORSIA. The first edition was adopted by the Council of ICAO on 27 June 2018 and became effective on 22 October 2018. It is now up to the states to translate this guidance material into national legislation (ICAO, 2018b). States and airlines need to build up the management system for CORSIA to make sure that the system is ready for operation in time (IATA, 2018).

7. The likelihood of international action

The implementation of a market-based measures system creates a certain complexity and administrative burden for the operators. The chosen option for aviation – an offsetting system – is the simplest and most flexible system under discussion. For international aviation, a global system would be the most effective and efficient system to control and reduce emissions, far better than any regional or local system. It would make it much easier to minimize any competitive impact on operators than a regional or local approach. The ICAO work has taken this into account and designed a balanced system, which needs to be made operational and successful now. It is the first and the only mandatory system for a global industry sector to address emissions reduction.

In concluding and looking to the future, there is a technical aspect to be mentioned, which is the link between the Paris Agreement and CORSIA. The Paris Agreement has changed the UNFCCC world. The instruments developed under the Kyoto regime need to be adjusted to the new Paris world. This is of special interest for the aviation sector as project-based instruments are needed to produce the emissions compensation necessary for CORSIA.

But of higher importance is the political dimension behind CORSIA. Counteracting climate change will be an ongoing challenge of increasing intensity. It is encouraging to see that international organisations like ICAO and its member states in cooperation with NGOs and the airline sector demonstrate their capability work together, to act and move forward.

References

ATAG – Air Transport Action Group. (2015). *A letter from the commercial aviation industry on climate change.*

IATA – International Air Transport Association. (2013). *Technology roadmap.* 4th ed. Geneva: IATA.

IATA – International Air Transport Association. (2018). *An airline handbook on CORSIA.* 3rd ed. Geneva: IATA.

IATA – International Air Transport Association. (2019). *Fact sheet CORSIA.*

ICAO – International Civil Aviation Organization. (2016). *On board. A sustainable future, environmental report.* Montreal.

ICAO – International Civil Aviation Organization. (2018a). *Annex 16 to the convention on international civil aviation.* Montreal.

ICAO – International Civil Aviation Organization. (2018b). *The Environmental Technical Manual (Doc 9501), Volume IV – procedures for demonstrating compliance with the Carbon Offsetting and Reduction Scheme for International Aviation (CORSIA).* Montreal.

UN – United Nations. (1998). *Kyoto protocol to the United Nations framework convention on climate change.*

World Bank. (2018). *State and trends of carbon pricing.* Washington, DC: World Bank.

7 ICAO's new CORSIA scheme at a glance – a milestone towards greener aviation?

Sven Maertens, Wolfgang Grimme
and Janina Scheelhaase

1. Introduction

After a long process, ICAO's Carbon Offsetting and Reduction Scheme for International Aviation (CORSIA), aiming at reducing CO_2 emissions from international air transport worldwide, became effective in January 2019. Partly building up on an earlier paper by the authors (Scheelhaase et al., 2018), this chapter looks at the genesis and key environmental and competitive impacts of CORSIA, also compared with the established EU ETS for aviation whose future is still unclear.

2. Background and genesis of CORSIA

Air transport is a major contributor to anthropogenic climate change, and it keeps growing at an enormous pace, with the International Air Transport Association (IATA) forecasting passenger figures to double between 2016 and 2036 (IATA, 2017). According to OECD/IAE figures, international aviation accounted for some 1.6% of global CO_2 emissions from fuel combustion in 2015.[1] If various non-CO_2 emissions like NO_x, SO_x, H_2O, soot and contrails as well as domestic flights are also considered, the sector's total contribution to radiative forcing is estimated to come close to 5% (Lee et al., 2009) or more.

Already in 1997, while it did not explicitly contain provisions for the limitation of emissions from international aviation,[2] Article 2 of the Kyoto Protocol had tasked the International Civil Aviation Organization (ICAO) to develop policy measures for the limitation or reduction of international aviation's greenhouse gas emissions (UNFCCC, 1997). This marks the start of a long-lasting political process which eventually resulted in Assembly Resolution A39–3 from October 2016, in which the ICAO states agreed to set up CORSIA (ICAO, 2016).

Like emission trading schemes or levies, CORSIA belongs to the family of market-based measures which tend to be more economically efficient than traditional "command and control" politics (see, e.g., Dales, 1968; Siebert, 1976). This is because the former "guarantee" to achieve a predefined environmental target in a cost-efficient manner as they directly or indirectly price emissions

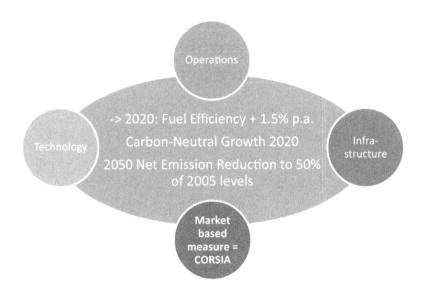

Figure 7.1 Air transport emission goals and related measures.

Source: Own figure based on IATA (2018a).

to incentivize producers to reduce or eliminate negative externalities (see e.g. Nordhaus, 1982; Smith, 2015).

CORSIA was developed in close consultation with the industry. In 2009, IATA airlines and other stakeholders agreed on three global climate goals for the international aviation sector: An average annual improvement in fuel efficiency of 1.5% between 2009 and 2020, a freeze of the sector's net CO_2 emissions from 2020 (labelled as CNG – "carbon-neutral growth"), and eventually their reduction to 50% of 2005 levels by 2050 (IATA, 2018a). Furthermore, the sector's representatives defined four different measures to reach these goals, labelled as "global and sectoral approach" (see Figure 7.1):

- An increasing use of new technologies, including alternative fuels.
- More fuel-saving operations like continuous descent approaches (CDA).
- Infrastructure improvements, especially in modernizing air traffic management.
- Finally, a single global market-based measure to fill any remaining emission gap – which has now been given birth as CORSIA.

3. Emergence and design of the EU ETS for aviation

In the meantime, in 2012, as a response to the slow progress at the ICAO level (Preston, Lee and Hooper, 2012), the EU had introduced its own market-based measure to regulate CO_2 emissions from community air transport, the EU ETS for aviation (see, e.g., EU, 2009a, 2009b; Anger and Köhler, 2010).

Originally, almost all flights from or to EU airports were planned to be included in the scheme, except for very few exemptions, according to the scheme's "de-minimis" provisions which include certain flights performed under the rules of public service obligations (PSO), or operators emitting less than 10,000 tonnes of CO_2 per year. However, acknowledging strong international opposition (Bartels, 2012) and the need to ease the ongoing CORSIA negotiations at ICAO level, the Commission's "stop the clock" decision eventually reduced the scheme's scope to intra-EEA (European Economic Area) traffic only (EU, 2013). Hence, both European and the occasional non-European operators flying within the EEA are obliged to surrender allowances for their CO_2 emissions.

The "stop the clock" regime was originally planned to last until 2016. However, by regulation (EU) 2017/2392, the EU is maintaining the reduced scope of the EU ETS from 2017 onwards, in order to take into account the emergence and initial effects of CORSIA in a next review and possible amendment of the EU ETS. The current legal framework implicates a return to the original, full-scope regime in case no amendment is going to be agreed on (EU, n.y.a, 2017).

A so-called cap is the core of the EU ETS for aviation: From 2013 to 2020, the total number of allowances to be allocated to aircraft operators for flights within the EEA represents 95% of the average historical emissions in this area in the years 2004–2006. Some 82% of these allowances are granted free of charge, according to an efficiency benchmark, while 15% are auctioned and 3% are allocated to a special reserve for distribution to new entrants and fast-growing airlines (EU, n.y.b, 2009a). Additional allowances exceeding 2004–2006 levels have to be purchased from other sectors, whereby EU Allowances (EUA) and permits from the Kyoto-based "Clean Development Mechanism" (CERs) and "Joint Implementation" (ERUs) are accepted for compliance.

The EU ETS for aviation was the subject of a number of research papers. Anger and Köhler (2010) reviewed a number of ex-ante studies on the possible environmental (= CO_2 reduction) and economic impacts to be expected from the scheme, which were overall found to be small with expected single-digit emission reductions and almost no (−0.002%) GDP impact. Preston, Lee and Hooper (2012) investigated the global coverage of the EU ETS for aviation. They calculated that in the full scope option, which did not materialize due to the "stop the clock" decision, some 35% of global air transport emissions would have been regulated under the EU ETS, while this share goes down to a small double-digit figure in the "stop the clock" regime.

Papers from the airline perspective, which mainly aim at assessing ETS-related costs for the carriers, include Meleo, Nava, and Pozzi (2016) and Albers et al. (2009). Using a route-based cost and demand simulation approach, the latter found that ETS-related cost changes would be small (between €9 and €27 per route for a carbon price scenario of €20 per ton) and therefore unlikely to stimulate network reconfigurations. The former assessed the cost and fare impacts of the EU ETS on Italian carriers, which depend on different emission permit price and cost pass-through scenarios. Likewise, they found the effects of the EU ETS for aviation to be rather small as they expect final price increases to stay below 1% even assuming a pass-through rate of 100%.

Cost increases for affected carriers could have competitive impacts in cases in which they compete against carriers that mainly operate on routes not being subject to the scheme. Earlier work by Schaefer et al. (2010) suggested significant competitive disadvantages for European network carriers compared to non-European airlines in the originally envisaged full scope scenario of the EU ETS, as the former would have to operate all flights from and to their hubs under the scheme's provisions, while the latter would be affected only on direct routes into the EU, but not elsewhere.[3]

A relatively recent research topic is the potential inclusion of non-CO_2 effects into the EU ETS, to better capture the full climate effects of the air transport sector. Scheelhaase (2019) finds that such a move would result in much larger cost effects, which will also depend on the length and altitude of each flight.

To our best knowledge, the interesting question of how to best continue with the EU ETS for aviation after CORSIA has been set in operation has not yet been tackled in academic research.

4. Design and functioning of CORSIA

Unlike the EU ETS, CORSIA is a global offsetting scheme in which the international airline sector, subject to some exceptions, will be obliged to offset any growth in CO_2 emissions on international routes above 2020 levels. For this, tradable certificates or permits representing the right to emit one tonne of carbon dioxide or its equivalent, so-called "carbon credits", are used for compliance and have to be purchased by the carriers according to their post-2020 emission growth on route tackled by CORSIA. As a consequence, airlines will choose to offset their emissions whenever this is cheaper than to reduce them directly.

These carbon credits are issued by greenhouse gas reduction projects like reforestation which, in return, shall deliver measurable reductions in emissions. This way, international aviation's net CO_2 emissions shall be stabilized while the other emissions reduction measures shown in Figure 7.1 (new technologies and fuels, operational and infrastructural improvements) will be further pursued. Emissions from domestic operations are not regulated under CORSIA as they are covered by the UNFCCC Paris Agreement, and because the ICAO is competent only for international air traffic.

Figure 7.2 illustrates the design and functioning of the scheme, which are ruled in Assembly Resolution A39–3 (ICAO, 2016) and in the related Standards and Recommended Practices (SARPs) document "Annex 16 to the Convention on Civil Aviation, Vol. IV" (ICAO, 2018a).

At first, the air transport world is divided in flights within and outside of CORSIA's scope, respectively. Not tackled by CORSIA are not only emissions stemming from domestic flights, but also emissions from small operators (< 10,000 t CO_2 p.a.), from small aircraft (< 5.7 t MTOM) and rotorcraft, and those from humanitarian, medical and firefighting operations (Assembly

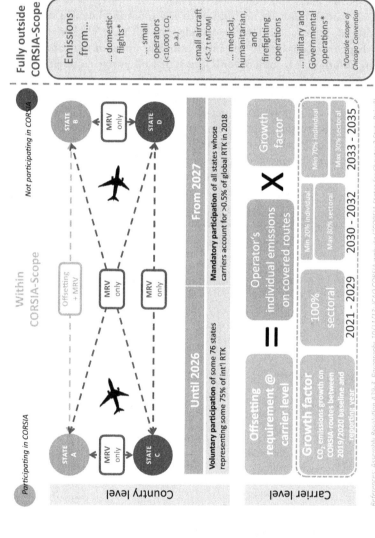

Figure 7.2 Design and Functioning of CORSIA scheme.

Source: Own figure based on ICAO (2016), Assembly Resolution A39–3, Paragraphs 10/11/13; ICAO (2019a).

Resolution A39–3, §13). In addition, military and governmental aviation are excluded as they are not subject to the Chicago Convention.

All other emissions from international civil aviation are regulated by the scheme, i.e. "within CORSIA's scope". However, actual offsetting requirements exist only for emissions from flights between the participating states, in the following also referred to as "CORSIA-states" (§10a). Emissions from flights between CORSIA states and non-CORSIA states, or entirely between non-CORSIA states, in contrast, are not subject to any offsetting but will still have to be monitored, reported and verified under the CORSIA scheme (§10b, §10c). This happens according to the internationally uniform standards ruled in Annex 16, Volume IV. In other words, the actual offsetting requirements of any airline in the world will solely depend on the airline's emissions on routes between CORSIA states, while the remaining emissions from international flights will just have to be monitored, reported and verified.

Until 2026, participation in the scheme is voluntary (§9a, §9b). As of January 2019, more than 75 states whose carriers represent almost 77% of international aviation activity measured in revenue tonne kilometres (RTK) have decided to voluntarily join CORSIA from its outset (see Table 7.1) – a list

Table 7.1 Voluntarily participating CORSIA states (as of 15 January 2019)

Albania	Guatemala	Poland
Armenia	Guyana	Portugal
Australia	Hungary	Qatar
Austria	Iceland	Republic of Korea
Azerbaijan	Indonesia	Republic of Moldova
Belgium	Ireland	Republic of North Macedonia (FYROM)
Bosnia and Herzegovina	Israel	Romania
Botswana	Italy	San Marino
Bulgaria	Jamaica	Saudi Arabia
Burkina Faso	Japan	Serbia
Cameroon	Kenya	Singapore
Canada	Latvia	Slovakia
Costa Rica	Lithuania	Slovenia
Croatia	Luxembourg	Spain
Cyprus	Malaysia	Sweden
Czech Republic	Malta	Switzerland
Denmark	Marshall Islands	Thailand
Dominican Republic	Mexico	Turkey
El Salvador	Monaco	Uganda
Equatorial Guinea	Montenegro	Ukraine
Estonia	Namibia	United Arab Emirates
Finland	Netherlands	United Kingdom
France	New Zealand	United States
Gabon	Nigeria	Zambia
Georgia	Norway	
Germany	Papua New Guinea	
Greece	Philippines	

Source: ICAO (2019a).

which includes not only the EU states and other big players like Australia, Canada, Indonesia, Korea, Japan, Mexico, Qatar, Turkey, the UAE and the US, but also smaller or developing states like Armenia, Botswana, Jamaica or Zambia. Large countries still missing on the list include the BRIC states Brazil, Russia, India and China.

From 2027, then, all states have to participate in CORSIA, with the exception of small islands, least developed countries, land-locked developing countries and states whose carriers account for less than 0.5% of 2018 international revenue tonne kilometres (RTK), unless they decide to volunteer (§9e).

From 2021, at an annual level, the airline sector will then have to offset any emissions from "CORSIA-flights" exceeding the so-called CORSIA baseline which is defined as the average emissions from CORSIA routes in 2019 and 2020. Hence, in the baseline period, countries are already obliged to report their carriers' revenue tonne kilometre volumes and route-based emissions, to feed ICAO with the necessary data for calculating the baseline emissions. If new countries join CORSIA in the forthcoming years, this baseline will have to be recalculated.

Actual offsetting occurs at the carrier level, under supervision of the responsible competent authority. To calculate an airline's offset obligation, in each year from 2021 to 2029, the airline's individual emissions from CORSIA-routes have to be multiplied with the sectoral global emission growth rate (over all carriers) since the baseline period (§11).

> **Example:** Imagine an airline's emissions subject to CORSIA offsetting amount to 4,912,000 tonnes of CO_2 in the year 2021, and the sector's emission growth factor on CORSIA routes in that year compared to the baseline period is 3.8%. In this case, the carrier's offset requirement would be 4,912,000 × 0.038 = 186,656 tonnes of CO_2.

The reason for uniformly applying the average sector mission growth to all carriers in the early years is to get the right balance between the offsetting requirements for older and new carriers, respectively. Otherwise, young and fast-growing airlines, e.g. from the Middle East or China, would have to shoulder most of the burden, while large but stagnating carriers like the big US, Japanese or European network airlines would hardly show any individual emission growth and therefore have no or only very moderate offsetting obligations. From 2030, however, individual emission growth will be attributed to the carriers to an increasing extent.

Apart from the aforementioned general exceptions for very small carriers (< 10,000 tonnes of CO_2) and aircraft (< 5.7 tonnes MTOM), which remain completely outside the scheme's scope, §12 of the Resolution makes special provisions for new carriers. New entrants will be free from any offsetting obligations for a period of up to three years if their annual emissions do not surpass 0.1% of global emissions in 2020 at an earlier point.

In June 2018, the ICAO Council adopted the First Edition of Annex 16 – Environmental Protection, Volume IV – Carbon Offsetting and Reduction

Scheme for International Aviation (CORSIA) (ICAO, 2018a). It contains common rules surrounding monitoring, reporting and verification (MRV), to make sure that the scheme's implementation and handling do not strongly differ between countries.

In addition, ICAO has published the first edition of the "Environmental Technical Manual (Doc 9501)" (ICAO, 2018b) which was approved by the ICAO Committee on Aviation Environmental Protection (CAEP). It contains "the most recent information available to administrating authorities, aeroplane operators, verification bodies and other interested parties in a timely manner, aiming at achieving the highest degree of harmonization possible" (ICAO, 2019b).

In another move to achieve a high degree of worldwide harmonization, ICAO has inaugurated Buddy Partnerships in which technical experts provided by some 15 donor states work together with the CORSIA focal points of almost 100 recipient states to provide on-site trainings and related follow-up on the implementation of the recipient states' CORSIA MRV systems (ICAO, 2018c).

5. Expected impacts and limitations

Aviation stakeholders and their industry associations are promoting CORSIA as a success. Examples include a website named Klimaschutz-Portal.aero, jointly run by different industry associations from the air transport sector and the German air navigation service provider DFS, which stresses the carbon neutrality of post-2020 international air transport growth (Klimaschutz-Portal, 2019). Likewise, the website "Aviation: Benefits Beyond Borders", run by the Air Transport Action Group consisting of "members include airports, airlines, airframe and engine manufacturers, air navigation service providers, tourism and trade partners, ground transportation and communications providers" (ATAG, 2019) communicates CORSIA as an instrument allowing "aviation to achieve its shared goal of carbon-neutral growth from 2020" as "airlines and other operators will offset any growth in CO_2 emissions above 2020 levels" (Aviation Benefits Beyond Borders, 2019).

Such communication neglects two main issues which have a significant impact on the scheme's environmental effectiveness: its coverage in terms of emissions compensated, and the quality of the offsets. It has already been shown that considerable CO_2 emission shares stemming from the air transport sector are not tackled by the scheme: Apart from domestic aviation, which does not fall under ICAO's supervision but, in 2016, held a worldwide emission share of approximately 36% (*Source*: DLR analysis using 4D-Race emission calculation tool based on global OAG passenger flight plan), emissions from flights from and to non-participating states and the whole 2019–2020 baseline emissions are not subject to compensation.

Accounting for this, Scheelhaase et al. (2018) have shown that – in the beginning in 2021 – only some 1.4% of the worldwide emissions stemming from civil air transport will actually be offset. This estimate was based on some 71 voluntarily participating states as of 29 June 2017, including China, which would represent about 87.7% of global, international RTKs. As China, however, withdrew from the list of participants in summer 2018 (Reuters, 2018), the coverage rate has in the meantime gone down to some 78 states representing about 77% of international RTKs. Accounting for this, the initial share of compensated emissions is expected to be just about 1.2%. If emissions from domestic flights and from routes from and to non-participating states, as well as (parts of) the baseline emissions were also subject to offsetting, the environmental impact would be much greater.

The EU ETS in contrast, while it only covers intra-European flights, has its baseline much more in the past (average of the years 2004–2006), meaning that all growth since then has to be compensated in buying certificates from other sectors, and 15% of the baseline emissions are subject to auctioning. As a result, Scheelhaase et al. (2018) have estimated a compensation rate of about 2.8% for 2021.

However, the share of emissions offset within the CORSIA scheme could rise to some 12% in 2030, and to about 18% in 2039 (Scheelhaase et al., 2018), accounting for an expected global CO_2 growth rate of international air transport of about 3.2% p.a., on average.

Apart from the initially small coverage rate of CORSIA, the environmental success of the scheme will heavily depend on the quality and availability of the carbon credits (offsets) and related projects. Although the Paris Agreement does not refer to the air transport sector, key principles for internationally transferred mitigation as stated in Article 6, like environmental integrity, robust accounting and transparency, will also be critical for CORSIA (UNFCCC, 2015). Becken and Mackey (2017) have shown that voluntary offset schemes offered by airlines in many cases lack consistent and accurate information, as well as a straightforward definition of what offsetting actually is.

While the scheme's Monitoring, Reporting and Verification standards have already been published (ICAO, 2018a), allowing for on-time implementation globally, the ICAO Council's decision on eligible emission units is still pending (as of January 2019; see, e.g., IATA, 2018b). It seems, however, likely that only those carbon credits which meet internationally recognized standards like the Gold Standard (Gold Standard, 2019) will be accepted within the scheme, which assure environmental integrity e.g. through the so-called "additionality", which means that a reduction of emissions elsewhere will actually be achieved in order to compensate air transport emissions.

The competitive impacts of CORSIA have also been discussed by Scheelhaase et al. (2018): Although most international traffic will be covered by CORSIA, and offsetting requirements depend only from the routes served and not from the carriers' place of registration, there might be some risk of competitive distortion between routes and between destinations, as CORSIA routes and non-CORSIA routes can be in competition.

- In cases in which the home country of a major hub carrier does not participate, all routings via this hub will (ceteris paribus) have a cost advantage over competing indirect routings. For example, until 2026, Aeroflot and the Chinese carriers will be able to connect Europe with Asia without any additional costs stemming from the purchase of offsets, while carriers from the EU and from countries like Thailand, Switzerland, the UAE, Qatar, Turkey and Singapore will have to offset their emission growth on most routes. This especially applies to the voluntary phase when, as it looks now, major countries like the BRIC states are not yet part of the scheme. From 2027, however, competition between the leading carriers globally will be less blurred by CORSIA as the BRIC states will have to join the scheme then.

- In addition, flights to certain destinations will be subject to CORSIA, while those to competing destinations might be exempt. For example, as things stand now, a routing like Dubai-Phuket will be regulated by the scheme, while there will be no offset requirements for, e.g., Dubai-Male, unless the Maldives decided to opt in voluntarily.

6. Conclusion

Under the new CORSIA scheme, which has already become effective in January 2019 for administrative purposes, any emissions growth from routes between participating states will be subject to offsetting from the year 2021 onwards.

Referring both to previous research and to CORSIA's legal provisions like the Assembly Resolution A39–3 and the related Standards and Recommended Practices (Annex 16, Vol. IV), we presented the design and main characteristics of the scheme and discussed its main achievements and drawbacks.

Given the wide range of different interests in global aviation, CORSIA – the first global CO_2 mitigation measure of any industry sector – can undeniably be regarded as a major international milestone towards greener aviation, and it may serve as a blueprint for other sectors like the shipping industry. However, the scheme's environmental effectiveness will be rather limited in the first years. This is, on the one hand, because of a rather unambitious baseline and, on the other hand, due to some key markets like the BRIC states which are unlikely to participate before 2027.

Notes

1 The IEA (International Energy Agency) "CO_2 Emissions from Fuel Combustion" database for 2015, published in 2017 (IEA, 2017), reports total CO_2 emissions from fuel combustion of 32,294 million tonnes, including some 529.7 million tonnes from international aviation. This makes a share of 1.6%.
2 In a similar way, the Paris Agreement by the UN Framework Convention on Climate Change (UNFCCC, 2015) also does not explicitly refer to international aviation.
3 Interestingly, in the "stop the clock" regime, the relative degree of competitive distortion can even be higher as non-EU carriers are now virtually free from any ETS burden (provided they do not offer any 5th freedom intra-Community routes) while the whole intra-EU networks of EU carriers are still fully subject to the scheme.

References

Albers, S., Bühne, J.A. and Peters, H. (2009). Will the EU ETS instigate airline network reconfigurations? *Journal of Air Transport Management*, 15, pp. 1–6.

Anger, A. and Köhler, J. (2010). Including aviation emissions into the EU ETS: Much ado about nothing? A review. *Transport Policy*, 17, pp. 38–46.

ATAG – Air Transport Action Group. (2019). *Who we are.* [Online] Available at: https://www.atag.org/about-us/who-we-are.html [Accessed 30 Nov. 2019].

Aviation Benefits Beyond Borders. (2019). *CORSIA explained.* [Online] Available at: https://aviationbenefits.org/environmental-efficiency/climate-action/offsetting-emissions-corsia/corsia/corsia-explained/ [Accessed 30 Nov. 2019].

Bartels, L. (2012). The WTO legality of the application of the EU's emission trading system to aviation. *European Journal of International Law*, 23, pp. 429–467.

Becken, S. and Mackey, B. (2017). What role for offsetting aviation greenhouse gas emissions in a deep-cut carbon world? *Journal of Air Transport Management*, 63, pp. 71–83.

Dales, J.H. (1968). *Pollution, property and prices.* Toronto: University of Toronto Press.

EU. (2009a). Directive 2008/101/EC of the European Parliament and the council of 19 November 2008 amending directive 2003/87/EC so as to include aviation activities in the scheme for greenhouse gas emission allowance trading within the community. *Official Journal of the European Union 52*, L8, 13 Jan.

EU. (2009b). Directive 2009/29/EC of the European Parliament and of the council amending directive 2003/87/EC so as to improve and extend the greenhouse gas emission allowance trading system of the community. *Official Journal of the European Union*, 52, L140, 5 June.

EU. (2013). Decision No 377/2013/EU of the European Parliament and of the council of 24 April 2013 derogating temporarily from directive 2003/87/EC establishing a scheme for greenhouse gas emission allowance trading within the community (1). *Official Journal of the European Union*, 56, L113, 25 Apr.

EU. (2017). Regulation (EU) 2017/2392 of the European Parliament and of the council of 13 December 2017 amending directive 2003/87/EC to continue current limitations of scope for aviation activities and to prepare to implement a global market-based measure from 2021. *Official Journal of the European Union*, 60, L350, 29 Dec.

EU. (n.y.a). *Reducing emissions from aviation.* Available at: https://ec.europa.eu/clima/policies/transport/aviation_en [Accessed 20 Jan. 2019].

EU. (n.y.b). *Allocation to aviation.* [Online] Available at: https://ec.europa.eu/clima/policies/ets/allowances/aviation_en [Accessed 22 Jan. 2019].

Gold Standard. (2019). [Online] Available at: http://www.goldstandard.org/resources/ [Accessed 22 Jan. 2019].

IATA – International Air Transport Association. (2017). *2036 forecast reveals air passengers will nearly double to 7.8 billion.* Press Release No.: 55, 24 Oct. [Online] Available at: https://www.iata.org/pressroom/pr/Pages/2017-10-24-01.aspx [Accessed 22 Jan. 2019].

IATA – International Air Transport Association. (2018a). *Fact sheet climate change & CORSIA*, May. [Online] Available at: https://www.iata.org/pressroom/facts_figures/fact_sheets/Documents/fact-sheet-climate-change.pdf [Accessed 22 Jan. 2019].

IATA – International Air Transport Association. (2018b). *An airline handbook on CORSIA.* 3rd ed. Revised, Nov. [Online] Available at: https://www.iata.org/policy/environment/Documents/corsia-handbook.pdf [Accessed 25 Jan. 2019].

ICAO – International Civil Aviation Organization. (2016). *Resolutions, adapted by the assembly.* Assembly – 39th Session. Provisional Edition, Oct., Montréal.

ICAO – International Civil Aviation Organization. (2018a). *International standards and recommended practices, environmental protection, annex 16 to the convention on international civil aviation, volume IV, Carbon Offsetting and Reduction Scheme for International Aviation (CORSIA).* Montréal. [Online] Available at: https://www.unitingaviation.com/publications/Annex-16-Vol-04/ [Accessed 23 Jan. 2019].

ICAO – International Civil Aviation Organization. (2018b). *Environmental technical manual (Doc 9501), volume IV, procedures for demonstrating compliance with the Carbon Offsetting and Reduction Scheme for International Aviation (CORSIA).* 1st ed. Montréal. [Online] Available at: https://www.unitingaviation.com/publications/9501-Vol-04/#page=1 [Accessed 23 Jan. 2019].

ICAO – International Civil Aviation Organization. (2018c). *Act CORSIA buddy partnerships.* [Online] Available at: https://www.icao.int/environmental-protection/CORSIA/Pub lishingImages/Pages/CORSIA-Buddy-Partnerships/ACT_CORSIA_Map_11_12_18_ rev1.jpg [Accessed 2 Jan. 2019].

ICAO – International Civil Aviation Organization. (2019a). *CORSIA states for chapter 3 state pairs.* Updated information on the States that intend to voluntarily participate in CORSIA from its outset. [Online] Available at: https://www.icao.int/environmental-protection/ CORSIA/Pages/state-pairs.aspx [Accessed 23 Jan. 2019].

ICAO – International Civil Aviation Organization. (2019b). *Environmental technical manual – volume IV.* [Online] Available at: https://www.icao.int/environmental-protection/COR SIA/Pages/ETM-V-IV.aspx [Accessed 30 Nov. 2019].

IEA – International Energy Agency. (2017). CO_2 *emissions from fuel combustion.* Excel database. [Online] Available at: https://www.iea.org/media/statistics/CO2Highlights.XLS [Accessed 23 Jan. 2019].

Klimaschutz-Portal. (2019). *CORSIA: Weltweit einzigartige CO_2-Kompensation.* [Online] Available at: https://www.klimaschutz-portal.aero/co2-kompensieren/corsia/ [Accessed 30 Nov. 2019].

Lee, D., Fahey, D., Forster, P., et al. (2009). Aviation and global climate change in the 21st century. *Atmospheric Environment,* 43, pp. 3520–3537.

Meleo, L., Nava, C.R. and Pozzi, C. (2016). Aviation and the costs of the European Emission Trading Scheme: The case of Italy. *Energy Policy,* 88, pp. 138–147.

Nordhaus, W.D. (1982). How fast should we graze the global commons? *American Economic Review,* 72, pp. 242–246.

Preston, H., Lee, D.S. and Hooper, P.D. (2012). The inclusion of the aviation sector within the European Union's emissions trading scheme: What are the prospects for a more sustainable aviation industry? *Environmental Development,* 2, pp. 48–56.

Reuters. (2018). *China no longer participating in start of aviation emissions deal.* [Online] Available at: https://www.reuters.com/article/us-climatechange-aviation/china-no-longer-partici pating-in-start-of-aviation-emissions-deal-idUSKBN1JU2CR [Accessed 22 Jan. 2019].

Schaefer, M., Scheelhaase, J., Grimme, W. and Maertens, S. (2010). The economic impact of the upcoming EU emissions trading system on airlines and EU member states-an empirical estimation. *European Transport Research Review,* 2(4), pp. 189–200.

Scheelhaase, J. (2019). How to regulate aviation's full climate impact as intended by the EU council from 2020 onwards. *Journal of Air Transport Management,* 75, pp. 68–74.

Scheelhaase, J., Maertens, S., Grimme, W. and Jung, M. (2018). EU ETS versus CORSIA – a critical assessment of two approaches to limit air transport's CO2 emissions by market-based measures. *Journal of Air Transport Management,* 67, pp. 55–62.

Siebert, H. (1976). *Analyse der Instrumente der Umweltpolitik.* Göttingen: Schwartz Verlag.

Smith, V.K. (2015). Environmental economics. In: *International encyclopedia of the social & behavioral sciences.* 2nd ed. Amsterdam: Elsevier, pp. 726–732.

UNFCCC – United Nations Framework Convention on Climate Change. (1997). *Kyoto protocol to the United Nations framework convention on climate change.* [Online] Available at: http://unfccc.int/resource/docs/convkp/kpeng.pdf [Accessed 25 Apr. 2018].

UNFCCC – United Nations Framework Convention on Climate Change. (2015). *Adoption of the Paris agreement, conference of the parties, twenty-first session (COP 21).* Paris, 12 Dec. [Online] Available at: http://unfccc.int/resource/docs/2015/cop21/eng/l09r01.pdf [Accessed 13 Nov. 2017].

8 Voluntary carbon offset schemes in the airline industry

Why did they fail?

Andreas Knorr and Alexander Eisenkopf

1. Introduction

The market for voluntary carbon offsets, i.e. those outside the strictly regulated Kyoto framework for tradable carbon emission permits, is growing with a vengeance. The number of such commercial as well as not-for-profit organizations is much higher than 20 years ago (Carbonify, 2020) – the vast majority of which entered the trade only after 2005 (Gössling et al., 2007, p. 231). This trend has not eluded the world of commercial aviation. By contrast, and starting in the early millennium years, voluntary carbon offsetting schemes seem to have become a serious concern for the top management of some of the world's leading airlines. Carriers as diverse as Air Canada, British Airways, Ethiopian Airways, Qantas (incl. its subsidiaries QantasLink and Jetstar), Continental, Cathay Pacific, Japan Air Lines, Air France/KLM, the SAS Group, EasyJet and Virgin Blue, to name just a few, then began to actively encourage their passengers to pay for the "neutralising" services of select carbon offset providers on top of the ticket price whenever they book a flight. Finally, some large online travel agencies such as Expedia and Travelocity, as well as leading car rental companies such as Avis, also opted to invite their customers to purchase carbon offsets. However, as this chapter will demonstrate, both the economic efficiency and ecological effectiveness of voluntary carbon offsetting as a tool to address the challenge of climate change should be considered very limited.

2. Aviation and climate change

It is not surprising that the transportation sector, and aviation in particular, have moved into the focus of climate policy. Today, the contribution of the transport sector as a whole to worldwide CO_2 emissions is estimated at around 23% (International Energy Agency, 2017, p. 44), although it accounts for only 11% of all greenhouse gas (GHG) emissions (IPCC, 2014, p. 599ff.). The corresponding figure for the European Union is pretty much the same, whereas the overall contribution of the transportation sector to GHG emissions at the OECD level is estimated at about 30% (ECMT, 2007).

While the contribution of the aviation sector to GHG emissions does not appear excessive, at about 3% of the global total (OECD, 2012, p. 7), whereas 19% are caused by road transport (EEA, 2007), its total impact on climate change might be substantially higher. This is due to the remaining scientific uncertainty about the true impact of aviation's emissions essentially occurring at high altitude. Therefore, their climate effects may be amplified by radiative forcing by a factor of two or three (ECMT, 2007).

Given its above average growth rates compared to most other GHG emitting industries, within and outside the transport sector, commercial aviation caught the attention of the Intergovernmental Panel on Climate Change (IPCC) as early as 1999. In its special report "Aviation and the Global Atmosphere" (IPCC, 1999), the IPCC investigated the potential effects of air travel on the global climate in general and on atmospheric ozone concentrations in particular.

3. Policies to mitigate the climate change impact of air transport: some efficiency considerations

3.1 Efficiency criteria for climate policy

Any economically rational climate policy must attempt to reduce greenhouse gas emissions at the lowest possible costs to society. In other words, GHG reduction efforts must be truly global in scope, covering all, or at least all major, emitting activities as well as all the countries with the highest absolute GHG emissions. It would also have to follow the same efficiency criteria as environmental policy in general. In this context, economists point primarily to the criteria of static and dynamic efficiency of political measures (Fritsch, 2018).

Static efficiency means that any politically desired amount of emissions' reduction should be reached at the lowest possible costs to society. The solution for this problem is that marginal costs of reduction should be the same in each sector concerned, i.e. the equimarginal principle is fulfilled (Fees and Seeliger, 2013). To apply a uniform target for the reduction of emissions to all sectors or countries concerned, for example, hence does not meet the goal of static efficiency, because the marginal cost of avoidance usually differs significantly between sectors. Accordingly, under real-world conditions, sector- and country-specific mitigation approaches do not at all qualify as first-best solutions.

Static efficiency is also affected by the transaction costs caused by a political measure. Therefore, a rational climate change policy also requires a rigorous comparative assessment of the transaction costs of different measures before adopting them to get a clear understanding of the likely abatement costs.

An even more important criterion is the dynamic efficiency of a political measure. Climate change policy should give incentives for an effective reduction of emissions and for technological progress (Fritsch, 2018). If polluters have to pay for the volume of emissions caused by their economic activities, there is a strong incentive to reduce GHG emissions either by reducing the volume of the transactions itself or by searching for and adopting technological improvements which help to minimize the emissions in question.

A third crucial point is the issue of ecological effectiveness. Generally speaking, ecological effectiveness requires that the instruments used by environmental policy are indeed conducive to reach the ecological target. With respect to the problem of climate change, we therefore have to assess whether the measures chosen actually contribute to reducing the amount of emitted GHG as much as aimed at by climate policy.

Irrelevant from an efficiency point of view – although politically salient – are the distributive effects of alternative reduction measures. It is obvious that the instruments of climate policy will affect consumers, firms and the government in a different manner. This is not a topic of static or dynamic efficiency, however, but affects the political appeal of these measures, i.e. the voters' preferred choice of policy. Hence, fairness with respect to sharing the economic burden of GHG reduction efforts between the affected parties (if these are domestic voters) will and must be a key factor in all political considerations, which are additionally influenced by the activities of special interest groups including non-governmental organizations (NGOs). If, for example, consumers are likely to bear the brunt of the use of an efficient and effective measure against global warming, politicians may refuse to adopt it nevertheless for fear of losing voters. They may therefore prefer the usage of a different measure with less evident economic consequences. On the other hand, industrial lobbies will – sometimes successfully – oppose measures that they feel will put most of the burden on their industry. In general, politicians will prefer measures that do not clearly disclose the true costs to the affected societal groups, because this increases the chance of implementation.

3.2 GHG reduction instruments: survey and brief assessment

Using the efficiency criteria derived in the preceding chapter, we can now try to assess the pros and cons of alternative measures of climate policy in order to get an idea of their economic efficiency and ecological effectiveness. This may lead to a sensible assessment of the efficiency and effectiveness of carbon offsetting for air transportation. Looking at the air transport sector as a whole, we can say that air transport is not affected by climate policy at the moment in most countries. In particular, there are no special taxes or levies on the use of aviation fuel. Air transportation is not subject to the requirements of the Kyoto Protocol (Grimme, Schaefer and Scheelhaase, 2007). Third country airlines serving the EU currently are also not covered by the EU ETS; however, ICAO is in the process of implementing an aviation-specific emissions trading scheme, the Carbon Offsetting and Reduction Scheme for International Aviation (CORSIA).

On the other hand, CO_2 emissions of the air transport sector are growing very fast due to the expansion of traffic volume as argued here. While significant progress was made in the past three decades with respect to the reduction of fuel consumption by specific commercial aircraft (with three- and four-engine aircraft having largely been replaced by twinjets, etc.), the massive growth in traffic led to a net rise of the total demand for fuel and hence to an increase in the carbon emissions resulting from air travel.

3.2.1 Supply side measures

Measures to reduce the CO_2 emissions of air transportation may be applied on the demand side or the supply side of the industry. Supply side measures are supposed to provide potentially strong incentives for the airlines themselves to reduce the specific fuel consumption of their aircraft. This results simply from market pressure and rising fuel prices. Fuel consumption per passenger kilometre may be reduced by a variety of measures such as the use of new technologically improved engines or new types of aircraft, by reducing the weight of the aircraft through different measures and by an improvement of capacity utilization (load factors) or by introducing more efficient operational procedures. However, the economic pressure to implement such measures is heavily contingent on the oil price, which has displayed massive volatility in recent years, swinging from an all-time high a few years ago to a long-time low in mid-2015.

However, there are two possible avenues for indirect public intervention on the supply side which merit further exploring. First, there is the possibility to promote public or private research and development in this sector. Objects for future research may include the optimization of fuel consumption of aircraft or the development of alternatives to fossil fuels (e.g. the use of biofuels, which is being tested by Lufthansa, or of liquid natural gas, which was proposed by Qatar Airways). Economists are usually sceptical of government interventions in the field of applied research, which should on efficiency grounds essentially remain a private-sector affair (Eisenkopf, 2007). Therefore, the government should mainly try to design a suitable institutional framework to promote research and development in the air transport sector but not set precise targets or mandate a politically preferred technology.

Another task for transport policy, especially in Europe, is to finally develop a framework for a harmonized, centralized air traffic control system and to create a truly Single European Sky. Obviously, the harmonization of aerial surveillance would lead to an optimization of aircraft operations that has the potential to reduce fuel consumption and carbon emissions. Although the scale of possible reductions is considerable, we have to bear in mind that the economic and ecological dividend from such improvements would essentially be a one-off effect.

3.2.2 Demand side measures

Currently, the public discussion of possible measures to fight global warming is largely focused on the demand side of the market. This is especially true with respect to aviation. The objective is to dampen demand for air transport services to a sustainable level by means of suitable measures which fully internalize the social costs of air transport-related GHG emissions. The common attitude to the air transportation market is that flying is "too cheap" at the moment because the price of the ticket does not reflect the external costs of this activity. Despite the existence of the insurmountable problem of methodologically and practically measuring the external costs of additional GHG emissions in a precise manner for all sectors, including all sectors of the transport market, with a high degree of precision, the theoretical solution proposed by simple welfare economics is relatively straightforward: internalization by means of one of the instruments available to policy-makers. As it would be beyond the scope and purpose of this chapter to discuss their respective advantages and disadvantages,[1] we shall confine ourselves to the most relevant instruments in the field of commercial aviation: taxes or levies on fossil fuels and the inclusion of air transport into a system of tradable emission permits like the EU's ETS, as these alternatives shall serve as the benchmark for the assessment of voluntary carbon offsetting schemes later on.

FOSSIL FUEL TAXES

If taxes increase the fuel price for air transportation, they will have a dampening effect on air travel demand and as a result reduce the GHG emissions of the airline industry in absolute terms. In this standard textbook scenario, that outcome is contingent upon the assumption of an elastic demand curve. But a closer look reveals some serious limitations of the use of fossil fuel taxes as a tool to substantially reduce GHG emissions:

- Taxes on the fuel consumption of air transportation have to be introduced by an international agreement; otherwise, it would result in severe distortion of competition between airlines registered in and/or operating to and from countries with taxes and others which do not. While this might be a negligible scenario for short- to medium-range non-stop or direct travel, it might strongly impact hub competition for long-distance connecting services. Moreover, given some countries' strong resistance to the idea, its universal implementation seems extremely unlikely in the foreseeable future.
- The implementation issue aside, there is also significant doubt about the economic efficiency and the ecological effectiveness of a fossil fuel tax. Static efficiency requires that the marginal costs of reduction are the same for every emission source of CO_2 (or any other GHG). This will not be true for a tax levied on the fuel consumption of aircraft, if there is no similar tax imposed on all other modes of transport (or any other activity) which burn carbon fuels too. In the German context, for example, for historical reasons road infrastructure has in large part been financed by means of a fuel tax and rail infrastructure out of general tax revenues (with track access charges as an additional source more recently). By contrast, the infrastructure costs of air transport have generally been covered by all sorts of user fees imposed upon airlines and passed on to passengers (and cargo forwarders). Therefore, any aviation-specific fossil fuel tax would inevitably distort intermodal competition.

- Third, for the reasons given earlier, the ecological effectiveness of a fuel tax remains doubtful because it is very difficult to precisely estimate the reaction of the consumers concerned and hence, the elasticity of demand.
- Finally, the main argument against the use of fossil fuel taxes for the internalization of externalities of carbon emissions results from allocative considerations. Due to a high income elasticity of air travel demand, even a high tax might not dampen demand substantially; this seems to be proven by the fact that passenger numbers and pkm continue to rise, the ever higher "fuel surcharges" levied by most major airlines in reaction to soaring oil prices notwithstanding.

TRADABLE EMISSION PERMITS

Current knowledge does not allow any reliable prediction as to which sector of the economy will be able to reduce energy consumption at the lowest costs to society. Moreover, if one follows the IPCC's stance, there seems to be a strong case in favour of an upper target for the amount of GHG emissions which may be released into the atmosphere. The economic consequence of all this is that climate policy should be based on a system of tradable permits. This is for two reasons. First, at least in the world of economic textbooks (though not necessarily in the real world), emission trading schemes (ETSs) are widely considered to be superior in terms of ecological effectiveness for the very reason that the absolute number of permits, and hence, the volume of GHG emissions, is fixed by policy-makers (for some discussion, see Fichert, Forsyth and Niemeier in this volume). Second, ETSs are also economically efficient, because emissions will be reduced in the sector with the cheapest abatement cost; in other words, the equimarginal principle applies.

The main problem, however, is to put theory to practice. This has several aspects. Obviously, on efficiency grounds, any real-world ETS should cover any meaningful emitter around the globe, regardless of location, industry and activity. At the moment, the largest such scheme which is in operation, the EU's ETS, is of regional significance only and so far does not cover all sectors as was stated earlier; aviation was included in 2012, but flights to and from Europe to non-European countries are currently exempted due to a long-standing dispute between the EU and most other leading aviation nations (see Morrell in this volume). International air transport will be covered by ICAO's CORSIA mechanism from 2020 (see Maertens et al. and Haag in this volume). The process of implementation has already started.

An important, though politically unlikely step towards a rational climate policy would therefore be to include all other large-scale producers of GHG, including the air transport sector, but also all non-CO_2 GHG emitters, such as agriculture in particular, and to implement it globally. The inclusion of air transport into the EU's ETS was therefore certainly a first step in the right direction. However, if this were to remain an EU-only effort, it would also lead to a massive competitive disadvantage for EU airlines and airports vis-à-vis competing non-EU carriers and airports (Grimme, Schaefer and Scheelhaase,

2007). Moreover, the inclusion of air transport as the only mode of transport would distort intermodal competition on a similar scale as was already discussed in the context of a selective fossil fuel tax regime. If on an even higher level, air transport, but not all of the other large-scale emitters were included, too high a share of adoption costs would be imposed on the sector while other industries would enjoy a free ride. From an economy-wide perspective, this breach of the equimarginal principle would invariably result in an inefficient overall allocation of resources

4. Assessment of voluntary carbon offset schemes

Against this background we will now turn our attention to carbon offset schemes. For this purpose, we will begin by analysing the structure of alternative types of carbon offset regimes and the behavioural incentives they create for providers and consumers alike. In a second step, we will compare the mechanism of carbon offsetting with the two alternative internalization tools which were discussed in the previous section.

4.1. Excursus: key terms[2]

The carbon footprint is the estimated amount of carbon dioxide emissions resulting from a particular activity. Due to the fact that in many cases not only CO_2 is emitted but other GHG as well, it appears more appropriate to measure the total climate effect of any activity or human being in CO_2 equivalent units. The climate effects of the emission of one unit of methane, for example, are equivalent to the emission of 21 units of CO_2.

A carbon sink is a condition, or a reservoir, such as trees or the oceans, which store more CO_2 than they release, resulting in a net reduction of CO_2. The process of uptaking and storing carbon is called carbon sequestration.

An offset is a counterbalancing equivalent. With regard to GHG emissions, it refers to the "act of reducing or avoiding GHG emissions in one place in order to 'offset' GHG emissions occurring somewhere else" (Trexler Climate + Energy Services, 2006). The ecological background is that contrary to local pollutants, which should be addressed at their very source, it does not matter where on the globe GHG emissions are mitigated. Moreover, carbon offset offers the opportunity to take advantage of the "radically different costs and practicalities of achieving GHG emission reductions by sector and geography" (ibid.). The term *carbon neutrality* describes a situation when all CO_2, though not necessarily all GHG emissions resulting from whatever activity, have successfully been offset.

The Kyoto Protocol, signed in 1997, is an international agreement under the umbrella of the United Nations Framework Convention on Climate Change (UNFCCC) which legally binds its signatories to reduce the emissions of some GHG by 5.2% in the 2008–12 period compared to the base year 1990. The protocol covers a total of six GHG: carbon dioxide (CO_2), methane (CH_4), nitrous oxide (N_2O), sulphur hexafluoride (SF_6), hydrofluorocarbons (HFC), and perfluorocarbons (PFC), but not water vapour, which accidentally is the most important GHG in absolute terms, though not with respect to its global warming potential.

4.2. An overview of the carbon market

4.2.1 The regulated carbon market under the Kyoto Protocol

The Kyoto Protocol has created a market for GHG emission permits and credits. It is based on a cap and trade system which imposes national emission quotas – caps – upon its Annex I signatory states, all of which are developed countries. It was not ratified by the USA, which is the largest GHG emitter in absolute terms. Moreover, most developing countries, commonly referred to as Annex II countries, are not subject to any binding reduction goal under the protocol. This includes China, the world's second largest GHG emitter and likely to surpass the USA in the very near future. Most importantly from an economic perspective, the Kyoto Protocol gave rise to the emergence of carbon markets by allowing signatories to meet their reduction obligation by means of any of three Flexible Mechanisms established by the protocol: the Clean Development Mechanism (CDM), Joint Implementation (JI) and emissions trading (like under the EU's ETS scheme).

CDM allows signatories to meet their own reduction obligations by implementing projects in developing countries which reduce or even avoid GHG emissions; if done successfully, this will earn them a corresponding number of tradable emission credits called Certified Emissions Reduction (CER), with one tonne of carbon reduction equalling one CER. Credits will be generated only if the project in question meets strict quality standards; in particular, it must be proven that the emission reductions generated are purely additional, i.e. they would not have happened anyway, but represent an extra gain. Applying additionality tests, certain authorized bodies are in charge of verifying and certifying any project before it will be permitted to participate in the CDM. JI follows the same rationale and procedures, the only difference being that emission reduction projects will be implemented in other developed countries. The tradable emission credits created under the JI framework are called Emission Reduction Units (ERU). Finally, under emission trading schemes such as the ETS, emission allowances – the so-called Assigned Amount Units (AAU) or, in the ETS context, EU Allowances (EUA) – are defined and allocated to the signatory states, which in turn will reallocate them to national emitters. In aggregate, their supply reflects the CO_2 emission reduction target agreed upon.

4.2.2 The voluntary carbon offset market

In contrast to the regulated carbon market described in the previous section, its voluntary counterpart has come into being without government action and "is

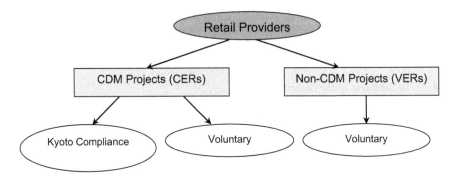

Figure 8.1 The carbon market.

Source: Adapted from Taiyab (2006, p. 8).

a place where anybody, from businesses, to NGOs, to individuals can participate in the business of offsetting" (House of Commons. Environmental Audit Committee, 2007, p. 8).

There are two main differences between the two. Firstly, instead of government regulations, non-binding voluntary standards and methodologies for creating credits are applied. Secondly, while credits created under the Kyoto Protocol's rules are perfectly fungible, i.e. may be used in any scheme, credits created on the voluntary market are not. This has resulted in a substantial lack of transparency with respect to the credibility of offset providers and real environmental benefits of the schemes they have on offer.

In reaction to this obvious shortcoming, however, several self-developed and hence non-binding standards such as the Voluntary Gold Standard (VGS) and the Voluntary Carbon Standard (VSC), which were in part conceived by reputable NGOs, are emerging to fill this vacuum and to provide guidance to potential buyers of offsets (House of Commons. Environmental Audit Committee, 2007, p. 9).

Overall, on all counts, the voluntary carbon market expanded rapidly since the beginning of the 21st century but has been stagnating. Demand was for 20 million tonnes of CO_2 equivalents in 2006, rising to about 100 million tonnes in 2011. In 2014 the total volume of the voluntary carbon market was 87 million tonnes; the corresponding turnover reached $395 million.

4.3 Voluntary carbon offset schemes in practice

4.3.1 Main providers

In 1989, the first carbon offset project was organized in the USA. At that time, Applied Energy Services committed to plant 50 million trees in the Western

Highlands of Guatemala in return for permission to build a coal-fired power station (Carbon Trade Watch, 2007, p. 14). In 1990, the Solar Electric Light Fund, the first carbon offset provider, started operations in the USA, followed in 1992, by Prima Klima Weltweit, a German organization. Today more than 40 competitors are active on the market, most of them based in the USA, the UK, Germany, Australia, and other rich OECD countries. Currently, there is not a single offset provider originating from a developing country. Among the leading carbon offsetters in the segment of aviation-related offsets, both non-profit and for-profit organizations coexist. Eminent examples include atmosfair (Germany, non-profit), myclimate (Switzerland, non-profit), Climate Care (UK, for-profit), and The Carbon Neutral Company (UK, for-profit).

4.3.2 Functioning

The idea behind voluntary offsets is to "neutralize that part of a carbon footprint not addressed through direct emissions reductions, the purchase of emissions-free electricity, or other means" (Trexler Climate + Energy Services, 2006, p. 1). Achieving carbon neutrality therefore requires a multi-stage approach. Ideally, in stage one, the exact size of the carbon footprint will be assessed. Stage two sees the implementation of reduction measures at the source. In stage three, the remaining unaccounted-for carbon emissions have to be calculated, after which in stage four, a sufficient number of GHG offsets must be purchased to cover this difference (ibid, 1).

The choice of offset projects differs substantially among offset providers. Most, however, prefer to finance the extension of land-based sinks, i.e. they focus on forestry- and plantation-based sequestration. Others, by contrast, opt to invest their funds in renewable energy projects, energy-saving schemes, etc.

4.3.3 Critical assessment

UNSOLVED ISSUES WITH RESPECT TO OFFSET SCHEMES

Aside from the fact that forestry-based offset projects, which are still the most popular ones but are likely to run into severe spatial constraints in the foreseeable future,[3] a number of specific problems exist.

METHODOLOGICAL UNCERTAINTIES REGARDING
THE CALCULATION OF THE CARBON FOOTPRINT

To help customers calculate the required number of offsets, almost all providers offer their own more or less sophisticated carbon calculators on their websites. However, even for identical itineraries, the results typically differ substantially. What is more, purchase prices for the offsets also vary substantially – often by a factor of 6, while at the same time many offsetters do not provide their (potential) customers detailed information about the nature of their projects.

As these surprising differences cannot be attributed to the nature of the offset provider's business models – non-profit vs. for-profit – calculator (in) accuracy as well as the lack of relevant data might be the main culprits. Indeed, the carbon footprint of a flight is not nearly as simple to calculate as it may appear, as a large amount of data and many types of effects must be considered. Crucial factors include, but are not limited to flight distance, cruising speed and altitude, type of aircraft (size, age, etc.), load factor, economy vs. business vs. first class travel, and weather conditions (which might affect contrail formation and radiative forcing, etc.) (Kollmuss and Bowell, 2007, p. 26ff).

DUBIOUS QUALITY OF SOME OFFSET PROJECTS

Three dimensions define – and possibly undermine – the overall quality of offset projects:

*   Additionality (which must be guaranteed)
*   Double counting (which must be avoided)
*   The provider's integrity

Obviously, ecological effectiveness can be achieved only if the providers of carbon offset schemes can ensure that consumer's investments actually result in an offset. In other words, additionality must be assured. While one indicator of additionality might be the fact that the project would not have been realized without the provider's financial support, this is not a simple task in practice, even if the available additionality tests are properly applied, for several reasons.

First of all, since most offset projects are forestry-based, providers must ensure that the carbon will remain sequestered permanently, or at least for a very long period of time (at least 50 years); otherwise, a carbon sink will be transformed into a carbon source due to natural processes (rotting) or as a result of human action (slash and burn, etc.).

Second, double counting of offsets must be discouraged to prevent multiple stakeholders from claiming credits from the same offset activity. The most appropriate solutions to this problem would be to retire offsets once they have been sold (to prevent them from getting sold several times to different buyers).

Third, more information should be made available to potential customers of offset providers about the types of projects pursued and their success rate, and last but not least, the percentage of funds which is actually invested (as opposed to being used to cover administration costs and profit targets).

To summarize, in order to continue to see passenger numbers grow and simultaneously to maintain its eco-friendly image into the future, the industry will have to accept a mix of greater transparency and some form of self-regulation or governmental standards to overcome the existing information asymmetry. But the design of standards and the evaluation of offset programmes will also result in non-trivial transaction costs (Parliamentary Office of Science and Technology, 2007).

It is fair to assume that carbon offsetting, for being a voluntary contribution, is highly unlikely to reduce the demand for air travel – the very source of aviation-related GHG emissions – significantly. The manifold design flaws regarding the functioning of carbon offsetting notwithstanding, this result could nevertheless be considered acceptable if the airlines' voluntary carbon offsetting schemes were broadly accepted and heavily used by passengers. Unfortunately, the opposite is true. However, most airlines are reluctant to publish participation figures, and the few academic studies on passengers' willingness to participate focus on motivational factors (Fang-Yuan, 2013) rather than gather evidence on pick-up rates. The first hint on the ineffectiveness of voluntary carbon offsetting schemes in the airline industry was provided by British Airlines which admitted in a parliamentary hearing that passengers chose to offset only 3,000 tonnes out of a total of 27 million tonnes emitted since the introduction of carbon offsetting in September 2005 – less than 0.01% of the total (Davies, 2007). Afterwards, pick-up figures improved slightly but remain insignificant from a climate policy perspective; in 2009, 126,000 out of 33,117,000 passengers opted in, 0.3% of the total (British Airways, 2009, p. 37). In 2011, British Airways scrapped its voluntary carbon offsetting scheme, replacing it with its One Destination Carbon Fund which will invest passengers' donations in CDM-conforming projects in the UK.

Lufthansa does not make data on the number of passengers who have chosen to purchase offsets available to the public. However, the company's annual Balance report – an overview of the company's CSR strategy and projects – provides at least some indirect evidence in its 2014 edition Lufthansa Group, 2014, pp. 52, 78). According to this corporate source, in 2013, Lufthansa passengers bought offsets for the equivalent of 14,000 tonnes of CO_2 emissions. In the same years, the passenger division of Lufthansa (i.e. excluding cargo and the other airlines of the Lufthansa Group) emitted 21,016,246 tonnes. This means that only 0.06 per cent of total CO_2 emissions were voluntarily offset. According to a comparative study of voluntary carbon offset regimes published in 2011 (Eijgelaar, 2011), current sales of flight offsets compensate less than 1% of all aviation emissions (about 700 million tonnes in 2013).

As always, there are some exceptions. Qantas reports that over 10% of passengers have been offsetting their flights. Since 2007, the airline has offset 3 million tonnes of carbon emissions. Recently it has been giving frequent flyer points to passengers who offset, and this has led to an increase in offsets (Hatch, 2019).

Therefore, in comparison to alternative internalization strategies, economic pressure to reduce fuel consumption and, as a result, GHG emissions, based on voluntary schemes is quite limited. In other words: while carbon taxes or the participation in an ETS would, ceteris paribus, provide incentives for technological and operational improvements, voluntary carbon offsetting translates into minimal dynamic efficiency in the airline industry.

Nevertheless, from a lobbying perspective, the attractiveness of carbon off-setting for airlines is obvious. Offset schemes may be pushed by industries like aviation for the benefits they create in helping airlines by providing them with ample PR opportunities to "greenwash" their products and services, and creating a good CSR image, without their incurring any adaptation costs (Transnational Institute, 2007). More transparency, including public disclosure of the low participation rates, is therefore not in the interest of the airline industry, although it is clearly warranted in the ongoing debate on the efficiency and effectiveness of climate change policies.

5. Conclusion

Given the global nature of GHG emissions, as well as the validity of the equimarginal principle, the idea to offset them in some other sector of the economy, or even in a different country, is not dubious per se. On efficiency grounds, however, voluntary carbon offsetting cannot nearly replace, and not even complement in any meaningful way, a well-designed and well-run system of tradable emission permits (or GHG taxes), i.e. a mandatory, comprehensive and truly global scheme. The main role of the airlines' voluntary carbon offset schemes therefore seems to be a dual one, benefitting both themselves and their passengers: They provide a socially accepted excuse for guilt-ridden travellers who do not wish to reduce their flying activities, let alone foregoing flying altogether, while at the same time granting the airlines the welcome image of acting as environmentally responsible corporations.

Notes

1 In the following, we will not discuss further instruments like regulatory measures or standards. For a short survey of potential instruments, see Umweltbundesamt/European Economic and Social Committee (2007).
2 This subsection and subsection 4.2 draw heavily on Kollmuss and Bowell (2006), Taiyab (2006), Trexler Climate + Energy Services (2006), House of Commons. Environmental Audit Committee (2007), World Bank (2007), and World Bank (2018).
3 According to calculations by Boon, Schroten and Kampman (2006), the area available globally for afforestation will be filled by 2050 by aviation alone, should all its climate effects be offset in this way.

References

Boon, B.H., Schroten, A. and Kampman, B. (2006). Compensation schemes for air transport. In: *Proceedings of the Tourism and Climate Chance Mitigation Conference*, 11–14 June, Westelbeers.
British Airways. (2009). *British Airways 2009/10 annual report and accounts*. London.
Carbon Trade Watch. (2007). *The carbon neutral myth*. Amsterdam. [Online] Available at: http://www.carbontradewatch.org/pubs/carbon_neutral_myth.pdf. [Accessed 29 Nov. 2019].
Carbonify. (2020). *Carbon offset/green tags directory*. [Online] Available at: http://www.carbonify.com/finder/offset-tag-companies.htm [Accessed 13 Mar. 2020].

Davies, N. (2007). The inconvenient truth about the carbon offset industry. *The Guardian (Online edition)*, June 16. [Online] Available at: http://www.guardian.co.uk/environment/2007/jun/16/climatechange.climatechange. [Accessed 29 Nov. 2019].

ECMT – European Conference of Ministers of Transport. (2007). *Cutting transport CO_2 emissions. What progress?* Paris.

EEA – European Environment Agency. (2007). *Annual European community greenhouse gas inventory 1990–2005 and inventory report 2007*. Submission to the UNFCCC Secretariat, technical report No 7, Copenhagen.

Eijgelaar, E. (2011). Voluntary carbon offsets a solution for reducing tourism emissions? Assessment of communication aspects and mitigation potential. *European Journal of Transport and Infrastructure Research*, 11(3), pp. 281–296.

Eisenkopf, A. (2007). Wettbewerb und Innovation. Die Grenzen staatlicher Innovationspolitik. In: G. Koch and B.J. Warneken, eds., *Region – Kultur – Innovation, Wege in die Wissensgesellschaft*. Wiesbaden: VS Verlag für Sozialwissenschaften, pp. 201–214.

Fang-Yuan, C. (2013). The intention and determining factors for airline passengers' participation in carbon offset. *Journal of Air Transport Management*, 29, pp. 17–22.

Fees, E. and Seeliger, A. (2013). *Umweltökonomie und Umweltpolitik*. 4th ed. Munich: Vahlen.

Fritsch, M. (2018). *Marktversagen und Wirtschaftspolitik, Mikroökonomische Grundlagen staatlichen Handelns*. 10th ed. Munich: Vahlen.

Gössling, S., Broderick, J., Upham, P., Ceron, J-P., Dubois, G., Peeters, P. and Strasdas, W. (2007). Voluntary carbon offsetting schemes for aviation: Efficiency, credibility and sustainable tourism. *Journal of Sustainable Tourism*, 15(3), pp. 223–248.

Grimme, W., Schaefer, M. and Scheelhaase, J. (2007). CO_2-Emissionshandel: Welche Kosten für Passagiere und Airlines? *Internationales Verkehrswesen*, 59, pp. 166–168.

Hatch, P. (2019). Qantas points push sees green flyers take off. *The Sydney Morning Herald*, 28 July. [Online] Available at: https://www.smh.com.au/business/companies/qantas-points-push-sees-green-flyers-take-off-20190726-p52b8a.html. [Accessed 29 Nov. 2019].

House of Commons. Environmental Audit Committee. (2007). *The voluntary carbon offset market*. Six Report of Session 2006–07, London, 23 July. [Online] Available at: http://www.publications.parliament.uk/pa/cm200607/cmselect/cmenvaud/331/331.pdf [Accessed 29 Nov. 2019].

IEA – International Energy Agency. (2017). *Tracking clean energy progress 2017*. Vienna. [Online] Available at: https://www.iea.org/publications/freepublications/publication/TrackingCleanEnergyProgress2017.pdf. [Accessed 29 Nov. 2019].

IPCC – Intergovernmental Panel on Climate Change. (1999). *Aviation and the global atmosphere*. Cambridge: Cambridge University Press.

IPCC – Intergovernmental Panel on Climate Change. (2014). *Climate change 2014 mitigation of climate change*. Working Group III Contribution to the Fifth Assessment Report of the Intergovernmental Panel on Climate Change, New York. [Online] Available at: https://www.ipcc.ch/site/assets/uploads/2018/02/ipcc_wg3_ar5_chapter8.pdf [Accessed 29 Nov. 2019].

Kollmuss, A. and Bowell, B. (2006). *Voluntary offsets for air-travel carbon emissions*. Tufts University. Tufts Climate Initiative Carbon Offsets Paper, Apr. 2007, Medford. [Online] Available at: https://sustainability.tufts.edu/wp-content/uploads/TCI_Carbon_Offsets_Paper_April-2-07.pdf. [Accessed 29 Nov. 2019].

Lufthansa Group. (2014). *Balance*. Frankfurt am Main: Lufthansa Group.

OECD – Organisation for Economic Co-operation and Development. (2012). *Green growth and the future of aviation*. Paper prepared for the 27th Round Table on Sustainable

Development to be held at OECD Headquarters 23–24 Jan., Paris. [Online] Available at: https://www.oecd.org/sd-roundtable/papersandpublications/49482790.pdf [Accessed 29 Nov. 2019].

Parliamentary Office of Science and Technology. (2007). *Voluntary carbon offsets*. postnote Nr. 290, July. [Online] Available at: https://www.parliament.uk/documents/post/postpn290. pdf [Accessed 29 Nov. 2019].

Taiyab, N. (2006). *Exploring the market for voluntary carbon offsets*. London. [Online] Available at: https://pubs.iied.org/pdfs/G00268.pdf. [Accessed 29 Nov. 2019].

Transnational Institute. (2007). *The carbon neutral myth. Offset indulgences for your climate sins*. Amsterdam. [Online] Available at: https://www.tni.org/en/publication/the-carbon-neu tral-myth-0 [Accessed 29 Nov. 2019].

Trexler Climate + Energy Services. (2006). *A consumers' guide to retail offset providers*. Portland. [Online] Available at: https://climatetrust.org/wp-content/uploads/2013/05/A-Con sumers-Guide-to-Retail-Carbon-Offset-Providers-2006.pdf. [Accessed 29 Nov. 2019].

Umweltbundesamt / European Economic and Social Committee, eds. (2007). *Climate change and environmental issues in transportation*. Report, Brussels.

World Bank. (2007). *State and trends of the carbon market 2007*. Washington, DC. [Online] Available at: http://siteresources.worldbank.org/NEWS/MiscContent/21319781/State Carbon.pdf [Accessed 29 Nov. 2019].

World Bank. (2018). *State and trends of carbon pricing 2018*. Washington, DC. [Online] Available at: https://openknowledge.worldbank.org/bitstream/handle/10986/29687/978146481 2927.pdf?sequence=5&isAllowed=y [Accessed 29 Nov. 2019].

9 Roadmap to decarbonising aviation

Bill Hemmings, Andrew Murphy, Thomas Earl, Carlos Calvo Ambel, Lucy Gilliam, Jori Sihvonen and Laura Buffet

1. Introduction

Aviation is one of the fastest growing sources of greenhouse gas (GHG) emissions and the most climate-intensive mode of transport. Globally, aviation emissions have more than doubled in the last 20 years (EEA, 2017) and, when including the significant non-CO_2 climate effects of aircraft flying at altitude, the sector is responsible for an estimated 4.9% of total anthropogenic forcing (Lee et al., 2009) (Figure 9.1).

Aviation emissions in Europe have doubled since 1990, while globally they could, without action, double or treble by 2050. Such emissions growth needs to be reversed and brought to zero by 2050 if we are to meet the goals of the Paris Agreement. Otherwise, growth in aviation emissions could rapidly consume the limited carbon budget to remain within the 1.5 and 2 °C targets of that agreement (Lee et al., 2009).

The Intergovernmental Panel on Climate Change (IPCC) special report on limiting global warming to 1.5 °C (IPCC, 2018) made it clear: rapid and far-reaching transitions are needed in all sectors, including transport, in order to reach net zero emissions by 2050. This includes full decarbonisation of all sectors of the economy where this is technically possible. Europe, due to its historical contribution to climate change, should lead the way.

So far few effective policies are in place to address this emissions growth. The aviation emission trading scheme (ETS) in Europe is restricted to flights within Europe which cover about one third of total EU outbound emissions, yet emissions within Europe continue to grow each year and now represent 3.6% of total EU CO_2 emissions – up from 1.5% in 1990 (EEA, 2017). At the global level, ICAO's CO_2 standard for new aircraft has proven to be technology following while the global offsetting scheme CORSIA, due to start on a voluntary basis in 2021, addresses out-of-sector emissions and will have no impact on aviation CO_2 itself. There are no regulations in place addressing the sector's significant non-CO_2 climate impacts at altitude.

In November 2018, and following a request by European governments, the European Commission said it would present a strategy to decarbonise the economy in line with the Paris Climate Agreement. In this study, we examine

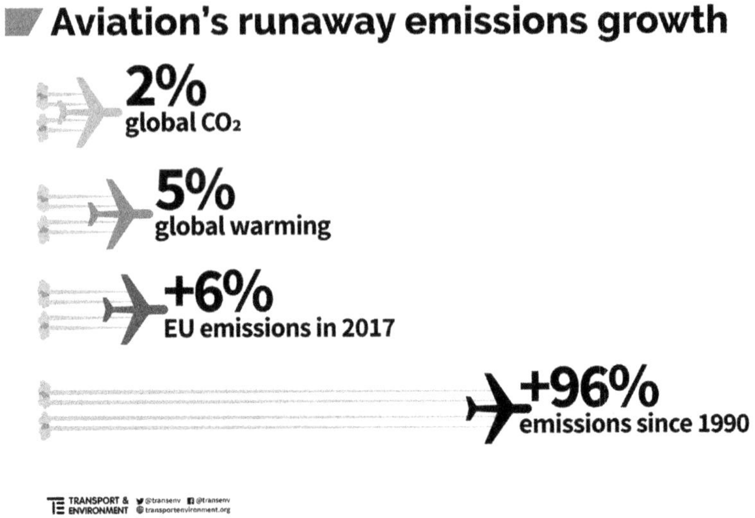

◥ Aviation's runaway emissions growth

2%
global CO2

5%
global warming

+6%
EU emissions in 2017

+96%
emissions since 1990

TRANSPORT & ENVIRONMENT @transenv @transenv transportenvironment.org

Figure 9.1 Global and European aviation growth.

whether a credible pathway to zero or near zero emissions exists for European aviation within the same timeframe. The scope of the study covers flights within and departing from Europe which matches the scope of including aviation emissions in the EU's 2030 reduction target. It takes broadly accepted passenger and emissions growth forecasts out to 2050, considers the role that various policies can play in reducing fuel demand from the sector, either by improving efficiency or reducing demand, and then proposes how the remaining fuel demand can be decarbonised.

The study first looks at likely emission scenarios out to 2050 and examines various design, technical and operational measures that, either within today's knowledge or being more ambitious, could impact that growth trend. We then consider various taxation options for pricing aviation carbon which, combined, would represent an effective carbon price of €150/tonne. An assessment is then made of the likely availability and price of sustainable alternative fuels (biofuels) against the background of the considerable and largely unsuccessful experience with such fuels in EU road transport. The remaining fuel demand is that which will need to be replaced with electrofuels, and we examine supply and price issues.

Background

While uncertainties exist, we do know that the sector will have a substantial fuel demand well into the 2030s, 2040s and beyond; the period when the European economy needs to increasingly decarbonise. This study finds that expected technology and operations efficiency improvements in the sector will not mitigate the expected fuel demand and emissions growth from aviation. Generating incremental efficiency improvements from current aircraft designs is becoming ever more costly and difficult. Further operational improvements remain possible but do not achieve decarbonisation and will require that the right policies be in place.

Aside from policies which will incentivise improvements in efficiency, measures which suppress the growing demand for air travel will be needed. Carbon pricing can and needs to play a central role in bringing forward further efficiency improvements and reductions in fuel demand. Exempt from kerosene taxation and with most European aviation emissions excluded from the EU ETS' intra EU scope, there is much to be done. We show that introducing fiscal measures that, combined, represent a carbon price equivalent to €150 a tonne can moderate fuel demand growth from the sector through reductions in traffic, incentivising a combination of design and operational efficiency improvements and modal shift. Other measures highlighted include stricter fuel efficiency standards and incentives to speed up fleet renewal. Combined, these measures could cut fuel demand by some 12 Mtoe, or 16.9% in 2050 compared to a business-as-usual scenario.

That still leaves substantial and increased fuel demand in 2050 which, based on today's technology, can be reduced only through the use of sustainable alternative fuels. Advanced biofuels could play a role; however, strict sustainability safeguards are needed to ensure advanced biofuels offer genuine emission savings. These are not yet in place. If fuels with poor environmental and climate credentials are excluded, we estimate that advanced sustainable alternative fuels could play a role – meeting up to 11.4% of the remaining 2050 fuel demand in our scenario. To close the gap, the study focuses on synthetic fuels, namely electrofuels, produced through combining green hydrogen with carbon from CO_2. With the hydrogen produced using additional renewable electricity, and with the correct source of CO_2 (direct air capture), such fuels can be close to near zero emissions and carbon circular. However, if electrofuels are the only way to decarbonise and fuel demand remains high, then there will be an enormous demand for renewable electricity, possibly equivalent in 2050 to some 28% of Europe's total electricity generation in 2015 – or 95% of the electricity using renewables currently generated in Europe.

We do not rule out the role that radical new aircraft designs, for example hydrogen or electric aircraft, could play in significantly reducing aviation emissions. However, such aircraft are not expected to be in operation in significant numbers until the 2040s, and it will be especially challenging to replace conventional aircraft for long-haul flights. Should hydrogen aircraft technology develop more rapidly, this would not be at odds with significant investment in synthetic fuels, as hydrogen is a key input for electrofuels.

Aside from decarbonising aviation fuels, the warming from aviation's non-CO_2 effects at altitude is considerable, and there remains a lack of policy focus and investment in scientific research on this topic. This failure to act means we are unable either to propose a suite of mitigation measures or to estimate their effects.

The case for acting on aviation emissions is clear – a failure to do so will fatally undermine efforts to achieve the goals of the Paris Agreement. We do not recommend offsetting, as this solution is incompatible with the decarbonisation logic of the Paris Agreement because the agreement requires emissions from all sectors to be reduced. The ICAO scheme CORSIA, due to start on a voluntary basis in 2021, addresses out-of-sector emissions and will have no impact on aviation CO_2 or non-CO_2 itself.

1.1 The context

Emissions from EU aviation increased 96% between 1990 and 2016 (EAA, 2017), while all other sectors, bar transport which grew 21%, reduced emissions. As a result, aviation emissions have grown from 1.5% of total EU emissions in 1990 to 3.6% today (UNFCCC, 2018). If the trend of traffic growth exceeding improvements in aircraft efficiency continues, the growth in aviation emissions threatens efforts under the Paris Agreement to keep global warming to 1.5 °C.

1.2 Can aviation be decarbonised?

Manufacturers are finding it increasingly difficult to deliver efficiency gains from new engines and aircraft designs, and incremental improvements are declining. With aircraft having a lifespan of 20–30 years and current models having orders up until the mid-2020s, aircraft being delivered now are locking us into decades of fossil fuel consumption. Truly sustainable alternative fuels are limited in volume and the significant price gap with tax-free kerosene is constraining uptake. Growth in air traffic remains strong; up 8.5% in Europe in 2017 (ACI, 2018), exceeding growth of 7.6% globally (IATA, 2018).

1.3 Regulating at what level?

Following the failure of efforts to include all aviation emissions in the EU ETS, Europe focussed on efforts to regulate these emissions at a global level through measures to be adopted by the UN's International Civil Aviation Organization

(ICAO). Two measures in particular were advanced – a CO_2 efficiency standard for new aircraft, and a global offsetting measure for emissions above 2020 levels.

These measures have been extensively critiqued elsewhere (ICCT, 2018). Neither will reduce emissions from the sector in a manner consistent with the goals of the Paris Agreement. ICAO suffers from a number of institutional flaws which, until resolved, make it highly unlikely that the organisation will deliver meaningful measures to cut emissions, let alone decarbonise aviation.

1.4 European efforts

Aviation emissions have long been a weak spot in European climate policy. After earlier consideration of taxation, the EU included aviation in its ETS from 2012 but backed down later that year in the face of intense resistance from industry and a group of foreign states. As a result, only flights within Europe are included for the time being. Meanwhile the sector continues to enjoy various tax exemptions (fuel duty, VAT), as well as state aid subsidies. ICAO CO_2 efficiency standards for new aircraft will have no significant impact on emissions (Hemmings, 2016), and the uptake of sustainable alternative fuels has been minimal (EASA, 2016).

In adopting its 2030 emissions target, the EU included all outbound aviation emissions – that is, emissions from all flights departing *from* Europe but not *to* Europe – so Paris–Madrid and Warsaw–New York are included but not Delhi–Rome. The 2030 target for the sector was set at 111 Mt CO_2e (Council of the EU, 2017) – below its current level of 148 Mt CO_2e. Achieving this target will require a significant uptake in new technologies or fuels, or alternatively an increase in ambition in other sectors. Long-term decarbonisation, which Paris demands, requires the sector to bring its own emissions to zero – both CO_2 and non-CO_2.

1.5 Europe's decarbonisation strategy

EU leaders agreed in December 2019 to endorse the objective of achieving climate neutrality by 2050 (European Council, 2019). The revised strategy is more stringent than the previous one and details Europe's contribution to the Paris Agreement objective of limiting a temperature increase to well below 2°C and pursuing efforts to limit an increase to 1.5°C. Considering that global temperatures have already risen at least 0.8°C (IPCC, 2018) and GHG concentrations are increasing rapidly, Europe must decarbonise all sectors by 2050.

The revised strategy needs to continue to cover outbound aviation, but it needs to provide greater detail on what measures/policies can be introduced to do this while making clear that the aviation sector too must commit to zero emissions by 2050. It also needs to address aviation's short-lived non-CO_2 climate effects, whose transient (days to weeks) climate warming impacts equal or exceed those of aviation's accumulated CO_2 emissions (Kärcher, 2018).

1.6 T&E decarbonisation pathway

This chapter presents a decarbonisation pathway for aviation out to 2050. The scope of the analysis is the same as the EU's 2030 target – all emissions from outbound flights.

T&E drew on aviation activity growth forecasts from the 2016 European Reference Scenario (European Commission, 2016) to project total outbound aviation emissions from European airports up to 2050. We then modelled the application of a range of measures to reduce fuel demand to what we believe is the maximum extent possible through fuel, technical and operational efficiencies or limiting passenger number growth through price signals. The result is what T&E believes fuel demand from the aviation sector can reasonably be reduced to by 2050. We then focus on how to decarbonise that remaining fuel demand through the use of sustainable advanced biofuels and synthetic e-fuels (power-to-liquid, or PtL). Full details of the modelling approach are found in the Appendices at the end of the chapter.

2. Measures to cut fuel demand

2.1 Business as usual

The business-as-usual (BaU) scenario was developed from the 2016 European Reference Scenario. It assumes a constant fuel price, so that policy measures can be analysed in isolation.

The result is that aviation energy demand in 2050 under our BaU scenario is projected to be 71.3 Mtoe, compared to 65.5 Mtoe in the Reference Scenario. As passenger activity in the Reference Scenario draws only on intra-EU and domestic flights, an analysis of the available seat kilometres from aircraft transponder data was used as a proxy to extend this to all EU departing flights. In 2050 we calculate EU outbound passenger activity to be 6753 Gpkm, compared to the 1,177 Gpkm projected for intra-EU flights in the Reference Scenario.

2.2 Design and operational efficiency

The design and deployment of more efficient aircraft and engines can play an important role in reducing fuel demand from the sector. We have divided our forecasting into the maximum possible reductions based on currently available technologies and what more radical designs may start to deliver closer to the 2050 timeline. We note here that there are trade-offs between reducing engine fuel burn (CO_2) and aircraft NO_x emissions, for example, which highlight the need for more work in both areas (Freeman, 2018).

The EU Reference Scenario includes in its aviation energy demand projections an increase in fleet efficiency, measured in terms of fuel burn per passenger km, of 41% by 2050 compared to 2010. We take this to be a combination of technical and operational improvements, as a 41% improvement from current aircraft designs alone is not deemed possible.

This 0.9% improvement per annum is towards the higher end of what is possible. However, it's also true that this is below what is possible in terms of design improvements – in line with what ICAO's independent fuel burn expert group found.

Our forecasting envisages a situation where governments adopt a more ambitious range of measures to encourage both new designs and their deployment. For example, the progressive implementation of an effective carbon price up to €150 a tonne will encourage new designs and their deployment across the fleet as well as accelerated phase-outs of older aircraft. Europe could introduce other policies to encourage fleet-wide efficiencies – for example, fuel taxation, additionally taxing dirty aircraft to accelerate phase-outs or linking the auctioning of slots at airports to aircraft efficiency. Europe could also introduce more effective aircraft efficiency standards through the EASA (European Union Aviation Safety Agency, based in Cologne) certification process.

Additional operational improvements could come about through the effective implementation by member states of the single European sky, accelerated upgauging (deployment of larger aircraft) and increased passenger density by curbing first and business class travel.

Our forecasting also takes into account potentially more radical aircraft designs entering the fleet from about 2040 onwards – strut systems, bubble designs, flying wings, hybrid and short-haul electric aircraft. A move to hydrogen-powered aircraft will require enormous investments for manufacturers and airports. The contribution of electric powered aircraft is not yet clear.

Our estimates presume additional fleet-wide efficiency improvements of 0.2% per annum over the BaU. From 2040, more radical designs are assumed to be 30% more efficient than existing technologies. Aircraft and operational efficiency improvements could reduce fuel demand 6.3 Mtoe (or 8.8%) by 2050.

2.3 Pricing aviation and eliminating subsidies

To decarbonise aviation, measures such as carbon pricing, other forms of taxation and the phasing out of subsidies will be essential – to curb demand and to incentivise design and operational efficiencies and the uptake of low or lower carbon fuels. Details of the underlying elasticities we have used in making the following estimates of reductions in demand due to pricing aviation are shown in Appendix B.

Carbon pricing is the charging of those who emit carbon emissions based on the level of their emissions. It is increasingly recognised as an essential, though by itself insufficient, measure to achieve the Paris Agreement target. However, the aviation sector remains lagging in the introduction of such pricing. Only flights within Europe, accounting for around 40% of the region's emissions (Transport & Environment, 2016), are included in EU ETS, leaving long-haul flights completely unregulated. Domestic aviation is included in New Zealand's carbon market. Domestic fuel taxation exists in some jurisdictions, such as Japan, Brazil and India and to a limited extent in the US.

Other forms of taxation can also play a role in reducing fuel demand and the growth in passenger numbers. Ending subsidies such as state aid to airports and airlines is a further obvious measure. Estimates put a Paris-compliant carbon price at €30 a tonne now, rising to €150 by 2050. There is an ongoing debate over what constitutes an appropriate carbon price. Research to date suggests that in the aviation sector, a price in excess of €100 is required due to that sector's higher mitigation costs (Schafer et al., 2015). We chose a price of €150 which, as outlined in this chapter, is eminently achievable. While raising revenue is secondary to the objective of decarbonisation, it is not unrelated. Additional revenues could be used to reduce other taxes (e.g. labour taxes) or help governments fund the necessary investments in decarbonising the economy as a whole or of specific sectors.

2.3.1   *Options for carbon pricing*

FUEL TAXATION

Fuel uplifted for international aviation remains mutually tax exempt owing to language introduced in bilateral aviation agreements, known as Air Service Agreements (ASAs), built up after the Second World War. Those exemptions remain in place and are a barrier to the immediate introduction of kerosene taxation into international aviation. Globally, the exemption is valued at €60 billion a year (Murphy, 2015).

European Council Directive 2003/96/EC, known as the Energy Taxation Directive (ETD) 2003, permits taxation of kerosene for domestic aviation; however, within the EU, only the Netherlands did so together with Norway and Switzerland. The ETD also permits two or more member states to introduce kerosene taxation for fuel used on flights between those states provided this is agreed bilaterally (Pache, 2019). So far this has not happened – one reason being that air services agreements continue to provide mutual fuel tax exemptions for foreign carriers operating intra-EU flights. These operations have decreased dramatically and an intra-EU kerosene fuel tax could be introduced with a de minimis provision which de facto exempts all foreign carrier operations up to a certain level. Amendments to the relatively few ASAs exempting foreign carriers when operating intra-EU flights should also be pursued (CE Delft, 2019).

Applying kerosene taxation to fuel uplifted for flights from Europe requires the abolition of the mutual fuel tax exemption in ASAs. This could start on a bilateral basis with non-EU countries. If all departing flights in Europe paid the ETD minimum tax on fuel uplifted, this would be equivalent to a CO_2 price of €130/tCO_2. A minimum price is precisely that – the level of the tax could be increased to achieve this chapter's target of €150 a tonne, or higher if that would deliver greater mitigation benefits.

EMISSIONS TRADING SCHEME

Only flights within Europe are currently covered by Europe's emissions trading scheme (EU ETS). A further exemption for flights to and from Europe was granted in 2017 until the end of 2023. In recent years, the system has suffered from an oversupply of allowances, bringing prices to as low as €5 a tonne, far below the sort of carbon pricing required to incentivise emission reductions. Combined with free allowances received by the sector, the scheme cost airlines only €150 million in 2015 compared to EU airline profits of €7.4 billion (IATA, 2017).

Since then, allowance prices have begun to recover, trading at over €25 a tonne by September 2018. Revisions to European legislation mean that from 2021, the number of aviation allowances issued each year will begin to decline, as is already the case for other sectors covered by ETS. There is also a commitment to review the number of allowances which are granted to airlines for free, rather than auctioned.

The effectiveness of the aviation ETS – in terms of revenues raised and emissions cut – will depend on the scope, the cap and allowance price. Were all emissions from Europe to be included in an effectively functioning ETS, then a path to the eventual decarbonisation of outbound flights would be clear. However, achieving this scenario will require significant political ambition.

2.3.2 Other options for taxing aviation

TAXES

Ticket taxes now cover more than half the EU aviation market (CE Delft and SEO, 2019). They are taxes levied on the act of passengers departing an EU airport. They usually vary based on flight distance or class of travel with costs built into ticket prices. Ticket taxes are simple to administer and can raise substantial sums of money; €3 billion a year in the UK alone. There is no legal barrier to member states introducing such taxes, at whatever rate. They have survived numerous legal challenges from airlines. Ticket taxes are a common feature of many aviation markets around the world.

Per plane taxes, or "movement" taxes, would be levied on aircraft/airlines by virtue of an aircraft departing an EU airport and paid directly by carriers to tax authorities with the additional costs built into ticket prices.

The per plane tax can be based on various environmental criteria – the aircraft's certified noise rating or its certified Maximum Take Off Weight (MTOW) which is a proxy for aircraft size and noise/air pollution. The tax could also approximate the flight's CO_2 emissions – which depend on the aircraft type and distance flown (CE Delft, 2018).

VAT

Though most European states levy VAT for domestic flights, the exemption on tickets for intra-EU flights is applied by all states. None apply VAT to extra-EU flight tickets. VAT exemptions are supposed to be primarily for essentials (medicines, food), but as with kerosene taxation, the VAT exemption is a convenient hangover for airlines from an earlier era when all international aviation was tax free. The exemption distorts the market – encouraging consumers to spend money on this carbon-intense mode of transport instead of other, potentially lower-carbon, expenditures including rail travel. The EU should amend its VAT legislation so that member states could levy VAT on the full price of the ticket at the single rate of the country of departure.

OTHER SUBSIDIES

As well as the indirect subsidies from tax exemptions, aviation also receives direct subsidies, for example through state aid for airports and airlines and government-backed financial support granted to manufacturers. Though the EU has largely reduced direct investment in airport capacity, particularly following a damning report by the European Court of Auditors (ECA, 2014), there is still some support granted to airport expansion from the European Investment Bank (EIB, 2018).

At a member state level, substantial amounts of state aid continue to be granted to airports – including operational aid to airlines, which has the most distortive effect on competition. The levels of state aid are difficult to quantify, and the European Commission, rather than attempting to rein in such aid, facilitates its provision and abuses by, for example, adding to the general bloc exemptions (European Commission, 2017). State aid to this carbon intensive sector has no future in a Paris-compliant scenario. The ending of these subsidies is factored into the €150 carbon price.

Our estimates are that introducing a carbon price of €150, on top of the design and operational efficiency measures, can reduce total emissions a further 5.8 Mtoe (or 8.9%) by 2050. A carbon price of €150 would result in an increase in ticket prices of approximately 19% in real terms.

2.4 Modal shift

Shifting passengers from air travel to other modes of transport, especially rail, can play a role in reducing overall emissions. Rail has a viable pathway to decarbonisation through reliance on 100% renewable electricity. However, it is important not to overstate the potential emission reductions.

Flights under 600 km account for only 7% of total aviation emissions in Europe (Transport & Environment, 2016). Modal shift is not possible for many of these routes – due to the high cost of building rail alternatives for what may be low frequency routes, or due to geography. There are certainly routes in Europe where the development of better and faster connections as well as additional high-speed rail (HSR) services can help cut aviation emissions provided high train load factors are maintained. Retention and reopening of night trains could facilitate a shift from aviation to rail for longer journeys. However, the opportunities are limited, and there may be an excessive financial and environmental cost from expanding HSR.

Developing rail as an alternative to aviation will require closing the price gap – through taxation and, for example, introducing stronger labour laws in the aviation sector to reduce the unfair competition from wage undercutting. Far greater competition in the rail sector is also needed.

Modal shift can also occur through businesses finding alternatives to flying, such as greater use of video conferencing or rationalising the amount of business travel. Demand reduction could also take place in leisure travel – choosing closer destinations or taking fewer but longer holidays.

Our forecast is that modal shift will have only a limited impact in reducing fuel demand in 2050. As these reductions are limited, they are included in the passenger demand reductions resulting from carbon pricing as such carbon pricing is the policy measure expected to contribute most to modal shift. As shown in Figure 9.2, the combined measures described previously could reduce the final aviation energy demand by 12.1 Mtoe, or 16.9%.

3. Decarbonising aviation fuels

The above measures are estimated to bring down the sector's fuel demand from 71.3 Mtoe under a BaU, to 59.2 Mtoe. Decarbonising aviation by 2050 will therefore depend on decarbonising that remaining fuel demand. We look at two pathways to do this – deploying sustainable advanced biofuels, and renewable fuels of non-biological origin (RFNBO).

3.1 Advanced biofuels

Advanced biofuels are defined as biofuels produced from waste and residues. The issues with many, particularly first generation, biofuels are well documented. Europe's experience with mandates for the road transport sector demonstrated that many of the biofuels used resulted in total emissions which were greater than the fossil fuels they replaced (Transport & Environment, 2018). This was due to what is known as indirect land use change – the use of land to grow crops for biofuels displaces land which was previously used to grow crops for food. This displacement sparks further deforestation and conversion of grassland to ensure sufficient land is cultivated for both fuel and food and an increase in emissions. In addition, even if we were to ignore these Indirect Land Use Change (ILUC) effects, the amount of land required to produce significant volumes of aviation biofuels would be enormous. (Powering the world's aviation fully with biofuels in 2050 would, directly or indirectly, require more than 3.5 million km^2 of land; T&E's own calculations indicate that international aviation will consume around 800 Mt of fuel in 2050. The NCV of kerosene is 44.1 TJ/kt. That equals 35.28 EJ = 843 Mtoe by 2050. 1Ha produces 100 GJ of biofuel.) This would run counter to the efforts to increase negative emissions and carbon sinks, which will be required as part of the Paris Agreement.

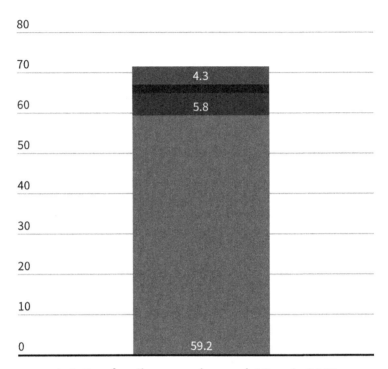

Aviation fossil energy demand, Mtoe in 2050

● Remaining energy demand, covered by fossil

● Reduction from €150/tCO2 carbon price

● Reduction from Gen II aircraft from 2040

● Reduction from 0.2% p.a. improvement conventional fleet

Figure 9.2 Contributions of technology, operational efficiency, and carbon pricing on kerosene demand in 2050. Note that 59.2 Mtoe of kerosene is 183 Mt CO_2, approximately equivalent to business as usual 2025 emissions.

We limit our availability forecast to only those advanced biofuels from waste and residues which deliver real and sustainable reductions in emissions. Such feedstocks are incidental to other processes and so will be limited in availability. Our projection is that in 2050, availability of sustainable advanced biofuels for the aviation sector will total 7500 kilotonnes of oil equivalent (ktoe), meeting 11.4% of European aviation fuel demand (if the above efficiency and carbon pricing measures are realised; otherwise, advanced biofuels could make up to 10.5% of BaU oil demand).

This is based on previous T&E research on the future availability of sustainable advanced biofuels (Transport & Environment, 2017a). In making this projection, our assumption is that other sectors, particularly road transport, will have transitioned entirely to direct electric or renewable hydrogen propulsion and by 2050 won't need to decarbonise through the use of alternative fuels.

Sustainable advanced fuels will contribute to decreasing greenhouse gas (GHG) emissions, but there are not so many which show pathways towards zero or negative emissions through their life cycle. If some fuels, for example, achieve 80% emission reductions, then their use will still result in emissions from the sector; i.e. not achieve decarbonisation. To contribute to the decarbonisation of aviation, their production and entire life-cycle impact (including indirect impacts) must be zero carbon. Therefore, decarbonising aviation is coupled with broader efforts to decarbonise the economy, as reducing the carbon intensity of other activities such as heat, industrial processes and electricity generation will help reduce the lifecycle emissions from advanced biofuels. It is crucial for EU policies to account for all GHG emissions (also indirect) from advanced fuels. For accounting purposes, we assign zero emissions to these fuels in our modelling exercise.

Our forecast is that an availability of 7500 ktoe of alternative fuels will contribute to reducing fossil kerosene demand by 6.8 megatonnes of oil equivalent (Mtoe) – or 11.4% – of aviation fuel demand in 2050 (an increasing uptake or blend of biofuel will reduce the CO_2 price, and the associated demand reduction.

3.2 Synthetic e-fuels

In this study, renewable fuels of non-biological origin (RFNBO) refers to the use of additional renewable electricity to extract hydrogen from water through electrolysis, which is then combined with CO_2 captured from the atmosphere to produce a drop-in liquid hydrocarbon fuel. These fuels are referred to here as electrofuels, and we examine only drop-in electrofuels i.e. electrofuels which can be used by aircraft through combustion in a jet turbine with minimal or no modifications to the aircraft, engines or ground refuelling infrastructure. This draws a line with other types of fuel, such as hydrogen, which requires completely new aircraft designs and new airport refuelling infrastructure, the potential emission reductions out to 2050 of which are accounted for under Section 2.2. However, importantly, a hydrogen scenario has similar, though slightly lower, implications to synthetic fuels in terms of costs and additional electricity needs.

The emission reductions resulting from the use of electrofuels depend mainly on what electricity is used to produce the hydrogen, and the choice of the source of CO_2 leads to different impacts. Using CO_2 from a fossil carbon origin, such as the one being emitted in a steel or a power plant, means the fuel is not carbon circular because the CO_2 ends up in the atmosphere anyway. Designing a synthetic fuel production chain around carbon capture risks locking in one sector to decarbonise the other, creating a disincentive to move towards full decarbonisation. In a 2050 timeframe, the alternative is to use CO_2 captured directly from the atmosphere – a more expensive process, but one which ensures the electrofuel is fully circular.

Despite these cost impacts, our decarbonisation proposals argue that as fuel efficiency improvements will not decarbonise aviation, and with sustainable advanced biofuels unable to meet all of aviation fuel demand in 2050, if the sector wishes to decarbonise, it must steadily and in a sustainable manner increase electrofuels production to meet the remainder of its fuel demand, at least until more radical technology breakthroughs become available.

However, the cost implications of electrofuels will remain substantial. Direct air capture costs are falling but will remain considerable for some time. And while renewable electricity costs are falling, and in some cases reaching parity or falling below non-renewable electricity costs, the fact that electrofuel production requires enormous quantities of electricity means that its cost will likely exceed that of untaxed kerosene.

It's also unlikely that, even with carbon pricing, electrofuels will reach cost parity with kerosene. As a result, policies will need to be put in place to ensure the uptake of electrofuels. These policies are detailed later in this chapter, but any policy which requires airlines to purchase a more expensive fuel will result in an overall increase in operational costs. At least some of that increase can be expected to be passed onto consumers, increasing the price of tickets and thereby reducing demand. In our forecasts, we factor in the impact that this reduced demand will have on air traffic and thus the overall demand for fuels.

It's worth noting the impact that electrofuels uptake will have on overall electricity demand. Our forecasts are that meeting aviation fuel demand with electrofuels will require 912 TWh. This amount is equivalent to 28.2% of Europe's total electricity generation of 3234 TWh in 2015, or 94.4% of the 966 TWh of renewables generation (Directorate General for Energy, 2017) (Figure 9.3). Note that this electricity used in the production of electrofuels will have to be renewable and additional for the resulting fuel to be considered zero carbon. Also, other sectors, such as industry, are expecting to use some types of electrofuels as a way to decarbonise. Such demand will have a considerable impact on broader efforts to decarbonise the European economy – it could mean that additional renewable electricity is used to create electrofuels, when it could have been used in a more efficient manner by other sectors of the economy. These competing demands for additional renewable electricity need to be taken into account to assess the realistic amounts of electrofuels which could be used in aviation.

In the production of electrofuels, only a portion will be suitable for use in the aviation sector. We've put that share at 80% – a very optimistic assessment – meaning there will be residual fuels from this process which may be of use to other sectors.

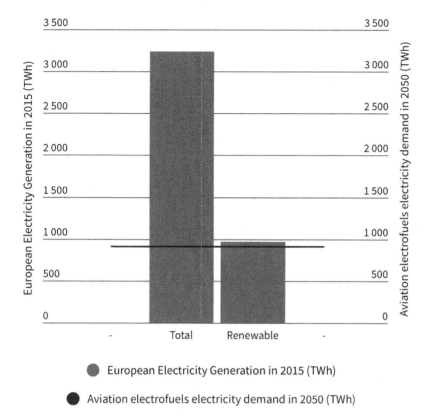

Figure 9.3 Electricity required to produce electrofuels for EU aviation in 2050.

As with sustainable advanced fuels, there is a risk of some residual emissions from electrofuels. And as stated earlier, the zero carbon status of these fuels is dependent on their potential displacement impacts, the manner of their production and therefore on the broader decarbonisation of the economy.

In our scenario, electrofuels are produced from 100% additional renewable electricity using direct air capture CO_2. With a cost of €2100 per tonne in 2050, electrofuel uptake will increase ticket prices a further 23% compared to a ticket price with a €150/tonne CO_2 equivalent price, resulting in a 28% reduction in projected passenger demand compared to a business-as-usual scenario.

3.3 Safeguards

3.3.1 Advanced sustainable biofuels

The legislative basis for use of advanced sustainable biofuels in Europe is the revision to the Renewable Energy Directive (RED II). Contrary to the 2009

RED, the new law does not force member states anymore to support first generation biofuels and will phase out the support to those first generation biofuels which have the most damaging impact on the climate and the environment.

However, the REDII revision falls short of ensuring that only sustainable biofuels which deliver maximum emission reductions are used. To deliver that outcome, the revision would have had to completely phase out the support to first generation biofuels and contain sustainability criteria including for indirect impacts. When it comes to advanced biofuels listed in Annex IX of the Directive, no matter whether they are used in road or aviation, the list still includes some problematic items such as unsustainable forest feedstocks. In addition, the sustainability criteria are not fit to tackle impacts of this variety of biofuels on soil carbon, for example. There is also uncertainty on how biofuels produced from feedstocks not in this Annex or which are not crop biofuels will be treated.

In order to ensure that these fuels are a partial long-term sustainable option for aviation, support should be limited to biofuels produced from wastes or residues, in line with the waste hierarchy, which delivers significant GHG savings after taking into account both direct and indirect impacts and other concerns such as loss in biodiversity, soil degradation or water pollution. This will greatly limit the availability of advanced sustainable biofuels, and it is the reason biofuels cannot be relied on to fully decarbonise aviation.

3.3.2 Electrofuels

Safeguards are essential in order to ensure that electrofuels result in actual emission reductions, without negative side effects on other sectors. As discussed previously, the two areas of concern are the supply of electricity and the supply of CO_2.

The RED II Directive addresses neither of these concerns effectively. The Directive doesn't include a requirement for electrofuels to use air capture and doesn't ensure that only renewable electricity will be used to produce electrofuels and will be additional. The Commission is expected to develop a methodology which could address these issues.

Our recommendations, and the related projections, are that strict sustainability safeguards are put in place (Transport & Environment, 2017d). Briefly, electrofuels should be produced from additional renewable electricity, the CO_2 source should be from air and strict sustainability criteria should be developed regarding land and water use.

3.4 Current limits to fuel blending

The industry certifying body ASTM (formerly the American Society for Testing and Materials) currently sets different blending limits for alternative fuels (biofuels and synthetic) which depend on the fuel and vary from as low as 10% to up to 90%. These limits are set to ensure an appropriate level of safety and to guarantee the smooth operation of aircraft engines because lubricity can be an issue with alternate fuels. These blending limits obviously restrict the emission reductions currently possible from using alternate fuels. Over time, these blending restrictions may be reduced or potentially abolished through new approaches to engine tuning or the development of engine additives. Our study is based on the expectation that such solutions will be found.

3.5 Achieving fuel switching

Our forecasts are that, in part owing to the necessary safeguards for both sustainable alternative biofuels and electrofuels and the electricity requirements for electrofuels, a significant price gap will exist between these alternative fuels and the kerosene they are seeking to replace.

Currently, limited measures are in place to encourage an uptake of aviation alternative fuels. The EU ETS recognises alternative fuels, with airlines able to reduce their allowance purchase obligations if they can demonstrate alternative fuel use. However, low prices of allowances in recent years removed any incentive for airlines to switch to alternative fuels.

Important for aviation in the REDII is a de facto binding 2030 target of 7% for advanced biofuels including biofuels from waste and residues, electrofuels, renewable electricity and recycled carbon fuels. Renewable energy use in aviation can be counted towards achieving the overall 14% target of renewable energy use by 2030, and after 2020 the contribution of advanced fuels used in the aviation sector will be counted as 1.2 times the fuel's actual energy content towards meeting the 7% sub-target for advanced fuels. This is meant to incentivise fuel producers to bring alternative fuel into aviation, but it is unclear whether a multiplication factor of 1.2 will actually result in such fuels going to the aviation sector. The majority of the targets are likely to be filled by the road sector. Our projected carbon price of €150 may encourage some fuel switching towards fuels which are on the lower end of the price spectrum. However, full fuel switching will require different measures.

Fuel mandates have a chequered history in terms of environmental effectiveness; for example in Europe, where a fuel mandate for the road transport sector has resulted in the wide-scale use of food-based biofuels to reach the required targeted. As a result, any obligation on fuel supplied to the aviation sector in Europe will need to be crafted so as to ensure it does not incentivise the production of alternative fuels with negative environmental effects, such as crop-based biofuels.

One avenue to ensure that a fair share of advanced fuels is targeted at aviation would be by requiring fuel suppliers to split their advanced fuels target proportionally between land and air transport (Transport & Environment, 2017c). Such a policy for advanced aviation fuels, which would cover both sustainable biofuels and synthetic fuels, needs to be based on these fuels' climate performance, not just on whether they are labelled 'renewable' or not.

So member states should be encouraged to adopt a low carbon fuel standard, as this offers the best framework for incentivising the delivery of renewable advanced low carbon fuels. The REDII allows member states to change their energy targets into a low carbon fuel standard provided the required level of renewable energy is realised by 2030. When all direct and indirect emissions are accounted for, it provides a performance-based differentiation and a competition for best performing technologies while giving clear market signals and incentives for clean fuel investments in the EU (ActionAid et al., 2016). Germany, for example, regulates alternative fuels through a GHG target.

3.6 A new dedicated EU policy for alternative fuels in aviation

However, it is unclear whether member states will implement the RED II in a way which will enable a real uptake of advanced fuels in aviation. One way to overcome this would be for the EU to develop a specific amendment to the policy framework, in the form of a dedicated GHG target, i.e. a low carbon fuel standard for sustainable advanced fuels in aviation. Such a standard would require fuel supplied on the EU aviation market to meet a progressively lower GHG intensity by using only sustainable advanced fuels.

At the same time, it would be crucial to ensure that such an additional policy tool does not lead to an increased demand in overall volumes for advanced biofuels compared to what is already required by the RED II. This is especially relevant for sustainable advanced biofuels feedstocks which are available only in limited quantities. Additional growth should be focused on electrofuels – which can be scaled sustainably – and the law should be crafted in a way that achieves this goal.

3.7 GHG – low carbon fuel standard for aviation

The Commission could propose an amendment to the REDII which requires suppliers placing aviation fuel on the EU market to comply with a gradually lower carbon intensity. Suppliers would be given several years to meet each level of the GHG intensity target which would apply either across the EU or at the member state level. Member states would be required by EU legislation to enforce the GHG intensity target at the member state level in a similar manner to the way Fuel Quality Directive (FQD) standards are currently implemented. A system of registration of aviation fuel suppliers would need to be established (that for road fuel suppliers was established through the tax provisions of the Energy Tax Directive). The legislation could include a malus/bonus penalty on fuel suppliers for not achieving/over-achieving the requirement. "Aviation fuel suppliers" would need to be defined to include refiners, airport fuel farms and fuel importers, etc.

All fuel uplifted for commercial aviation in the EU would be affected – i.e. for both intra- and extra-EU flights. The retail price of fuel sold to airlines across the EU would rise to reflect suppliers' higher costs. Safeguards might need to be considered to ensure suppliers did not cross-subsidise higher aviation fuel costs by passing some of the increased costs onto the road sector. The low carbon fuel standard would need to be drafted in such a way as to ensure suppliers acted in tandem across the EU to avoid regional price distortions and potentially airline tankering.

Policy

- Introduce sufficient safeguards to ensure that sustainable alternative biofuels and electrofuels deliver promised emission reductions without negative consequences on sustainability.
- Member states should require fuel suppliers to split their advanced fuels target proportionally between land and air traffic and adopt a GHG target/ low carbon fuel standard as this offers the best framework for incentivising the delivery of renewable advanced low carbon fuels.
- An amendment to the RED II requiring all fuel suppliers placing aviation fuel on the EU market to meet a decreasing carbon intensity, with the purpose of bringing all fuel sold to near zero carbon by 2050.

4. Decarbonising aviation results

From this discussion, Table 9.1 summarises the scenarios, the assumptions and the resultant effect on aviation energy demand and aviation passenger activity. In a BaU (business as usual) scenario, passenger activity is expected to grow by 80% from 2015 to 2050, i.e. from 722 million departing passenger movements to 1117 million. Full details of the calculation methodology can be found in the Appendices.

The results of the different measures are presented in this section. A sensitivity analysis is provided in the Appendices.

Figure 9.4 (left) shows the CO_2 emissions trajectories from 2000 to 2050. Rapid decarbonisation is shown to occur from 2030 onwards, where the combined measures of demand reduction, efficiency measures, advanced biofuels and electrofuels curb CO_2 emissions to approximately 2010 levels. From that point on, and with the increasing uptake of electrofuel and renewable electricity production, a rapid decrease ensues. In 2050, the CO_2 emissions from the departing flights in the EU are zero. Figure 9.4 (right) shows how the measures stack up in terms of liquid fuel consumption.

One of the biggest measures in and of itself is the reduction in demand from introducing PtL. Note that in 2050, the demand reduction from the charges equivalent to €150/tonne of CO_2 have been nullified, as the kerosene no longer has a fossil component. Aside from being a driver for more efficient aircraft and their operations, the importance of the carbon pricing can be seen in the cumulative emissions savings. They have been calculated to reduce emissions by 180 Mt CO_2 cumulatively over the 2020–2050 period, compared to no price. With the remaining 39.2 Mtoe, at the price of 2,100€/t of fuel, this equates to an annual fuel bill for airlines fuelling in Europe exceeding €82 billion. This compares to approximately €35 billion today spent on fossil kerosene.

The passenger activity for the BaU and the two scenarios that affect passenger demand are shown in Figure 9.5. As can be seen, this analysis shows

Table 9.1 Summary of aviation CO$_2$ mitigation scenarios

Scenario	Energy demand	Passenger demand	Notes
BaU	The fleet is assumed to improve 1% p.a.	No Change	Taken from Reference Scenario 2016. Energy demand increases 23% from 2015 to 2050. Fleet improvement is a combination of technical and logistical improvements. The Reference Scenario assumes 940€/ktoe for fuel in 2050. With the same methodology as is used to reduce demand with an increase in price, the BaU energy demand is increased with a constant and lower €600/ktoe price.
Fleet efficiency	Additional fleet improvements of 0.2% p.a.	No Change	No rebound considered from cheaper tickets based on lower fuel consumption
Gen II aircraft	30% more efficient than conventional fleet, picks up 1% demand p.a.	No Change	No rebound considered from cheaper tickets based on lower fuel consumption. Gen II are bubble type, strut wings, etc.
Aviation pricing	Reduction driven by change in passenger demand	€150/tCO$_2$ results in 12% reduction in demand.	There is 3.15 tCO$_2$ per tonne of fuel. Fuel cost assumed to be 25% of short haul ticket price and 20% of long haul. Passenger weighted elasticities (see Appendix B) from InterVISTAS and long-term income elasticities are adjusted to −0.48 for all EU departing flights. Ticket prices increase 17% over BaU.
Biofuels	7500 ktoe available in 2050	No Change	Growth following an S-curve, beginning from 2020
PtL demand	100% aviation demand met by 2050	Demand reduces from additional cost.	Reduced demand from €150/tCO$_2$ is nullified. PtL consumption from 2020 follows an S-curve.

that passenger demand levels off from 2030 with an increasing share of PtL, owing to both its uptake and price. The 2050 passenger activity is equivalent to the business-as-usual activity in the early 2030s; thus an increase in overall passenger activity is still envisaged in this analysis. However, as passengers will be travelling further, this does not equate to a greater number of total flights. Modal shift will be most successful for short-haul flights, while longer flights contribute significantly to the passenger activity metric as a single flight can usually take more passengers a multiple further. Thus, growth in activity does not justify increasing the capacity of airports, particularly in Western Europe where many airports are at capacity. Limiting growth by simply avoiding airport expansion is an effective way to keep downward pressure on demand.

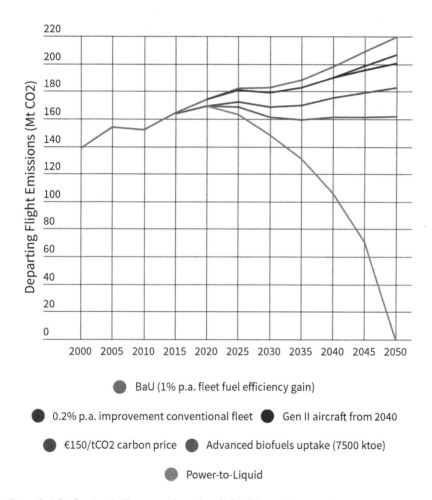

Figure 9.4 Reduction in European departing flight CO_2 emissions and PtL consumption of European departing flights in 2050 after demand reduction measures have been applied.

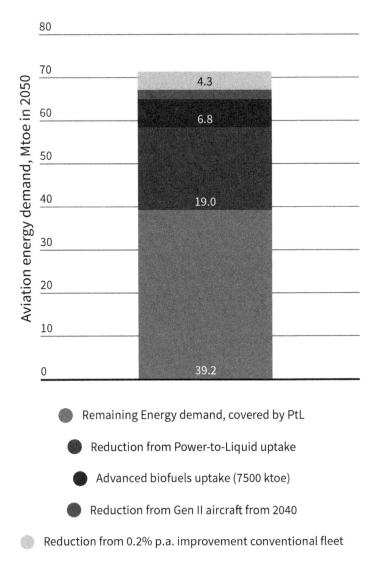

Legend:

● Remaining Energy demand, covered by PtL

● Reduction from Power-to-Liquid uptake

● Advanced biofuels uptake (7500 ktoe)

● Reduction from Gen II aircraft from 2040

● Reduction from 0.2% p.a. improvement conventional fleet

Figure 9.4 (Continued)

5. Aviation's non-CO_2 effects

Aviation's non-CO_2 climate effects include NO_x emissions at altitude, contrails, cirrus cloud formation, soot and water vapour, etc., and can equal or exceed the climate impact of aviation CO_2. Despite the ongoing uncertainties as to how these effects impact the climate and their extent, it is essential when drawing up an aviation decarbonisation strategy that policies to address these non-CO_2 effects are included, particularly where varying the fuels aircraft use is being considered.

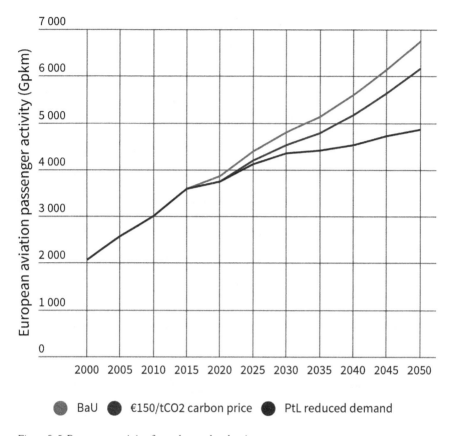

Figure 9.5 Passenger activity from demand reduction.

There are currently no measures in place to address aviation's non-CO_2 climate impacts. When aviation was being included in the EU ETS Directive in 2008, Parliament sought to add a non-CO_2 multiplier to airlines' obligations to purchase allowances, but this was rejected. A study for the Commission proposed the imposition of a cruise NOx charge with distance, but this was not acted upon (Transport & Environment, 2017b). Since then, research into determining the exact climate impacts of these non-CO_2 effects has continued. The understanding of contrail-cirrus effects and their climate impact has improved over the years, and potential measures involving changed flight trajectories so as aircraft avoid climate sensitive areas are being put forward (REACT4C, 2014). On the other hand, the aerosol-cloud effects of aircraft, if they exist, remain largely unknown. Sulphate aerosols from jet engines which may vary with fuel properties might change the properties of low level clouds which cool, while emitted soot particles might trigger cirrus which might cool or warm.

In the 2017 revision of the EU ETS Directive, a requirement was included for the Commission to come forward by January 2020 with proposals to address these non-CO_2 effects if appropriate (Art 30(4) of the revised Directive). In the meantime, further research is expected to be published which might reduce uncertainties regarding the climate warming impact of some of the non-CO_2 effects.

Measures to reduce fuel demand and thus commercial traffic will reduce non-CO_2 effects insofar as they result in less flight activity. And since non-CO_2 effects are transient – hours or months (with the exception of CH_4 cooling from NO_x emissions, which will diminish in decades) – the reduced warming will be immediate – whereas emitted CO_2 persists in the atmosphere along with its warming impact at diminishing levels for hundreds of years.

The exhaust from biofuels and e-fuels will contain less soot than that from kerosene and can be expected to result in some reduction of non-CO_2 effects (DLR, 2016), but because water vapour and NO_x will continue to be emitted from the engines, the principal sources of aviation non-CO_2 warming will persist. So the overall non-CO_2 impact of a switch to using cleaner fuels cannot be quantified here.

When aircraft operate at certain flight levels and atmospheric conditions conducive to ice crystals forming (as the hot and humid exhaust cools and mixes with the environment), climate warming contrails and cirrus clouds can form. If aircraft are rerouted (changed flight levels, route deviations) to avoid these atmospheric conditions, then the contrails/cirrus will not form. How much climate warming can be mitigated in this way is open to debate, but estimates suggest very significantly (Grewe et al., 2017). Changing flights levels and deviating may incur small additional flying time and fuel burn penalties/costs which are the main reasons why industry opposition has ensured such measures have not been adopted. Such opposition is likely to continue, but the sorts of CO_2 reductions outlined in this decarbonisation pathway would far exceed any CO_2 penalties from aircraft rerouting and allow a clear case to be made for adopting measures to have aircraft avoid climate sensitive areas. Such measures would require much improved weather forecasting 12 hours out, to identify sensitive climate areas and allow for flight plans to be changed.

We have not sought to quantify the possible reductions from these alternatives. Neither are the possible impacts of a transition to electric or hydrogen aircraft on non-CO_2 effects considered here, because the deployment of such aircraft in a meaningful commercial quantity is beyond the 2050 timeline we have analysed, the technologies remain speculative and the science about non-CO_2 impacts remain unclear.

5.1 Policy

Mitigating aviation's non-CO_2 effects must be included in any long-term emissions reduction strategy. Rerouting around climate sensitive areas holds promise and needs to be considered as a viable option. Reductions in CO_2 burn from measures we have outlined would likely more than compensate from any fuel burn penalty or rerouting. A switch to cleaner fuels may well reduce non-CO_2

impacts, but these cannot be quantified here. Any aviation decarbonisation strategy must include the provision of significant additional funding into non-CO_2 issues and in particular to understand the non-CO_2 impacts of low/zero carbon fuels, the potential reductions in non-CO_2 warming of flights by avoiding climate sensitive areas, and the enhanced weather forecasting capabilities, etc., that such measures would require. The Commission has little time now to meet its obligations under the revised EU ETS Directive to come forward with potential non-CO_2 mitigation measures by January 2020.

6. Conclusions

Since its deregulation, European aviation emissions have taken off. Artificially cheap tickets through tax exemptions and through government subsidies have propped up and propelled the industry. Unfortunately, there is little awareness of the severe climate impacts and dangers that this mode of transport causes. As it stands, aviation flies in the face of the Paris Agreement, the goals of which are essential for the environment, society and the economy.

If Europe is to pursue a zero carbon economy, it must address this major and rapidly growing source of emissions. Europe's climate policy to date has either neglected this sector or pursued false solutions such as offsetting. The IPCC's most recent report warns that time is rapidly running out to limit a dangerous increase in temperatures; there is no more time for delay.

This study outlines the measures needed to put aviation on a pathway to decarbonisation, and it does not shy away from the challenges this poses. Fuel demand can be cut substantially, but only when aggressive policy measures are put in place. Its fuel can be decarbonised, but there are substantial challenges. Non-CO_2 effects must finally be addressed if we are serious about arresting aviation's climate impact.

The longer action is delayed, the greater the challenge of decarbonisation will be. With the EU revising its long-term decarbonisation strategy, now is the time to ensure Europe acts. This study therefore shows one of many possible pathways to decarbonise aviation. Passenger demand must not increase to the levels that many analysts predict, but largely plateau, and as soon as possible. This will mean ending the tax breaks, the government subsidies and the airport expansions.

Significant effort and resources will be required to collect and process sustainable feedstocks to produce the maximum amount of advanced biofuels to reduce the amount of electrofuels required to cover the remaining kerosene demand. This pathway therefore requires significant amounts of additional renewable electricity to be rapidly installed, which will be required to produce electrofuels at considerable cost.

Finally, the decarbonisation pathway presented in this study requires active engagement from policy makers to ensure a decarbonised future. They represent concrete, feasible and legally sound measures that policy makers, politicians and citizens can press to be urgently implemented.

Appendix A
Calculations and inputs

In order to calculate the effects of efficiency gains and pricing policies on the future of European aviation, the 2016 EU Reference Scenario is used as a basis to generate a BaU scenario in this study. The key factors we used are shown in Table 9.2 for two salient years. Alternative fuel uptake is assumed to increase in line with a logistic function (or an S-curve); other measures are assumed to increase linearly.

There are several assumptions already built into the EU Reference Scenario that we take advantage of. The first is the fleet efficiency, which improves on average 1% per year from 2010 to 2050. As mentioned above, the price of fuel in the 2016 Reference Scenario is projected to increase to approximately €930/t; we correct the aviation demand for this by assuming that the fuel price remains constant at €600/t, which results in a 13% cheaper ticket price. This is calculated based on the assumptions detailed in Appendix B. This step was undertaken in an attempt to unpick the demand reduction measures built into the Reference Scenario to avoid double counting them, and to avoid relying on an increase in fuel price to reduce demand. Further inputs are shown in Table 9.3.

When applying efficiency measures, no rebound effect is assumed that may result from airlines passing on fuel savings to customers. Similarly, the introduction of advanced biofuels is assumed to cause no reduction in demand due to their higher price, to simplify the analysis. As these fuels attain only a blend of 13%, if they were double the price of kerosene, the change in ticket price would be around 3%, implying a demand in reduction of only 1.5% in 2050.

The measures are applied in the same order as outlined in the study: The fuel fleet and operational efficiencies are applied, on top of which a carbon price, followed by advanced biofuels, and finally electrofuels. The implication of this is that an uptake of biofuels has the effect of reducing the CO_2 price proportionally to the blend. The remaining fossil kerosene is then replaced by electrofuels, which reduce the carbon price to zero by 2050. However, owing to the 2050 price of €2100/t (equivalent to the effect of a carbon price of €500/t), there is still a significant drop in demand resulting from the uptake of this fuel. The way in which fuel and carbon prices affect the ticket price, and thus passenger demand, are described further in Appendix B.

Table 9.2 Parameters for scenarios – part 1

Parameter	2015	2050	Description/notes
Aviation Energy Demand (Mtoe)	53.3	71.3	All departing flights from the EU. Final demand adjusted from 65.5 Mtoe to account for differences in fuel cost.
Population (million)	505	522	The GDP per capita over this period is
GDP (in billion €$_{2013}$)	13,400	22,500	thus projected to increase by 62%.

Table 9.3 Parameters for scenarios – part 2

Parameter	2020	2050	Description/notes
Kerosene price (€/t)	600	600	Assumed constant
Fuel price fraction of ticket price (domestic & intra-EU)	25%	25%	See Appendix B for how the extra-EU flights increase their share
Fuel price fraction of ticket price (extra-EU)	20%	20%	
Extra improvement on fleet compared to the BaU	0%	6%	0.2% per annum from 2020. This metric includes fuel and operational efficiency.
Gen II aircraft	0%	3%	From 2040, 1% per year ingress of 30% more efficient aircraft design.
Advanced biofuels (ktoe)	50	7500	In 2020 the amount of 50 ktoe is assumed to be available (EASA, 2018), requires 33% year on year growth.
CO$_2$ price (€/t)	30	150	From ETS, VAT, kerosene tax
PtL price (€/t)	5000	2100	Malins (2017)
PtL conversion efficiency	38%	50%	Schmidt and Weindorf (2016); Malins (2017)

As mentioned previously, electrofuel uptake is assumed to follow an S-curve, increasing from small amounts in 2020, reaching half the required capacity in the year 2045 (denoted y_0) and meeting 100% of fossil kerosene demand in 2050. The growth rate factor, k, was 0.2, where the amount of PTL produced for a given year, y, is:

$$PTL_y = \frac{PTL_{2050}}{1 + e^{-k(y-y_0)}}$$

The Reference Scenario includes only passenger activity for the intra-EU segments, while included energy demand for all outbound flights. From a combination of analysis of transponder data from PlaneFinder, Eurostat passenger numbers, and an assumption that in 2050, extra-EU flights will on average be 7000 km, the passenger activity from all departing passengers was calculated and projected to 2050.

Appendix B
Elasticities

This Appendix gives greater detail on how each measure affects aviation demand.

Price elasticities

A number of factors influence air travel demand, as outlined by IATA's *Air Travel Demand* study (Smyth and Pearce, 2008). In most general terms, increasing the cost of flying reduces its demand. The reduction is not universal across the market, as it depends on factors such as the choice and utility of other modes of transport to undertake the journey (such as train, bus or car), and how wealthy the passenger is. In this study, price and income elasticities are calculated based on *Air Travel Demand* and are described in further detail in this Appendix. Furthermore, the income elasticities are modified in the context of more recent studies, such as Gallet and Doucouliagos (2014) and Department for Transport (2017).

In the first step, the relevant elasticity coefficients for the flight segments based on distance band, price increase coverage, and geography are listed (Table 9.4).

Combining the appropriate factors gives the following price-based demand elasticities (Table 9.5).

According to these elasticities, an increase in ticket price of 10% for an intra-EU flight will result in a 8.4% reduction in demand.

Income elasticities

The price elasticities just described will not tend to be constant in time. Another key driver of aviation demand is wealth, whereby as people become richer, they tend to fly more. Income elasticities are computed from the segments for flights originating from developed economies. An elasticity of greater than 1 tends to indicate a luxury item (Table 9.6).

Combining the appropriate factors gives the following income-based demand elasticities (Table 9.7):

Table 9.4 Elasticity coefficients

Code	Disaggregation of flight segments	Elasticity coefficient	Description
LH	Long haul	1	Short-haul flights have more options available to
SH	Short haul	1.1	avoid the flights (such as car, train, bus)
RL	Route level	1.4	Route level taxes can push passengers to
NL	National level	0.8	cheaper routes (highly price sensitive), and
SL	Supra-national level	0.6	national taxes can result in re-routing to other countries. This study assumes EU-wide measures, i.e. at the supra-national level, which reduces passenger options for modal shift.
EU	Intra-EU	1.4	Geographical location determines the cost
TA	Trans Atlantic	1.2	sensitivity based on fast-growing developing
AS	EU–Asia	0.9	markets, and mature developed markets.

Table 9.5 Demand elasticities (based on segments)

Segment	Elasticity	Elasticity coefficient combination
Domestic	−0.92	−1 * SH * SL * EU
Intra-EU	−0.84	−1 * LH * SL * EU
Extra-EU	−0.63	−1 * LH * SL * (TA + AS) / 2

Table 9.6 Income elasticities

Code	Segment	Elasticity	Description
SH	Short haul	1.3	As people become wealthier, they tend to demand
MH	Medium haul	1.4	more air travel. Long-haul and very-long-haul
LH	Long haul	1.5	flights become increasingly desirable with wealth.
VH	Very long haul	2.2	

Table 9.7 Income elasticities (based on segments)

Segment	Elasticity	Elasticity coefficient combination
Domestic	1.3	SH
Intra-EU	1.5	(MH + LH) / 2
Extra-EU	1.9	(LH + VH) / 2

According to these income elasticities, a per capita increase in wealth (or increase in GDP per capita) of 10% will result in an increase in 15% of intra-EU flights, *ceteris paribus*, assuming ticket prices remain stable. As can be seen from Appendix A, Europeans are projected to be 62% wealthier in 2050 than they were in 2015 based on GDP. It is not clear to what extent the EU Reference Scenario has used these elasticities, but it is assumed that these elasticities are causes in accelerating aviation demand to the levels that are projected. These elasticities have been used to compute the passenger share evolution in each flight segment, as described later.

There is evidence that as markets mature, these elasticities reduce. Gallet and Doucouliagos (2014) suggest that when taking both income and price elasticities into account, the income elasticity would be 0.633. The UK Department for transport foresees long-term income elasticities of 0.6, also significantly lower than those presented in the IATA study. This assumes that the market is mature.

Accounting for price and income elasticities

When combining price and income elasticities, the standard approach would be to sum the net effects of both elasticities on the demand. For example, if a ticket price increase would result in a 10% reduction in passengers, but an increase in wealth would increase demand by 5%, the net effect would be a 5% reduction. In this analysis, however, passenger demand is assumed to have price and income elasticities built in. Therefore, the standard approach is not suitable in this case.

In this study, the income elasticity of 0.6 is applied directly to the price demand in 2050. If wealth considerations were not included, the segment weighted elasticity in 2050 would be −0.79. However, adjusting the elasticities based on wealth considerations gives a final segment and wealth-adjusted price demand elasticity of −0.48 in 2050. This indicates a mature market where wealthier travellers are less affected by price increases.

The underlying reasoning behind using price and income elasticities is to see how pricing mechanisms such as a CO_2 price can reduce aviation passenger demand, which will reduce the amount of electrofuels the EU would need to produce. These elasticities are highly uncertain, however. To have a clearer view of how this can change the results, a sensitivity analysis is conducted and is presented in Appendix C.

Evolution of aviation segments projections

The income demand elasticities show that long-haul and very-long-haul flights are expected to increase at a greater rate than domestic and intra-EU flights. The departing passenger numbers, P, of 2016 provided by Eurostat (2018) have their 2050 projections weighted by the income elasticities, E, as per the following formula:

$$P_{i,2050} = \sum P_{i,2015} \cdot L_i \cdot (1+G) \frac{E_i \cdot P_{i,2015} \cdot L_i \cdot (1+G)}{\sum E_i \cdot P_{i,2015} \cdot L_i \cdot (1+G)}$$

Table 9.8 Passenger numbers and growth rates

Flight segment	Departing passengers 2015 (millions)	Growth in pkm (2015–2050)	Departing passengers 2050 (millions)
Domestic	158.0	33%	210.2
Intra-EU	393.2	48%	583.6
Extra-EU	170.7	89%	323.3

For the domestic, intra-EU and extra-EU segments, i, with total passenger number growth measured in pkm $G = 75\%$, taken directly from the reference scenario projections between 2015 and 2050. The passenger-weighted average length of the domestic and intra-EU segments are calculated from transponder data in 2016 and are assumed to be constant. Extra-EU flight segment lengths are assumed to be 7000 km on average. This results in the following growth rates for each segment, shown in passenger numbers (Table 9.8).

Appendix C
Sensitivity analysis

This chapter presents policy requirements that Europe needs to pursue in order to decarbonise aviation by 2050. This Appendix explores additional scenarios, where efficiency measures, SAFs and other demand reduction measures are not taken, and the sensitivity analysis on the use of income elasticities. The results of this analysis are presented in Table 9.9.

The results (see Figure 9.6) show that if short-term measures are not applied as a long-term strategy to decarbonisation, the required PtL production will increase by 31%, or to 36.8% of 2015 EU generation of 3234 TWh. Between Scenarios 1 and 2, there is no difference between passenger demand, as when there is 100% SAFs and electrofuels in the blend, there is no CO_2 price demand reduction. Passenger demand is 28% less than projected in 2050, or roughly equivalent to 2030 levels. Scenarios 3 and 4 show the effect of applying unadjusted price elasticities. In the case where price elasticities were to be constant, the price of electrofuels would result in nearly halving the passenger demand from the business-as-usual scenario, equivalent to passenger activity in 2020. The implication is that with lower passenger activity, there is less requirement to produce electrofuels. Finally, Scenario 5 shows the electrofuel required in the case where no advanced biofuel is available to aviation, which may be the case based on the demand from competing sectors for biomass and from increasingly stringent sustainability criteria that may be legislated for. The result here shows that almost 20% more additional and renewable electricity would be required to produce enough electrofuels.

Selection of appropriate elasticities is thus crucial to approximating the future passenger and energy demand of aviation, particularly how they will evolve over the next 30 years to 2050. There is an underlying assumption that elasticities are constant irrespective of the price change. From the literature review conducted to attain the elasticities used in this study, there has been no discussion on the fairness of this assumption. For example, the assertion that a proportional change in demand will be the same for a 5% change in price compared to a 50% change is not verifiable. The main takeaway from this analysis is that demand reduction is necessary to reduce the amount of additional renewable electricity capacity required in the EU, irrespective of whether long-term elasticities change or not. The final values attempt to give an order of magnitude appreciation of how much additional renewable electricity this will equate to.

Table 9.9 Sensitivity analysis scenario

Sensitivity analysis scenario		2050	
		Passengers' activity in Gpkm* (% reduction from BaU in 2050)	Electricity demand for electrofuel in TWh** (% EU 2015 generation)
0	Business as usual	6753	N/A
1	Pathway to decarbonisation as detailed in this chapter	4853 (−28%)	912 (28.2%)
2	No efficiency, alternative fuels or demand reduction	4853 (−28%)	1191 (36.8%)
3	Scenario 1 with no long-term income elasticity adjustment	3587 (−47%)	628 (19.4%)
4	Scenario 2 with no long-term income elasticity adjustment	3587 (−47%)	880 (27.2%)
5	Scenario 1 without advanced biofuels	4853 (−28%)	1086 (33.6%)

* Giga passenger-kilometres
** Terawatt hours

Reduction in fossil kerosene consumption in EU28

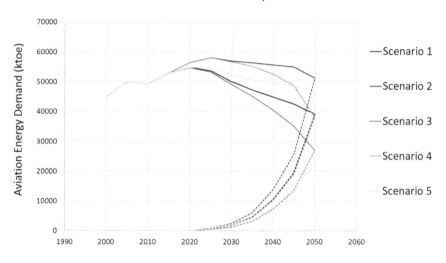

Figure 9.6 Results of sensitivity analysis scenarios. Dashed lines indicate the PtL production curve following an S-curve required to meet fuel demand by 2050.

References

ACI – Airports Council International Europe. (2018). [Online] Available at: https://www. aci-europe [Accessed 6 Feb. 2018].

ActionAid, Fern, BirdLife Europe and Transport & Environment. (2016). *NGOs recommendations for post-2020 sustainable low carbon transport fuels policy.* [Online] Available at: https:// www.transportenvironment.org/sites/te/files/publications/28%2010%202016%20 NGO%20letter%20low%20carbon%20fuels%202030.pdf. [Accessed 30 Nov. 2019].

CE Delft. (2018). *A study on aviation ticket taxes.* Delft.

CE Delft. (2019). *Taxing aviation fuels in the EU.* Delft.

CE Delft and SEO. (2019). *Taxes in the field of aviation and their impact.* Report prepared for the European Commission, Brussels.

Council of the EU. (2017). *Non-ETS (ESR):WPE 2 March – commission presentation on 2030 GHG emission reduction target.* WK 2017/2017. [Online] Available at: https://www.trans portenvironment.org/sites/te/files/WK_2310_2017_INIT_2.pdf [Accessed 30 Nov. 2019].

Department for Transport. (2017). UK aviation forecasts – moving Britain ahead. [Online] Available at: assets.publishing.service.gov.uk/government/uploads/system/uploads/attach ment_data/file/674749/uk-aviation-forecasts-2017.pdf [Accessed 30 Nov. 2019].

Directorate General for Energy (European Commission). (2017). *EU energy in figures.* Statistical pocketbook 2017. [Online] Available at: https://publications.europa.eu/en/pub lication-detail/-/publication/2e046bd0-b542-11e7-837e-01aa75ed71a1/language-en/ format-PDF/source-search [Accessed 30 Nov. 2019].

DLR. (2016). *Condensation trails from biofuels/kerosene blends scoping study.* European Commission. [Online] Available at: https://ec.europa.eu/energy/sites/ener/files/documents/ Contrails-from-biofuels-scoping-study-final-report.pdf [Accessed 30 Nov. 2019].

EASA – European Union Aviation Safety Agency. (2016). *European aviation environmental report.*

EASA – European Union Aviation Safety Agency. (2018). *European aviation environmental report.*

ECA – European Court of Auditors. (2014). *EU-funded airport infrastructures: Poor value for money.* [Online] Available at: https://www.eca.europa.eu/Lists/ECADocuments/SR14_21/QJAB 14021ENC.pdf [Accessed 30 Nov. 2019].

EIB – European Investment Bank. (2018). *Denmark: EIB renews backing for Copenhagen Airport.* [Online] Available at: http://www.eib.org/en/infocentre/press/releases/all/2018/2018-219-eib-renews-backing-for-copenhagen-airport.htm [Accessed 30 Nov. 2019].

European Commission. (2016). *EU reference scenario 2016.* [Online] Available at: https:// ec.europa.eu/energy/en/data-analysis/energy-modelling/eu-reference-scenario-2016 [Accessed 30 Nov. 2019].

European Commission. (2017). *State aid: Commission simplifies rules for public investment in ports and airports, culture and the outermost regions.* [Online] Available at: https://europa.eu/rapid/ press-release_IP-17-1341_en.htm [Accessed 30 Nov. 2019].

European Council. (2019). *European Council meeting (12 December 2019) – Conclusions.* [Online] Available at: https://www.consilium.europa.eu/media/41768/12-euco-final-conclusions-en.pdf [Accessed 13 Mar. 2020].

European Environmental Agency. (2017). *Aviation and shipping – impacts on Europe's environment.* EEA Report No. 22. [Online] Available at: https://www.eea.europa.eu/publica tions/term-report-2017 [Accessed 30 Nov. 2019].

Eurostat. (2018). *Table: Avia_paoc.* [Online] Available at: http://appsso.eurostat.ec.europa.eu/ nui/show.do?dataset=avia_paoc&lang=en [Accessed Sept. 2018].

Freeman, S., Lee, D.S., Lim, L.L., Skowron, A. and de Leon, R.R. (2018). Trading off aircraft fuel burn and NO_x emissions for optimal climate policy. *Environmental Science & Technology,* 52, pp. 2498–2505.

Gallet, C.A. and Doucouliagos, H. (2014). The income elasticity of air travel: A meta-analysis. *Annals of Tourism Research,* 49, pp. 141–155.

Grewe, V., Dahlmann, K., Flink, J., Frömming, C., Ghosh, R., Gierens, K., Heller, R., Hendricks, J., Jöckel, P., Kaufmann, S., Kölker, K., Linke, F., Luchkova, T., Lührs, B., Van Manen, J., Matthes, S., Minikin, A., Niklaß, M., Plohr, M., Righi, M., Rosanka, S., Schmitt, A., Schumann, U., Terekhov, I., Unterstrasser, S., Vázquez-Navarro, M., Voigt, C., Wicke, K., Yamashita, H., Zahn, A. and Ziereis, H. (2017). *Mitigating the climate impact from aviation: Achievements and results of the DLR WeCare project.* Aerospace, 4(3). doi:10.3390/ aerospace4030034.

Hemmings, B. (2016). A flying fairy tale: Why aviation carbon cuts won't take off. *Climate Home News.* [Online] Available at: https://www.climatechangenews.com/2016/02/23/a-flying-fairy-tale-why-aviation-carbon-cuts-wont-take-off/ [Accessed 30 Nov. 2019].

IATA – International Air Transport Association. (2017). *Economic performance of the airline industry.* [Online] Available at: https://www.iata.org/whatwedo/Documents/econom ics/IATA-Economic-Performance-of-the-Industry-mid-year-2017-report.pdf [Accessed 30 Nov. 2019].

IATA – International Air Transport Association. (2018). *2017 marked by strong passenger demand, record load factor.* [Online] Available at: https://www.iata.org/pressroom/pr/Pages/ 2018-02-01-01.aspx [Accessed 30 Nov. 2019].

ICCT – International Council on Clean Transportation. (2018). *ICAO's CORSIA scheme provides a weak nudge for in-sector carbon reductions.* [Online] Available at: https://theicct.org/ blog/staff/corsia-carbon-offsets-and-alternative-fuel [Accessed 30 Nov. 2019].

IPCC – Intergovernmental Panel on Climate Change. (2018). *Special report – global warming of 1.5 °C.* [Online] Available at: https://www.ipcc.ch/sr15/ [Accessed 30 Nov. 2019].

Kärcher, B. (2018). Formation and radiative forcing of contrail cirrus. *Nature Communications,* 9. doi:10.1038/s41467-018-04068-0.

Lee, D.S., Fahey, D.W., Forster, P.M., Newton, P.J., Wit, R.C.N., Lim, L.L., Owen, B. and Sausen, R. (2009). Aviation and global climate change in the 21st century. *Atmospheric Environment,* 43(22–23), pp. 3520–3537. doi:10.1016/j.atmosenv.2009.04.

Malins, C. (2017). *What role is there for electrofuel technologies in European transport's low carbon future?* Cerulogy.

Murphy, A. (2015). Responsible flying grounded by aviation's fuel tax exemption. *Euroactiv,* 16 Apr. [Online] Available at: https://www.euractiv.com/section/climate-environment/ opinion/responsible-flying-grounded-by-aviation-s-fuel-tax-exemption/ [Accessed 30 Nov. 2019].

Pache, E. (2019). *Kerosene tax analysis parts I and II.* [Online] Available at: https://www.trans portenvironment.org/publications/legal-analysis-implementation-aviation-kerosene-tax ation-europe [Accessed 30 Nov. 2019].

REACT4C. (2014). *Project REACT4C.* [Online] Available at: https://www.react4c.eu/ [Accessed 30 Nov. 2019].

Schafer, A., Evans, A., Dray, L. and Reynolds, T. (2015). Costs of mitigating CO_2 emissions from passenger aircraft. *Nature Climate Change,* 6, 412–417.

Schmidt, P. and Weindorf, W. (2016). *Power-to-liquids. Potentials and perspectives for the future supply of renewable aviation fuel.* Dessau-Roßlau: Umweltbundesamt.

Smyth, M. and Pearce, B. (2008). *Air travel demand.* IATA Economics Briefing No 9. [Online] Available at: www.iata.org/whatwedo/documents/economics/air_travel_demand.pdf [Accessed 30 Nov. 2019].

Transport & Environment. (2016). T&E analysis of UNFCCC and aircraft transponder data from PlaneFinder (2016). Transponder data were coupled with the ICAO fuel burn calcu-lator methodology, and flights analysed based on journey type.

Transport & Environment. (2017a). *A target for advanced biofuels.* [Online] Available at: https:// www.transportenvironment.org/sites/te/files/2017_06_Advanced_biofuels_target.pdf [Accessed 30 Nov. 2019].

Transport & Environment. (2017b). *The non-CO_2 impacts of aviation must be tackled.* [Online] Available at: https://www.transportenvironment.org/sites/te/files/publications/2017_06_ non-CO2_aviation_briefing_final_0.pdf [Accessed 30 Nov. 2019].

Transport & Environment. (2017c). *How to incentivise renewable aviation fuels through the renewable energy directive.* [Online] Available at: https://www.transportenvironment.org/publications/how-incentivise-renewable-aviation-fuels-through-renewable-energy-directive [Accessed 30 Nov. 2019].

Transport & Environment. (2017d). *Electrofuels – what role in EU transport decarbonisation?* [Online] Available at: https://www.transportenvironment.org/sites/te/files/publications/2017_11_Briefing_electrofuels_final.pdf [Accessed 30 Nov. 2019].

Transport & Environment. (2018). *10 inconvenient facts about the EU biofuels sector.* [Online] Available at: https://www.transportenvironment.org/what-we-do/biofuels/10-facts [Accessed 30 Nov. 2019].

UNFCCC. (2018). *Member state reporting.* [Online] Available at: https://unfccc.int/process/transparency-and-reporting/reporting-and-review-under-the-convention/greenhouse-gas-inventories-annex-i-parties/national-inventory-submissions-2018 [Accessed 30 Nov. 2019].

10 Intermodal dimension of climate change policy

Werner Rothengatter

1. Risk of climate change and challenges for transportation

The "Representative Concentration Pathways" (RCP) presented by the IPCC (2015) in their 5th Synthesis Report describe a wide range of possible greenhouse gas (GHG) and pollutant emission scenarios until the year 2100. The widened range of scenarios compared with the 4th Synthesis Report indicates that an increase of the world temperature of 5 °C and more is possible if the production and consumption trends continue (see IPCC, 2015, p. 9, Figure SPM.5). This message has been further emphasized in the Special Report of the IPCC (2018). Based on these findings the World Climate Conference of Katowice of 2018 has reconfirmed the agreements of the Paris and the Marrakech Conferences (2015, 2016) and postulates the reduction of global warming to an increase below 2 °C worldwide until the end of this century, aiming at even 1.5 °C, to achieve a sustainable development path for most regions of the earth.

The treatment of climate impacts in economics is not homogenous because of different basic assumptions (see Musso and Rothengatter, 2013):

1   Future damages can be managed, and damage costs can be quantified (trading-off possible).
2   Most serious impacts can be reduced by adaptation measures, and others can be treated according to assumption 1 (trading off possible).
3   Most serious impacts are irreversible and cannot be compensated (no trading-off possible).

The neo-classical approaches start from assumption 1, i.e. from the calculation of future damage costs. These costs are estimated for future decades and discounted by a social rate of discount. When the social discount rate is high enough, even high future damages of climate change show low present values. The much-read and commented *Stern Review* (2007) applies a very low discount rate assuming that the rate of social time preference is 0.1%.[1] The review concludes with the result that one EUR invested in mitigation yields five EUR cost reductions of avoided future climate damages. Nordhaus (2007) and other authors showed that discount rates of 3% or higher – as they are used in cost-benefit studies and guides – would put the Stern results in question. This underlines that the empathy of the present generation with respect to the living conditions of future generations – expressed by the choice of social discount – plays a crucial role in the discussion about necessary mitigation or adaptation policies.

Assumption 2 is based on the expectation that major damages of climate change can be substantially reduced by adaptation measures. For instance, high dikes and flood protection could prevent the negative impacts of higher sea levels. In this case the economic valuation would sum up the discounted costs of adaptation actions and the remaining damage costs of climate damage (e.g. cost of migration of inhabitants from sunken islands or coastal areas). In most neo-classical approaches the economic costs per tonne of CO_2 or GHG come out comparatively low,[2] such that the climate change impacts don't play a dominant role in cost-benefit analysis or marginal cost pricing in transport (see European Commission, 2014b).

Assumption 3 can be found in the literature on ecological economics (e.g., Costanza, 1991; Baumol, Oates and Blackman, 1979; Baumol and Oates, 1988). The basic philosophy is that major impacts on nature and human life cannot be reversed such that safe minimum values for emissions have to be defined and controlled. The economic costs can then be estimated by calculating the costs of all actions necessary to achieve the safe minimum values (avoidance or mitigation costs). In the case of GHG this leads to the consequence that international agreements are necessary first on the target reduction levels and secondly on the actions to be taken by the different countries. The resulting costs per tonne of CO_2 can even exceed 200 EUR for developed countries (Musso and Rothengatter, 2013).

The aforementioned World Climate Conferences are following the issues according to assumption 3 and have set a clear safe minimum value for GHG (2° or even lower, down to 1.5°). Furthermore, the recent conferences defined regional mitigation targets. One hundred ninety-six countries attended the Paris conference, and 174 countries signed the agreement and started its adoption. The US withdrawal has weakened the international climate alliance but didn't change the climate reduction agreements of the other signatories. The EU has agreed to the terms and conditions of the long-term reduction target and announced a GHG-reduction of 40% until 2030, compared to 1990. The targets for the transport sector until 2019 were: a 60% reduction until 2050 (compared to 1990), a 20% reduction until 2030 (based on 2008). In the EU Green Deal of November 2019 these targets have been tightened for achieving carbon neutrality in 2050. This reflects the unsatisfactory development of the transport sector. While energy and production sectors are on track (they are widely included into the European emission trading scheme, or ETS) the transport emissions have increased by 7% (60 Mt) between 2013 and 2017. In particular, aviation emissions increased by 9% in this period and meanwhile have a share of 13.3% of EU transport emissions (2016). Therefore, mitigation policies like shifting traffic from road and air to rail are components of the overall GHG reduction strategy.

In Section 2 we go into some details of the climate impacts of the transport sector and their contribution to the external costs of the different transport modes. As the challenges of climate change for air transport are the focus of this book, we will limit the comparisons to passenger transport on competitive rail/air distances. In Section 3 we look at state actions to stimulate the market players in order to take avoidance measures. Section 4 deals with concrete options for shifting transport from air to rail. The case study on the Spanish high-speed rail (HSR) network and its planned extension, as described in Section 5, will indicate the potentials and limits for a "shift" strategy from air to high-speed rail (HSR). Section 6 will give the conclusions.

2. Climate impacts and contribution of different transport modes

The transport sector produces about one fifth of the global CO_2 emissions and shows high growth dynamics. In the EU 28, the emission share of transport is 24.3% (European Commission, 2016, in terms of CO_{2eq}); the shares of modal contributions are 72% for road, 14% for navigation (including maritime), 13% for air and less than 1% for rail (values for 2016; see European Commission, 2018). Climate change impacts are a part of the external costs of transport, i.e. costs that are not covered by the producers and would have to be internalized through public interventions to create fair market conditions for the transport modes. In this section we first analyze the specific CO_2 emissions of the different transport modes, and secondly place them into the framework of external costs.

A study of the climate efficiency of different transport modes has to be related to the emissions per unit of traffic activity, e.g. per passenger kilometres (pkm). However, the transport modes compete only on particular distance bands, i.e. car/HSR on shorter and HSR/air on medium distances. Therefore, such comparisons require specifying a number of conditions:

Distance of travel: For air transport the emissions in the landing/take-off cycles are dominant on short distances; consequently, the comparative CO_2 advantage of land-borne modes decreases with distance.

Type of vehicles: Aircraft use is optimized according to distance and traffic volume of origin-destination (OD) pairs. In the case of HSR, there can be a number of stations in a corridor which provide sufficient patronage and determine the assignment of capacity (single or double train sets, one or double deck carriage, frequency of service).

Occupancy of vehicles: In aviation the load factors are between 75% and 85% for financially viable services. For HSR this depends on the service strategy. In the case of fixed service schedules (e.g. hourly), the average occupancy is low, as for instance in Germany where less than 50% are recorded. If the frequency is adjusted to the peaks of travel demand, as for instance in France, Japan or China, the occupancy rates are 70% or even higher, e.g. in Japan and China on the main corridors.

Activity dependent or total emissions: Most economic studies on external costs of transport are focusing on the travel dependent ("marginal") costs (see e.g. European Commission, 2014b). In these approaches the emissions caused by the provision of infrastructure and vehicles are neglected. However, a fair comparison of climate efficiency of different transport modes requires considering the total emissions.

Weighing of emissions: In most publications on climate impacts, the emissions of aircraft flying at high altitudes are weighed by a factor of 2. According to IPCC (2015), this factor can be estimated between 2 and 5, although there is no clear scientific evidence. This is argued to be because of the higher impacts on radiation, e.g. through contrails and synergetic reactions of exhaust products in high altitudes (see Grewe in this volume).

The railway organizations offer CO_2 and other emission calculators which show the advantage of rail on medium distances. The example in Table 10.1 is taken from the UIC calculator.

It is obvious that the percent advantage of rail declines with increasing distance. However, it has to be taken into account that the rail traveller needs about 47 hours on the route from Lisbon to Stockholm and has to change trains ten times such that only a few railway enthusiasts will take this alternative into account. Using the CO_2 calculator developed by the IFEU Institute (2019) – based on the TREMOD model (2016) – the relative advantages of HSR come out almost constant (a factor of 6) for distances up to 1,250 km (see Table 10.2).

This means that, depending on the essential assumptions, the operational climate advantage of rail on short flight distances compared with air is between

Table 10.1 Results from UIC emission calculator

City pair	Distance (km Air)	Kg CO₂ rail	Kg CO₂ car	Kg CO₂ air	Travel time rail (hrs)
Frankfurt–London	640	19.6	82.7	130.3	6.30
Lisbon–Stockholm	2990	94.4	373	277	47

Source: UIC.www.ecopassenger.org

Table 10.2 CO_{2e} emissions[3] (in kg) dependent on distance

Travel distance	500 km	750 km	1000 km	1250 km
Car	94.5	141.8	189.0	236.3
Air	105.7	158.5	211.3	264.1
Rail/HSR	17.8	26.7	35.6	44.5

Source: IFEU (2016).

Basis: Well-to-wheel consumption of CO_{2e}, without emissions stemming from vehicle production/maintenance and infrastructure provision. Average mix of energy production for rail.

the factors of 4 and 6 in Europe. In Japan the CO_2 advantage for Shinkansen trains vs. short-distance air transport can be much larger, up to a factor of 10, on very busy corridors (e.g. Tokyo–Osaka). A life-cycle comparison shows that the share of infrastructure provision to CO_2 production is much higher for rail compared with air (1.6 vs. 0.07 g/pass.-km or 11% vs. 0.06% of specific CO_2 production).[4] The break-even point is calculated at 4,000 passengers per day[5] while the actual patronage on the Tokyo–Osaka link is about 230,000 passengers per day (Hayashi et al., 2014).

It is noteworthy that for the existing Tokaido line, which became operational in 1964, the very low break-even point of 4,000 passengers per day is due to the low number of bridges and tunnels along this line. The planned new MAGLEV line between Tokyo, Nagoya and Osaka will cross the mountainous area of central Honshu and includes many expensive engineering structures such that the CO_2 production of infrastructure provision will be much higher. The environmental advantage of a MAGLEV connection – providing a maximum speed of about 500 km/h – vs. aviation is reduced to an estimated factor of 3, even under optimistic assumptions for patronage and energy efficiency of the system (see Hayashi et al., 2014).

3. Market interventions by taxation, emission trading and subsidization

3.1 Taxation and emission trading

Savings of CO_2 emissions is the major external cost advantage of railways when compared with aviation (see for instance European Commission, 2014b). The widely recommended economic instrument for internalization of external costs is taxation, as it is described in many textbooks in the form of "Pigou taxes" (difference between marginal social and private costs). Climate taxes are suggested by many prominent economists, including Nobel Prize laureates like W.D. Nordhaus, J.E. Stiglitz or G.A. Akerlof (Kaufman, 2019). Such taxes can be directly related to the carbon footprint, as for instance implemented in Norway, Finland or British Columbia, Canada. Many countries apply energy taxation systems which tax the consumption of fossil fuel and generate impacts comparable to climate taxes. However, the systems of direct or indirect climate taxation are highly heterogeneous and very hard to coordinate for the avoidance of undesired distortions of competition. Furthermore, fuel taxation is not very popular and the plan to increase green taxation in France has led to massive citizens' protests ("yellow jackets"). The protagonists of climate taxation, therefore, suggest redistributing the revenues on a per capita basis to compensate for the negative impacts of this instrument on income distribution.

The differential treatment of rail and air with respect to energy taxation and value added taxes (VAT) plays a role for intermodal competition. International aviation is exempted from VAT according to ICAO rules,[6] while the situation of railways varies by country (VAT 2018 in the UK: 0%; in France: reduced rate of 10%; in Germany: 19% for long-distance rail transport). It may happen that the VAT which a customer has to pay for a rail ticket from Berlin to Paris is higher than the price of a low-cost flight including all taxes. This results from national taxation schemes, which provokes pressure from the rail lobby and environmental NGOs in high VAT countries to reduce the VAT rate for long-distance rail accordingly.

Ticket taxes can be raised for all flights, including international flights, such that the tax exemption rules for kerosene and VAT will not apply and countries can set the tax rates independently. These rates can be differentiated according to the ticket category which may increase acceptance by the users (as for instance in the UK). Presently, ticket taxes are very low such that there is some potential for their increase, to use them as a surrogate for climate taxation.[7]

Against the background of the most heterogeneous systems of direct and indirect taxation – which serve a bundle of public objectives beyond climate protection – emission trading has become a favoured economic instrument. It is regarded as market conforming because the CO_2 producing agents can choose the way of reaction – either buying emission certificates or reducing emissions. This implies that economic sectors which can implement mitigation of emissions at low costs will show the highest CO_2 reductions while sectors (like aviation) for which reduction technologies are most expensive or even not existing today would have to buy emission allowances accordingly. The EU introduced the emission trading scheme (ETS) in 2005. It functions by setting caps and trading the allowances. The caps set for 2020 foresee that the sectors covered by the system will produce 21% less GHG in 2020 and 41% less GHG in 2030 compared with 2005. Thirty-one countries are included (28 EU countries plus Iceland, Liechtenstein and Norway) and around 45% of EU's GHG emissions are covered. This indicates that important emitters are not included like several industrial sectors, agriculture, the transport sector and households.

In the aviation sector the ETS applies only to flights between airports in the European Economic Area. The initial endowment was given free of charge to the carriers while they have to buy additional emission allowances. The price for a one-ton emission allowance is presently about 25 EUR (September 2019). Although it has increased within one year from a much lower level, it has little impact on the intra-European flight tariffs. Taking the emission volumes for short-distance flights of up to 1,000 km, this would increase tariffs by 2–4 EUR per flight if additional allowances were needed. For international flights, the ICAO member countries decided in 2016 to introduce a Carbon Offsetting and Reduction Scheme for International Aviation (CORSIA), which will be gradually implemented after 2021. It is the aim of this scheme to achieve carbon neutrality of the growth of international aviation after 2020. Air carriers which operate on routes included in the scheme have to compensate for the growth of GHG emissions either by investing in GHG reducing projects (worldwide) or by buying certificates which are used to finance the carbon offsetting projects. This scheme is still to be worked out in detail and could replace the ETS for aviation in the EU after 2023.

3.2 Subsidization of operation, infrastructure provision and manufacturing

3.2.1 Aviation

Although air transport is a private business in most countries of the world, it is supported by a host of state aid instruments.[8] Gössling, Fichert and Forsyth (2017) give a comprehensive overview of the variety of subsidies given to airlines, airport operators, infrastructure providers and aircraft manufacturers (see Table 10.3). The EU has set competition rules in the course of air market liberalization (ICAO, 2013) which limit the state aids for preventing the EU member states from subsidy races. Operating aids are in principle not compatible with EU competition rules. The widely practised operating aid for regional airports (with fewer than three million passengers per year) through public recovering of operating losses is allowed only for a transitional period under certain conditions (e.g. permitted public service obligations). Also, start-up aids to airlines are permitted only for a limited time period. As the airports are obliged to recover their full operating costs at the end of the transitional period, it has become more difficult to attract airlines through zero or low take-off/landing fees.

The liberalization of the air transport market in the EU after 1990 has induced a "boom" for establishing new regional airports because many regions hoped to

Table 10.3 State aids for the aviation sector

	Manufacturers		Infrastructure providers		Airlines
	Aircraft	Suppliers	Air Traffic Control	Airports	
Grants:					
Research & Development	X	X	X	X	X
Exports	X	X	X	X	X
Investments	X	X			
Loss coverage					
Equity infusions	X		X	X	X
Loans & loan guarantees	X	X		X	X
Grants to provide air transport				X	X
services to remote regions					X
Dedicated transfers to					
residents buying tickets					
Hidden subsidies:					
Reduced infrastructure fees	X			X	X
Cross-subsidisation				X	X
Monopoly rights				X	X
No or reduced taxes:					
Fuel					X
Value Added Taxes					X
Frequent flyer programs					X

Source: Gössling, Fichert and Forsyth (2017)

create new "job machines" by investing public money into this dynamic market. Most investments in regional airports were publicly financed, partly with co-financing from the EU. The European Court of Auditors (ECA, 2014) published a disillusioning assessment on the effectiveness of this financial support after auditing 20 airports. About one half of the audited airports, in particular the smaller airports, were loss making; in many cases investment undertaken was unnecessary, delayed or too costly. Traffic demand was overestimated in about 50% of the forecasts. It should be considered that this evaluation refers to a small share of the aviation market.[9]

The revised EU Guidelines on State Aid to Airports and Airlines (2014/C 99/03) try to streamline these investment activities to avoid investment in "white elephants" and to stop financial aids for non-profitable airports until 2024 unless criteria for public service obligations for connecting remote regions are fulfilled. But public aids for airport infrastructure are not only a phenomenon for small airports. The Berlin airport project, for instance, shows that the state is acting as a risk taker of last resort if an airport project is overrunning the estimated costs by orders of magnitude.[10] Little information is available from airport investment costs and their recovery in the Emirates (Abu Dhabi, Dubai) or in Turkey (Istanbul New Airport). The Partnership for Open & Fair Skies (2015) reports massive state investments in airports to subsidize national air carriers.

Aircraft development and manufacturing are co-financed by the state as well. For instance, in the US, Boeing benefits from military projects and their spin-offs to civil aviation; while in the EU, Airbus Industries receives development aids. In the case of the Airbus A 380 project, these financial aids amounted to 6.5 billion EUR, partly given as low-interest loans, to be repaid from sales revenues. After the decision to stop the A 380 manufacturing, Airbus Industries argued that the loans can be regarded as public risk capital such that repayment is not necessary. Without entering into this labyrinth of legal, half-legal or illegal subsidies (the World Trade Organization (WTO) has estimated that the illegal subsidies given to Airbus Industries between 1989 and 2006 amount to 18 billion USD while Boeing had received 5.3 billion USD illegally in the same time period),[11] one can conclude that the state aids given to manufacturers for development and production of aircraft are influencing intra- and intermodal competition in a relevant order of magnitude.

Other hidden subsidies beyond tax exemptions, which in particular influence competition between HSR and low-cost carriers (LCC) on shorter air distances, stem from unfair social conditions for pilots, cabin and ground personnel. Ryanair has applied special labour contracts which include self-employment of pilots and other neglections of corporate social responsibility. This has raised conflicts with labour unions and led to the inclusion of the problem of social conditions in aviation, road freight and maritime transport on the agenda of future EC policy (see European Commission, 2016; European Parliament, 2015).

3.2.2 Railways

The railway sector has a long tradition of public subsidization since the state took over the governance in many countries by the end of the 19th century after spectacular bankruptcies of private railway companies and increasing importance for military purposes. While the predominant aim in the first phase was to consolidate and coordinate the heterogeneous networks and services, the subsidization in a second phase (between the world wars) was motivated by the protection of railway operators against upcoming (private) road competition. In the past decades, the protection of the environment and the fight against climate change has developed the predominant motivation for subsidizing the railways. In the case of HSR, subsidies for operation and services do not play a major role,[12] and there is also no open subsidization of technology development (except for new MAGLEV technologies which don't play a role in the market until now).[13] Basic research is supported by national R&D policy (railway research institutes) and EU framework research programs (like Shift2Rail in the EU Horizon 2020 program). The manufacturers of HSR rolling stock do not enjoy direct financial support (except of noise protection technology), while it is hard to estimate the extent to which the national rolling stock and control technology suppliers are benefitting from technological protectionism of the states.

The main public HSR subsidization is dedicated to rail infrastructure provision and maintenance. The first HSR investments in Japan and Europe were commercially sound projects and could recover the invested capital costs. The following HSR projects needed public co-financing, which is revealed by public-private partnership (PPP) constructions. For instance, the French Tours–Bordeaux HSR link opened in 2017, and it receives direct public co-financing of 38% and a co-funding of the public infrastructure company of 12%. This 8 billion EUR project presently serves as a prototype for public-private partnership for HSR investments with a total public share of 50%. Other large projects show much higher needs for public money as, for instance, the German link Stuttgart–Ulm which includes complex regional and urban components ("Stuttgart 21" presently estimated to exceed a cost of 10 billion EUR – twice as much as the estimation of 2010). The development of the Spanish HSR network gives an outstanding example for a national strategy to use HSR for enhancing regional equity and environmental quality at the price of huge commercial losses. This case will be discussed further in Section 5.

The European Commission (2010) has published a brochure on high-speed Europe which foresees a tripling of the HSR network length from 10,000 km to 30,750 km in 2030. The Transeuropean Network plans of 2013 have taken up this issue and assigned high priority to HSR investments through the definition of a core network and core network corridors (CNC) to be finalized until 2030. The total investment volume for CNC has been estimated at 623 billion EUR (Schade et al., 2015, 2018), of which about two thirds are planned for rail improvements (infrastructure, control system ERMTS). Roughly estimating that more than half of the rail budget will be used for providing the key performance parameters for an interoperable rail freight network and its intermodal connecting nodes, results in a remaining budget which will by far not be sufficient to implement an additional 20,000 km of HSR until 2030.[14]

The European Court of Auditors (ECA, 2018) has characterized the present EU HSR network in its special report as an ineffective patchwork. The European Commission has co-financed HSR investments between 2000 and 2017 with grants of 23.7 billion EUR, which makes 11% of the total investment of 215 billion EUR. Furthermore, 4.5 billion EUR has been invested into the control system ERMTS (used by different types of trains) and 29.7 billion EUR has been given as loans from the European Investment Bank (EIB) with special conditions. The ECA finds that the success for EU's co-funding for HSR is at risk. Some points of the disillusioning diagnosis are:

- More than 40% of the co-financed HSR projects have not achieved a benchmark of 9 million passengers per year, which indicates financial sustainability.[15]
- The costs invested per minute saved are partially extremely high. Four out of ten lines audited showed costs of more than 100 m EUR and the highest costs went up to 369 million EUR per minute saved (Stuttgart–Ulm).[16]
- High speeds of 250 km/h and more are not in any case necessary, and HSR trains often run on much lower average speeds due to frequent stops.
- There is little progress for developing the CNC, the implementation times are high (16 years on average for large projects) and the target of 30,000 km in 2030 is an illusion against the background of 9,000 km HSR in operation and 1,700 km under construction (status 2017).

The ECA (2018)[17] does not question that HSR can achieve environmental progress by diverting traffic from road and air to rail. It also supports major improvements of trans-border links to generate positive international cohesion effects as they have been estimated by integrated transport/economic studies (see Schade et al., 2015, 2018). But this requires a combination of HSR with regional development strategies and coordinated long-term planning with strict monitoring, linking EU support to strategic priority projects, harmonizing the legal processes for permitting cross-border projects and major organizational changes to provide seamless connections between HSR, conventional rail and regional public transit.

3.2.3 Modal comparison of subsidization

One can conclude from this discussion that both modes, rail and air transport, are heavily subsidized, while rail is supported in a much higher dimension because of the more expensive infrastructure. For both modes, it is most difficult to quantify the subsidization amounts accurately, in particular if investments are widely financed publicly as is the case with railways and regional airports. Yoshino, Helble and Abidhadjaev (2018) suggest treating the state like a private investor and estimating the additional tax revenues which are created by HSR or airport investments and balance them with the invested public money. Stillman (2018) recommends emitting "tax kicker bonds" for future public tax prospects for infrastructure financing. By applying such instruments, the extent to which public financing leads to long-term net subsidization becomes more transparent – this holds for publicly financed HSR as well as for airport investments. Obviously, the quantification of such impacts requires a life-cycle analysis including wider economic impacts (see Rothengatter, 2017).

4. Potential of modal shift in long-distance transport

It is necessary to divert a substantial traffic volume from air to rail for achieving a measurable environmental advantage in a transport system. Dobruszkes, Dehon and Givoni (2014) have analysed the impact of HSR on aviation in Europe by means of an econometric ex-post analysis comprising 162 city pairs. In 31 city pairs the air service was abandoned after introducing HSR, in 131 cases air service remained. Also, for the latter city pairs an influence, could be statistically proven, which came out most strongly if the travel time for HSR was 2.5 hours and below. HSR travel time had a similar effect on offered seats and the number of flights, i.e. a structural impact on flight frequency and aircraft used could not be confirmed. Feeder/connection flights to hub airports were partially substituted by HSR which, according to the authors, might be welcomed by airlines at congested airports because capacity is freed for long-distance and inter-continental flights. Albalate and Bel (2015) have compiled worldwide examples and show that the introduction of HSR on busy corridors had a substantial impact on the modal split between rail and air (see Table 10.4).

Table 10.4 Impacts of new HSR connections on modal split on distances between 250 and 600 km (market shares in %)

OD link	Air market share before	Air market share after
Madrid–Seville (470 km)	40	13
Madrid–Malaga (513 km)	72	14
Madrid–Valencia (391 km)	61	14
Paris–Lyon (427 km)	31	7
Paris–Brussels (312 km)	7	2
Hamburg–Frankfurt (524 km)	10	4
Taipei–Kaoshsiung (345 km)	28	5
Taipei–Tainan (308 km)	14	2
Taipei–Chiayi (246 km)	4	0
Seoul–Daegu (326 km)	15	0
Seoul–Busan (442 km)	42	17

Source: Albalate and Bel (2015).

For decades the forecasting studies of consultancies and rail companies focused on travel time, which is illustrated in a brochure of UIC (2018). Also, the statistical analysis of Dobruszkes, Dehon and Givoni (2014) follows this approach and even neglects travel costs as an argument of modal decisions because of the statistical difficulties to quantify the cost inputs correctly. Indeed, there are a wide range of tariffs which are set according to optimal marketing strategies. However, the high relevance of pricing strategies is underlined by the development of low-cost carriers, which serve about one third of the EU air transport market (EU share in July 2018: 34%; see DLR, 2018). This gives rise to the assumption that the price elasticity has become increasingly important, in particular after the world economic crisis in 2008.

An empirical study of Ortega et al. (2016) for Spain, which is based on a combined revealed/stated preference analysis performed in 2014, exhibits a quantitative indication of the preference changes. The coefficients for travel time/cost are −0.005/−0.021, i.e. the cost factor appears to be four-times more important than the time factor. Although this result has to be interpreted with care against the background of the economic downturn in Spain after the world economic crisis, one should not expect that the increasing weight of costs versus time is only a temporary phenomenon.[18] Table 10.5 exhibits the direct and cross elasticities with respect to costs for rail, coach, car and air.

Table 10.5 underlines the strong asymmetry of user reactions. A 1% increase of air tariffs will lead to a 1.54% decrease of air and a 0.1% increase of rail transport demand (only). In other words, a 1% decrease of rail tariffs would shift much more traffic from air to rail compared with a 1% increase of air tariffs (e.g., induced by an internalization of external costs of aviation). This supports the hypothesis that improving on railway productivity for offering the rail service at lower prices can be more successful compared with achieving moderate time savings by costly HSR investments.

The success of low-cost carriers has motivated some rail companies to reconsider their pricing strategies. In France, the OUIGO low-cost HSR service has been introduced by SNCF in April 2013 on the route from the Paris region (Marne-la-Vallée) through Lyon (airport) to Montpellier/Marseille (see Delaplace and Dobruszkes, 2015). Although the salary conditions correspond to the general conditions of SNCF, there are substantial cost savings through a flexible labour management (e.g. multi-tasking, variable working days) but are

Table 10.5 Direct and cross cost elasticities for HSR services in Spain

Cost	Train	Coach	Car	Air
Train	−0.583	0.608	0.632	0.692
Coach	0.205	−0.662	0.406	0.424
Car	0.047	0.088	−0.480	0.102
Air	0.097	0.169	0.197	−1.537

Source: Ortega et al. (2016).

still far from achieving the labour cost savings level of low-cost air carriers. The trains provide more seats (634 vs. 510 of a double-deck TGV), which can be doubled by coupling two trains, and offer less service (single class, no bar, no luggage rack). The trains pay lower rail track charges compared with the usual TGV because they do not use the Paris central terminals. They perform more runs per day because of reduced service times at both ends. The train occupancy is slightly higher compared with the usual TGV; figures for 2014 indicate a load factor to 80% but, it has to be noted, there is a no-show rate when people buy several low-tariff tickets while not using all of them. The fare structure varies between 10 and 85 EUR, depending on age, day and time of reservation. E-ticketing is obligatory. No lounge, vending machines or WiFi are offered, and the check-in-time is 30 minutes before departure. With these changes, SNCF aims at saving about 50% of the variable costs compared with traditional TGV service such that the tariffs on routes with competition by low-cost air carriers are substantially lower.[19]

In Spain, the railway undertaking RENFE has introduced a new pricing scheme in February 2013. This pricing scheme is similar to that of air carriers. It sets prices depending on the hour of the day, the category of user, the expected demand and the time of booking (see Ortega et al., 2016). The tariffs were reduced by about 11% on average. For promotional tickets the discounts are up to 70%. As a result, the average occupancy rate of HSR went up from 66% to 74%. Long-distance travel profited in particular, such as Madrid–Barcelona (621 km, +16%) and Barcelona–Seville (1,121 km, +88%, starting from a low basis). On long distances, the main part of diverted traffic came from air transport (in the case of Madrid–Barcelona, 14 out of 16%). On the busiest link between Madrid and Barcelona, the general observation is confirmed that HSR will become the dominant market player in long-distance travel as soon as the travel time is lower than three hours. Presently the travel time with AVE (the Spanish HSR) is 2.5 hours and the overall modal share (including all alternatives like air, bus, car) is more than 50%. But there are also examples for successful HSR connections which take about four hours, as for instance the ICE connection Munich–Berlin for sprinter trains (regular trains: 4 hours, 25 minutes). The modal split figures for rail/car/air changed from (23/29/48)% to (46/24/30)%, i.e., rail could double its market share one year after opening in December 2017.

One can conclude from these examples that HSR can become the predominant transportation mode on distances between 300 and 800 km, dependent on speed, frequency of service and tariffs offered. In exceptional cases the critical distance for competition can be even higher if very high speeds are offered (e.g. Beijing–Shanghai). Low-cost and flexible tariff strategies like in France and Spain have reinforced the modal shift. However, the positive examples are found for connections between large cities and densely populated corridors. Less densely populated areas in between HSR stations or with poor accessibility to the HSR network enjoy little benefits or may suffer even from backwash effects. The Spanish transport investment strategy is trying to avoid such negative regional impacts by constructing a high-density HSR network. This strategy will be discussed in the following section.

5. HSR network expansion: limits to growth

5.1 Planned HSR network in Spain

Spain has developed the second largest HSR network in the world (3,200 km in 2018) after China (25,000 km). The Spanish PEIT infrastructure plan of 2005 foresees an investment expenditure for HSR in an order of magnitude of 83.5 billion EUR until 2020. The planned length of the HSR network is more than 5,000 km. The main motivation behind this policy is regional equity and environmental sustainability. It is presumed that HSR is environmentally friendlier than air and road transport and that HSR brings new prospects for regional development. Every region in Spain should be connected to the capital Madrid within 4 hours. Ninety per cent of Spanish inhabitants should reach the next HSR station within a distance of 50 km. These political goals imply constructing an HSR network with the highest density in the world in terms of km/capita and km/km². Due to the lower population the average passenger-km per km on Spanish HSR links is one fifth of the French and one ninth of the Japanese figures (see Albalate and Bel, 2015), which will go down further in the future with the planned extension of the network.

The HSR investments in Spain have been substantially supported by EU co-funding for three reasons: First of all, Spain was defined a "cohesion country" (like Ireland, Portugal and Greece and the "accession countries" after 2004) and enjoyed dedicated funding to link this peripheral country better to the EU central area. Secondly, Spain had a wide-gauge rail system which could be widely changed to the standard gauge corresponding to the interoperability goal for EU infrastructure systems. Thirdly, the Commission had developed plans to develop a 30,000 km HSR network in Europe until 2030, and the Spanish government was willing to join this initiative. Against this political background, Spain received 47.3% of the total EU HSR grants between 2000 and 2017 (altogether 23.7 billion EUR). While the average co-funding rate for HSR investments in the EU was about 11%, Spain received the top rate of 26%.

Only the first HSR investments in Spain (Madrid–Seville; Madrid–Barcelona) were economically viable (although not recovering the full investment costs). The European Court of Auditors (ECA, 2018) mentions several Spanish HSR links which show traffic volumes far below the critical benchmark of 9 million passengers per year. Also, the analyses of Zembri and Libourel (2017), Albalate and Bel (2015, 2017) and Beria et al. (2018) conclude that the HSR plans in Spain are oversized from the economic point of view.

In this context the border crossings need special attention because their improvement is a major goal of EU transport policy. The core network corridors (CNC) of Transeuropean Networks are defined in a way that they connect at least three countries. Examples are CNC corridors linking Spain with France and Portugal through the Mediterranean and the Atlantic corridors. Provision of both corridor connections with HSR would by far not fulfil the ECA criterion for an economically viable passenger volume in the medium term (see Doll, Rothengatter and Schade, 2015). But they are regarded necessary to overcome the border resistances between Portugal, Spain and France and to meet the connectivity goal for European corridors.

These examples illustrate the dilemma with border crossing HSR links: The rail traffic volume is presently much too low to economically justify HSR investments. Therefore, a high rate of EU and national co-financing is needed, hoping that removed bottlenecks at border crossings, combined with massive regional development aids, will induce long-run benefits alongside the European core network corridors. It remains to be shown that a sufficient potential for long-run benefits can arise with some probability, which would imply an analysis of long-term wider economic impacts (see Section 5.3).

5.2 Other examples for risks of over-investment in HSR

Spain has been taken as an example because the dominance of regional development and environmental quality goals over economic viability are politically transparent and obvious regarding the performance statistics. Similar observations hold for other parts of the planned EU HSR network, as for instance:

*   Rail Baltica, an HSR connection between Warsaw and Tallinn (870 km), eventually to be extended by a tunnel to Helsinki (50 km). While the benefits for freight transport appear reasonable (resulting in the plan to operate 2–3 freight trains per hour) it is questionable whether the high-speed design (250 km/h) for passenger transport is economically justified (four trains per day planned between Tallinn and Warsaw; HSR travel time 6 hours, 47 minutes). Estimated costs without tunnel, 5.8 billion EUR; with tunnel, 15–19 billion EUR).
*   Lyon–Turin, a 270 km trans-alpine link including a 57 km base tunnel, decided by a treaty between Italy and France, designed for HSR and conventional freight trains, heavily criticized because of high costs (estimated 8 billion EUR for the tunnel, 25 billion EUR for the total project) and overestimation of future transport volumes.
*   Stuttgart–Munich giving an example for huge cost overruns (meanwhile approaching 13 billion EUR), while the connected corridor Munich–Verona gives an example for patchwork investments, with a fast implementation of the Brenner Base tunnel (estimated 10 billion EUR) while the access links from the German and the Italian side are partly undecided and partly planned to be realized after 2040.
*   Various parallel investments, e.g. alongside the Baltic–Adriatic, Mediterranean, Rhine Danube or Orient–East Mediterranean corridors. In particular in South-East Europe, the CNC plan of the European Commission

(2019) foresees a high density of the HSR network, although the forecasted patronage is low (see the transport and market chapters of the CNC studies).[20]

The examples just presented demonstrate that a number of HSR projects are not guided by an economically rational calculus. National or regional prestige motives and the hope for high co-financing by the European Commission can influence the propagation of over-dimensioned projects and parallel investments. Therefore, it seems necessary to adjust the HSR development plans to the financial constraints by strictly streamlining the CNC plans and setting priorities right.

5.3 Checks for sustainability of airport and HSR investments

From the scientific point of view, several improvements of planning and evaluation are appropriate to avoid investment failures for airport and HSR projects in the future:

*   Integrated network-based planning.
*   Life-cycle analysis including wider economic impacts.
*   Opportunity cost calculus.

5.3.1 Integrated planning and assessment

In most cases the planning of airports and HSR projects is project-based, assuming that there is little interdependency with other projects. This project-based approach – assessed by cost-benefit analysis – should be substituted by the planning and assessment of network configurations. This would reveal the interdependencies among projects, avoid parallel investments and help in determining the optimal design of projects. A second characteristic of integrated planning is the consideration of the close interdependency between transport, economy, environment and social systems. The European Commission has launched several projects for integrated assessment, as for instance TransTools, HighTool, ASTRA (System Dynamics) or Trimode.

Integrated assessment would extend the narrow cost-benefit analysis (CBA), which has in the past fostered the risk of a patchwork-type HSR investment strategy because the individual projects were assumed to be independent of each other. A further caveat generated by conventional CBA consists in inducing adverse incentives for the stakeholders. If moderate assumptions are used, then it is easy for project opponents to bring forward the argument of missing economic profitability, and it will be hard even for promising projects to leap the parliamentary hurdles. Therefore, project promoters often prefer to press consultancies (charged for feasibility studies) to apply very optimistic assumptions for forecasting and evaluation for ending up with CBA figures passing the thresholds set for positive decisions.

5.3.2 Life-cycle analysis including wider economic impacts

Large transportation projects have a long life and develop their synergistic effects with other facilities after decades. Therefore, integrated assessment has to be combined with a life-cycle analysis for the whole lifetime of a project – and not for 30 years only, as it is assumed in many project applications as well as in the example calculations of the CBA guide of the European Commission (2014a). A life-cycle analysis also makes transparent the major maintenance and re-investment needs of a project. In particular publicly financed projects often abstract from future follow-up costs of an investment decision while the latter may be partly considered in PPP contracts if the contractor has to return the project to the public after the end of the concession period in good condition.

Life-cycle analysis also offers the option to include the long-term interdependencies between transport and the economy into the assessment calculus. Wider economic impacts which are not considered in conventional CBA are, for instance, technological spillovers (changing productivity of sectors, creating new market opportunities, knowledge transfer), multiplier/accelerator effects in underemployed economies or the exploitation of regional potential through (international) connectivity effects, combined with regional structural policy.

On the financial side, life-cycle analysis prepares a base for monitoring the financial flows stemming from a project. This concerns on the one hand the long-term follow-up costs (in particular for maintenance and re-investment) of an investment decision and the associated financial obligations. On the other hand, it allows the estimation of the long-term returns of investment for the public in terms of additional future tax revenues. If the long-term wider economic impacts are estimated, it is then possible to derive the direct and indirect taxes (according to the national taxation systems) which can be expected by the state. This approach can generate a quantitative figure of the long-term net subsidization (see Yoshino, Helble and Abidhadjaev, 2018).

5.3.3 Opportunity calculus

It has been shown in Section 5.1 and 5.2 that HSR investments are not always motivated by economic efficiency goals. But the question remains as to what extent better regional accessibility and contribution to GHG savings can justify financial losses from HSR or airport investment. The answer to this question can be given by an explicit opportunity calculus comparing alternative network configurations. For instance, instead of providing a dense HSR network, the combination of a coarsely meshed HSR backbone network with conventional long-distance and regional transit networks, offering synchronized connections between major cities and sub-centres in their catchment areas, may provide similar regional and environmental benefits at much lower investment costs.

An integrated life-cycle assessment of alternative plans would be needed for identifying the best configuration. In this context aviation and airports can be considered as constitutive components of an integrated transport service concept. In particular, regional airports can play a role in remote or low-density regions because the environmental impacts of constructing airports are comparatively low and the service can be adjusted to the users' needs, while HSR would cause high irreversible investment costs and yield only low environmental benefits in such regions.

Applying an opportunity calculus using integrated life-cycle assessment methods (as they are, for instance, described in Rothengatter, 2017, 2019) goes beyond the standard approaches of feasibility studies and requires a higher input of scientific expertise. But it helps in avoiding the application of arbitrarily set benchmarks as for instance the weakly based 9 million passengers/year criterion for economic HSR viability, which the ECA (2018) has used.

6. Conclusions

Ex-ante and ex-post studies show that HSR has an impact on aviation. On origin-destination connections between large metropolitan areas, it can lead to a massive diversion of travellers towards rail transport. In a number of cases, air transport has been completely abandoned after starting HSR operation. However, such effects concentrate on main corridors and on the major cities supplied with HSR stations, if travel times don't largely exceed total flight travel times. For such relationships, substantial environmental advantages and positive economic agglomeration impacts can be identified.

But good HSR connections between major agglomerations may lead to backwash effects for regions in between agglomerations or in remote areas (see Vickerman, 2015). The Spanish HSR development concept tries to avoid such undesired impacts with a high-density HSR network. It is driven by the political goals of regional equity and environmental sustainability while the goal of economic viability is less important. This raises the general question as to what extent improvements of equity and environmental quality can compensate for economic deficits.

The analysis of this chapter raises doubts that HSR is an appropriate instrument to improve regional equity and environmental sustainability if the expected passenger volumes remain comparatively low. The paper advocates the application of an opportunity calculus, comparing alternative multi-modal network configurations by means of integrated life-cycle assessment, to find out the best investment strategy for fostering the sustainability goals. Combining a lean HSR network with well-connected conventional intercity service and regional transit systems may deliver the same regional and environmental benefits at lower investment costs. The provision of regional airport infrastructure can also be integrated into such a concept, connecting less densely populated regions which cannot be linked to HSR at reasonable costs.

Notes

1 The widely applied "Ramsey formula" for calculating the rate of social discount r is $r=\gamma+\mu g$, where γ represents the rate of time preference of the present generation ("rate of rapacity"), μ the marginal elasticity of utility for consumption and g the growth rate

of future consumption. Stern argued that γ should be set close to zero for ethical reasons and chose $\gamma=0.1$ while g is set around 1.3% and $\mu=1$.

2 The estimation of about 85 USD per tonne of CO_2 in the *Stern Review* (2007) is one of the highest values coming out of neo-classical approaches.

3 The influence of other pollutant emissions on radiation is considered by equivalence factors.

4 This implies that the operational CO_2 advantage (factor 10) is reduced to about 8.5 if the infrastructure provision is included in the comparison.

5 This would correspond to about 1.5 million passengers/year, which appears very low.

6 VAT could be introduced on the domestic feeder flights for international flights. This option is not applied to avoid a distortion of competition between airports.

7 This is sharply opposed by the airline industry. See IATA (2016).

8 See European Commission (2014c) which refers to the relevant articles of the Treaty of Functioning of the European Union (TFEU).

9 Small airports with fewer than 1 million passengers/year serve 4% of the air passenger volume (medium sized with 1–5 million passengers) serve 18%, and main hub airports 78%.

10 Estimated costs at the beginning of construction work 2006: 2 billion EUR. Estimation 2019: 7.3 billion EUR.

11 Both parties question this ruling of WTO. See Gössling, Fichert and Forsyth (2017).

12 In the EU the variable infrastructure costs are financed by rail track charging.

13 The public support for the Chinese HSR industry is not reported, in particular after the merger of rail manufacturers in 2015 to establish the CRRC (China Railway Rolling Stock Corporation).

14 If the average infrastructure costs are estimated at 25 million EUR/km, the HSR extension would require 500 billion EUR.

15 The ECA (2018, p. 46) mentions only one scientific literature source from 2007 to support this benchmark. This indicates that such a general figure has to be interpreted with care. Other sources, e.g. Albalate and Bel (2015), mention lower benchmarks of about 6 million passengers/year.

16 The protagonists of this project will argue that the ECA has assigned the total costs to HSR while the project includes substantial improvements to regional and urban transport.

17 "High-speed is a beneficial mode of transport which contributes to the EU's sustainable mobility objectives" (ECA, 2018, p. 19).

18 It should also be considered that the sample of questioned users was rather small (220 interviews).

19 As the OUIGO stations are located at the periphery of Paris or Lyon, additional costs for feeder service may occur. In the case of Lyon, they can be higher than the special OUIGO rate.

20 Available on the web page of the EU Commission.

References

Albalate, D. and Bel, G. (2015). *La experiencia internacional en alta velocidad ferrovia.* Documento de Trabajo. 2015–02. Universitat de Barcelona.

Albalate, D. and Bel, G., eds. (2017). *Evaluating high-speed rail. Interdisciplinary perspectives.* London and New York: Routledge.

Baumol, W.J. and Oates, W.E. (1988). *The theory of environmental policy.* 2nd ed. Cambridge, MA: Cambridge University Press.

Baumol, W.J., Oates, W.E. and Blackman, S.A. (1979). *Economics, environmental policy, and the quality of life.* Englewood Cliffs: Prentice Hall.

Beria, P., Grimaldi, R., Albalate, D. and Bel, G. (2018). Delusions of success: Costs and demand of high-speed rail in Italy and Spain. *Transport Policy,* 68, pp. 63–79.

Costanza, R. (1991). *Ecological economics.* New York: Columbia University Press.

Delaplace, M. and Dobruszkes, F. (2015). From low-cost airlines to low-cost high-speed rail? The French case. *Transport Policy,* 38, pp. 73–85.

DLR. (2018). *Low cost monitor 2/2018*. Cologne.

Dobruszkes, F., Dehon, C. and Givoni, M. (2014). Does European high-speed rail affect the current level of air services? An EU-wide analysis. *Transportation Research Part A*, 69, pp. 451–475.

Doll, C., Rothengatter, W. and Schade, W. (2015). *Results and efficiency of railway infrastructure financing within the EU*. Study on behalf of the European Parliament's Committee on Budgetary Affairs. Karlsruhe.

ECA – European Court of Auditors. (2014). *Special report. EU-funded airport infrastructures: Poor value for money*. Brussels.

ECA – European Court of Auditors. (2018). *Special report. A European high-speed rail network: Not a reality but an ineffective patchwork*. Brussels.

European Commission. (2010). *High speed Europe. A sustainable link between cities*. Brussels.

European Commission. (2014a). *Guide to cost-benefit analysis of investment projects*. Brussels.

European Commission. (2014b). *Handbook on external costs of transport*. Prepared by Ricardo et al., Brussels.

European Commission. (2014c). *Guidelines on state aids to airports and airlines* (2014/C 99/03). Brussels.

European Commission. (2016). *Commission staff working document the implementation of the 2011 white paper on transport "Roadmap to a single European transport area – towards a competitive and resource-efficient transport system" five years after its publication: Achievements and challenges*. SWD (2016) 226 final, Brussels.

European Commission. (2018). *EU transport in figures*. Brussels: Statistical Pocketbook.

European Commission. (2019). *Corridor studies*. [Online] Available at: https://ec.europa.eu/transport/themes/infrastructure/ten-t-guidelines/corridors/corridor-studies [Accessed 30 Nov. 2019].

European Parliament. (2015). *European parliament resolution of 9 September 2015 on the implementation of the 2011 white paper on transport: Taking stock and the way forward towards sustainable mobility* (2015/2005(INI)).

Gössling, S., Fichert, F. and Forsyth, P. (2017). Subsidies in aviation. *Sustainability*, 9(1295), pp. 1–19.

Hayashi, Y., et al. (2014). Importance of intercity passenger transport for climate change issues. In: Y. Hayashi, S. Morichi, T.H. Oum and W. Rothengatter, eds., *Intercity transport and climate change*. New York: Springer, pp. 1–30.

IATA – International Air Transport Association. (2016). *Airline taxation is taxing economies*. [Online] Available at: https://airlines.iata.org/analysis/airline-taxation-is-taxing-economies [Accessed 30 Nov. 2019].

ICAO – International Civil Aviation Organization. (2013). *EU competition rules*. Document ATConf/46-IP/4.

IFEU Institute. (2016). *Der persönliche CO_2 Fussabdruck*. [Online] Available at: https://www.ifeu.de/projekt/der-persoenliche-co2-fussabdruck/ [Accessed 30 Nov. 2019].

IFEU Institute. (2019). *TREMOD*. [Online] Available at: https://www.ifeu.de/methoden/modelle/tremod/ [Accessed 30 Nov. 2019].

IPCC – Intergovernmental Panel on Climate Change. (2015). *5th synthesis report 2014*. Geneva.

IPCC – Intergovernmental Panel on Climate Change. (2018). *Special report. Global warming of 1.5°C*. Geneva.

Kaufman, N. (2019). *Leading economists offer 5 carbon tax recommendations: 3 1/2 are basic principles of economics*. [Online] Available at: https://energypolicy.columbia.edu/research/commentary/leading-economists-offer-5-carbon-tax-recommendations-3-12-are-basic-principles-economics [Accessed 30 Nov. 2019].

Musso, A. and Rothengatter, W. (2013). Internalization of external costs of transport – a target driven approach with a focus on climate change. *Transport Policy*, 29, pp. 303–314.

Nordhaus, W.D. (2007). *The "Stern Review" on the economics of climate change*. NBER Working Paper Series No w/12741, New Haven.

Ortega, A.A., Guzman, V., Felipe, A., Preston, J. and Vasallo-Magro, J.M. (2016). Price elasticity of demand on the high-speed rail lines of Spain: Impact of the new pricing scheme. *Transportation Research Record*, 2597, pp. 90–98.

Partnership for Open & Fair Skies. (2015). *Massive Subsidies are distorting the international aviation market*. [Online] Available at: http://www.openandfairskies.com/wp-content/themes/custom/media/White.Paper.pdf [Accessed 30 Nov. 2019].

Rothengatter, W. (2017). Wider economic impacts of transport infrastructure. Relevant or negligible? *Transport Policy*, 59, pp. 124–133.

Rothengatter, W. (2019). Megaprojects in transportation networks. *Transport Policy*, 75, pp. A1–A15.

Schade, W., Krail, M., Hartwig, J., Walther, C., Sutter, D., Killer, M., Maibach, M., Gomez-Sanchez, J. and Hitscherich, K. (2015). *Cost of non-completion of the TEN-T*. On behalf of the EU Commission, Karlsruhe.

Schade, W., Maffii, S., Hartwig, J., de Stasio, C., Fermi, F., Martino, A., Welter, S. and Zani, L. (2018). *The impact of TEN-T completion on growth, jobs and the environment – methodology and results*. Final Report. Part I. On behalf of the EU Commission, Karlsruhe and Milan.

Stern, N. (2007). *Stern Review: The economics of climate change*. Cambridge: Cambridge University Press.

Stillman, G.B. (2018). Introducing the tax-KickerBond for infrastructure. In: N. Yoshino, M. Helble and U. Abidhadjaev, eds., *Financing infrastructure in Asia and the Pacific. Capturing impacts and new sources*. Tokyo: Asian Development Bank Institute, pp. 453–471.

UIC – Union Internationale des Chemins de fer. (2018). *High speed rail. Fast track to sustainable mobility*. Brussels.

Vickerman, R. (2015). Highspeed rail and regional development: The case of intermediate stations. *Journal of Transport Geography*, 42, pp. 157–165.

Yoshino, N., Helble, M. and Abidhadjaev, U., eds. (2018). *Financing infrastructure in Asia and the Pacific. Capturing impacts and new sources*. Tokyo: Asian Development Bank Institute.

Zembri, P. and Libourel, E. (2017). Towards oversized high-speed rail systems? Some lessons from France and Spain. *Transportation Research Procedia*, 25, pp. 368–385.

11 Scenarios for future policies – potential costs and competitive impacts of different market-based measures for the limitation of all climate relevant species from aviation

Janina D. Scheelhaase, Katrin Dahlmann, Martin Jung, Hermann Keimel, Hendrik Nieße, Robert Sausen, Martin Schaefer and Florian Wolters

1. Introduction

Climate relevant emissions from air transport are CO_2, H_2O, NO_x, SO_x, soot, contrails and triggered contrail cirrus (see for instance Sausen et al., 2005). Lee et al. (2010) have estimated that the full climate impact of air transport on global radiative forcing was 4.9% in 2005 with CO_2 alone contributing about 1.6%. While aviation's CO_2 emissions have been regulated in the European Union, New Zealand, South Korea and other countries in the last years and will be addressed by the global offsetting scheme CORSIA from 2020 onwards, this is not the case for air transport's non-CO_2 emissions. As the air transport sector is expected to grow in the medium and long term, addressing the full climate impact of this sector is necessary from an environmental point of view.

Against this background, the German Aerospace Center (DLR) analysed how the full climate impact of aviation could be regulated by market-based measures and which environmental and economic impacts would be associated with these policies. This analysis has been conducted in the interdisciplinary research project AviClim (Including *Avi*ation in International Protocols for *Clim*ate Protection). To our knowledge, this project is the first of its kind investigating market-based measures for limiting the full climate impact of air transport. For an in-depth literature review and discussion, see Scheelhaase et al. (2014) and Scheelhaase et al. (2016). AviClim has been funded by the German Federal Ministry of Research.

This chapter presents selected economic results of AviClim. It is organized as follows: Section 2 provides an overview of AviClim's methodological approach. In Section 3, selected results for the costs and competitive impacts are presented and discussed. In Section 4, recommendations are given.

2. AviClim methodological approach

Climate relevant species addressed within AviClim are CO_2, NO_x, H_2O and contrails. In this research project, three market-based measures have been investigated alternatively:

- a climate tax;
- an open emission trading scheme for regulating all climate relevant emissions from aviation;
- a NO_x emission charge combined with an open CO_2 trading scheme and operational measures (50% of flights operated between 30 and 60°N and on an altitude between 9 and 12 km will be flying 2000 ft lower to avoid contrails).

For the selection of these market-based measures, both the findings of environmental economics and institutional economics theory as well as the relevant recent developments on the international level (UNFCCC, ICAO, EU) have been taken into account.

Since the possible introduction of market-based measures for the limitation of aviation's climate relevant emissions has been a controversial issue on the international level for the last decade, different geopolitical scenarios have been designed within AviClim. These scenarios differ concerning the level of international support for the climate protecting measure under consideration. In this way, they take the global dimension of the issue and the challenges associated with the international negotiations on climate change into account. Based on the political discussions on the EU, ICAO and UNFCCC levels in the last years, three scenarios seem worthwhile to consider in this chapter:

- The first geopolitical scenario assumes that the political measure under consideration will be implemented by the member states of the European Union (EU27) plus Norway, Iceland and Liechtenstein, but not by the rest of the world. This scenario is called "Greater EU".
- A second scenario which presumes that the US, Canada, South Korea, Japan, Singapore, Russia, Australia, India, China, Brazil and the United Arab Emirates will introduce this political measure in addition to the "Greater EU" states (EU27, Norway, Iceland, Liechtenstein and Switzerland). This way, the major players and emitters in international aviation will be addressed. Accordingly, this scenario is called "Great Aviation Countries".
- Finally, the scenario "World" is assuming a worldwide implementation of the climate protecting measure under consideration.

As a reference development, a business-as-usual scenario has been developed. In this scenario, the absence of climate protecting measures in aviation, other than those implemented until 2010, is assumed. For all scenarios investigated, an autonomous fuel efficiency improvement of 1.4% p.a. has been assumed.

The selected market-based measures have been combined with the three geopolitical reduction scenarios. The comparison of the environmental and economic impacts of these different market-based measures and geopolitical scenarios allows for conclusions on the environmental, economic and competitive impacts of the political measures under consideration.

The cost, demand and competition impacts of these political measures as well as the impacts on employment have been estimated by employing economic simulation models. The environmental and climate effects have been investigated by DLR-developed metrics and models; see Schaefer (2012) and Dahlmann (2012) for details.

Both long-lived CO_2 and short-lived non-CO_2 species, such as NO_x, H_2O or contrails and associated cirrus, contribute to aviation's full climate impact. The latter depend on flight altitude, geographical location, day time, weather and other factors (e.g. Fichter et al., 2005; Mannstein, Spichtinger and Gierens, 2005; Fichter, 2009; Frömming et al., 2012). Since the lifetimes of non-CO_2 species differ and their climate impact depends to a great extent on the location of emission, the climate impact induced by aviation's non-CO_2 species is not proportional to the CO_2 emissions. Against this background, the application of a suitable metric is important for the appropriate translation of the non-CO_2 effects into equivalent CO_2. According to Dahlmann (2012), the so-called "Average Temperature Response" (atr) is an adequate metric for the comparison of aviation's non-CO_2 effects with each other and with CO_2 and the translation of the non-CO_2 effects into equivalent CO_2. Within AviClim, time horizons for the metric atr of 20 and 50 years (atr 20 and atr 50) are investigated. This means the mean changes in near surface temperature averaged over 20 and 50 years, respectively, are taken into account. In this chapter, we concentrate on the effects calculated for the metric atr 50.

Within AviClim, three different price development paths for CO_2 and CO_2 equivalents have been assumed alternatively:

- a "High Price Path" where prices per tonne CO_2 equivalent range from 10 USD in the year 2010 up to 80 USD in the year 2030,
- a "Low Price Path" where a price development of 10 USD per tonne CO_2 equivalent (2010) to 30 USD per tonne in 2030 has been assumed and
- a 'Mixed Price Path' which combines low CO_2 equivalent prices for both trading schemes under investigation and high CO_2 equivalent prices for the climate tax and the NO_x charge. This way, the probable advantages of emission trading models which become evident in lower prices for emission permits (as compared to taxes and charges) can be shown more explicitly.

The costs for the market-based measures will increase the production costs of the airlines under the regulatory scheme. Under the simplifying assumption that the airlines will act as profit maximizers, they will try to pass through the full costs of complying with the regulation scheme. Accordingly, prices for air services will increase. How will demand react? As it is difficult to predict this demand reaction (see for instance Oum, Waters and Yong, 1990, 1992; Lu, 2009), different price elasticities of demand have been assumed alternatively. The corresponding demand reactions range from a perfectly inelastic reaction (quantitative demand for air services remains unchanged as compared to the business-as-usual development); a moderate demand reduction (quantitative demand reduction is under-proportionate to the price increase); and a highly elastic reaction (quantitative demand reduction is disproportionate to the price increase by the airlines).

If demand reacts by a quantitative reduction, airlines' revenues will be affected negatively. As a next step, the airlines are expected to change their flight plan (supply side effect). Implicitly, equality of supply and demand has been assumed here. This is plausible after a certain time. These developments will affect employment and air traffic in the timeframe analysed. In case air traffic will decrease as compared to the business-as-usual development, less fuel will be used. This will lead to less climate relevant emissions and a reduced climate impact from aviation.

3. Selected economic results

The following section provides an overview of AviClim's selected results on the costs and competition impacts of the market-based measures climate tax and emission trading for all climate relevant species. Here, modelling results for the geopolitical scenarios "Greater EU", "Great Aviation Countries" and "World" combined with the "High Price Path" as well as the "Low Price Path" and the metric atr 50 are presented. This selection of market-based measures and scenarios allows for most meaningful results in terms of cost and competitive impacts. Scheelhaase et al. (2014) presents and discusses AviClim's economic and environmental results in full.

In the next section, at first, cost impacts for the aviation sector under the respective market-based measure are presented. This is followed by an analysis of the cost and competition impacts on the airlines' level.

3.1 Costs for the aviation sector under the market-based measure

Under the assumption that the airlines' potential to abate climate relevant emissions by technological measures will be already tapped in the business-as-usual scenario, which is reasonable to believe as fuel costs are an important driver today, the costs for the market-based measures will increase the production costs of the airline sector, as mentioned earlier. AviClim results show that total costs for the airline sector depend to a great extent on the market-based measure, the geopolitical reduction scenario and the CO_2 equivalent prices assumed. The following figures provide an overview of the costs modelled for the airlines under the respective market-based measure and geopolitical scenario.

As Figures 11.1, 11.2 and 11.3 show, total costs for complying with the respective market-based measure increase within the timeframe analysed. This

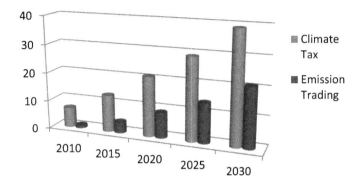

Figure 11.1 Cost impacts in the scenario "Greater EU", in USD million, Low Price Path. AviClim modelling results. In 2012 prices. Results for the metric atr 50.

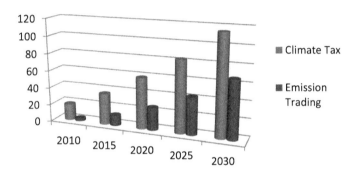

Figure 11.2 Cost impacts in the scenario "Great Aviation Countries", in USD million, Low Price Path. AviClim modelling results. In 2012 prices. Results for the metric atr 50.

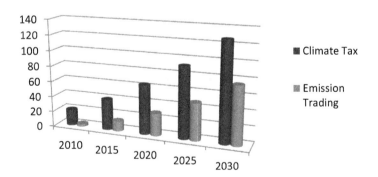

Figure 11.3 Cost impacts in the scenario "World", in USD million, High Price Path. AviClim modelling results. In 2012 prices. Results for the metric atr 50.

development can be explained by the expected air traffic growth in 2010–2030. This leads to rising climate relevant emissions and increasing costs for the climate tax and the emission trading scheme.

With regard to the geopolitical reduction scenario investigated, total costs are the highest for the scenario "World", as expected. As a maximum, total costs of about 339 USD million can be expected in the year 2030 (climate tax, High Price Path). Costs calculated for the "Great Aviation Countries" are almost at the level of the results for the "World" scenario. This is because the delta between both reduction schemes is less than 10 per cent of the global flights. In contrast, costs estimated for the airlines under the "Greater EU" scenario are comparably low. Here costs ranging from 1 USD billion (emission trading, Low Price Path) in the year 2010 to 105 USD billion (climate tax, High Price Path) in the year 2030 have been modelled. Overall, these differences in costs are caused by the number and the emission characteristics of the flights under the respective geopolitical reduction scenario.

An analysis of the market-based measure assumed reveals that the emission trading scheme for all climate relevant species causes significantly lower costs than the climate tax. This is the case for all geopolitical scenarios and price paths investigated. The differences in costs are the highest in the beginning of the time period under investigation and diminish partly until 2030. In the "Greater EU" scenario, for example, total costs for the emission trading scheme amount up to 1 USD billion in 2010 while costs for the climate tax are expected to be about 7 USD billion in that year (High Price Path). In the year 2030, however, total costs for complying with the emission trading scheme are expected to be about 57 USD billion and total costs for the climate tax are estimated at 105 USD billion (High Price Path). These differences between the market-based measures can be explained by their fundamental discrepancies in the modes of functioning: while the climate tax charges from the first unit of CO_2 equivalent, under an emission trading scheme 85 per cent of 2010's emissions are free of charge because for this amount, emission permits are allocated for free. This rate of permits issued free of charge to the airlines under the scheme is due to AviClim's assumptions for the emission trading scheme analysed. Consequently, at the beginning of the timeframe under consideration, a relatively small number of permits has to be purchased additionally. This leads to smaller costs as compared to the climate tax. In the course of time the number of required permits rises as air traffic is expected to grow. As a result costs for complying with the emission trading scheme for the airline sector increase until 2030 but stay on a lower level than the costs for the climate tax. Overall, AviClim modelling results indicate that a global emission trading scheme limiting aviation's full climate impact would be advantageous to minimise airlines' costs as compared to a climate tax.

At the same time, environmental benefits from the emissions trading scheme are significant: For the scenario "World", for instance, a reduction in temperature change of up to about 70 per cent in the year 2100 has been estimated as compared to a business-as-usual development. See Scheelhaase et al. (2014) for full environmental results.

3.2 Costs and competitive impacts for airline groups under the market-based measure

3.2.1 Airline groups investigated

As total costs probably will be distributed differently within the airline sector, competitive distortions may be caused by the climate protecting measures. To investigate these questions, different airline groups were created in respect to the country of origin and the business model of the airlines under consideration.

1   Geopolitical Scenario "Greater EU":

*   Top 10 "Greater EU" Full Service Network Carrier (FSNC);
*   Top 10 Non-"Greater EU" Full Service Network Carrier (FSNC);
*   Top 10 "Greater EU" Low-Cost Carrier (LCC)/Holiday Carrier.

2   Geopolitical Scenario "Great Aviation Countries":

*   Top 10 "Great Aviation Countries" Full Service Network Carrier (FSNC);
*   Top 10 Non-"Great Aviation Countries" Full Service Network Carrier (FSNC);
*   Top 10 "Great Aviation Countries" Low-Cost Carrier (LCC)/Holiday Carrier.

3   Geopolitical Scenario "World":

*   Top 10 "World" Full Service Network Carrier (FSNC);
*   Top 10 "World" Low-Cost Carrier (LCC)/Holiday Carrier.

This grouping was conducted for two reasons: Firstly, an analysis on individual companies' level would be associated with too many uncertainties. This is because airline's management strategies and market developments play an important role on this level, which are difficult to foresee for external parties. Secondly, an investigation of the total of some 250 airlines listed in the global flight schedule OAG (Official Airline Guide, 2011 ff.) would be too time-consuming and would probably not lead to very meaningful results as the assignment of the individual airlines to the different airline business models will be questionable in a number of cases.

Regional carriers have been excluded from this analysis because in most cases, these airlines can be characterized as being not very important in terms of ASK (available seat kilometres) offered, RTK (revenue tonne kilometres) operated as well as revenues realized and distances operated as compared to the rest of the sector. Also, regional carriers operate their flights mostly within national or close continental boundaries. Against this background, distinctive results cannot be expected for these groups of airlines.

Tables 11.1, 11.2 and 11.3 provide an overview of the assignment of individual airlines to the respective airline groups explained here, differentiated by

Table 11.1 Geopolitical reduction scenario "Greater EU": airline groups investigated

Top 10 "Greater EU" – Full Service Network Carrier	Top 10 Non- "Greater EU" – Full Service Network Carrier	Top 10 "Greater EU" – Low Cost Carrier/Holiday Carrier
Lufthansa, Air France, British Airways, KLM, Iberia, Virgin Atlantic Airways, Alitalia, TAP Portugal, Scandinavian Airlines (SAS) and Finnair.	Delta Air Lines, American Airlines, United Airlines, Emirates, Continental Airlines, China Southern Airlines, Qantas, Cathay Pacific, US Airways and Air China.	Ryanair, easyjet, Air Berlin, Thomson Airways, Thomas Cook Airways (UK), Condor Flugdienst, Air Europa, TUIfly, Monarch Airlines and Aer Lingus.

Source: Own compilation on the basis of Airline Business (2011). Airline assignment on the basis of the country of origin and main business model used. Only airlines with flights under the reduction scheme are taken into account.

Table 11.2 Geopolitical reduction scenario "Great Aviation Countries": airline groups investigated

Top 10 "Great Aviation Countries" – Full Service Network Carrier	Top 10 Non- "Great Aviation Countries" – Full Service Network Carrier	Top 10 "Great Aviation Countries" – Low Cost Carrier/Holiday Carrier
Delta Air Lines, American Airlines, United Airlines, Emirates, Lufthansa, Continental Airlines, Air France, China Southern Airlines, British Airways and Qantas.	Thai Airways International, Qatar Airways, Turkish Airlines (THY), Malaysia Airlines, Saudi Arabian Airlines, LAN Airlines, China Airlines, Air New Zealand, South African Airways and Garuda Indonesia Airways.	Southwest Airlines, Ryanair, easyjet, JetBlue Airways (US), Air Berlin, Thomson Airways, AirTran Airways, GOL Linhas Aereas Inteligentes, Thomas Cook Airlines (UK) and WestJet Airlines (Canada).

Source: Own compilation on the basis of Airline Business (2011). Airline assignment on the basis of the country of origin and main business model used. Only airlines with flights under the reduction scheme are taken into account.

Table 11.3 Geopolitical reduction scenario "World": airline groups investigated

Top 10 "World" – Full Service Network Carrier	Top 10 "World" – Low Cost Carrier/Holiday Carrier
Delta Air Lines, American Airlines, United Airlines, Emirates, Lufthansa, Continental Airlines, Air France, China Southern Airlines, British Airways and Qantas.	Southwest Airlines, Ryanair, easyjet, JetBlue Airways (US), Air Berlin, Thomson Airways, AirTran Airways, GOL Linhas Aereas Inteligentes, Thomas Cook Airlines (UK) and WestJet Airlines (Canada).

Source: Own compilation on the basis of Airline Business (2011). Airline assignment on the basis main business model used.

geopolitical reduction scenario. This assignment has been conducted on the bases of empirical passenger data (RPK) for the year 2010 (Airline Business, 2011). This base year had to be chosen because all models used within AviClim base upon this year. In this respect, the ranking of the different Top 10 airlines' groups is not up to date anymore in some cases. And some of the airlines listed in the following table do not exist as individual companies anymore today. For instance, Continental Airlines and United Airlines merged in 2010–2011 and the brand "Continental" has been abandoned since. On the other hand, an in-depth analysis of the rankings 2009–2013 reveals that the changes in ranking predominantly rest upon position changes within the "Top 10 groups" or company mergers. Against this background the respective Top 10 airlines groups can be characterized as being relatively stable in the timeframe 2009–2013.

Not surprisingly, the Top 10 groups of the FSNC as well as the LCC/ Holiday carrier in the scenarios "Great Aviation Countries" and "World" are identical in ranking and composition, as the last two tables illustrate. An in-depth analyses and comparison of the competitive impacts for the airlines groups under both reduction scenarios is still worthwhile to conduct, because in the "World" scenario all global flights are subject to the respective market-based measure, whereas in the scenario "Great Aviation Countries" only the flights to, from and within these countries are under the respective reduction instrument.

3.2.2 Methodological approach for modelling the cost impacts of the market-based measures under consideration

The modelling of the cost impacts of the climate tax and the emission trading scheme for all climate relevant species from aviation has been conducted as follows. First, the revenue tonne kilometres (RTK) of the years 2010–2030 under the respective geopolitical reduction scenario have been calculated for the individual airlines. According to AviClim's main assumptions, all flights to, from and within the countries participating in the geopolitical scenario are subject to the market-based measure under consideration. Second, the corresponding climate relevant emissions (in tonnes CO_2, NO_x, H_2O, contrails) for these flights have been estimated.

The costs for the climate tax have then been modelled by weighing the climate relevant emissions under the reduction scenario on the airlines' level with the specific metric for CO_2, NO_x, H_2O, contrails, respectively. The metric atr_{50} translates the climate impact of the non-CO_2 species into equivalent CO_2. This metric varies with the flight position p (see the equation that follows) and the climate relevant species. This way, the different climate relevant species can be directly compared with each other and the total amount added up in tonnes CO_2 equivalent. As a next step, the total amount of CO_2 equivalent subject to the reduction measure has been multiplied by the assumed price per tonne CO_2 equivalent, differentiated by the three price scenarios and years explained previously.

These modelling steps can be conducted by using the following formula

$$climate\,tax = price * \sum_{p \in Flight} CO_{2_{(p)}} + NO_{x_{(p)}} * atr_{50_{(p)}}^{(NO_x)} + H_2O_{(p)} * atr_{50_{(p)}}^{(H_2O)}$$
$$+ dist_{(c)} * atr_{50_{(p)}}^{(Cont)}.$$

Where: $NO_{x(p)}$ is the amount of NO_x emitted on the different flight altitudes, degrees of longitudes and latitudes (identical with flight position p) at different points in time. The climate relevant species H_2O, CO_2 and contrails are differentiated by the flight position p as well, because these species diversify with the local atmospheric conditions and the actual thrust-setting of the engines. Since the climate impact of CO_2 does not depend on the altitude of emission, it is not necessary to take the flight altitude ($atr_{CO2,p}$) into account for this climate relevant species.

The climate tax has been calculated for all flights and airlines under the respective reduction scenario on a flight-by-flight-basis. The summation of the individual airlines' costs for the Top 10 airline groups analysed equates to their total costs for the climate tax.

The costs for complying with the emission trading scheme have been calculated within three consecutive steps. The starting point was the estimation of the emissions cap for the respective geopolitical reduction scenario. Within AviClim the emissions cap has been set at 2010 levels. This means that aviation's emissions are limited to the amount of CO_2 equivalent emitted in the year 2010. This cap has been calculated in tonnes of CO_2 equivalent applying the methodology explained earlier. For all emissions exceeding this cap, permits have to be purchased by the airlines. Since the aviation sector is expected to grow in the timeframe 2010–2030, aviation will be a net buyer on the emission permits market. Furthermore a free allocation of 85% of 2010 emissions has been assumed; this assumption has been inspired by the free allocation rule in the EU ETS. The remaining 15% of permits have to be auctioned by the airlines. Applying these rules, the amount of climate relevant species under the emission trading scheme and the amount of emissions exceeding the cap can be calculated. For the latter, emission permits have to be purchased. The number of permits allocated free of charge to the individual airlines will be determined by a so-called benchmark, which has also been inspired by the related regulations in the EU ETS for aviation. But within AviClim, we decided to abstain from introducing the numerous exceptions within the EU ETS and to keep the benchmark rules relatively simple. The benchmark applied within AviClim stays constant throughout the whole timeframe analysed, the same as the EU ETS. But it differs between the geopolitical scenarios because the absolute amount of CO_2 equivalent emitted as well as the RTK subject to the reduction schemes vary.

The method of calculating the benchmark for aviation has been described in literature; for instance, see Scheelhaase, Grimme and Schaefer (2010) for details. In short, the total amount of CO_2 equivalent of the base year (AviClim: 2010) is weighed with the share of emission permits allocated for free (AviClim: 85%). The result will then be calculated as a ratio of the total RTK for 2010. This benchmark in turn will be multiplied by the absolute number of RTK submitted by the airline for 2010 to calculate the individual number of permits allocated free of charge. This way, very environmentally efficient airlines will get a higher number of emission permits for free, while relatively inefficient aircraft operators will receive a smaller number of permits per RTK. Thus, early movers in terms of efficiency will be rewarded for their past steps.

The benchmark applied within AviClim can be regarded as a measurement for the environmental efficiency of the flights under the reduction scheme. In the geopolitical "Greater EU" scenario the benchmark is 2.817 tonnes CO_2 equivalent/1,000 RTK, in the scenario "Great Aviation Countries" it is 2.940 tonnes CO_2 equivalent/1,000 RTK and in the scenario "World" it is 2.952 tonnes CO_2 equivalent/1,000 RTK. Here, the existing differences in the environmental efficiency of flights and airlines already show. Apparently the flights to, from and within the countries of the "Greater EU" scenario in 2010 are a little more environmentally efficient than the other flights analysed here. Whether this can be explained by the environmental efficiency of the airlines or the specific characteristics of the flights under the regulation scheme will be investigated in the following.

The cost impact of the emission trading scheme on the individual airlines can be calculated by subtracting the number of permits allocated free of charge from the absolute amount of CO_2 equivalent emitted. The delta is the number of permits which has to be purchased on the emission permits market. This delta will be multiplied with the assumed price for CO_2 equivalent. The costs for complying with the emission trading scheme on the level of individual airlines result. The summation of the costs of the respective Top 10 groups equates to their total costs for this market-based measure.

3.2.3 Results for different airline groups

Tables 11.4 and 11.5 provide an overview of the costs calculated for the different airline groups, market-based measures, geopolitical reduction scenarios and price paths explained earlier.

Tables 11.4 and 11.5 show that both the absolute cost impact and the specific costs implied by the climate protecting measure differ quite clearly from each other with regard to the geopolitical reduction scenarios analyzed. In absolute numbers the highest cost impact can be expected for airlines based in one of the countries supporting the respective climate protecting measure. The climate tax, for instance, will lead to additional costs for the Top 10 FSNC from a "Greater EU" country of about 15.53 USD billion in the year 2030 (Low Price Scenario). Their competitors from outside the "Greater EU" countries will have to bear additional costs of about 6.23 USD billion in the same year and scenario. This discrepancy is caused by the fact that the predominant number

Table 11.4 Absolute costs for the climate tax and the emission trading scheme for different airline groups, in USD million

Scenario/Group of Airlines	Low Price Path					High Price Path				
Emission Trading all species	2010	2015	2020	2025	2030	2010	2015	2020	2025	2030
Top 10 "Greater EU" Network Carrier	399	1696	3677	6513	8753	399	2827	7354	15631	23342
Top 10 Non-"Greater EU" Network Carrier	152	669	1451	2378	3647	152	1116	2902	5707	9727
Top 10 "Greater EU" LCC/Holiday Carrier	141	487	1001	1526	2193	141	811	2002	3662	5849
Top 10 "Great Aviation Countries" Network Carrier	1040	3363	7753	12835	19600	1040	5605	15506	30803	52267
Top 10 Non-"Great Aviation Countries" Network Carrier	155	816	1862	3143	4777	155	1360	3723	7544	12739
Top 10 "Great Aviation Countries" LCC/Holiday Carrier	242	819	1631	2481	3578	242	1365	3261	5955	9540
Top 10 "World" Network Carrier	982	4158	8892	14342	21533	982	6930	17784	34420	57420
Top 10 "World" LCC/Holiday Carrier	249	843	1680	2145	3693	249	1406	3360	4487	9847

Scenario/Group of Airlines	Low Price Path					High Price Path				
Climate Tax	2010	2015	2020	2025	2030	2010	2015	2020	2025	2030
Top 10 "Greater EU" Network Carrier	2658	5085	8195	12160	15530	2658	8474	16390	29184	41414
Top 10 Non-"Greater EU" Network Carrier	1013	1960	3173	4530	6230	1013	3267	6345	10871	16612
Top 10 "Greater EU" LCC/Holiday Carrier	938	1682	2595	3518	4584	938	2804	5190	8444	12224
Top 10 "Great Aviation Countries" Network Carrier	6934	12204	19541	27569	37282	6934	20340	39082	66167	99419
Top 10 Non-"Great Aviation Countries" Network Carrier	1036	2137	3622	5344	7418	1036	3561	7245	12826	19782
Top 10 "Great Aviation Countries" LCC/Holiday Carrier	1613	2875	4372	5908	7690	1613	4792	8745	14180	20507
Top 10 "World" Network Carrier	6546	10683	20020	28252	38225	6546	17805	40040	67804	101933
Top 10 "World" LCC/Holiday Carrier	1661	2962	4504	5160	7929	1661	4936	9008	10896	21145

Source: AviClim modelling results. In 2012 prices. Results for metric atr 50.

Table 11.5 Specific costs for the climate tax and the emission trading scheme for different airline groups, in USD/RTK

Scenario/Group of Airlines	Low Price Path					High Price Path				
Emission Trading All species	2010	2015	2020	2025	2030	2010	2015	2020	2025	2030
Top 10 "Greater EU" Network Carrier	0.005	0.016	0.028	0.041	0.045	0.005	0.027	0.056	0.098	0.120
Top 10 Non-"Greater EU" Network Carrier	0.005	0.017	0.029	0.037	0.046	0.005	0.028	0.057	0.090	0.122
Top 10 "Greater EU" LCC/Holiday Carrier	0.005	0.015	0.026	0.034	0.042	0.005	0.026	0.052	0.081	0.111
Top 10 "Great Aviation Countries" Network Carrier	0.006	0.015	0.027	0.038	0.045	0.006	0.024	0.053	0.091	0.119
Top 10 Non-"Great Aviation Countries" Network Carrier	0.005	0.018	0.032	0.042	0.050	0.005	0.030	0.063	0.100	0.134
Top 10 "Great Aviation Countries" LCC/Holiday Carrier	0.006	0.017	0.028	0.036	0.045	0.006	0.028	0.056	0.087	0.120
Top 10 "World" Network Carrier	0.005	0.018	0.030	0.040	0.049	0.005	0.030	0.061	0.096	0.130
Top 10 "World" LCC/Holiday Carrier	0.006	0.017	0.029	0.032	0.046	0.006	0.029	0.057	0.066	0.122
Average	0.005	0.017	0.029	0.037	0.046	0.005	0.028	0.057	0.089	0.122

Scenario/Group of Airlines	Low Price Path					High Price Path				
Climate Tax	2010	2015	2020	2025	2030	2010	2015	2020	2025	2030
Top 10 "Greater EU" Network Carrier	0.032	0.049	0.063	0.077	0.080	0.032	0.081	0.126	0.184	0.213
Top 10 Non-"Greater EU" Network Carrier	0.033	0.049	0.061	0.071	0.078	0.033	0.082	0.125	0.171	0.209
Top 10 "Greater EU" LCC/Holiday Carrier	0.036	0.053	0.068	0.078	0.087	0.036	0.088	0.136	0.187	0.232
Top 10 "Great Aviation Countries" Network Carrier	0.039	0.053	0.067	0.081	0.085	0.039	0.088	0.134	0.196	0.226
Top 10 Non-"Great Aviation Countries" Network Carrier	0.030	0.047	0.061	0.071	0.078	0.030	0.078	0.123	0.171	0.208
Top 10 "Great Aviation Countries" LCC/Holiday Carrier	0.041	0.059	0.075	0.086	0.096	0.041	0.098	0.150	0.207	0.257
Top 10 "World" Network Carrier	0.036	0.046	0.068	0.078	0.086	0.036	0.076	0.137	0.188	0.230
Top 10 "World" LCC/Holiday Carrier	0.042	0.061	0.077	0.076	0.098	0.042	0.101	0.154	0.160	0.262
Average	0.036	0.052	0.068	0.077	0.086	0.036	0.087	0.136	0.183	0.230

Source: AviClim modelling results. In 2012 prices. Results for metric atr 50.

of flights operated under this geopolitical reduction scenario is performed by airlines based in one of the "Greater EU" countries, while flights from their competitors from outside the "Greater EU" – with very few exceptions – are operated only to and from Europe. For instance, in this geopolitical scenario, about 90% of Lufthansa's RTKs will be operated under the climate protecting measure, while United Airlines only has to comply with the climate protecting measure under consideration for 18% of its RTKs operated. This leads to the conclusion that a competitive disadvantage can be expected for those aircraft operators whose country of origin is supporting the respective climate protecting measure and which operate flights to and from other world regions.

An analysis of the specific costs (USD/RTK) shows a heterogeneous picture: On the one hand, the specific costs implied by the market-based measures are lower for some airlines based in a "Greater EU" or a "Great Aviation Country", as compared to their competitors from outside the respective geopolitical regulation scheme. This is especially true for the costs caused by the emission trading scheme for the years 2015–2030. On the other hand, for the climate tax a partly opposing trend can be noticed. For instance, the specific costs for the Top 10 FSNC based in one of the "Great Aviation Countries" will increase by 0.085 USD per RTK due to the climate tax in the year 2030, while the specific costs for the Top 10 FSNC from outside this group of countries rise by only 0.078 USD/RTK.

Apart from the absolute and specific costs, the average specific emissions, i.e. tonnes CO_2 equivalent per 1,000 RTK, are a decisive factor for the airlines' financial burden implied by the market-based measure under consideration. Also, the free allocation of emission permits in relation to the required number of permits on the airlines' level is an essential variable for the costs caused by the emission trading model. Table 11.6 presents the specific emissions und their development in the timeframe investigated. Furthermore, the table shows the development of the percentage of free allocation of emission permits in relation to the required number of permits for the different airline groups investigated.

As illustrated by Table 11.6, the specific climate relevant emissions are expected to decrease within the timeframe 2010–2030. This is the case for all groups of airlines investigated: On average the specific climate relevant emissions will decrease from 3.65 tonnes CO_2 equivalent per 1,000 RTK in the year 2010 to about 2.93 tonnes CO_2 equivalent/1,000 RTK in 2030. Here the influence of autonomous technological efficiency gains on the environmental performance of the aviation sector shows.

Not surprisingly, a comparison of the specific climate relevant emissions of the different groups of airlines reveals wide differences. Especially those groups of carriers operating very fuel efficiently (LCC and Holiday carrier) have significantly higher specific climate relevant emissions than other groups of airlines at the beginning of the timeframe analyzed. The Top 10 LCC/Holiday carrier based in one of the "Greater EU" countries, for instance, emitted about 3.63 tonnes CO_2 equivalent per 1,000 RTK in 2010, while the Top 10 FSNC from one of the "Greater EU" countries caused about 3.42 tonnes CO_2

Table 11.6 Development of the specific emissions (tonnes CO_2 equivalent/1,000 RTK) and of the free allocation of emission permits in relation to the required number of permits (in per cent) in the timeframe 2010–2030

Scenario/Group of Airlines	Specific emissions (t CO_2 equivalent/1000 RTK)					Percentage of free allocation of emission permits					
	2010	2015	2020	2025	2030	2010	2015	2020	2025	2030
Top 10 "Greater EU" Network Carrier	3.42	3.44	3.33	3.15	2.83	85%	67%	56%	49%	45%
Top 10 Non-"Greater EU" Network Carrier	3.30	3.25	3.14	2.91	2.69	85%	64%	52%	46%	40%
Top 10 "Greater EU" LCC/Holiday Carrier	3.63	3.55	3.39	3.12	2.88	85%	71%	62%	57%	53%
Top 10 "Great Aviation Countries" Network Carrier	3.74	3.52	3.38	3.11	2.86	85%	69%	58%	51%	46%
Top 10 Non-"Great Aviation Countries" Network Carrier	3.26	3.30	3.22	2.97	2.73	85%	63%	50%	43%	37%
Top 10 "Great Aviation Countries" LCC/Holiday Carrier	4.07	3.94	3.77	3.47	3.26	85%	71%	63%	58%	54%
Top 10 "World" Network Carrier	3.62	3.59	3.45	3.17	2.92	85%	66%	55%	49%	43%
Top 10 "World" LCC/Holiday Carrier	4.18	4.05	3.87	3.62	3.30	85%	71%	63%	58%	54%
Average	3.65	3.58	3.44	3.19	2.93	85%	68%	57%	51%	47%

Source: AviClim modelling results. In 2012 prices. Results for the metric atr 50.

equivalent per 1,000 RTK. These differences can be explained by the techno-logically given "trade-off" between fuel (and thus CO_2) optimization of air-craft engines on the one hand, and a NO_X (and other climate relevant species) optimization of these engines on the other. Today's engines can technologically be optimized in only one or the other way. By a step-wise introduction of innovative engine technology which allows for the reduction of both CO_2 and non-CO_2 emissions at the same time in the timeframe analyzed, the differences between the specific emissions of the LCC/Holiday carriers and the other airline groups investigated diminish. In 2030, for instance, the Top 10 FSNC based in one of the "Greater EU" countries are expected to emit about 2.83 tonnes CO_2 equivalent per 1,000 RTK, and the Top 10 LCC/Holiday car-rier from one of the "Greater EU" countries will cause circa 2.88 tonnes CO_2 equivalent/1,000 RTK.

The percentage of free allocation in relation to the required number of allowances is also an important factor, as mentioned previously. This is because this percentage determines the number of permits airlines have to purchase for maintaining their operations. In 2010, this percentage is 85 per cent regardless of the business model of the airlines and the geopolitical scenario assumed, due to AviClim's main assumptions for the emission trading scheme. Since the num-ber of permits allocated for free stays constant in the timeframe 2010–2030 and the climate relevant emissions caused rise in this period, the number of emis-sion permits required by the airlines increases. Correspondingly, the percentage of free allocation in relation to the required number of permits decreases. On average, this percentage decreases from 85 per cent in 2010 to about 46.8 per cent in 2030. In other words: in 2030, the airline sector has to purchase emis-sion permits for more than half of its climate relevant emissions.

An analysis by airline business model reveals some distinctive differences: From 2015 onwards, the Top 10 LCC/Holiday carrier groups have the high-est percentage of free allocation in relation to the required permits, as compared to both Top 10 groups of FSNC in the respective scenario. This is the case in all geopolitical reduction scenarios investigated. Further remarkable is that FSNC based in a country supporting the market-based measure will always receive a higher percentage of free allocation of emission permits as compared to the competing FSNC based outside the geopolitical reduction scenario. In 2020, FSNC from one of the "Great Aviation Countries" will receive free emission permits for about 57.7 per cent of their climate relevant emissions in that year, for instance. In contrast, their competitors based outside the "Great Aviation Countries" will get a free allocation of emission permits of only about 50.4 per cent in 2020.

Two main reasons explain these findings. Firstly, there are the growth rates of air traffic in the timeframe analyzed. In the medium term these growth rates differ clearly depending on the world region: The European and North American air traffic markets are expected to be relatively mature. In contrast, for the Asian market noticeable growth is forecasted (Airbus, 2013). Accord-ingly, the absolute amount of climate relevant emissions will develop unevenly in the future, depending on the world region. As the airlines serve these world regions differently, this will influence their share of free emission permits in relation to the number of required permits.

Secondly, the specific climate relevant emissions (tons CO_2 equivalent/1,000 RTK), i.e. the emission characteristics of the flights under the emission trading scheme, play an important role. The smaller the specific climate relevant emissions of the flights, the better for the free allocation rate of permits. AviClim modelling results show that especially on long-haul flights, the ratio tonnes CO_2 equivalent/flight kilometre is relatively disadvantageous as compared to short- and medium-haul flights. This is mainly because NO_x emitted on high altitudes (i.e. cruise levels) may have an increased climate effectiveness (Lee et al., 2009, 2010). Consequently, short- and medium-haul flights of LCC/Holiday carriers operated within the geographical boundaries of the respective geopolitical scenario are treated in favour because of their rather short flight length. The same applies to short- and medium-haul flights by FSNC as well as their feeder and de-feeder flights if these flights are operated within the geographical boundaries of the respective scenario.

According to these findings, the rate of free allocation of emission permits will be lower for FSNC from outside the geopolitical reduction scenario as compared to their competitors based in a country supporting the emission trading scheme. Remarkably, this can be interpreted as a competitive disadvantage for airlines whose country of origin does not support climate protecting measures in aviation actively. Whether or not this presumably small competitive advantage will compensate the disadvantage caused by the absolute financial burden of the market-based measure for airlines based in a country supporting this measure remains to be seen.

4. Conclusions and recommendations

Modelling results indicate that a global emission trading scheme for limiting aviation's climate relevant emissions would be advantageous in terms of airlines' costs as compared to a climate tax. At the same time, competitive distortions can be avoided.

An analysis for different groups of airlines reveals that in absolute numbers the highest cost impact can be expected for airlines based in one of the countries supporting the respective climate protecting measure. This leads to the conclusion that a competitive disadvantage can be expected for those aircraft operators whose country of origin is supporting the respective climate protecting measure and which operate flights to and from other world regions.

An in depth-analysis of the specific emissions and the rate of free allocation of permits shows that the world regions served by the airlines under consideration as well as the length and the emission characteristics of the flights are important factors for the economic impacts of the market-based measures. Also the airline business model is a distinctive determinant for the costs and competitive effects. LCC and Holiday carriers are treated in favour by the emission trading scheme on short- and medium-haul flights. FSNC based in a country supporting the respective market-based measure will gain a competitive advantage as compared to their competitors from outside the geopolitical reduction scenario. This is because the share of free allocation of emission permits will always be lower for the latter. This is remarkable since these results for the limitation of aviation's full climate impact are contrary to the respective findings for an emission trading scheme for the limitation of CO_2 alone (see Scheelhaase, Grimme and Schaefer, 2010, for instance). Whether this presumably small competitive advantage compensates for the disadvantage caused by the absolute financial burden of the market-based measure for airlines based in a country supporting this measure remains to be seen.

Clearly, the best option would be the implementation of an emissions trading scheme as assumed in AviClim on a global level. Only by implementing such a scheme can competitive distortions be avoided and environmental benefits maximized. If a global emission trading scheme for aviation turns out to be not agreeable, the second best approach would be an implementation of an emissions trading scheme in the "Great Aviation Countries". This is because the delta between both reduction schemes is less than 10 per cent of the global flights.

References

Airbus. (2013). *Global market forecast 2013–2032*. Blagnac Cedex.

Airline Business. (2011). *Top 200 passenger operations ranked by traffic 2011*.

Dahlmann, K. (2012). *Eine Methode zur effizienten Bewertung von Maßnahmen zur Klimaoptimierung des Luftverkehrs*. Cologne: DLR-Forschungsbericht 2012–05.

Fichter, C. (2009). *Climate impact of air traffic emissions in dependency of the emission location and altitude*. Cologne: DLR-Forschungsbericht 2009–22.

Fichter, C., Marquart, S., Sausen, R. and Lee, D.S. (2005). The impact of cruise altitude on contrails and related radiative forcing. *Meteorologische Zeitschrift*, 14, pp. 563–572.

Frömming, C., Ponater, M., Dahlmann, K., Grewe, V., Lee, D.S. and Sausen, R. (2012). Aviation-induced radiative forcing and surface temperature change in dependency of the emission altitude. *Journal of Geophysical Research*, 1(D19104). doi:10.1029/2012JD018204. ISSN 0148-0227.

Lee, D.S., Fahey, D.W., Forster, P.M., Newton, P.J., Wit, R.C.N., Lim, L.L., Owen, B. and Sausen, R. (2009). Aviation and global climate change in the 21st century. *Atmospheric Environment*, 43, pp. 3520–3537.

Lee, D.S., Pitari, G., Grewe, V., Gierens, K., Penner, J.E., Petzold, A., Prather, M.J., Schumann, U., Bais, A., Berntsen, T., Iachetti, D., Lim, L.L. and Sausen, R. (2010). Transport impacts on atmosphere and climate: Aviation. *Atmospheric Environment*, 44, pp. 4678–4734.

Lu, C. (2009). The implications of environmental costs on air passenger demand for different airline business models. *Journal of Air Transport Management*, 15, pp. 158–165.

Mannstein, H., Spichtinger, P. and Gierens, K. (2005). A note on how to avoid contrail cirrus. *Transportation Research Part D*, 10, pp. 421–426.

Official Airline Guide (OAG) (2011 ff.) *MAX flight schedule database*. Luton.

Oum, T.H., Waters, W.G. and Yong, J.S. (1990). *A survey of recent estimates of price elasticities of demand for transport*. World Bank Working Papers, WPS 359, Washington, DC.

Oum,T.H.,Waters,W.G. andYong,J.S. (1992). Concepts of price elasticities of transport demand and recent empirical estimates. *Journal of Transport Economics and Policy*, 26, pp. 139–154.

Sausen, R., Isaksen, I., Grewe,V., Hauglustaine, D., Lee, D.S., Myhre, G., Köhler, M.O., Pitari, G., Schumann, U., Stordal, F. and Zerefos, C. (2005). Aviation radiative forcing in 2000: An update on IPCC (1999). *Meteorologische Zeitschrift*, 14, pp. 555–561.

Schaefer, M. (2012). *Development of a forecast model for global air traffic emissions*. Cologne: DLR Forschungsbericht 2012–08.

Scheelhaase, J., Dahlmann, K., Jung, M., Keimel, H., Murphy, M., Nieße, H., Sausen, R., Schaefer, M. and Wolters, F. (2014). *Die Einbeziehung des Luftverkehrs in internationale Klimaschutzprotokolle (AviClim)*. Cologne: Endbericht, Dec.

Scheelhaase, J., Dahlmann, K., Jung, M., Keimel, H., Nieße, H., Sausen, R., Schaefer, M. and Wolters, F. (2016). How to best address aviation's full climate impact from an economic policy point of view? Main results from AviClim research project. *Transportation Research Part D: Transport and Environment*, 45, pp. 112–125.

Scheelhaase, J., Grimme, W. and Schaefer, M. (2010). The inclusion of aviation into the EU emission trading scheme – impacts on competition between European and non-European network airlines. *Transportation Research Part D: Transport and Environment*, 15, pp. 14–25.

12 Inclusion of international aviation emissions under the Paris Agreement's Nationally Determined Contributions (NDCs)

Andrew Murphy

1. Overview

The Paris Agreement (PA), adopted by 195 countries in December 2015, commits its parties to taking action in order to limit an increase in pre-industrial temperatures to 1.5 °C/well below 2 °C. In order not to exceed these increases, all states must over time adopt economy-wide emission reductions and achieve a global net balance of anthropogenic emissions and sinks (i.e. to decarbonise) in the second half of this century. International shipping and aviation are major economic sectors and significant sources of emissions.

The most recent study of shipping emissions by the UN agency with responsibility for regulating the sector, the International Maritime Organization (IMO), found that the sector is responsible for CO_2 equalling 1,000 Mtonnes CO_2 or 3.1% of annual global CO_2 emissions (IMO, 2014). That same study forecasts that, unregulated, emissions from the sector could grow 120% by 2050 and represent 10% of total global emissions at that time. The aviation sector has a similar CO_2 profile, though with a greater projected increase in emissions due to the expected growth in passenger demand over the coming decades (ICAO, 2016). However, aviation has an additional climate impact due to the effect that its emissions have at higher altitudes. This non-CO_2 effect is estimated to result in the sector contributing to 4.9% of global warming (Lee et al., 2009).

The PA's predecessor, the Kyoto Protocol (KP), made specific reference to these emissions, requesting developed states to work though the specialised UN agencies – ICAO for aviation and IMO for shipping – to limit and reduce emissions from these sectors. At the UNFCCC COP where that Protocol was adopted, that body's Subsidiary Body for Scientific and Technological Advice (SBSTA) were encouraged to "further elaborate on the inclusion of these emissions in the overall greenhouse gas inventories of Parties" (UNFCCC, 1997). However, the PA is silent on any role for ICAO or the IMO in meeting the Paris goals while at the same time calling for economy-wide decarbonisation under Article 4.

However, there remains some uncertainty as to who is responsible to reduce these emissions. This presents a threat to the goals of the Paris Agreement, as emissions from these sectors are substantial and growing. The aviation sector in particular has an emissions impact and growth which, if not adressed, could consume one-quarter of the carbon budget under a 1.5 degree scenario (Carbon Brief, 2016).

Taking into account this overall goal, and that measures have been adopted to date by both states and through international agencies, these emissions should, where not already done so, be included in nationally determined contributions (NDCs), the pledges submitted by parties to the PA. Such an inclusion would encourage states to take action, both at the national and international ICAO and IMO levels as appropriate, to address emissions from these sectors. Including these sectors in NDCs would reduce incidents of states adopting less progressive stances at ICAO/IMO than at UNFCCC, as these states would welcome more effective climate action by these agencies in order to assist in meeting their NDC goals.

2. Paris Agreement wording on international transport emissions

The UNFCCC was adopted in 1992 and commits parties to reducing their emissions from all sectors, including transport. The convention does not distinguish between modes of transport, and where it excludes types of emissions, it does so explicitly – e.g. it excludes those emissions covered by the Montreal Protocol (Art 4(1)(a) UNFCCC).

The obligations of parties to the UNFCCC were elaborated in a number of subsequent decisions and agreements – the most notable being the PA and the KP. The PA differs from the KP in a number of key respects. The first is that it sets specific temperature targets (1.5 °C/well below 2 °C; Art 2.1) which require all sectors of the economy to rapidly decarbonise. Neither UNFCCC nor KP set such a clear objective. That the PA agreed to such a target demonstrates that climate change is now recognised as an existential threat, requiring action from all sectors. The second is that it calls for parties to undertake rapid *economy-wide* emission reductions (Art 4.4). In parallel, it foresees that developing countries should adopt such economy-wide targets over time. Finally, unlike the KP which requested that developed states work through ICAO/IMO to limit and reduce emissions, there is no such reference in the PA.

The achievement of PA temperature targets is conditional upon humanity not emitting more GHG than the remaining finite carbon budgets as advised by the 5th assessment report (IPCC, 2014). These emission limits, set in terms of carbon budgets, encompass all sectors, including international aviation and shipping. For this reason the temperature targets of the PA require all sectors of the economy to act. Aviation and shipping are clearly part of economy-wide emissions, and the PA makes no specific reference to ICAO or IMO. Since economy-wide decarbonisation is the responsibility of parties to the PA, states should make clear in their NDCs what actions they propose to take to reduce these emissions.

3. Examination of NDCs and action taken to date

A number of NDCs pledge economy-wide emission reductions, e.g. the NDCs submitted by the US, EU, Canada, South Korea and Russia, which, without a clear statement to the contrary, should be taken to include international aviation and shipping emissions. A number of other major NDCs refer to a reduction in emissions per GDP – a 'GDP carbon intensity' target. In this type of target, states commit to reducing emissions per GDP output. Such targets are included in the NDCs of China and India, among others. International aviation and shipping are part of a party's GDP and are therefore, implicitly, included in the carbon intensity NDC commitment. Excluding emissions from these sectors from NDCs would give a distorted view of a party's progress on reducing its GDP/carbon intensity.

Including these emissions in NDCs is also a recognition that a good part of the activity which can be taken to mitigate emissions from these sectors needs to be taken at a national level. The list of possible national actions is extensive and ranges from fuel taxation and other taxation – e.g. sales tax, removal of subsidies – state aid, passenger taxes, levies, emissions trading and other measures, a moratorium on airport capacity expansion, R&D, mandates for alternative fuels, and aircraft. States can also agree on a bilateral/multilateral basis to remove existing exemptions on taxing aviation fuel or ports can institute such schemes as port discounts and/or mandates for zero emission vessels (ZEVs), CO_2/air pollution charges, virtual arrival and slow steaming. Many states are already adopting such measures: for example, differentiating port charges to reward more efficient ships, or adopting transparent monitoring and reporting rules for ships, or even mandating zero emission vessels (ZEVs) for specific routes or environmentally sensitive areas. Many parties are also rationalising their airspace in order to improve operational efficiency, or putting money into researching alternative fuels and better aircraft design.

Many of the activities undertaken by states affect both domestic and international emissions. For example China's 13th Five Year Plan (2016–2020) calls for operational efficiency improvements, reduction in carbon intensity per passenger/km and the uptake of alternative fuels. If successfully implemented, such policies will impact both domestic and international emissions, and it is necessary that these emissions and the related actions are explicitly recognised and included in NDCs if there is to be an accurate accounting of progress towards the Paris goals. The United States and the EU, for example, have similar approaches to aviation, supporting alternative fuel development and modernising/rationalising airspace management systems, which if successful may reduce emissions from international aviation.

Where parties do take action, it is also both appropriate and essential that they are able to claim credit for the resulting emission reductions. Otherwise, an incentive to reduce these emissions would be removed. Conversely, excluding these emissions could see parties allow these emissions to expand uncontrolled, with no implications for their national climate efforts. Such an outcome would be inconsistent with the aims of the PA.

4. Attribution of emissions

The attribution of emissions to parties should not be confused with the differentiated responsibility of parties to take action on those emissions via NDCs. Discussion on how to attribute emissions from international aviation and shipping dates back to the first meeting of the parties to the UNFCCC in 1995. At that meeting the UNFCCC's Subsidiary Body for Scientific and Technical Advice (SBSTA) was requested to address the issue of the allocation and control of emissions from international bunker fuels and report on this work to COP 2.

The UNFCCC secretariat prepared a paper that included eight allocation options for consideration. The SBSTA meeting at COP2 in 1996 considered the eight options and agreed that five of these options should be the basis for further work.[1] The original eight are listed in Table 12.1.

Efforts to resolve the attribution issue by selecting one of these options remain ongoing and as a result there is no commonly agreed means to allocate these emissions. In the meantime, Parties to the UNFCCC were requested to report all fuel sales for international transport as a separate item in their national inventories. This can be considered as a "no allocation" method in practice.

From a climate policy perspective, however, "no allocation" cannot be considered appropriate. It permits parties to take action which expands emissions from the respective sectors, for example through agreeing trade deals or providing subsidies to aviation, without accounting for the resulting increase in emissions. And while the "No allocation" option may have been credible under

Table 12.1 Allocation options proposed by SBSTA

Options brought forward for further consideration
1) No allocation
2) Allocation of global bunker fuel sales and associated emissions to Parties in proportion to their national emissions
3) Allocation to Parties according to the country where the bunker fuel is sold.
4) Allocation to Parties according to the nationality of the transport operator, the country where the aircraft is registered, or the country of the operator
5) Allocation to Parties according to the country of destination or departure of aircraft or vessel. Alternatively the emissions related to the journey of an aircraft or vessel could be shared between the country of departure and the country of arrival

Options considered less practical
6) Allocation to Parties according to the country of destination or departure of passengers or cargo.
7) Allocation to Parties according to the country of origin of passengers or owner of cargo.
8) Allocation to the Party of all emissions generated in its national space

Source: UNFCCC (1996).

Kyoto, it provides a clear conflict with the requirement of Paris for parties to adopt "economy-wide" emission reductions and for parties to balance all anthropogenic sources and removals of emissions.

Which of the remaining four options are therefore preferable? Option 2 is "Allocation in proportional to national emissions", where the total international emissions were distributed to parties based on their total emissions – i.e. if international aviation represented 2% of total emissions, then each party would increase their emissions by 2%. As SBSTA noted, this would provide an incentive for parties to agree to action at international level, as reductions globally would reduce the total emissions of each party. However, unsaid but a corollary of this position, is that such allocation would reduce incentives for parties to take action at a national level. If a party were to, for example, rapidly expand its airport capacity, the positive emissions impact would be shared by all contracting parties.

Option 3 – allocation of emissions to where bunker fuel is sold – would be relatively easier to administer, and for aviation would generally reflect the level of aviation activity by each party. However, for shipping, where a small number of parties are responsible for a disproportionate share of bunker fuel sales, such an allocation would result in an uneven distribution of emissions. For example, the Netherlands, under a 2000 modelling of such an allocation, would be responsible for 9.1% of total global shipping emissions, over four times that of the neighbouring UK (CE Delft, 2000). An allocation method should aspire to avoid a disproportionate burden on some parties unless there is a clear policy benefit or reasoning for this.

Option 4 – allocation of emissions to nationality of the transport operator – also raises issues of fairness. Many major airlines are registered in relatively small states; for example, Ryanair has its aircraft operator certificate with Irish authorities. Such an allocation would result in emissions from flights which have no connection to Ireland or the Irish economy being allocated to that country. Importantly, there are no known legal mechanisms for Irish authorities to directly regulate that airline's emissions for flights disconnected from that economy. Emissions would be included in a party's NDC, but without an ability for that party to regulate those emissions.

Option 5 – "Allocation to Parties according to the country of destination or departure of aircraft or vessel" – presents the most favourable option for allocation of emissions. It protects the principle that actions by parties which increase or reduce emissions from these sectors will be accounted for under this allocation method.

When considering this option in 1996, SBSTA noted that this option would require sharing of information between parties, and methodologies for counting emissions would be needed. However, since this 1996 discussion, efforts to track emissions from these sectors have improved considerably. ICAO's Carbon Offsetting and Reduction Scheme for International Aviation (CORSIA) is based on a global monitoring, reporting and verification (MRV) system which, launched at the start of 2019, is intended to cover all emissions from international aviation (not just on routes covered by CORSIA). Prior to CORSIA, there was and still is the MRV provisions under the EU ETS, which cover all flights within Europe, regardless of nationality of the carrier.

The future interaction of CORSIA and EU ETS is unknown, but early implementation of CORSIA in Europe has taken place under the EU ETS Directive, providing a possibility that the two schemes, or at least their MRV provisions, will co-exist.

Similar developments have occurred in shipping, with the IMO adopting a global MRV scheme which came into force in 2018. The EU were first movers in this regard, adopting an MRV scheme for all ships calling to port at the EU, which came into force in 2015 and which the EU is now considering how to reconcile with the IMO MRV scheme.

These MRV schemes can be used as a basis to implement the fifth allocation option. A barrier, however, may be access to the relevant information. Under the ICAO CORSIA MRV scheme, airlines report their emissions to the country of AOC, though that country of AOC does not take responsibility for them (which, if they were to, would be Option 4). To ensure operationalisation of Option 5, parties would need access to the emissions data of operators AOCed elsewhere for routes departing from that party. For example, the United States would need access to the emissions data of Air France flights departing from that territory. This is provided for under the ICAO CORSIA rulebook, known as the Standards and Recommended Practices (SARPs), where access to such emissions data is made possible upon request.

Parties are therefore in a position to adopt Option 5 unilaterally, through gathering data collected under international MRV schemes or, in the case of the EU, through their existing MRV schemes. This can be considered a bottom-up approach, where parties do not wait for agreement at SBSTA level on an allocation method. However, such a bottom-up approach is consistent with the Paris Agreement, which permits parties to expand the scope and ambition of their NDCs.

Agreement at SBSTA on an allocation method would be preferable, and efforts to achieve this should be encouraged. But as the status quo of de facto "no allocation" so clearly contradicts the Paris Agreement requirement for parties to regulate all emissions, parties seeking to align their NDCs with the objectives of the Agreement should not await the consensus required to achieve agreement.

5. What role for IMO and ICAO

Acting on these emissions through NDCs may raise the question of how action taken at the international level, through ICAO and IMO, can be accounted for. As for many sectors of the economy, international cooperation plays an essential role in facilitating climate ambition. However, there should be no suggestion that joining international efforts means that a party is excluding these emissions, in this case international aviation and shipping, from their commitments, and therefore is not under an obligation to take early or additional and complementary national action.

Parties working though ICAO and IMO are at different stages in adopting targets and measures to help address these sectors' climate impact. ICAO has established a target offsetting CO_2 emissions above 2020 levels and, at its 2016 triennial assembly, requested its Council to begin work on establishing a long-term emission reduction strategy beyond 2020. In April 2018 the IMO agreed on a long-term goal of at least a 50% reduction by 2050 from 2008 levels as a start towards decarbonisation, but it is only the beginning work as discussions on actual reduction measures have yet to start in order to achieve this target. The adoption and implementation of these measures may take many more years.

Parties working through ICAO and IMO aim for the broadest possible participation in their collective action. Experience over the past 20 years shows the level of ambition for collective action at the ICAO and IMO levels will continue to remain below what is required under the Paris Agreement. While states must continue to work to boost ambition in these agencies by agreeing to more effective measures and more urgently, and in particular align the positions they adopt in ICAO/IMO with the positions adopted in UNFCCC, ultimately states will likely need to pursue additional ambition on a national, regional or bilateral basis. This ambition may be complementary or subsumed partly or wholly in whatever measures and targets are adopted by ICAO/IMO. In some areas, such as fuel taxation, ICAO has no competence and so is not in a position to adopt the measure that is widely used in other transport modes. Any move at the IMO on marine fuel taxation/levy would require all major flag and port states to agree and strictly enforce a global levy. Such a levy could be implemented only through the adoption and ratification of a new international treaty, which would take 10–15 years to put in place. Some measures, such as taxation of shore-side electricity and environmentally friendly port charges as well as investment in the development and deployment of zero emission fuels/propulsion technologies, is even outside the remits of the IMO.

6. Level of ambition resulting from inclusion in NDCs

Inclusion of these sectors within NDCs does not prejudge or imply a level of ambition in terms of emission reductions. The Paris Agreement provides parties with the right to determine the level of ambition of their NDCs overall, and the level of ambition applied to each sector within the NDCs. The only requirement is that they do not reduce a level of ambition once adopted – the "no backsliding" provision of Article 3.

Inclusion does not prescribe a level of ambition. However, its purpose is to ensure that parties examine all sectors of their economy and, on the basis of evaluating the cost and efficiencies of reducing emissions from specific sectors, makes a determination as to the level of ambition required economy-wide and for different sectors. There is also the issue of linkages between different sectors – for example, efforts to electrify or use alternative fuels to reduce emissions from shipping and aviation will have implications for efforts to reduce emissions from other sectors by, for example, diverting renewable electricity or increasing demand for crop-based biofuels. Adopting economy-wide NDCs covering all sectors therefore allows for a more thorough analysis of the impact of reducing emissions from each sector.

7. Conclusion and recommendations

Excluding international aviation and shipping from national and regional efforts, sectors which if they were states would both be top ten emitters, risks fatally undermining the objective of the Paris Agreement. It is therefore appropriate that they are included by parties in their NDCs. This would reduce incidents of states not aligning their UNFCCC positions with their ICAO/IMO positions, and inclusion would therefore boost ambition in these agencies. The absence of a commonly agreed method for allocating emissions is not a barrier to states taking action, including committing to do so in their NDCs. States should adopt national measures and targets, additional to measures and targets agreed at ICAO/IMO, to address emissions from these sectors.

Note

1 For the remaining three options, that meeting added that they were "considered to be less practical because of data requirements or inadequate global coverage".

References

Carbon Brief. (2016). *Analysis: Aviation could consume a quarter of 1.5C carbon budget by 2050.*
CE Delft. (2000). *National allocation of international aviation and marine CO₂ emissions.* Delft.
ICAO – International Civil Aviation Organisation. (2016). *Environment report.* Montreal.
IMO – International Maritime Organisation. (2014). *Third greenhouse gas study.*
IPCC – Intergovernmental Panel on Climate Change. (2015). *5th synthesis report 2014.* Geneva.
Lee, D.S., Fahey, D.W., Forster, P.M., Newton, P.J., Wit, R.C.N., Lim, L.L., Owen, B. and Sausen, R. (2009). Aviation and global climate change in the 21st century. *Atmospheric Environment*, 43(22–23), pp. 3520–3537. doi:10.1016/j.atmosenv.2009.04.024.
UNFCCC. (1997). *COP 3, decision 2.*
United Nations Framework Convention on Climate Change. (1996). *Communication from parties included in annex I to the convention: Guidelines, schedule and process for consideration: Addendum: Detailed information on electricity trade and international bunker fuels.*

13 Review and further directions

Peter Forsyth

1. Introduction[1]

The objective of this book has been to analyse the economics of policies directed towards lessening the harmful effects of air transport on climate change. It is recognised that air transport has a significant and growing impact on carbon and other emissions, and that under business as usual, it will be responsible for a growing share of emissions. Several policies have been suggested, and in some cases implemented, which are directed towards lessening emissions. These policies have several aspects – technological, legal and economic. The primary purpose of this volume is to analyse the economic aspects of such policies. In doing this it is useful to outline the mitigation problem in broader terms, taking note of the technological aspects of the policies, and putting them into the overall policy perspective.

It makes good sense to begin with some technological background. This is done in the first two chapters. The chapter by Grewe discusses the way air transport affects climate change. Carbon emissions are clearly important, but air transport's total effect is significantly greater than just these. The way in which air transport adds to other emissions and effects is outlined briefly. A second technical chapter is that by Roth, which focuses on renewable fuels for aviation. In the medium to longer term, air transport will need to make much more, and in time exclusive, use of renewable or synthetic fuels unless offsets and carbon sequestration can be used extensively. At this stage, there are many ideas and there is much experimentation, but there will need to be extensive research and development before these fuels become widespread.

The chapter by Fichert, Forsyth and Niemeier is intended to provide an analytical background to several of the major policies which have been suggested, and in some cases implemented, for air transport. These include emission trading schemes (ETSs), the Carbon Offsetting and Reduction Scheme for International Aviation (CORSIA) and voluntary offsets, and this chapter provides an introduction to policies which are discussed in more detail in other chapters, along with a discussion of taxes. An important aspect which has not been given the attention it deserves is that of how these policies interact with one another.

Perhaps one of the most significant policy options yet tried has been the EU ETS. The workings of this policy, and especially its impact on airline costs, are examined in detail by Morrell. A question for all ETSs is, how are, and should, permits be allocated – free to the airlines, auctioning or other means? The chapter by Knorr and Eisenkopf looks at voluntary offsetting schemes. These are very popular – most airlines have them. However, the take up by passengers has not been very great, and as a result, they are not regarded as very successful. In addition, there are questions about how genuine the offsets are (see Hemmings et al.). Another way of addressing air transport's emissions is through modal shift. This option is examined by Rothengatter. Some other modes, especially car, also create high emissions, but rail, including high-speed rail, is much less emissions intensive than air. Rothengatter concludes that there is a role for high-speed rail as a substitute for air, though its costs mean that investment should be judicious.

In the years to come, CORSIA may be a significant policy. This is a policy developed by the International Civil Aviation Organization (ICAO) to achieve carbon-neutral growth in international air transport from 2021, to be applied to a large and growing number of airlines and routes. The role of ICAO in developing this policy is explored in the chapter by Haag. The gradual process by which CORSIA was arrived upon is discussed in this chapter. How CORSIA will operate is discussed in detail by Maertens, Grimme and Scheelhaase. While the creation of an international scheme is an achievement, this chapter also highlights some of the limitations. One of these concerns the gradual (and initially voluntary) process under which airlines will be brought into the scheme, and another is that it will take a long time before a significant proportion of air transport's emissions are offset. Both international shipping and air transport are to be handled by supranational authorities such as ICAO. Murphy provides a useful comparison of the ways shipping and aviation have been handled.

The chapters by Hemmings et al., and Scheelhaase et al. both discuss the broader policy scenario. Hemmings et al. look at the problem of decarbonising air transport in Europe. They evaluate the different options and pay particular attention to the role that renewable and synthetic fuels might play and provides an estimate of how different policy measures might be used to address the decarbonisation problem. Scheelhaase et al. analyse some options to reduce all emissions, not just carbon emissions. The options include a climate tax as well as an ETS covering all emissions. The simulation analysis makes estimates of the costs of achieving reduction targets for specific groups of airlines.

1.1 The road ahead

The objective of this book has been to provide a summary of work that has been done in terms of economic analysis and policy in the area of air transport and mitigating its impact on climate change. In most of these areas there is scope for more research, and this is particularly so when it comes to the measurement of air transport's impact on climate, the design of ETSs and tax instruments, and on newer areas such as the economic analysis of CORSIA. However, there are several broad areas, as distinct from specific policies like taxes or ETSs, which have not been covered. Some of these have been discussed briefly in the chapters of this book, but others have not been explored either in other studies, or at all. In future some of these could turn out to be important areas for further study.

This final chapter continues with an outline of some of these neglected issues and concludes with a menu of policy choices. It is not feasible to provide a simple ranking of policies, since there are many different aspects to the policies. However, it is possible to draw up a menu of possible policies and their effects and characteristics.

The questions which might be highlighted include the following:

- *What is the task at hand (discussed in Sections 2.1 and 2.3)?* Is it eliminating air transport's own emissions, or is it one of reducing (or eliminating) *all* emissions from *all* industries at minimum cost? Many commentators talk about an "air transport emissions problem" – it can be argued that this is misleading and guides one to propose unnecessarily high-cost solutions.
- *Can the wider economic benefits of air transport be reaped in a way which is consistent with addressing emissions reductions (Section 2.4)?* Some policies reduce emissions while not reducing air transport by much, and thus but do not reduce the wider economic benefits – these can be factored into the policy mix.
- *Can different policies be combined so that they are complementary rather than redundant (in particular, avoiding the "waterbed" effect) (Section 3.1)?* It should not be assumed that more policies are necessarily better. If a ticket tax or a fuel tax is imposed on an industry which already is subject to an ETS, it will have precisely zero effect on overall carbon emissions unless there are mechanisms to avoid this outcome.
- *Is it always desirable to allow permit trading between industries in an ETS (Section 3.3)?* Not necessarily – this is because the emissions from air transport are different, and higher, than the emissions from other industries, and ETSs often cover only CO_2 emissions.
- *How can the fiscal aspects of different policies (taxes, subsidies) be allowed for (Section 3.4)?* Other things being equal, taxes are a more efficient form of addressing externalities than others (subsidies or revenue neutrality) – the notion of a "green dividend".
- *How can emissions of other gases best be handled (Section 4.1)?* Addressing all the greenhouse gases at once is a very large task. But it is quite possible to take emissions of non-CO_2 gases into account when evaluating each of the available policies. This is rarely done. It can lead to unexpected results – the more blunt ticket taxes may prove better in reducing non-CO_2 emissions than often preferred instruments.
- *How do airlines act in response to free permits as compared to permits which they have to pay for (Section 4.2)?* Free versus paid for permits or allowances has implications for incidence, but the issue also has implications for how

much airlines emit. Profit-maximising airlines behave differently from non-profit-maximising airlines. It is one issue which has hardly been analysed.

- *What are the key political economy questions in reducing emissions in air transport (Section 4.3)?* Some relevant questions concern the public good nature of emissions reduction, balancing the interests of governments, airlines and their customers, and the ability to "export taxes".
- *How can a country preserve the competitiveness of its airlines while implementing emissions reductions policies (Section 4.4)?* If a country imposes emissions reduction policies on airlines, it may find that foreign airlines gain a competitive advantage.

These questions, and many others which are discussed in this book, are summarised in Tables 13.1 and 13.2. The tables summarise the policies on offer, and enable the benefits and costs of these policies to be recognised, sometimes evaluated and compared.

2. By how much should air transport reduce its emissions?

2.1 Setting out the (air transport) emissions problem

It is often said that there is an "air transport emissions" problem. This view is, however, much too narrow. Rather, there is a general emissions problem, which causes or contributes to climate change, and air transport emissions contribute in a significant way to this problem. The emphasis in this book has been to document air transport's contribution to this problem and discuss policies which can address air transport's contribution to the overall emissions problem in a minimum-cost way.

It is common, though unhelpful, to compartmentalise the emissions problem into this industry's problem or that country's problem. Thus, there is talk of the "air transport" emissions problem, the "maritime" emissions problem or the "tourism industry's" problem. However, doing so perpetuates a misconception that there are many emissions problems, rather than one overall problem.

This "silos" mentality has harmful effects in terms of policy making, which prevents resolving a costly problem at least cost. Thus, policymakers address the energy emissions problem, the maritime emissions problem and the air transport emissions problem with no recognition that they are all part of the same overall problem, and that the best way to address them is to solve them all jointly. This does not always happen, fortunately – for example, the European Union ETS links air transport with other industries. The silos mentality is very much present when it comes to international air transport (note, not *air transport*, but only *international* air transport) which is now being addressed through the CORSIA approach. As this stands, there is no trading between international and domestic air transport or any other industry, other than the industries which supply the offsets. This means that it will be more expensive than it needs to be.

This silos mentality is very much apparent when it comes to target setting (such as zero carbon growth). A good example of this confusion of thought is with the UK Government's target for aviation as discussed by the UK Committee on Climate Change (2009), and recently reviewed in its 2019 Report (2019). The Committee estimates the growth in emissions from air transport to 2050 and concludes that this growth implies a level of emissions which is far above the target level. But why have an *air transport* target level in the first place? Surely what is important is the level of the overall emissions, not just the emissions from one industry in one country. Arbitrarily set targets are expensive to meet. It is also the case that air transport industry bodies, such as ICAO and the International Air Transport Association (IATA), tend to show a silos mentality, in the sense that they treat air transport as separate from other industries. This is evident in the CORSIA approach, though this may have been inevitable given the difficulties in getting agreement amongst disparate nations.

There will need to be some sort of overall target or constraint setting by the government (or group of governments in the case of regions such as the EU). Over the medium to longer term, the Paris Agreement sets targets which most countries have accepted. The government will need to specify what level of emissions it will permit. A government will also need to set out the phasing of the constraints over time – typically, it will start low, to allow industries to adjust, and then it will tighten the constraints. It is possible that, rather than set a constraint, a government may set a price – for example, it may set a carbon tax and leave it to the market to determine the level of emissions (the result will be that some industries reduce emissions a lot, and others rather little). The top level constraint, as set by the government, may be determined on a cost-benefit basis, with the government estimating the costs of emissions reduction and comparing this to the expected benefits through the reduction in harmful climate change (see Teusch and Braathen, 2019). This is essentially done in the Stern Report (Stern, 2007), and also the approach taken by Nordhaus (Nordhaus, 2013). In reality, the process is likely to be more rough and ready than this. Once the government has determined the top level constraint, it is not needed to set targets for individual industries – the more the industries can be integrated, the better in terms of lessening the costs of reducing emissions.

It may be that by 2050 emissions from air transport will need to be zero – if the total allowable emissions from all industries are set at zero, there will be no scope for trading between industries. However, it is possible that emissions offsetting will be sufficiently reliable by this time to enable the zero net emissions constraint to be met, in part, by offsetting (and trading between industries will be feasible). In this case, there need not be a zero constraint for aviation emissions.

Perhaps the primary objection to lessening emissions on an industry-by-industry (or on a country-by-country) basis is that it is more costly. If there is an ETS approach to emission reduction in a country, it is cheaper to include all emitting industries within the same ETS. If it is easier to reduce emissions in one industry (e.g. electricity generation) than another (air transport), then it is efficient to allow trading in permits or allowances between the industries (subject to the qualification raised in Section 3.3). If carbon taxes are the chosen instrument, it is cheaper to have the same carbon tax rate for all industries, not an environment where one industry pays a high tax rate and another no tax. This principle applies also to different jurisdictions. Costs are minimised by spreading out the burden of reducing emissions over several regions or countries, so that the marginal cost of reducing emissions is equated in different industries and countries. Thus, the EU ETS lessens the cost of emissions reduction as compared to an arrangement in which all countries have separate ETSs. Of course, it may take time to integrate industries and countries into larger mechanisms, but the object should always be to broaden the base and facilitate trade.

For many observers the idea of trade does not come easily. They feel that if air transport creates emissions, it should be responsibility of the industry to reduce them on its own (see, for example, Committee on Climate Change, 2009, 2019). They observe that the emissions from air transport are growing steadily and that the share of air transport is growing to be quite significant. From this they conclude that there is an "air transport emissions problem", which can be addressed only by high taxes, arbitrary restrictions and draconian limits to travel, starting immediately.

A growing share of total emissions due to air transport need not mean that there is an insuperable problem if climate change policy is handled efficiently. Suppose that a country relies on an ETS as its main emissions reduction mechanism. With air transport emissions growing more rapidly than those of other industries, air transport will need to be a net buyer of permits, and the share of bought permits will need to rise. Air travel will be more expensive but still very affordable. Alternatively, suppose that the country chooses to implement a carbon tax, sufficient to meet its climate policy obligations. In this case, the reduction in emissions from the air transport industry will be small relative to the reductions in other industries. A higher carbon price than for other sectors is not cost-efficient.

As often is the case, there are qualifications to this general rule. So far, the discussion of problems and policies has implicitly assumed that all of air transport's emissions are the same. In reality the problem is much more complicated. Air transport generates more than just CO_2 emissions. It is often suggested that the effective emissions of greenhouse gases from air transport are around 2 to 3 times its emissions of CO_2. There is a range of emissions of gases which air transport emits, and there are contrails. The science of what emissions air transport creates is subject to ongoing study (see Grewe in this volume, as well as Section 4.1). When the science is resolved, the question of how to limit the multiple emissions needs to be resolved.

Here, the policy question is not a simple one. It is not a matter of choosing a policy instrument and multiplying it by 2.5 or some other factor (see Scheelhaase, 2019). Different policies have different effects on the different emissions. For example, a (simple) passenger tax, which works only on the demand side, may reduce all (and not only CO_2) air transport emissions in the affected geographical markets, since it will likely reduce air transport output there. Other policies, such as fuel taxes, are more complex. A (fossil) fuel tax may be designed to reduce CO_2 in a given market, in which case it will reduce CO_2 through lessening demand, and it will also have an effect on technology and stimulate the use of renewable and synthetic fuels, also to reduce CO_2 emissions. But it will also have an effect on emissions of other gases. However, a policy such as CORSIA, which is specifically linked to reducing CO_2 emissions through the offset mechanism, will primarily work to reduce CO_2 emissions.

It becomes even more complicated when several policies are implemented at the same time. Consider imposing a passenger tax when air transport is part of a multi-industry ETS. This is likely to have no net effect on CO_2 emissions in the geographical area affected by the ETS. The CO_2 emissions from air transport will fall, since demand for air transport will fall. However, under an ETS, total industry emissions of CO_2 will remain the same, since other industries emit more as air transport emissions fall (the ETS automatically ensures that total emissions of CO_2 remain fixed, unless there are specific mechanisms in place to counteract this effect; see Fichert, Forsyth and Niemeier in this volume, and also see Section 3.1 for some discussion of the "waterbed" effect). In addition, if airlines react to declining demand in the ETS area in shifting flights or aircraft to markets not covered by the scheme, overall CO_2 emissions may even increase. However, emissions of other gases will actually fall in the ETS area, since air transport output will fall (and the emissions of non-CO_2 gases are not constrained by the ETS, though see Section 3.1). Curiously, a policy of taxing air transport to "decarbonise" air transport may not have any effect on carbon in the regulated geographical area, but it may have a useful effect on reducing other harmful emissions there.

While some of the (more technological) chapters in this book discuss CO_2 and other emissions, most of the policy papers are directed to lessening CO_2 emissions (such as Morrell on ETSs, Maertens, Grimme and Scheelhaase on CORSIA and Knorr and Eisenkopf on offsets) only. It is important to analyse the effects of policies on CO_2 emissions as a first step toward analysing the effects on all emissions. In the literature, this task is far from complete. As noted, some policies have effects on only CO_2, while others have effects on a range of gas emissions. Some policies reduce CO_2 and other emissions, while others reduce CO_2 at the cost of increasing other gas emissions. Combinations of policies add to complexity since policies interact.

The argument here has been that it is efficient to address all emissions, not just the emissions of specific industries. If this happens, the reduction in emissions from air transport is likely to be significantly less than the reduction in other industries, at least in the short to medium term. It is possible that this will not be enough, and that a move to a zero emissions economy is needed by 2050. If this is the case, all industries, including air transport, will need to operate with zero emissions.

2.2 The tax and policy environment

Before dealing with the details of how best to develop polices to address emissions in air transport, it is useful to look at air transport taxes in the wider context. There are several policy interventions, which could be subsidies, taxes or quantitative measures, and which, ideally, need to be considered to gain an overall perspective. The more important ones of these for air transport, and in particular international air transport, are as follows:

- *The role of air transport in generating revenues for a government.* As with other industries, there is a role for taxation to enable the government to gain sufficient revenues to cover its outgoings. Ideally taxes should be structured as outlined by Ramsey (1927) and developed in more detail by Diamond and Mirrlees (1971a, 1971b) – for some implications, see Section 3.4. In practice, governments opt for simpler systems, such as Value Added Tax (VAT) or GST (Goods and Services Tax). Some countries apply VAT to domestic air transport, but international air transport is not subject to it. In addition, some aspects of tourism, a complementary industry for (air) transport, are not taxed. Often tourism accommodation is not subject to tax, and tourists can often gain VAT rebates on leaving the country (which may be subject to tax in the tourist's home country). To this extent, air transport is under-taxed, especially as compared to other industries (see Keen and Strand, 2007; Keen, Parry and Strand, 2013).
- *There may be benefits from air transport which are not always taken into account.* These benefits are termed "wider economic benefits" (WEBs), and they are linked to the benefits of increased connectivity. This is an area of study which has become better analysed of late – for a brief discussion, see Section 2.4. To the extent that these benefits exist, air transport is underprovided, and ideally, interventions such as subsidies might be called for.
- *Sometimes there may be a case for "exporting taxation", where a country gains from other countries.* This is a variant of the optimal tariff argument. It is particularly relevant for air transport and its complement, tourism. Put simply, a country may be able to gain by putting a tax on a good or service which is paid by residents of other countries. An example is an air transport tax which is paid by non-residents. For a case study on Australia, see Forsyth et al. (2014).
- *A final policy intervention is where a government levies a tax to correct for a negative externality, such as greenhouse gas emissions, or subsidises positive externalities (see Keen, Parry and Strand, 2013).* As has been discussed throughout this book, there are many policy mechanisms which can be used to reduce emissions.

As can be seen, developing the right set of policies to take account of all of these aspects is more complex than simply setting a tax to limit emissions. Ideally, all of the aspects discussed here need to be addressed by appropriate policies. Analysing how to do this is beyond the scope of this book. The objective here has been to focus in on the ways of addressing the costs of emissions, which form part of the solution to the overall problem.

A possible way of addressing the emissions externality will depend on what is being done to address the other issues as discussed. An industry should be subject to a revenue tax (such as VAT), and a tax to address externalities (such as a carbon tax if there is no ETS in place). If there are wider economic benefits from this industry's output, a reduction in tax or a subsidy could be called for. Export taxes make good sense for the country levying them, but they are paid for by other countries – thus these should be eliminated if global welfare is the objective. Taxation arrangements in the complementary industry, tourism, are relevant as well. Overall international air transport is relatively lightly taxed, though for some countries, export taxes are high. If there is a VAT being levied in a country, this will have an impact on emissions generated – this is also true if there is an export tax on aviation and tourism. There may be other taxes levied on air transport to address other externalities – for example, a noise tax. All these need to be taken into account when a policy to lessen emissions is being designed.

2.3 Low demand elasticities and high costs of emissions reduction: does including air transport matter?

It is granted that aviation contributes a significant and growing share of greenhouse gas emissions. But is it important to include aviation in policies to reduce emissions? This is not a trivial question. Just because aviation contributes a significant share does not necessarily mean that imposing policies to reduce it will make much of a difference to the amount of emissions, especially in the short term. It is quite possible that the cost of leaving aviation out of the policy mix may be small, and when taking into account administrative costs, on balance negative. In short, a case needs to be made for including aviation (for a discussion, see Forsyth, 2014).

This is because air transport (especially international air transport) for some countries can be relatively unresponsive to policies, both on the demand side and the cost/technology side. The demand for long-haul air transport is often fairly inelastic – though this is not the case with short-haul low-cost carriers (LCCs). This means that policies, such as taxes, even if they are optimally set, will not make much of a difference to the amount of emissions unless set at a very high level. On the cost/technology side, it is difficult to determine ways of reducing emissions at a low or moderate cost. This means that the effect of general policies, such as carbon taxes, do not produce much emissions reduction when applied to air transport, at least in the short term.

A few examples can make this point. Suppose that there is an industry-wide ETS in a country. If the costs of emissions reduction are to be minimised, trading between industries should be permitted. As the air transport grows rapidly, emissions from the industry will exceed the permits allocated to it, and it will be a net buyer of permits. The air transport industry will not reduce its own emissions by very much. Alternatively, suppose that there is an industry carbon tax. With low demand elasticities and limited ability to change technology in the short term, again the reduction in emissions will be low.

If it is not very difficult to impose a policy, then it might as well be done, even though the effects in terms of emissions reduction may not be large. Furthermore, things change over time. Elasticities tend to rise, as more options come into the market. On the technology side, there will be developments over time, and there will be more options for emissions reduction. It would be better to have a policy, such as an ETS, in place, even though its effects on emissions reduction may be small in the early years. In addition to this, as noted earlier, air transport tends to be already taxed rather lightly.

The low elasticity problem has a bearing on the choice between a single industry option (e.g. an aviation-only ETS or a ticket tax) or multiple industry options. A single industry option will be hard to justify in terms of effectiveness. A ticket tax will need to be very high to have much effect, and an aviation-only ETS will result in high increases in fares if it reduces emissions by much. It will be seen as ineffective and not worth the while. Multi-industry policies (such as ETSs and industry-wide carbon taxes) produce emissions reductions for less cost and the impact on one industry – air transport – will be much less (and much more acceptable). This will be so even though the reduction in aviation emissions will be relatively small.

A response to the low elasticity problem might be to set high taxes on air transport, so that emissions are reduced significantly. This might be seen as air transport "doing its share" of emissions reduction. While superficially appealing, this is a costly way to reduce emissions – this would mean that the marginal cost of reducing emissions from air transport would be much higher than that in other industries.

Furthermore, the incentives for investment, for example in emissions reducing technology, needs to be recognised. Prices act as a signal for investment. If there are no costs to generating emissions, there may not be much investment in technologies to lessen emissions, and over time, the technologies which are effective in lessening emissions will not be available (see Flues and van Dender, 2017). Pricing may not be worthwhile at a point of time, but it may be worthwhile over time.

There may also be other objectives beyond reducing emissions at minimum cost for policy. It might be argued that there is an equity reason for imposing a policy even though it has little effect. Users of air transport are imposing a cost through their contribution to emissions, and some would argue that they should pay this cost, for example, in a tax or through an ETS. If this argument were to be used, it is important that it be used carefully – for example, it should not be used to justify inefficient policies (such as single industry ETSs) which look better than they really are.

In short, the suggestion that air transport should be exempt from emissions reduction policies could have some limited merit in some situations. However, perhaps the best approach is to set efficient policies, which will produce small emissions reductions in the short run. However, in the long run, emissions reduction policies will have greater effect. In addition, if there is already a general policy in place, such as a multi-industry ETS, it would most likely be easy to include air transport.

2.4 The implications of the wider economic benefits of air transport

In recent years, there has been an interest in the potential "wider economic benefits" (WEBs) of ground transport. The idea has been that there may be more benefits from ground transport than have been normally recognised in policy analysis. For example, there may be more benefits than are normally counted in typical cost-benefit analysis (Vickerman, 2013). A related idea is that there may be broader "wider economic impacts" (WEIs). Most of this discussion has taken place at the level of ground transport, though it is now being recognised that there may be wider economic benefits of air transport. At this point, research is at an early stage, and it is not clear whether the WEBs from air transport are minor, or large, as some have claimed (for early studies, see InterVISTAS, 2006; Pearce and Smyth, 2007). The WEBs from different types of traffic may well differ. The notion of WEBs is closely linked to the belief that greater airline or network connectivity gives rise to benefits. It is important to recognise that wider economic *benefits* have the same metric as negative externalities such as greenhouse emissions – broader wider economic *impacts* (a broader metric), such as those on GDP or jobs, should not be, since they have a different metric.

This has implications for emissions reduction policies as applied to air transport. A simple idea might be that emissions reduction policies would always be in conflict with ensuring that the benefits of air transport, including the WEBs, are maximised. Thus, it might be argued that higher output of air transport creates WEBs and this is good, but the same higher output generates more emissions, and that is bad. It will be difficult to determine whether policies, such as ticket taxes, are good or bad.

However, matters are more complex than this (fortunately). Not all emissions reduction policies lead to less air transport. A policy which stimulates the use of low carbon fuels may reduce emissions at little cost in terms of WEBs. Several other policies, such as those operating through increasing engine efficiency and reducing aircraft miles though more direct routes, may also reduce emissions without reducing air transport.

The upshot of this is that different policies to reduce emissions have differing effects on the gains from air transport, including WEBs. The impact on WEBs is only one of the factors which need to be taken account of. To choose the best policies, it is necessary to evaluate all policies in terms of the relevant criteria (e.g. impact on non-carbon gases, cost of implementation, etc.). This can, to some extent, be done using partial equilibrium techniques such as cost-benefit analysis, or general equilibrium techniques such as computable general equilibrium models.

The implications of WEBs are not a theoretical nicety – already the practical debate is being affected by studies which derive their results by using them, and the discussion of air passenger duties and their effects has been strongly influenced by them. The PwC studies of the UK duty, and more recent studies for other countries, assume very high WEBs from air transport – this is one of the reasons why these studies conclude that countries lose if they impose these duties (PwC, 2013). Recognising that air transport may have WEBs is no longer an option in the assessment of emissions reduction policies – it is essential.

This being so, accurate measurement of WEBs is a priority. Measurement of the WEBs of air transport is in its infancy, but some approaches are much more promising than others. In particular, studies based on Input-Output models or Economic Impact Analysis should be regarded with caution. These studies typically produce very large "impacts" and "benefits" of additional air transport, partly by ignoring the costs of producing the extra output. These results cannot be compared to the (smaller) impacts and benefits obtained by using more rigorous techniques such as cost-benefit analysis or computable general equilibrium modelling.

3. Minimising cost and maximising effectiveness

3.1 Are policies complementary or redundant (the waterbed effect)?

It is likely that a jurisdiction will not rely on a single instrument to address the emissions problem. A jurisdiction will often use several polices, all of which, hopefully will lower emissions. For example, a country might impose a ticket tax and also subsidise the use of biofuels. If several different policies are to be used, it is important to determine how these policies act together. Will they be additive, in the sense that implementing two policies will lead to a greater overall reduction on emissions? Or are these policies inconsistent, in that when one policy is implemented, such as an ETS, adding another policy, such as a ticket tax, will not have any additional effect on emissions (or indeed, could even make things worse)? These are important questions to answer, since several policies, especially ETSs and the proposed CORSIA, will not work as expected if other policies are being implemented.

If there is a single objective of a policy, such as reducing carbon emissions, then the easiest solution is to determine which is most efficient in achieving that objective, and simply implement that one – there is no point in adding other policies. It may be argued that the most efficient policy is a carbon fuel tax, which would directly address the emissions externality – provided the latter is straightforward to monetise. In any case, there should be a preference for trying to implement the most effective and efficient policy.

However, things may not be quite so simple. It could be that the preferred option is too difficult to implement, and that second best approaches will have to be used. This is especially so when there is uncertainty about how policies will work, or about the external cost/damage that would have to be internalised, and it may be advisable to use a mix of two or more policies (assuming that they are not inconsistent). In the literature on climate change policies under uncertainty, hybrid models have been suggested to get close to efficiency (Pizer, 2002). It is also quite possible that there will be more than one objective, such as that of reducing emissions at minimum cost. There may be a concern about not imposing too high a cost on the passenger or keep the cost burden on the air transport industry low. Thus, a mixture of policies could be the best approach. For example, a government may choose to implement a ticket tax on the airlines, coupled with a subsidy on biofuels. This could be budget neutral, with the proceeds of the ticket tax being used to finance the cost of the subsidy. This combination of policies would also lessen the cost to the passenger.

If more than one policy is to be implemented, it is critically important to analyse how the policies interact. This is not often done. Once one policy is in operation, it is easy to suggest additional policies, with the objective of further increasing the reduction in emissions. Sometimes this is likely to work – for example, when a ticket tax is added to a fuel tax or when making airlines liable for VAT. However, in some important cases, this will not work.

These cases rely on quantitative constraints, rather than prices, to lower emissions – the most important of these are ETSs. The new CORSIA mechanism, to come into operation in 2021 for international air transport, also poses problems when coupled with other policies. The workings of quantitative policies are described in the chapter by Fichert, Forsyth and Niemeier and in the chapter by Maertens, Grimme and Scheelhaase in this volume. An ETS sets a physical limit on the allowable (usually CO_2) emissions from the air transport industry, or a group of industries, and as a result, imposing additional policies has no additional effect on these emissions. Thus, if there is an ETS in operation in a given geographical market, a ticket or carbon tax, or a biofuel subsidy, will have precisely zero effect on emissions of CO_2 in this market, or may even be counter-productive if flights or aircraft are shifted to other, emerging markets outside the ETS's scope. These additional instruments are redundant, unless other mechanisms are introduced to counteract this result (see later in this chapter), or there are other objectives (such as revenue raising). This point has been recognised in the analysis of emissions reduction policies, and there is some literature on it (see Forsyth, Dwyer and Spurr, 2007; Fankhauser, Hepburn and Park, 2011), and it is sometimes termed the "waterbed" effect.[2]

This effect is explained in the chapter by Fichert, Forsyth and Niemeier in this volume. Figure 13.1 is taken from that chapter and deals with the case of an ETS. For simplicity, it is assumed that emissions vary in proportion to air transport output and that marginal and average costs are constant. The ETS limits the amount of emissions which may be produced by the air transport industry to an amount K. With a demand of D, and long-run average (and marginal) cost of LAC, emissions permits will be valuable. The price which passengers pay will be P_1, which adds the price of the permits to the costs of the airlines. Suppose the government imposes an additional policy instrument to reduce emissions, namely a tax set at t. This will have no effect on the quantity of emissions.

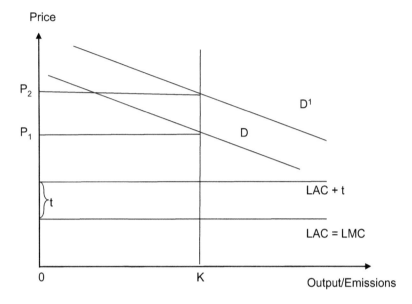

Figure 13.1 Interaction between ETSs and taxes.

The price of emissions permits will fall, in this case by the amount of the tax. The ticket tax will raise revenue for the government, but it will do nothing to reduce emissions of CO_2. Under an ETS, the amount of emissions is fixed, no matter what additional measures (e.g. biofuel subsidies or voluntary offsets) are imposed. These additional policies are redundant.

Suppose that there is an ETS which targets the CO_2 emissions of a number of industries including air transport, and that trading between industries is permitted. Suppose that aviation is a net buyer of permits. If the government imposes an additional policy, such as a ticket tax, what is the impact on emissions in the regulated region? Airline prices will rise, but all this will mean is that other industries will take up the slack – the total CO_2 emissions will remain unchanged (the waterbed effect). Aviation emissions will fall, and this may be of relevance if these other emissions, such as those of NO_x, are of concern. A ticket tax may will reduce the emissions of non-carbon emissions in the regulated market, but not carbon emissions.[3]

The waterbed effect can be avoided if, at the same time as the aviation tax is implemented, the total allowances in the ETS are reduced by the same amount as the likely reduction in emissions as a result of the tax. With the present form of the European ETS, individual countries have been taking action to reduce emissions – this is one of the reasons why the prices of allowances have been remaining unexpectedly low (the waterbed effect in action). However, in 2019 a market stability reserve (MSR) was introduced to lessen volatility in allowance prices. As part of this change, a mechanism has been introduced which will result in allowances being permanently removed from the market under certain conditions. To the extent that the additional tax triggers a reduction in allowances on the market, there will be something of a reduction in the waterbed effect (on the MSR, see Hepburn et al., 2016). As of 2019, it was not clear how effective this mechanism will be in addressing the waterbed effect, nor whether in future aviation will still be included in the EU ETS or handled by CORSIA.

It might be wondered why the additional action, such as an aviation tax, is needed since the avoidance of the waterbed effect requires a reduction in allowances to accompany it – why not reduce allowances without introducing the tax? For many industries this is a pertinent question, but there is an answer in the case of aviation. In the regulated geographical market, the aviation tax reduces both CO_2 emissions, and non-CO_2 emissions. Even if a tax is not effective in reducing regional CO_2 emissions, it still will be effective in reducing non-CO_2 emissions. There is also the fiscal effect, since the tax raises government revenue while the ETS will not raise much revenue if allowances are partly free, as is the case with the European ETS. Revenue raising is not just a matter of a transfer – see Section 3.4. However, inclusion of non-CO_2 emissions in the ETS may be another option, which could eliminate the need for additional taxes (for some discussion, see Scheelhaase, 2019).

CORSIA-type mechanisms have some of the same properties as ETSs, though in some ways they are similar to taxes which must be spent on offsets. There is a quantitative switching point to emissions, set at 2020 emissions for the system coming into being for international aviation. Airlines can generate more emissions, but only if they purchase offsets for the excess emissions they create. Taking the actual emissions and the offsets required into account, the airlines are limited to the 2020 emissions levels. In effect they are achieving zero carbon growth if offsets work perfectly – something which is strongly questioned by critics (see Hemmings et al. in this volume).

Suppose an additional policy is implemented – for example, a ticket tax. This will increase the cost to the passengers (airline average cost, plus offset cost, plus tax), and the amount of air transport will be reduced. The actual amount of emissions will fall, but so too will be the number of offsets purchased by the air transport industry. The net un-offsetted emissions will be the same. There will be no change in offsetted emissions if offsets are genuine and priced correctly. The net global emissions will be unchanged. In this sense the tax is redundant (though it increases government revenue, and it will have an effect on non-carbon emissions).

What has been shown here so far is the interaction between an ETS or CORSIA mechanism and other policies such as airline taxes. What happens if both a CORSIA scheme is combined with an ETS? In the EU, it may be that air transport still remains subject to the ETS, and CORSIA, though it also may be that only one mechanism will be used.

The answer is quite straightforward if both schemes impose fixed constraints – either the ETS determines emissions and CORSIA is redundant and has no

effect on emissions, or the reverse happens, and the CORSIA scheme determines emissions and the ETS is redundant. Things are different, though, when
trading with other industries is permitted. This is shown in Figure 13.2.

In Figure 13.2 the case of a tight ETS (air transport only) combined with
a slack CORSIA constraint is shown initially. Airlines are permitted to create
emissions up to a level C, beyond which they are required to purchase offsets
for all the extra emissions beyond C. However, the ETS sets an allowable maximum K. This constraint is binding, and the CORSIA constraint is redundant.
Alternatively, the case of a tight CORSIA could be shown.

Things become more interesting when air transport is part of a wider industry-
based ETS. In this case, there is no strict constraint on air transport emissions,
though there is a constraint on overall multi-industry emissions. Airlines will
need to obtain permits/allowances for emissions which will be available at a
set market price. Suppose that, initially, demand is shown by D_1. If the price of
permits is a, the price to the airlines will be P_3, and the CORSIA constraint
will be redundant.

Over time, the demand will increase to D_2, and the CORSIA constraint will
become effective. If the airlines' emissions exceed the CORSIA constraint C,
they will also be required to purchase offsets, in addition to ETS permits. At
this stage, both CORSIA and the ETS constraints have some effect. The price
of ETS permits, a, and the price of offsets, b, will be added to the LAC, to yield
a total price of P_4. In this case, the combination of the two policies will have
the effect of reducing overall net emissions of CO_2. Airlines are required to buy
ETS permits, but the overall industry-wide emissions will remain at Z (not
shown) if the waterbed effect is not addressed. Thus, if CORSIA is imposed
when there is already an ETS in operation, the net effect is that airlines will

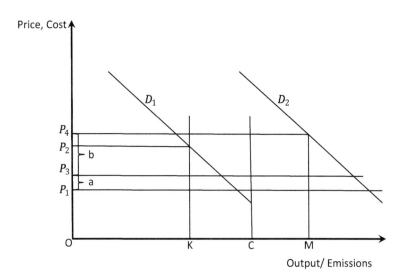

Figure 13.2 Interaction between ETSs and CORSIA.

be required to buy offsets for M–C emissions – air transport emissions will be reduced since the price has risen from P_3 to P_4, but this is matched by an increase in the same amount of emissions in other industries (the non-carbon emissions will be reduced). If the waterbed effect is addressed, there will be net fall in emissions in addition to the offsetted emissions.

It is not clear exactly what the rules governing a combined system of ETS and CORSIA will be in, for example, the EU, where the introduction of the market stability reserve which will reduce or eliminate the waterbed effect. Here, it has been assumed that airlines will be required to buy ETS allowances and CORSIA offsets. It might be regarded that this involves "double taxation". If so, airlines might be required only to buy either ETS permits or CORSIA offsets, not both. In this case, only one of the schemes is effective, and the impact on emissions will be less than if both schemes are in operation. In the case of the EU, the ETS covers only domestic and intra-European flights, and CORSIA only international flights; intra-European international flights might be – in theory – covered under both systems, though this has yet to be determined.

3.2 Targeted or direct policies

Policies can differ in that some are very targeted and affect objectives, such as the reduction of carbon emissions, very directly, or they may be very vaguely targeted and have only an indirect impact on the objective. The simplest way of defining targeted policies is to consider some examples. Consider first a fuel tax which discourages carbon emissions. This would be a very targeted or direct policy. Another policy could be a ticket tax which is based on whether a traveller makes a flight. This has an impact on carbon emissions, but it is not a very direct or targeted policy. Finally, consider a limit on the expansion of an airport. This policy may be designed to reduce carbon emissions from aviation, but it will only do so in a very indirect way, and it may not succeed at all.

The general rule is that the more tightly targeted a policy is, the more effective it is, and the lower the cost of achieving the main objective. Thus, it could be expected that the fuel tax of a given level will reduce emissions more than a ticket tax. One of the reasons for this is that a fuel tax works on both the demand and supply side – it will reduce the demand for air transport and also give airlines an incentive to adopt less carbon incentive methods of producing air transport services (say, by using lower carbon fuels). By contrast, a ticket tax will reduce demand, but it has no incentive effects on the way air transport services are produced. Thus, in choosing between different policies, an important determinant is how direct or targeted they are.

The notion of targeted or direct policies can help in designing better policies. A simple ticket tax is a relatively blunt instrument when it comes to lessening carbon emissions (often they have multiple objectives). However, it is quite straightforward to design more targeted policies. A ticket tax can be designed to take account of load factors, or to reward airlines with newer fleets, or be based partly on the size (and fuel efficiency) of the aircraft used (to become a movement tax) (for a discussion see Leicester and O'Dea, 2008). It may not be easy to implement carbon taxes in international aviation (though if bilateral partners agree, it may be feasible), but a well-designed ticket tax may be a reasonable substitute. Several countries are now imposing ticket taxes, and some countries are attempting to design them to be more effective in reducing carbon emissions.

Thus far in this discussion, it has been presumed that the objective is to reduce carbon emissions only. As noted in several places in this chapter, other emissions are damaging. This needs to be taken into account in choosing policies. A tax which is related to carbon emissions will be good at reducing carbon emissions – but what of the other emissions? If a policy is good at targeting carbon emissions, it is not necessarily the case that it will be good in reducing other emissions. It is quite possible that a ticket tax may be *superior* to CORSIA in reducing the overall emissions of air transport, since the emphasis of CORSIA is targeted to reduce/offset carbon emissions only. As always, it is necessary to determine all of the impacts of the policy options before concluding which is best.

3.3 Tradability – is trade always desirable?

It is not easy to find economists who oppose trade (those who do have to use more and more convoluted arguments why they do so). This applies in the discussion of emissions reduction policies – several of these policies involve the possibility of trade between regions and industries. It would normally be accepted that it would be efficient to allow trade between industries covered by ETSs (or, indeed, CORSIA-type arrangements if they were extended to other industries) rather than have separate ETSs for individual industries such as air transport and energy. It would also be expected that it would be efficient to allow trade in permits between countries all of which have ETSs covering their industries.

Hence, at first sight, the case for trade is straightforward also for air transport (see Fichert, Forsyth and Niemeier). Suppose that there is a choice between having an air transport-only ETS and including air transport in a more general industry-wide ETS. It can be shown that the costs of achieving a desired level of reduction of CO_2 will be minimised if the air transport ETS is integrated with the industry-wide ETS (this is shown in Figure 13.3, from Fichert, Forsyth and Niemeier). Given the moderate elasticity of demand for air transport, along with the inability of air transport technology to reduce emissions significantly in the short to medium term, it is very likely that air transport will be a net buyer of permits. Moving from an air transport-only ETS to a general industry ETS, with the same total reduction in emissions, results in increased air transport emissions and reduced emissions from other industries.

Despite the general rule in support of trade, there can be exceptions. Air transport emissions generates one of these. This comes about because of the fact

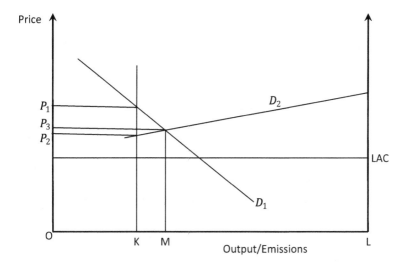

Figure 13.3 Trading in allowances/permits.

that air transport creates not only CO_2 emissions but also several other harmful emissions. As noted elsewhere, the total emissions from air transport could be of the order or 1.5 to 2 times as harmful than the emissions from CO_2 alone. However, most policies, such as the European ETS, are primarily directed to reducing CO_2 emissions. The presence of such other gases may then create problems since, when air transport joins an ETS dealing with CO_2 only, total CO_2 emissions remain the same as they fall under the cap, but emissions of other gases – caused by air transport activities – rise (though it should be noted that other industries emit non-CO_2 as well – for example, methane from agriculture).

This means that there is a cost to integrating aviation into an industry wide, CO_2-based ETS. This cost depends on how much the non-CO_2 gases rise by, and what the cost of these gases are. The efficiency gain from integration needs to be compared to the cost of such additional gases. If the additional gas emissions are large, and if the cost of these gases is high, it could be that integrating the ETSs to trade with other industries leads to less efficient overall outcome and hence may not be desirable. Thus a cost-benefit calculation which can be done relatively easily given the impact of the non-CO_2 emissions can be monetized in a serious way (see Teusch and Braathen, 2019). Opening up an ETS to trade with other industries may not be desirable.

There is ongoing research, e.g. in Germany, on the inclusion of non-CO_2 emissions within an ETS, which would eliminate the earlier arguments against trade and against the use of ETS as a single policy measure. There are proposals, which have yet to be brought into fruition, to include a range of emissions from air transport in the EU ETS (see Scheelhaase, 2019). If this happens, this problem with trade will be removed.

3.4 Taxes, subsidies and constraints – implications for the dead weight losses

Much discussion of climate change policies ignores the impact on the government budget. This is appropriate if the main objective of the discussion is to analyse the properties of the policies in a world without real-world complications. However, it is not sufficient if the policies are being discussed as practical options, with due consideration being given to complications which will be inevitably be present. There are budgetary implications for all real climate change policies. Taxes have very different implications for government budgets than subsidies. These budgetary aspects need to be taken into account.

In recent years there has been the development of effective ways of analysing fiscal aspects of policy options in the public economics literature. An early contribution to the theory of optimal taxation was that of Ramsey (1927). This contribution was not widely recognised until the work of Diamond and Mirrlees (1971a, 1971b). This work was a critical step in the way taxation was analysed, and in particular the way in which the efficiency costs of taxation were recognised and measured. It was the catalyst for measures of the dead weight loss, or efficiency cost, of taxation in real economies. Different measures abound, but often analysts (see, for example, Keen, Parry and Strand, 2013) use a measure of around 1.20 Euro as the cost of raising 1 Euro of taxation as an approximation.

The idea about the dead weight loss from taxation is as follows. In order to gain an extra Euro, a government increases taxes but, in so doing, it imposes additional distortions of the economy, so that the overall cost to the economy is 1.20 Euro. This is directly relevant for the assessment of climate change policies. If the policy involves setting a tax, such as a ticket tax, there is additional revenue which can be used for flood mitigation, defence, schools or hospitals. A subsidy, such as one for using biofuels, requires additional tax to be levied, and this could be used for other purposes, such as funding hospitals. Thus negative externalities, such as emissions, can be corrected in many ways, such as taxes or subsidies; but of these, subsidies are the most expensive, and taxes are the cheapest. There is a "green dividend" when a negative externality is corrected with a tax rather than in some other way, such as via a subsidy.

We can rank policies according to their cost in terms of dead weight losses. Taxes, such as fuel taxes, ticket taxes, and VATs, are best in that they lower dead weight losses in the economy. The same is true where there is an ETS where permits are auctioned. Policies which have a neutral effect on the budget include ETSs with free permits, airport restrictions (if these do not result in traffic moving to other countries), voluntary offsets and engine requirements. CORSIA is a neutral approach. Offering cash incentives to airlines and airports to make choices which they would not normally have made, such as using biofuels, and using electricity made from renewable sources, are the most expensive ways of achieving the emissions reduction objective, other things being equal.

If the objective is to lower emissions at least cost, these effects on the dead weight cost of raising taxation need to be taken into account, as are several other aspects. Thus, for example, a subsidy for airlines to use biofuels might be, in a particular case, the most cost-effective option when all factors are taken into account.

4. Broader aspects – handling non-CO_2 emissions and incidence

4.1 Beyond CO_2 – policies to reduce other greenhouse gases

The emphasis in this volume has been on lessening the emissions of CO_2. However, aviation produces several other gases and contrails which increase global warming and are harmful in general to the environment. These gases have been discussed in several chapters, though most of the discussion of policies has been of those primarily directed to lessening CO_2. There are several reasons for this. Much of the analytical work has been directed to CO_2. Further, perhaps even more of the emphasis in policy development and application has been on measures to lessen CO_2 emissions. The other greenhouse gases have been estimated to have had a significant impact on climate change (see Grewe in this volume). It is often suggested that the total damage caused by aviation is in the order of up to two times the damage caused by CO_2.

If these estimates are accurate, and if policy actions are concentrating on CO_2, then a significant part of the overall problem is not being addressed. Ideally, all harmful greenhouse gases and contrails should be addressed. Doing so is not a simple matter – it is not a matter of taking a policy directed to reducing CO_2 and making it three times stronger. The emissions of the different gases are not only imperfectly correlated, and some policies have conflicting effects. Thus, one policy, that of implementing a ticket tax to reduce aviation output may reduce all greenhouse gases in the geographical market where the tax is applied, while another policy, such as that of adjusting engines, may have the effect of reducing CO_2 emissions while increasing the emissions of NO_x.

Ideally there should be a separate policy directed to address each of the harmful emissions (which would be based on research as to the trade-offs between effects). This is not likely to happen in the near future. Given this, the best that can be hoped for is that the policies under consideration for implementation (directed primarily to reduce CO_2 emissions) are analysed thoroughly in terms of their effects on other gases. This will involve both technical and economic analysis. Results will depend not only on what policy is being considered, but also on the detail of the policy. For example, an ETS for carbon has different effects on NO_x emissions depending on whether trading is permitted or not.

The core reason for this is that not all emissions are the same – and aviation is different from other industries. Emissions from aviation are more harmful than emissions from (most) other industries, because of the additional emissions which accompany aviation emissions. A typical ETS targeting CO_2 does not take any recognition of this – for example, if there is trading, permits can be exchanged between industries even though the emissions from different industries will differ. This needs to be taken into account if policies are to be optimised. Some examples can make the point.

Suppose a choice between a ticket tax and a fuel tax. If there is a ticket tax, aviation output will be reduced in the affected market. All harmful gases will be reduced, though not necessarily in the same proportion. If there is a fuel tax, the higher price for air travel will also result in a reduction of all emissions. However, there are other effects. One might be that airlines will adjust their engines to lessen CO_2 emissions, but this might also result in additional emissions of NO_x under certain circumstances. While a fuel tax could be a more efficient option if reducing CO_2 is the only objective, if there are other objectives, such as reducing all harmful emissions, a ticket tax might be preferable, unless such other emissions would also be tackled by the fuel tax or, for example, an ETS (assuming that direct pricing of other emissions is not feasible).

A second example is with an ETS. If an ETS is directed solely to air transport, all greenhouse emissions will be reduced. However, if trading is permitted, as noted earlier, it is possible for there to be an increase in aviation's use of permits, and a decrease in the use by all other industries. This will have no effect on the overall level of CO_2 emissions. However, it could also lead to higher emissions of other gases, since aviation generates more of these than other industries.

A similar effect occurs when an ETS is combined with another policy, such as a ticket tax. As has been shown, as with the waterbed effect, imposing the ticket tax will have no effect on CO_2 emissions in the regional market where the tax is applied. However, it will have the effect of reducing emissions of other greenhouse gases from aviation in this area, since aviation's share of allowable permits will have been reduced. In short, imposing a ticket tax may be a desirable policy, not because of its (zero) effect on CO_2 emissions, but because of its effect of reducing other emissions. However, as mentioned earlier, a shift of flights to non-regulated world regions as reaction to such a tax could even have adverse impacts.

A final example is with CORSIA. If demand for air transport rises over time, airlines will have to buy additional offsets. These effectively keep CO_2 emissions constant, once allowance for offsets is made, if offsets work as effectively as they are supposed to. However, emissions of other gases will continue to grow, since offsets are directed towards CO_2 emissions and not other emissions.

As noted earlier, there is some discussion that the EU ETS could be broadened to take into account non-CO_2 emissions. In the same way, other mechanisms such as CORSIA could be extended to constrain emissions of non-CO_2 emissions, if suitable offsets for these are available.

4.2 Who pays? Determining the incidence

In this book, the question of what is the incidence of emissions reduction policies has not been given much coverage. In certain places, such as the chapter by

Fichert, Forsyth and Niemeier, there is some analysis of incidence (the pass through of taxes). This lack of coverage is not to imply that this question is unimportant. It reflects that fact that there has been relatively little research on the incidence question, and that some aspects of it are difficult to unravel. This is a brief outline of some of the major issues.

Policies may impose a cost on actors in the industry (ticket taxes), such as airlines and their passengers, or they give a benefit (subsidies for the use of biofuels), or they may attempt to be cost neutral (though an ETS with free permits may not be cost neutral for all who are affected). In most cases it will be the industry actors, such as airlines and airports, on which the incidence initially falls. The ultimate incidence will usually be, at least in part, on the final consumer, the passenger.

If all markets are competitive and there are no distortions, the final consumer, the passenger/shipper, will bear the full cost of the policy, if it raises prices, or the full benefit if it lowers prices. However, there are several market imperfections which will result in the airline (and airport sometimes) bearing some of the cost.

The presence of monopoly and oligopoly in airline markets is an important one of these imperfections; this is recognised in the study by OXERA (2003) and other studies. If airline markets are not perfectly competitive, and if there is a cost imposed on the airline, for example as a result of a ticket tax, the airline will be unable to pass on the full amount of the tax. This is an important qualification since airline markets are normally oligopolistic or, in some cases, monopolistic. When markets are characterised by monopoly or oligopoly, the firms will increase the prices to the consumer by the full amount of the cost increase if they seek to maximise their profits (for an econometric study of pass through of aviation fuel price increases in the US, see Ozmen, 2011). This has direct relevance for the analysis of measures such as ticket taxes or fuel taxes. Furthermore, airlines do not always behave in exactly the same way as a textbook monopoly/oligopoly. Theoretical analysis can go only so far – what is needed is empirical analysis. There has been little of this in the areas of interest here.

Another important example of a market imperfection comes about from the imposition of quantitative limits on behaviour. One case of this is with slot limits which are imposed in many busy airports. Another is when bilateral arrangements between countries limit the number of flights which airlines can operate between particular countries. These constraints limit the number of flights airlines may take to below the amount the airlines would like to offer and result in prices being set according to demand. Prices are above cost. If there is a cost increase, for example, due to a ticket tax being levied, there will be no effect on price or output which is fixed (see Fichert, Forsyth and Niemeier, 2014). The airline will be forced to absorb the cost increase, and passengers are unaffected. In this case there will be no reduction in emissions (see OXERA, 2003; Forsyth, 2008).

The most perplexing of these cases comes about when there is a quantitative limit on emissions and permits are allocated to airlines (at least partly) free of charge. This happens with the EU ETS and will happen when CORSIA is in operation (airlines will be required only to purchase offsets for their emissions which exceed their 2020 emissions). Airlines will be able to operate and create emissions if they buy allowances/permits or buy offsets. This arrangement creates a potentially significant gap between average and marginal cost of operation (Forsyth, 2009). How do airlines price their (now more valuable) flights? Do they set their prices according to the (low) average cost, which covers the price they pay for their allocated permits (zero), plus the price they have to pay for the permits for which they have to pay full price? Or do they set prices at the higher marginal cost, reflecting the full opportunity cost of the permits/allowances, and gain higher profits as a result? If the airlines are profit maximisers, they will do the latter. If permit prices are high, the airlines may be able to gain high profits as a result of the high value of the permits which are allocated for nothing. If airlines are pricing at average cost, why do they do this given that they are passing up profits? This is another empirical question on which empirical work is needed to shed light.

Whether permits are paid for, and how airlines respond to free permits, will have an impact on the effectiveness of the ETS to limit emissions. Firstly, while carbon emissions will be unaffected by how the airlines choose to behave, this will not be so for the non-CO_2 emissions. Air transport output will be higher if airlines practise average cost pricing than if they practise marginal cost pricing, and this gives rise to higher non-CO_2 emissions. Secondly, if there are free permits and airlines practise marginal cost pricing, rents will be created and there is the risk of rent seeking – waste of real resources to gain these resources. An example of this has been suggested by Flues and van Dender (2017), who argue that the presence of free permits distorts the incentives to invest in lower emissions technologies. In short, there is a case that it is more efficient to have paid for permits than free permits.

4.3 The political economy of emissions reduction in air transport

In this book, there has not been much in the way of discussion of political economy questions. Much of the discussion has been on the pure policy aspects, such as what the effects of a specific policy are likely to be. However, political economy aspects are important, especially in determining which policies do actually get implemented. The political economic of emissions reduction is a large topic which needs to be discussed in another forum. Here, three issues are discussed briefly:

- The public goods aspect of emissions reduction.
- The choice of instruments.
- The export tax aspect.

Emissions reduction is a global public good. This means that there is an incentive to free ride facing nations, individuals and industries. Emissions reduction will increase global welfare, but the benefits from action are not reaped by those taking the actions to reduce. Individuals sometimes have the opportunity to reduce their emissions, for example, by using the offset schemes offered by airlines. As noted by Knorr and Eisenkopf, the take-up of these is low. Airlines make some efforts, for example, by experimenting with biofuels, perhaps to ready themselves for when stronger measures are mandated. It will be governments, groups of governments (e.g., in the EU), and international organisations like ICAO which will set the standards or mechanisms in place to induce or compel businesses such as airlines and airports to reduce emissions.

Ultimately, actions are voluntary. The Kyoto Protocol and the Paris accord are voluntary agreements, and nations are not compelled to join (some countries have not). The desire to trade with other countries can be a spur to action – one country may refuse to trade with another if it considers that it is a free rider. ICAO is a voluntary organisation which cannot compel airlines to act. This said, it does have some power. For example, countries can ban aircraft from flying to their airports if they do not meet ICAO noise standards.

Many observers complain that progress in reducing emissions has been very slow. However, given the public good nature of emissions reduction, this is not surprising. In fact, it might be argued that there has been reasonable progress – in terms of countries implementing carbon taxes, ETSs and several other smaller mechanisms. ICAO has established CORSIA which, if it works as planned, will have a significant effect in avoiding the growth in un-offsetted CO_2 emissions from international air transport.

The second aspect deals with the choice of policies. Firms such as airlines and airports prefer to receive subsidies to implement a course of action than pay a tax if they do not. Governments often prefer to receive taxes or implement revenue neutral policies (such as an ETS with free permits) than provide subsidies. Ticket taxes, such as the UK air passenger duty (APD), have been very unpopular with the airline industry and passengers, though the EU ETS, which covers UK airlines, and which operates with partly free allowances, has achieved a measure of acceptance. CORSIA, which has yet (2019) to commence, is a scheme to achieve carbon-neutral growth – this means that emissions below 2020 levels are not taxed, and only emissions above require airlines to purchase offsets (which, in the early days, may be relatively cheap).

Ultimately, governments have the power to tax, at least at the domestic level, and can choose the policies they wish to impose on their industries, including air transport, be they ones which involve a tax burden on their industries and their residents, or ones which avoid a burden. By contrast, airlines and their customers will always object to taxes or equivalent burdens (the pass through of taxes on airlines will normally be less than 100% in the short to medium term, meaning that both airlines and customers suffer). To achieve action on emissions reduction, governments may need to concentrate on options which impose a small burden on their air transport industries and customers, such as ETSs with many free allowances, or mechanisms like CORSIA.

This said, there are further aspects of air transport taxes which can be of relevance. Having canvassed a range of considerations which make for difficulties in achieving emissions reductions in air transport, it is time to recognise one which *may* make it easy to reduce emissions. This comes about as a result of the possible "tax export" effect of air transport taxation. If a country imposes an air transport tax (e.g. a ticket tax or a fuel tax), it is possible that it may gain in terms of net benefits. This is because, if residents of other countries pay the tax, the country gains revenues which can be distributed to its residents. Most air transport taxes are paid, at least some part, by non-residents – in some cases, non-residents pay most of the air transport tax. If this is the case, the country may have a national interest in imposing the tax – which may have the desirable effect of reducing carbon and other emissions in the affected geographical market.

Whether or not this is the case for a particular country depends on a range of factors which have been discussed in various parts of this chapter. These include the WEBs of air transport, the effects of the tax on employment, the gains from inbound tourism and the costs of outbound tourism and other factors. While it is true that most studies of the economic impacts of air transport taxes conclude that the country suffers from imposing one (e.g. IATA, 2006), it must be said that these studies have used a faulty approach (EIA or Economic Impact Analysis). The few studies which have used the rigorous computable general equilibrium (CGE) approach have produced different outcomes, with the Australian study (Forsyth, Dwyer and Spurr, 2014) concluding that Australia gained by imposing a tax, and the UK study (PwC, 2013) concluding that the UK lost. The reasons why the results differ lie in different assumptions about employment, WEBs and other factors. Depending on these factors, it is certainly possible for countries to gain from imposing a tax, and by using a CGE approach, it is possible to determine under which conditions this will be so.

There will be a smaller export tax effect if a group of countries (e.g. the EU) all impose a tax – individual countries lose from their partners' taxes, though there is an export tax effect vis-à-vis countries not in the group, such as the US. It is possible that there may be too much of an incentive for countries to impose aviation taxes which others pay for. Globally, there are no net gains from export taxes – what one country gains, others lose. Countries may impose taxes for other than emissions reductions reasons; nonetheless, these taxes can reduce emissions.

4.4 Impacts on airline competitiveness

When a country or region imposes an emissions reduction policy which works through increasing the price of air transport services, there is a possible effect on its airlines' (international) competitiveness. This is often a concern when one country imposes a policy but other competitor countries do not, or when the tax is not equally applied to all airlines or passengers. The former has been a particular issue for Europe with its ETS, and both the former and the latter with individual countries with ticket taxes. The competitiveness issue arises with the application of the EU ETS (as shown by Morrell in this volume) and, to some extent, it also arises with the application of CORSIA, since not all countries will be part of CORSIA, either in the early days or possibly for a long time. In addition to the competitiveness issue, there is also an economic efficiency issue – if one airline is subject to a tax or required to purchase allowances/permits, and a competitor is not, there will be a situation in which the airline which has the lower overall costs will not be the airline which serves the market.

Morrell gives several examples of how the application of policies can lead to unlevel playing fields between airlines (especially had the EU ETS not been revised to exclude flights to and from Europe). To some, but usually to a lower extent, competitiveness issues can also arise with CORSIA (see Maertens et al. in this volume). In addition to issues relating to flights, the application of these policies can affect the competitiveness of hubs – for example, the use of European hubs such as Paris or Amsterdam relative to the use of Gulf hubs such as Doha and Dubai.

Competitiveness issues pose distinct problems in the design of emissions reduction policies. To a degree, problems can be alleviated by ad-hoc measures designed to fix specific problems. For example, feeder flights connecting to long-haul flights might need to purchase fewer allowances, and the ticket taxes can be designed to lessen the competitiveness problem. However, this may not be a satisfactory solution in the long run and it may create further problems. In essence, the problems of competitiveness come about because countries/regions are seeking to advance several conflicting objectives at once – they are seeking to increase the coverage of emissions reduction policies (often beyond the borders of the country), they may be seeking to increase government revenues (for example, with ticket taxes), and they are seeking to preserve their airlines' competitiveness. This is a difficult balancing act.

5. Reducing emissions from air transport

5.1 Progress so far

It may be thought that there has been slow progress in designing and implementing policies to reduce greenhouse gas emissions in air transport. This is perhaps a pessimistic viewpoint. Comparing the present to the situation say, ten years ago, there has been progress. Ten years ago, a number of policy options had been suggested though not implemented. In the period since, there has been a significant process of actually experimenting with policies, and setting up of medium-term arrangements. Some of these have been major initiatives, such as the setting up and operation of the EU ETS. Most of the main policy options have been tried, and there are results in terms of how they have been working (though for a more pessimistic view, see Gössling, 2018).

This can be outlined briefly:

- Ticket taxes (such as the UK APD) have been implemented in a number of countries. Several of these have not been primarily directed towards reducing emissions, though this is one of the effects at least in the geographical market where the tax is applied, subject to any shifting of flights or aircraft to other world regions. The impacts of these taxes have been studied (PwC, 2013; Forsyth et al., 2014), though many studies are not rigorous. There is a good knowledge basis on them. Their economic effects have been analysed to some degree. At the time of writing, there is renewed interest in ticket taxes as a way of reducing emissions.

- There has been rather less analysis of fuel taxes. There are a number of countries which are levying them in domestic air transport, though not in international air transport. This reflects the widespread belief that international treaties and agreements prohibit their use, though this belief is being challenged (see Hemmings et al. in this volume). There may be more scope for countries or groups of countries to implement fuel taxes than has been thought.
- Perhaps the most important emissions reduction policy to be applied to air transport has been the EU ETS. Air transport was included in the broader ETS in 2012, and it has continued to operate. This ETS allows (to an extent) trading between industries. There is ongoing research on its extension to non-CO_2 emissions.
- ICAO has been making progress towards setting carbon standards for engines.
- There is widespread, ongoing research into bio and other low carbon fuels, such as power-to-liquid-based kerosene (PtL). So far, a large number of airlines have been conducting experiments with biofuels. However, such fuels are all still in the experimental stage, and these have not yet been used extensively.
- At the time of writing (2019), ICAO is on track to implement the CORSIA mechanism to cap carbon emissions from international air transport at 2020 levels (see Maertens, Grimme and Scheelhaase, and Haag, in this volume). This mechanism will be voluntary initially, and it will cover an increasing number of countries. If it works as planned, it will be a significant step in freezing air transport net emissions growth from 2020, though it will not freeze total emissions.
- Over the past ten years, many airlines have introduced voluntary offset schemes for passengers (see Knorr and Eisenkopf in this volume). Some of these schemes have not had much of an impact, though some airlines, such as Qantas, have claimed that passengers have been offsetting around 5%–10% of their flights (Hatch, 2019). Increasingly, however, firms and other institutions seem to make use of such schemes for employee travel.
- Restrictions on the development of airports has been suggested as an emissions reduction measure. For example, the UK Committee on Climate Change has argued that air transport will need to reduce its emissions and that additional capacity at airports should be capped. However, other

airports and hubs, in the same or in other world regions, might at least partly take over unaccommodated traffic, thereby nullifying the effect on reducing emissions.

• Many airports are now claiming to be carbon neutral. This may not make a large difference to overall emissions from air transport, though it is a step in the right direction.

• Reforms to air traffic management may reduce emissions in several ways, such as by facilitating more direct flights. The yet-to-be-achieved Single European Sky holds out the promise of significant carbon reductions (at least per flight, seat or passenger) if actually implemented, but may also enable additional growth.

• Changes in operating procedures of airlines can reduce emissions. Airlines are exploring these and will respond to incentives such as those from fuel taxes.

In short, there is currently quite a lot going on, though several policies (voluntary offsets) are more symbolic than real. It is rather piecemeal, and there is little integration of policies. Some policies can be inconsistent with one another. A lot is experimental and limited. As far as one can tell, little has been done by way of evaluation of effectiveness, in terms of actually reducing emissions. Some have suggested that little by way of emissions reduction has been achieved. This may or may not be so, though it is likely that governments have not tried to make large differences intentionally – they are proceeding cautiously. If need be, they can ramp up their effects with the suite of policies measures at their disposal.

5.2 Which policies are best? A menu of policy options

Policy options differ quite widely. There has been a range of policies discussed in this book, and there are several which have not been given specific attention. Each of these policies has a range of different characteristics which may or may not be relevant in a specific situation. A number of these characteristics have been discussed in the chapter by Fichert, Forsyth and Niemeier in this book. In particular this deals with the economic efficiency of the policy, the transaction costs of implementing them, and their effectiveness. This chapter has brought into play a number of additional aspects or characteristics. All in all, the policy menu is rather complex.

A convenient way of handling these aspects is to summarise them in two tables. Table 13.1 comes from the chapter by Fichert, Forsyth and Niemeier, adds in a few extra policies and gives some examples of where these policies have been tried. Table 13.2 summarises the additional aspects introduced in this chapter.

It would be time-consuming to discuss all the cells of these tables. Instead, what can be done is provide a brief discussion of the key aspects of the policies, along with a few examples.

Table 13.1 Assessment of policy options

Policy	Efficiency	Transaction Cost	Effectiveness (emission reduction in the regulated market)	Examples
ETS – Paid Permits Part of Multi-Industry Scheme	Very high, but sensitive to fluctuations	Moderate	Very high	New Zealand
Part of Aviation-Specific Scheme	High		High	
ETS – Free or Subsidised Permits Part of Multi-Industry Scheme	High but sensitive to fluctuations	Moderate, though prone to rent seeking	High	EU
Part of Aviation-Specific Scheme	Moderately high		Low	
CORSIA	High though subject to errors	Higher than for ETS, as offsetting projects will also have to be monitored	High if most countries join the scheme and if offsets are genuine	Planned but yet to be implemented by ICAO
Aviation Fuel Tax	Very high except when airport slots are limited	Moderate	High	
Carbon Tax	Very high except when airport slots are limited	Low	High	
Passenger Taxes	Moderate except when airport slots are limited	Low	Low	UK, Germany
Limits to Airport Expansion	Very low	Low	Very low	Suggested for London airports
Reducing Airport Congestion	Moderate	Low though with political problems	Moderate	US airports a possible application
Reforming ATC	Moderate	High	Unknown	Possible reform of European ATC

Requirements on New Engines	Low	Low	Low to moderate	CAPE/ICAO stringency requirements
Subsidies for Low Carbon Fuels	Low	Moderate	Moderate	Voluntary trials
Voluntary Actions by Airlines, Airports and Passengers	Moderate	Low to moderate	Low to moderate	Many examples, airline offset schemes
Operating Procedures	Very high	Low	Effective but quantitively small	Airlines are reviewing and trialling
Carbon Free Airports	Not known	Not known	Quantitatively small	Many airports are going carbon neutral

Table 13.2 Assessment of policy options

Policy	Impact on WEBs	Consistency with other policies in the same geographical market	Targeted or Indirect?	Tradability	Fiscal Implications	Impact on Non-Carbon Emissions	Who Pays?
ETS – Paid Permits Part of Multi-Industry Scheme	−	Yes	++	++	++	0 (but may be considered in the future)	pax/al
Part of Aviation-Specific Scheme	−	Yes	++	−	++	0	pax/al
ETS – Free or Subsidised Permits- Part of Multi-Industry Scheme	−	Yes	++	++	0	0 (see above)	pax/al
Part of Aviation-Specific Scheme	−	Yes	++	−	0	0	pax/al
CORSIA	−	Yes	++	No	0	0 (see above)	pax/al
Aviation Fuel Tax	−	No	+	na	+++	?	pax/al
Carbon Tax	−	No	−	na	++	−?	pax/al
Passenger Taxes	−	No	−	na	++	−?	pax/al
Limits to Airport Expansion	−	No	−	na	− (lower tax revenues from sector and WEB)	+	Whole economy
Reducing Airport Congestion	+	No	−	na	0	+	na
Reforming ATC	+	No	−	na	0	+	na
Requirements on New Engines	−	No	++	na	0	?	pax/al
Subsidies for Biofuels	+	No	++	na	−	?	Whole economy
Voluntary Actions by Airlines, Airports and Passengers	0	No	+	na	0	0	pax/al/ap
Operating Procedures	0	No	++	na	0	?	pax/al
Carbon Free Airports	−	No	+	na	0	0	pax/al/ap

Key:
- Negative impact
-- Strongly negative impact
0 No impact
+ Positive impact
++ Strongly positive impact
pax Passengers affected
al Airlines affected

Three aspects are listed in Table 13.1:

Efficiency. Economic efficiency is an important aspect of all policies. ETSs are regarded as an efficient means of reducing emissions, as are fuel taxes. Ticket taxes are regarded as less efficient, and airport restrictions are likely to be inefficient.

Transaction costs. Some policies can be costly to set up and implement. ETSs may be costly, though airport restrictions are easy.

Effectiveness. Policies may be good in theory, but are they effective? Ticket taxes may not reduce emissions by much, while fuel taxes may be more effective.

Turning to the aspects listed in Table 13.2:

Impact on WEBs. Some policies work by suppressing the demand for air transport – if so, they risk reducing the wider economic benefits. ETSs and even more ticket taxes work in this way, while reducing airport congestion may increase air transport but not emissions.

Consistency with other policies. Policies which work through constraining output will result in no additional benefit from having other policies. Thus, imposing a ticket tax will have no effect on reducing carbon emissions if there is already an ETS in place and no mechanism to avoid the waterbed effect is in place.

Targeted policies. Targeted policies such as ETSs or fuel taxes are likely to have a stronger effect than less targeted policies such as ticket taxes or airport restrictions.

Tradability. Policies which embody the possibility of trading (between industries or countries) will have a lower cost. ETSs with trade between industries or countries will minimise costs – by contrast, CORSIA does not yet have any opportunity to trade.

Fiscal implications. There is a "green dividend" by imposing policies which create revenue for the government, such as a fuel tax. Policies which require subsidies, such as subsidies for the use of biofuels, impose a cost on the government and society.

Impact on non-carbon emissions. Some policies, such as ticket taxes, may be good in that they reduce non-carbon emissions as well as carbon emissions. By contrast, setting engine standards may reduce carbon emissions at the same time as they increase other emissions.

Who pays? Only a limited amount of research has been done on the incidence of emissions reduction policies. Clearly passengers pay a high proportion of the increase in costs in many cases. When airlines are imperfectly competitive and when excess demand at airports is rationed by slots, airlines pay some of or all of the costs. Exactly who pays when permits/allowances are granted to airlines at less than market price has yet to be determined.

The objective of these tables is to set out the various effects of different policies. They provide a checklist so that all the key aspects of policies can be determined. Too often only one or two of the key aspects of policies are considered in policy discussion. This results in misleading and incomplete assessments of these policies.

5.3 Priorities

What are the best ways of going forward in the task of reducing greenhouse gas emissions from air transport? As the previous section has indicated, selection of policies is a good deal more complicated than often assumed. Each of the policies has multiple aspects, such as impacts on non-carbon emissions, cost of implementation and impacts on the wider benefits of air transport, which need to be taken account of if the right policies are to be selected. So far, not much has been done to fill in the body of the table in the last section. Once this is done, the building blocks for the design of a good policy mix for air transport will be evident.

Several questions, some of them difficult, need to be answered to achieve progress.

- One of these concerns the trading and the broadness issue. Under what circumstances does it make sense to allow trading between air transport and other industries, or between different countries? Normally trading is desirable, in that it enables costs to be reduced, as is a broader base for a tax. However, when policies such as ETSs are targeted towards reducing only carbon emissions, but air transport creates other emissions as well, an air transport only ETS may be superior to a general industry ETS. This may not be a major problem, but it needs to be recognised and sorted out. The inclusion of non-CO_2 emissions in an ETS would overcome this issue.

- Another issue concerns the interaction and complementarity of different policies. Some policies do not work well together. This is particularly true with policies which rely on setting quantitative limits, such as ETSs. For example, imposing an air transport tax on an industry already subject to an ETS will not further reduce carbon emissions, but it may be of help in reducing non-carbon emissions in the regulated area. Again, this needs to be recognised and taken account of.

- Aviation creates carbon and other types of emissions. Some policies target carbon emissions, while others have an effect on all of the emissions of air transport. Fuel taxes may be better than ticket taxes at addressing the carbon problem, but ticket taxes can be better at reducing other emissions.

- The wider economic benefits of air transport may be very small, or very large. The answer to this question will have a bearing on what emissions reductions policies are best. How large WEBs are is an ongoing issue with research, and conclusive results are not likely soon. In the meantime, it is prudent to test the reliance on WEBs of policies which might be implemented.

- There is much work to be done on the design of different policies. There may be new policies which are suggested, but even if this is the case, alternative designs of existing policies can be explored. An example is ticket taxes – existing taxes are very blunt in their impact on emissions. However, it is now recognised that it is possible to design taxes which are much more effective in reducing emissions. Some design issues as that noted earlier are essentially economic in nature. Many of the more difficult design issues are technological – how to design better fuels or engines.
- How reliable and genuine are offsets? Several policies rely on offsets, and this will become more true once CORSIA is in operation.
- How do airlines respond to being given free emissions permits (or being able to emit up to the 2020 level in CORSIA)? Will they set prices based on the average cost they are facing, or the (higher) marginal cost they face? If they are profit maximisers, they would be expected to set prices according to their marginal cost, and they will enjoy substantial profits as a result of being in an ETS or CORSIA. Most commentators assume that they set prices based on their average cost and forego these high profits. The answer to this question will affect how an ETS or CORSIA works to reduce emissions.

Notes

1 I am grateful to Frank Fichert, Hans-Martin Niemeier, Kurt van Dender, Jonas Teusch, Samuel Ribansky and Sven Maertens for valuable comments. All errors are my own.
2 Let us imagine the following scenarios: Within the EU ETS scope (intra-EEA), Germany introduces a ticket tax. As a reaction to this, airlines may shift aircraft/flights from Germany to other EEA routes (with no net effect on CO_2), or even to regions outside the EU ETS scope, e.g. in selling aircraft to a country like Indonesia (again, no net effect on intra-EEA CO_2, this time due to the waterbed effect; but additional CO_2 emissions are generated in Indonesia).
3 Again, worldwide emissions may even grow if air transport supply is shifted to unregulated markets.

References

Committee on Climate Change (UK). (2009). *Meeting the UK aviation target – options for reducing emissions to 2050*. London: Committee on Climate Change.
Committee on Climate Change (UK). (2019). *Net zero technical report*. London: Committee on Climate Change.
Diamond, P. and Mirrlees, J. (1971a). Optimal taxation and public production. *American Economic Review*, 61(Mar.), pp. 8–27.
Diamond, P. and Mirrlees, J. (1971b). Optimal taxation and public production. *American Economic Review*, 61(June), pp. 261–278.
Fankhauser, S., Hepburn, C. and Park, J. (2011). *Combining multiple climate policy instruments: How not to do it*. Centre for Climate Change Economics and Policy, Working Paper No 48

and Grantham Research Institute on Climate Change and the Environment Working Paper No 38.

Fichert, F., Forsyth, P. and Niemeier, H-M. (2014). Auswirkungen der deutschen Luftverkehrsteuer auf das Passagieraufkommen – Eine Zwischenbilanz. *Zeitschrift für Verkehrswissenschaft*, 85(3), pp. 167–193.

Flues, F. and van Dender, K. (2017). *Permit allocation rules and investment incentives in emissions trading systems*. OECD Taxation Working Papers No 33, OECD, Paris.

Forsyth, P. (2008). Airport slots: Perspectives and policies. In: P. Forsyth, D. Gillen and H-M. Niemeier, eds., *Airport slots: International experiences and options for reform*. Aldershot: Ashgate, pp. 379–405.

Forsyth, P. (2009). The impact of climate change policy on competition in the air transport industry. In: OECD/International Transport Forum, ed., *Competition between Airports, airlines and high speed rail, OECD/ITF Round Table 145*. Paris: OECD, pp. 95–127.

Forsyth, P. (2014). Climate change policies, long haul travel and tourism. *Journal of Tourism Economics, Policy and Hospitality Management*, 1(1), pp. 1–17.

Forsyth, P., Dwyer, L. and Spurr, R. (2007). *Climate change policies and Australian tourism. Scoping study of the economic aspects*. Sustainable Tourism Cooperative Research Centre.

Forsyth, P., Dwyer, L., Spurr, R. and Pham, T. (2014). The impacts of the Australia's departure tax: Tourism versus the economy. *Tourism Management*, 40, pp. 126–136.

Gössling, S. (2018). Air transport and climate change. In: N. Halpern and A. Graham, eds., *The Routledge companion to air transport management*. London: Routledge, pp. 402–416.

Hatch, P. (2019). Qantas points to push green flyers. *The Age*, 29 July.

Hepburn, C., Neuhoff, K., Acworth, W., Burtraw, D. and Jotzo, F. (2016). Introduction. The economics of the EU market stability reserve. *The Journal of Environmental Economics and Management*, 80, pp. 1–5.

IATA – International Air Transport Association. (2006). *Economics briefing impact of the rise in UK air passenger duty*. Geneva: IATA.

InterVISTAS. (2006). *Measuring the economic rate of return on investment in aviation*. Vancouver: InterVISTAS.

Keen, M., Parry, I. and Strand, J. (2013). Planes, ships and taxes: Charging for international aviation and marine emissions. *Economic Policy*, 28, pp. 710–749.

Keen, M. and Strand, J. (2007). Indirect taxes on international aviation. *Fiscal Studies*, 28(1), pp. 1–41.

Leicester, A. and O'Dea, C. (2008). Aviation taxes. In: R. Chote, C. Emmerson, D. Miles and J. Shaw, eds., *The IFS green budget: January 2008*. London: Institute for Fiscal Studies, pp. 187–211.

Nordhaus, W. (2013). *The climate casino: Risk, uncertainty and economics for a warming world*. New Haven: Yale University Press.

OXERA. (2003). *Assessment of the financial impact of airlines of integration into the EU greenhouse gas emissions trading scheme*. Report for BAA External Emissions Trading Steering Group.

Ozmen, M. (2011). *In Icarus's slipstream: Emissions mitigation and cost transmission in the airline industry*. PhD Thesis, Monash University.

Pearce, B. and Smyth, M. (2007). *Aviation economic benefits*. IATA Economics Briefing 8.

Pizer, W. (2002). Combining price and quantity controls to mitigate climate change. *Journal of Public Economics*, 85, pp. 409–434.

PwC. (2013). *The economic impact of air passenger duty*. A study by PwC.

Ramsey, F. (1927). A contribution to the theory of taxation. *Economic Journal*, 37, pp. 47–61.

Scheelhaase, J. (2019). How to regulate aviation's full climate impact as intended by the EU council from 2020 onwards. *Journal of Air Transport Management*, 75, pp. 68–74.

Stern, N. (2007). *The economics of climate change: The Stern Review.* Cambridge: Cambridge University Press.

Teusch, J. and Braathen, N. (2019). *Are environmental tax policies beneficial? Learning from programme evaluation studies.* OECD Environment Working Papers No 150, OECD, Paris.

Vickerman, R. (2013). The wider economic impacts of mega-projects in transport. In: H. Priemus and B. van Wee, eds., *International handbook on mega-projects.* Cheltenham: Edward Elgar, pp. 381–397.

Index

Printed in the United States
by Baker & Taylor Publisher Services